JAPAN

TOP SIGHTS, AUTHENTIC EXPERIENCES

Rebecca Mil
Craig McLachlan
Spurling, Phillip Ta

Contents

Plan Your Trip

Sea of Okhotsk

RUSSIA

Asahikawa ◉

◉ Kitami
Nosappu-misaki ◉

HOKKAIDO
p220

◉ **Tomakomai**

◉ Muroran

◉ Hakodate

◉ **Aomori**

Hirosaki ◉

◉ **Akita**   ◉ **Morioka**

Sea of Japan

Yamagata ◉   ◉ **Sendai**

PACIFIC OCEAN

JAPAN ALPS
p154

◉ **Niigata**   ◉ **Fukushima**

◉ Nagaoka   ◉ Koriyama

◉ Iwaki

◉ **Toyama**

◉oka

◉zawa

◉ Nagano

Utsunomiya ◉

◉ **Maebashi**   ◉ **Mito**

◉ukui

Hachioji

◉ Urawa

TOKYO
p34

Kōfu ◉

◉ **Gifu**

◉oya

Shizuoka ◉

◉ Yokohama

FUJI
FIVE
LAKES
p166

◉ **Tsu**

Hamamatsu ◉

NARA
p140

KII PENINSULA
p260

N   0 ⊢———————⊣ 400 km
    0 ⊢———————⊣ 200 miles

Welcome to Japan

Japan is truly timeless, a place where ancient traditions are fused with modern life as if it were the most natural thing in the world.

There's an intoxicating buzz to Japan's urban centres, with their vibrant street life, glowing streetscapes, 24-hour drinking and dining scenes, architectural wonders that redefine what buildings – and cities – should look like. Leave them behind and you've got a country that is more than two-thirds mountains, with bubbling hot springs at every turn. In the warmer months there is excellent hiking, through cedar groves and fields of wildflowers, up to soaring peaks and ancient shrines (the latter founded by wandering ascetics). In the winter, all this is covered with snow and the skiing is world class. (And if you've never paired hiking or skiing with soaking in an onsen, you don't know what you've been missing.)

Travelling around the country offers numerous opportunities to connect with Japan's traditional culture. Spend the night in a ryokan (traditional Japanese inn), sleeping on futons and tatami mats, and padding through well-worn wooden halls to the bathhouse (or go one step further and sleep in an old farmhouse). Chant with monks or learn how to whisk bitter *matcha* (powdered green tea) into a froth. From the splendour of a Kyoto geisha dance to the spare beauty of a Zen rock garden, Japan has the power to enthral even the most jaded traveller.

... a country that is more than two-thirds mountains, with bubbling hot springs at every turn.

Arashiyama Bamboo Grove (p123), Kyoto
ABDERAZAK TISSOUKAI / 500PX ©

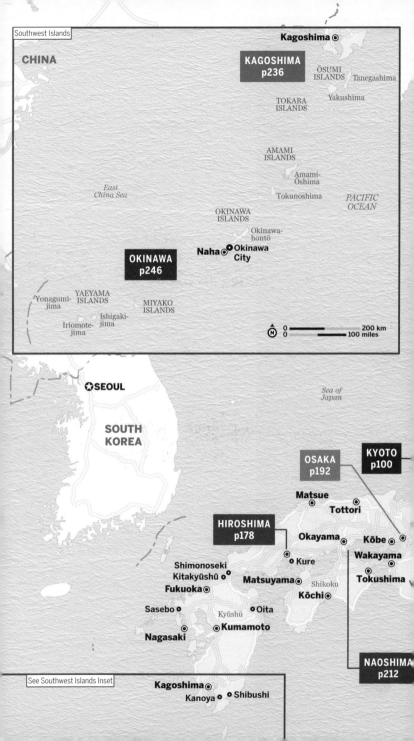

Southwest Islands

CHINA

Kagoshima ◉

KAGOSHIMA p236

ŌSUMI ISLANDS — Tanegashima

TOKARA ISLANDS — Yakushima

AMAMI ISLANDS

Amami-Ōshima

East China Sea

Tokunoshima

PACIFIC OCEAN

OKINAWA ISLANDS

Okinawa-hontō

Naha ◉ **Okinawa City**

OKINAWA p246

Yonagumi-jima — YAEYAMA ISLANDS

Iriomote-jima — Ishigaki-jima

MIYAKO ISLANDS

N — 0 — 200 km
0 — 100 miles

✪**SEOUL**

Sea of Japan

SOUTH KOREA

OSAKA p192

KYOTO p100

Matsue ◉

Tottori ◉

HIROSHIMA p178

Okayama ◉

Kōbe ◉

WAKAYAMA ◉

Shimonoseki
Kitakyūshū ◉

◉ **Kure**

Shikoku

Matsuyama ◉

Tokushima ◉

Fukuoka ◉

Kōchi ◉

Sasebo ◉

Kyūshū

◉ **Oita**

Nagasaki ◉

◉ **Kumamoto**

NAOSHIMA p212

See Southwest Islands Inset

Kagoshima ◉
Kanoya ◉ ◉ **Shibushi**

The Daibutsu (Great Buddha) in Nara's Tōdai-ji temple (p144)
WIBOWO RUSLI / GETTY IMAGES ©

Plan Your Trip
Japan's Top 12

SEAN PAVONE / SHUTTERSTOCK ©

Tokyo

The city that has it all

Tokyo is one of the world's reigning cities of superlatives – the dining, drinking and shopping are all top class. It's a city always in flux, which is one of its enduring charms, forever sending up breathtaking new structures and dreaming up new culinary delights. It truly has something for everyone, whether your ideal afternoon is spent in an art museum or racing through the streets of Akihabara in a go-kart.

From left: Kabukichō (p59); 21_21 Design Sight (p64)

1

Kyoto

Traditional culture at its finest

There are said to be more than 1000 Buddhist temples in Kyoto, Japan's imperial capital for over 1000 years. The city is a show-room for centuries of Japanese religious architecture, which pro-duced both the glittering Kinkaku-ji (Golden Temple; pictured top) and the stark Zen garden at Ryōan-ji. But don't equate religiosity with temperance here: Kyoto is also the city where geisha enter-tained in lantern-lit teahouses (and still do).

2

Japanese Alps

Soaring peaks and charming villages

The mountainous heart of Japan has fantastic hiking trails through alpine valleys and along former post roads; bubbling hot springs overlooking gorges; and plenty of photogenic vistas. Here's your chance to stay in an atmospheric country ryokan (traditional Japanese inn). Or travel to the remote village of Shirakawa-gō (pictured above), or, even more remote, Ainokura, and fall asleep to the sound of chirping frogs in a centuries-old thatched-roof farmhouse.

3

4

Nara
Buddhist treasures of early Japan

Nara was Japan's first permanent capital in the
8th century and the site of the country's first great
monumental building spree. There are numerous
grand temples here, older than those in Kyoto. The
highlight, of course, is the Daibutsu (Great Buddha;
pictured right). The statue is among the largest
gilt-bronze effigies in the world, and the temple
that houses it, Tōdai-ji, is among the world's largest
wooden structures.v

5

Kii Peninsula
Ancient temples and pilgrim trails

Not far from Osaka but a world away, this mountainous peninsula puts you in touch with ancient
Japan. Visit the temple complex Kōya-san, with its
moss-covered stupas and chanting monks. Then
head deeper into the peninsula where you can walk
a network of trails known as the Kumano Kodō, laid
down centuries ago by mountain ascetics seeking
spiritual enlightenment in what must have felt like
the ends of the earth. Right: Cemetery at Oku-no-in
(p266), Kōya-san

Naoshima

Island of contemporary art

Naoshima is Japan's top destination for contemporary art and architecture. An island in the Inland Sea, it functions as one big open-air museum, with buildings and installations from leading international creators – all designed to enhance the glorious natural scenery. Much of what visitors find so compelling, however, is the blend of avant-garde and rural Japan: there are villages here that remain a vital part of the island's artistic renaissance.

JENNY JONES / GETTY IMAGES ©

Hiroshima

Heartbreaking history and a message of hope

It's not until you visit the Peace Memorial Museum that the true extent of human tragedy wreaked by the atomic bomb in 1945 becomes vividly clear. A visit here is a heartbreaking, important history lesson and the park around the museum offers many opportunities for reflection. But the city's spirit of determination – as well as its food – will ensure that you'll have good memories to take with you when you leave. Above: Children's Peace Monument (p185)

7

Fuji Five Lakes

An iconic mountain and crystal-blue lakes

Even from a distance the perfectly symmetrical cone of Japan's highest peak will take your breath away. Fuji-san is among Japan's most revered and timeless attractions. Dawn from the summit? Pure magic. Hundreds of thousands of people climb it every year. Those who'd rather search for picture-perfect views can do so from the less-daunting vantage points in the foothills and hot springs of the scenic Fuji Five Lakes district.

9

Osaka

Vivacious city famous for its food

Something magical happens when the sun sets in the Land of the Rising Sun: the grey city streets turn into crackling canyons of neon. Nowhere is this light show more dramatic than along Osaka's Dōtombori canal. In fact, just about everything seems to be turned up a notch in Japan's third-largest city. It's a city that loves to let loose and lives to eat – the perfect stop for your urban Japan fix. From left: Dōtombori (p202); *tako-yaki* (octopus dumplings)

SATOSHI ISHIZU / GETTY IMAGES ©

Hokkaidō

Raw nature and outdoor adventures

Hokkaidō, Japan's northernmost island, is an untamed landscape of mountains that is pock-marked with crystal-blue caldera lakes and sulphur-rich hot springs. This is big mountain and snow country, where skiers carve snow drifts reaching several metres in depth. In the green season, hikers and cyclists are drawn to the island's wide-open spaces and dramatic topography. Clockwise, this page: Snowsports at Niseko (p224); Yōtei-zan volcano (p229); Noboribetsu Onsen (p230)

10

Okinawa

Beaches, diving and island life

There's more to Japan than most realise: the subtropical islands of Okinawa stretch hundreds of kilometres southwest, almost to Taiwan. Some of these islands, such as Ishigaki and the Kerama Islands, are known for their palm-fringed beaches of sugar-white sand and turquoise waters. Others, such as Iriomote-jima, are covered in primeval forest – some of the last virgin forest left in Japan – and offer a truly otherworldly experience. Above: Kabira-wan (p250), Ishigaki-jima

Kagoshima

Active volcanoes, hot springs and trekking

Kagoshima, roughly 1000km southwest of Tokyo, is an urban outpost with a distinctly different, rugged feel. Lording over the city is the smoking (quite literally) volcano Sakurajima. Kagoshima is also the jumping-off point for the island of Yakushima, which, with its ancient cedars, tangled vines and seaside springs, looks more like a *Star Wars* set than planet Earth. If you're after something a little different, this is the place for you. Above: Ibusuki Sunamushi Kaikan Saraku (p245)

Plan Your Trip
Need to Know

When to Go

Hot summers, mild winters
Warm summers, cold winters

Sapporo
GO Apr–Oct

Takayama
GO Apr–Oct

Tokyo
GO any time

Kyoto
GO Mar–Jun or Sep–Nov

Naha
GO Mar–Nov

High Season (Apr & May, Aug)

o Weather in April and May is generally fantastic; August is hot and humid but the season for summer festivals.

o Accommodation is pricey and hard to find during cherry-blossom season (late March to early April), Golden Week (early May) and O-Bon (mid-August).

Shoulder (Jun & Jul, Sep–Dec)

o June and July fall in the rainy season (except Hokkaidō); typhoons roll through in September.

o Prices and crowds increase in resort areas during autumn foliage season (November).

Low Season (Jan–Mar)

o Cold days and snowy mountains make this peak ski season, but affordable and uncrowded elsewhere.

o Many businesses close over the New Year period (end December to early January).

Currency

Yen (¥)

Language

Japanese

Visas

Visas are issued on arrival for most nationalities for stays of up to 90 days.

Money

Post offices and some convenience stores have international ATMs. Most hotels and department stores, but only some restaurants and ryokan, accept credit cards.

Mobile Phones

Purchase prepaid data-only SIM cards (for unlocked smartphones only) online, at airport kiosks or at electronics stores. For voice calls, rent a pay-as-you-go mobile.

Time

Japan Standard Time (GMT/UTC plus nine hours)

Daily Costs

Budget: Less than ¥8000

- Dorm bed: ¥3000
- Bowl of noodles: ¥750
- One temple or museum entry: ¥500

Midrange: ¥8000–20,000

- Double room at a business hotel: ¥10,000
- Dinner for two at an *izakaya* (Japanese pub-eatery): ¥6000
- Half-day cycling tour or cooking class: ¥5000

Top End: More than ¥20,000

- Double room in a nice hotel: from ¥25,000
- Dinner for two at a good sushi restaurant: from ¥15,000
- Taxi ride between city sights: ¥2500

Useful Websites

- **Lonely Planet** (lonelyplanet.com/japan) Destination information, hotel bookings, traveller forum and more.
- **Japan National Tourism Organization** (www.jnto.go.jp) Official tourist site with planning tools and events calendar.
- **Tokyo Cheapo** (https://tokyocheapo.com) Budget saving tips for Tokyo and travel in Japan.

Opening Hours

Note that some outdoor attractions (such as gardens) may close earlier in the winter. Standard opening hours:

Banks 9am to 3pm (some to 5pm) Monday to Friday
Bars from around 6pm to late
Department stores 10am to 8pm
Museums 9am to 5pm, last entry by 4.30pm; often closed Monday (if Monday is a national holiday then the museum will close on Tuesday instead)

Post offices 9am to 5pm Monday to Friday; larger ones have longer hours and open Saturday
Restaurants lunch 11.30am to 2pm; dinner 6pm to 10pm; last orders taken about half an hour before closing

Arriving in Japan

Narita Airport, Tokyo (p95) Express trains and buses run frequently to central Tokyo (around ¥3000; one to two hours) between 6am and 10.30pm. Taxis start at ¥20,000.

Haneda Airport, Tokyo (p95) Trains and buses (¥400 to ¥1200, 30 to 45 minutes) to central Tokyo run frequently from 5.30am to midnight; infrequent night buses. For a taxi, budget between ¥5000 and ¥8000.

Kansai International Airport, Osaka (p210) Express trains run frequently to Kyoto (from ¥2850, 75 minutes) and Osaka (¥1430, 35 minutes) between 6am and 10pm; infrequent night buses. A shared taxi service to Kyoto costs ¥3600; a standard taxi to Osaka starts at ¥14,500.

Getting Around

Train Fast, efficient, reliable and can get you just about anywhere; discount rail passes make train travel very affordable.

Bus The cheapest way to make long-haul journeys and the only way to get to some rural destinations.

Car Roads are great, driving is safe, and a car will give you plenty of freedom. Especially recommended in Hokkaidō, the Japan Alps and the Kii Peninsula. Drive on the left.

Air An extensive network of domestic flights and an increased presence of budget carriers makes air travel a good option for long distances or time-pressed itineraries.

For more on getting around, see p309

Plan Your Trip
Hotspots For...

Japanese Cuisine

Eating is one of the great pleasures of visiting Japan. And chief among those pleasures is discovering just how varied Japanese cuisine is, from region to region and season to season.

Kyoto (p100)
Japan's ancient imperial capital is the birthplace of *kaiseki* (Japanese haute cuisine) and the tea ceremony.

Kitcho Arashiyama
An elegant procession of seasonal dishes (p132).

Osaka (p192)
Colourful Osaka is Japan's capital of street food, where fierce competitions turn humble dishes to high art.

Wanaka Honten
Top for *tako-yaki* (octopus dumplings; p198).

Okinawa (p246)
Japan's southern islands have a tradition of their own. Try *gōyā champurū* (stir-fried bitter melon; pictured).

Yūnangi
Okinawan classics in an old-school *izakaya* (p257).

Art & Architecture

Japan has a sublime artistic tradition that transcends gallery walls, the pages of books and the kabuki stage to seep into everyday life.

Tokyo (p34)
Art museums, theatres and the creations of Japan's 20th-century architects.

Tokyo National Museum
The world's largest collection of Japanese art (p40).

Naoshima (p212)
An island of contemporary art, including several museums designed by Japanese architect Andō Tadao.

Art House Project
A village setting for art installations (p216).

Nara (p140)
Buddhist art and architecture from the dawn of the Japanese empire in the 8th century.

Tōdai-ji
Home of Nara's Daibutsu statue (p144; pictured).

Outdoor Adventure

Japan is a year-round destination for travellers keen to stretch their legs – on gentle strolls or up serious peaks. In winter, it's all about going down the mountains.

Fuji Five Lakes (p166)
Iconic Mt Fuji is the main draw, but the pretty lake district offers gentler hikes through the foothills too.

Mt Fuji
Watch the sunrise from Japan's highest summit (p170).

Kagoshima (p236)
Drive around an active volcano, get buried in sand or visit the island of Yakushima, a hiker's paradise.

Jōmon-sugi
Trek through Yakushima to this ancient tree (p240).

Hokkaidō (p220)
Japan's northernmost island is largely undeveloped and a playground for every sort of outdoor enthusiast.

Niseko United
A haven for powder hounds (p224; pictured).

Historic Sites

See the sights where Japan's history – that of the samurai warrior, the wandering ascetic and the farmer bent over their rice paddies – is brought to life.

Kii Peninsula (p260)
A wild, mountainous region of temperate rainforest believed by the ancients to have spiritual power.

Kumano Kodō
Pilgrim trails past hamlets and shrines (p264).

Japan Alps (p154)
The mountainous interior is home to the castle Matsumoto-jo (pictured) and well preserved post-towns.

Shirakawa-gō
Villages of thatched-roof farmhouses (p158).

Hiroshima (p178)
This city has numerous monuments to the day that changed history for Japan and the world.

Peace Memorial Museum
Evocative account of the bomb's aftermath (p185).

Plan Your Trip
Local Life

J. HENNING BUCHHOLZ / SHUTTERSTOCK ©

Activities

Volcanic Japan bubbles with onsen (hot springs). The Japanese have turned the simple act of bathing into a folk religion and the country is dotted with temples and shrines to this most relaxing of faiths. Many believe the waters to have curative properties; depending on the mineral content they can be hailed as having a positive effect on skin, circulation or digestion. At the very least, you will sleep very, very well after a soak.

Shopping

Tokyo is the trendsetter for all of Japan; Osaka, the shopping capital of western Japan, has a street-smart style of its own. Kyoto is the place to pick up traditional goods such as anything tea and tea-ceremony related. Around the country are pottery towns and others famous for local crafts.

Entertainment

Sumo, steeped in ancient ritual, is Japan's national sport. Tournaments take place in January, May and September in Tokyo and in March in Osaka – by all means see it if you can. However, while sumo has its devout followers, it's baseball that is the clear fan favourite. Even if you don't follow baseball, it's worth getting tickets to a game in Japan just to see the perfectly choreographed cheers. Baseball has a culture all of its own here, as spectators chomp on dried squid and buy beer from *uriko*, the young women with kegs strapped to their backs, who work the aisles with tireless cheer.

Eating

As visitors to Japan quickly discover, the people here are absolutely obsessed with food. You'll find that every island and region of Japan has its own *meibutsu* (local speciality) that is a point of pride. Japan's larger cities have a good spread of cuisines, so you can take your pick from restaurants specialising in different Japanese dishes or Chinese, Thai, French, Italian and more. Look to food courts in department stores and train stations for easy options.

CARL FORBES / SHUTTERSTOCK ©

In rural areas, the top foodie meals are often served at ryokan (traditional Japanese inns), where the dishes make ample use of local ingredients. Given the choice, most Japanese travellers book meals at their lodgings. As this is the case, be warned that in many rural or resort areas there may be few restaurants open for dinner.

Drinking & Nightlife

Any Japanese city of reasonable size will have a hankagai (繁華街), a lively commercial and entertainment district. Famous ones include: Tokyo's Kabukichō, Osaka's Dōtombori and Sapporo's Susukino. Such districts are stocked, often several storeys high, with a medley of drinking options that include *izakaya* (traditional pub-eateries), cocktail bars, Western-style pubs, jazz cafes, nightclubs and more – all awash in the neon lights that form Japan's urban signature.

You can't visit Japan without getting in a round of karaoke (カラオケ; kah-rah-oh-kay), a popular local pastime. In Japan, karaoke is sung in a private room among friends. Admission is usually charged per person per half-hour. Food and drinks (ordered by phone) are brought to the room. To choose a song, use the touch screen device to search by artist or title; most have an English function and plenty of English songs to choose from.

★ **Best Markets**

Tsukiji (p60), Tokyo

Nishiki (p114), Kyoto

Kuromon Ichiba (p203), Osaka

Daichi Makishi Kōsetsu Ichiba (p257), Naha

Ameya-yokochō (p43), Tokyo

From left: Sumo wrestlers face off in Tokyo; Food stall in Nishiki Market (p114), Kyoto

Plan Your Trip
Month by Month

January

🎎 Shōgatsu (New Year)

Families come together to eat and drink to health and happiness. The holiday is officially 1 to 3 January, but many businesses and attractions close the whole first week, and transport is busy. *Hatsu-mōde* is the ritual first shrine visit of the new year.

February

February is the coldest month and the peak of Japan's ski season.

🎎 Setsubun

The first day of spring is 3 February in the traditional lunar calendar, a shift once believed to bode evil. As a precaution, people visit Buddhist temples, toss roasted beans and shout *'Oni wa soto! Fuku wa uchi!'* ('Devil out! Fortune in!').

🎎 Yuki Matsuri

Two million visitors head to Sapporo's annual snow festival in early February. Highlights include the international snow sculpture contest, ice slides and mazes for kids and plenty of drunken revelry. Book accommodation very early.

April

Warmer weather and blooming cherry trees make this a fantastic month to be in Japan, though places like Kyoto can get very crowded.

🎎 Cherry-Blossom Viewing

When the cherry blossoms burst into bloom, the Japanese hold rollicking *hanami* (blossom viewing) parties. The blossoms are fickle and hard to time: on average, they hit their peak in Tokyo or Kyoto between 25 March and 7 April.

🎎 Takayama Spring Matsuri

On 14 and 15 April the mountain town of Takayama hosts the spring instalment of its famous festival. This is the more elaborate of the two (the other is in October), with parades of spectacular floats lit with lanterns

23

MARVIN MINDER / SHUTTERSTOCK ©

and a lion dance. Book accommodation well in advance.

May

May is lovely: it's warm and sunny in most places and the fresh green in the mountains is stunning. Be wary of the travel crush during the Golden Week holiday period (29 April to 5 May).

🎎 Sanja Matsuri

The grandest Tokyo festival of all, this three-day event, held over the third weekend of May, attracts around 1.5 million spectators to Asakusa. The highlight is the rowdy parade of *mikoshi* (portable shrines) carried by men and women in traditional dress.

June

By mid-June *tsuyu* (the rainy season) sets in, lasting until mid-July.

July

When the rainy season passes, suddenly it's summer – the season for festivals and *hanabi taikai* (fireworks shows). It does get very hot and humid; head to Hokkaidō or the Japan Alps to escape the heat.

🏔 Mt Fuji Climbing Season

Mt Fuji (p170) officially opens to climbing on 1 July, and the months of July and August are ideal for climbing the peak.

From left: *Hanami* crowds in Kyoto's Maruyama-kōen (p121); Sanja Matsuri, Tokyo

✿ Gion Matsuri

The most vaunted festival in Japan is held on 17 and 24 July in Kyoto, when huge, elaborate floats are pulled through the streets. Three evenings prior, locals stroll through street markets dressed in beautiful *yukata* (light cotton kimonos). Accommodation is expensive and difficult to find.

✿ Tenjin Matsuri

Held in Osaka on 24 and 25 July, this is one of the country's biggest festivals. On the second day, processions of *mikoshi* and people in traditional attire parade through the streets, ending up in hundreds of boats on the river.

☆ Fuji Rock Festival

Japan's biggest music festival takes place over one long (and often wildly muddy and fun) weekend at a mountain resort in late July. Big-name acts on the large stages; indie bands on the smaller ones.

August

School holidays mean beaches and cooler mountain areas get crowded. Many Japanese return to their home towns (or take a holiday) around O-Bon, so transit is hectic and shops may close.

✿ Peace Memorial Ceremony

On 6 August, a memorial service is held in Hiroshima for victims of the WWII atomic bombing of the city. Thousands of paper lanterns are floated down the river.

✿ O-Bon (Festival of the Dead)

Three days in mid-August are set aside to honour the dead, when their spirits are said to return to the earth. Graves are swept, offerings are made and lanterns are floated down rivers, in lakes or the sea to help guide spirits on their journey.

✿ Rōsoku Matsuri

Kōya-san's already deeply atmospheric Oku-no-in is lit with some 100,000 candles on 13 August for Rōsoku Matsuri during O-Bon.

✿ Daimon-ji Gozan Okuribi

Huge fires in the shape of Chinese characters and other symbols are set alight in the hills around Kyoto during this festival, which forms part of the O-Bon rites.

September

Days are still warm, hot even, but less humid – though the odd typhoon rolls through this time of year, which can ruin hiking plans.

☉ Moon Viewing

Full moons in September and October call for *tsukimi*, moon-viewing gatherings. People eat *tsukimi dango* – *mochi* (pounded rice) dumplings, shaped round like the moon.

October

☉ Roppongi Art Night

Held in mid- to late October, this weekend-long arts event (www.roppongi artnight.com) sees large-scale installations and performances taking over the streets of Roppongi in Tokyo.

November

Crisp and cool days with snow starting to fall in the mountains. Autumn foliage peaks in and around Tokyo and Kyoto, which can draw crowds.

December

December is cold across most of Japan. Many businesses shut down from 29 or 30 December for the New Year holiday.

✕ Toshikoshi Soba

Eating buckwheat noodles on New Year's Eve, a tradition called *toshikoshi soba*, is said to bring luck and longevity – the latter symbolised by the length of the noodles.

✿ Joya-no-kane

Temple bells around Japan ring 108 times at midnight on 31 December, a purifying ritual.

Plan Your Trip
Get Inspired

Read

Shogun (James Clavell; 1975) Based on the true story of a Brit who visited Japan in 1600 (and a fun way to learn Japanese history).

Norwegian Wood (Murakami Haruki; 1987) Coming-of-age story set in 1960s Tokyo by Japan's most popular living writer.

The Book of Tokyo: A City in Short Fiction (Edited by Michael Emmerich, Jim Hinks & Masashi Matsuie; 2015) Ten stories by contemporary Japanese writers.

Thousand Autumns of Jacob de Zoet: A Novel (David Mitchell; 2010) Historical novel set in a cosmopolitan enclave during Japan's period of isolation.

Watch

Osaka Elegy (Mizoguchi Kenji; 1936) A modern girl makes her way in Osaka.

Rashōmon (Kurosawa Akira; 1950) Psychological work set in feudal-era Japan by the master auteur of the golden age of Japanese cinema.

My Neighbor Totoro (Miyazaki Hayao; 1988) Studio Ghibli classic about two young sisters living in an enchanted country house.

Lost in Translation (Sofia Coppola; 2003) Disorienting, captivating Tokyo through the eyes of two Americans.

Your Name (Shinkai Makoto; 2016) Enormously popular anime about a city boy and country girl who swap places.

Listen

Furisodation (Kyary Pamyu Pamyu) Electro-pop earworm about coming of age from Japan's pop star *du jour*.

Shimanchu nu Takara (Begin) Love song to Okinawa with *eisa* (Okinawan folk-style) chanting.

Hanamizuki (Hitoto Yō) Tender ode to love and loss and a perennial karaoke favourite.

Tokyo, Mon Amour (Pizzicato Five) Moody lounge track from the '90s Shibuya indie scene.

Fujiyama (Dave Brubeck) Mournful meditation on Japan's iconic mountain, from the late composer's *Jazz Impressions of Japan*.

Above: Women in kimonos walking the arcades of Fushimi Inari-Taisha (p104), Kyoto

Plan Your Trip
Five-Day Itineraries

Kansai in Depth

Japan often feels like a destination that requires a long trip and lots of advanced planning, but it needn't be. The Kansai region is packed with top attractions – such as beautiful Kyoto and lively Osaka – all within in an hour of each other by train.

①

③

Kyoto (p100) Spend two or three days in this magical city exploring the centuries-old temples and gardens.
🚃 40 min to Nara

①

Osaka (p192) Eat till you burst in Japan's capital of street food.
🚃 40 min to Gokurakubashi, then 🚃 5 min to Kōya-san

③

②

Nara (p140) See the splendid Daibatsu (Great Buddha) and stroll through Nara-kōen.
🚃 40 min to Osaka

④

Kii Peninsula (p260) Spend your last night in a Buddhist temple in the otherwordly mountaintop monastery Kōya-san.

Tokyo & Mt Fuji

Between Tokyo and the attractions in its orbit, you can cover a lot of varied terrain, taking in both contemporary and traditional Japan with very little fuss. Base yourself in the capital taking advantage of its excellent dining scene and transit links.

Nikkō (p54) 17th-century World Heritage–listed shrines and temples. 🚃 2 hrs to Tokyo, then 🚃 2 ½ hrs to Mt Fuji

②

Fuji Five Lakes (p166) In summer climb Mt Fuji, catching dawn from the summit. The rest of the year, visit these placid lakes for mountain views.

Tokyo (p34) Museums, markets and parks by day; great food and nightlife after dark. 🚃 2 hrs to Nikkō

①

③

①

②

Plan Your Trip

10-Day Itinerary

The Grand Tour

This is a classic route for first-time visitors. It hits many of Japan's star attractions, can be done year-round and takes advantage of the excellent value and seamless travel offered by a Japan Rail Pass.

Himeji (p200) Spend a morning touring Japan's best-preserved castle.
🚃 1 hr to Hiroshima

Hiroshima (p178) Bear witness to the momentous history of the 20th century at Hiroshima's Peace Memorial Park. 🚢 40 min to Miyajima

Miyajima (p186) Watch the sunset over the island's floating *torii* gate and then bed down in a ryokan (traditional Japanese inn).

RICHIE CHAN / SHUTTERSTOCK ©

Kyoto (p100) Immerse yourself in Japan's traditional side, among the temples and shrines of the old Imperial capital. 🚄 40 min to Nara

①

Tokyo (p34) Get your bearings and a taste for urban Japan. 🚄 2 hrs to Kyoto

②

④ **③**

Nara (p140) Hop over to Nara to see the Daibutsu (Great Buddha). 🚄 40 min to Osaka

Osaka (p192) Budget an evening for the bright lights and big flavours of this fun-loving city. 🚄 40 min to Himeji

⑥

⑦

FROM LEFT: SEAN PAVONE / SHUTTERSTOCK ©; WORLDSTOCK / SHUTTERSTOCK ©

Plan Your Trip

Plan Your Trip
Two-Week Itinerary

Urban & Rural Adventures

This itinerary gives you four very different snapshots of Japan: the ultra-modern city in Tokyo; the Japan of old in Kyoto; the mountain heartland in the Japan Alps; and the laid-back island villages of Okinawa. You'll need a sense of adventure, as this takes you off the beaten track.

Tokyo (p34) Take in the highlights of the capital – the night views, the pop culture and more. 🚃 3 hrs to Nakatsugawa (for Magome)

Japan Alps (p154) Hike through the Kiso Valley, then rent a car to head to mountain hamlets and hot springs. 🚃 2 hrs to Kyoto

Kyoto (p100) Dive deep into Japan's storehouse of traditional culture. ✈ 2½ hrs to Okinawa (Ishigaki), from Kansai International Airport

Okinawa (p246) Explore the beaches, jungles, picturesque villages and cuisine of the remote – and stunning – Yaeyama Islands.

MATT MUNRO / LONELY PLANET ©

Plan Your Trip
Family Travel

Japan for Kids

Safe, clean and full of mod cons, Japan is a great place to travel with kids. The downside is that many cultural sights (shrines, temples and museums) may bore them; you'll want to work in plenty of activities to keep things fresh. Teens will love the pop culture and neon streetscapes.

Planning

Very little special planning is necessary for travellers with children, but do bring any medicines that your child takes regularly (or may need), as Japanese pharmacies don't sell foreign medications (though similar ones can be found). The *shinkansen* (bullet train) is very smooth, but if your child is very sensitive you might consider preventative measures; winding mountain roads here are as nausea-inducing as they are anywhere. The only other thing you might want to pack are small plastic forks and spoons, as not all restaurants have these on hand.

Sleeping

Most hotels can provide a cot for an extra fee (providing there's enough room for one). Some hotels have triple rooms, but quads or rooms with two queen-sized beds are rare. Hostels often have family rooms (or at worst, a four-person dorm room that you can book out). These also often have kitchen facilities.

Local families often stay in traditional accommodation (ryokan and *minshuku*) with large tatami rooms that can hold up to five futons, laid out in a row.

Eating

Local families take a lot of meals at 'family restaurants' (ファミレス; *famiresu*), chains like Gusto, Jonathan's, Saizeriya and Royal Host that have kids' meals, high chairs, big booths and nonsmoking sections. High chairs are not as common as in the West. Supermarkets, bakeries, fast-food restaurants and convenience stores stock sandwiches and other familiar foods; supermarkets carry baby food.

If you plan to stay at a ryokan with a meal plan, discuss any menu modifications when you book (places that regularly get foreign tourists should be accommodating); you can also book a stay without meals.

Getting Around

Children between the ages of six and 11 years ride for half-price on trains (including bullet trains), while those aged under six ride for free. Most train stations and buildings in larger cities have lifts; however, some attractions, such as temples and castles, may not have ramps. You won't get much sympathy if you get on a crowded train during morning rush-hour (7am to 9.30am) with a pram. If you must, children under 12 years can ride with mums in the less-crowded women-only carriages.

Beware that side streets often lack pavements, though fortunately traffic is generally orderly in Japan.

★ Best for Kids

Skiing at Niseko United (p224)

Visiting the Ghibli Museum (p61)

Sun and sand in Okinawa (p25)

Cycling in Hida (p165)

Baseball at Tokyo Dome (p93)

Travelling by car is often a good strategy for families, as it makes child- and luggage-wrangling easier. Destinations that are good for driving include pretty much anywhere outside the major cities.

Child seats in taxis are generally not available, but most car-rental agencies will provide one if you ask in advance.

From left: Kabira-wan (p250), Ishigaki-jima; Ghibli Museum (p61)

Ginza & Marunouchi
(p60)

TOKYO

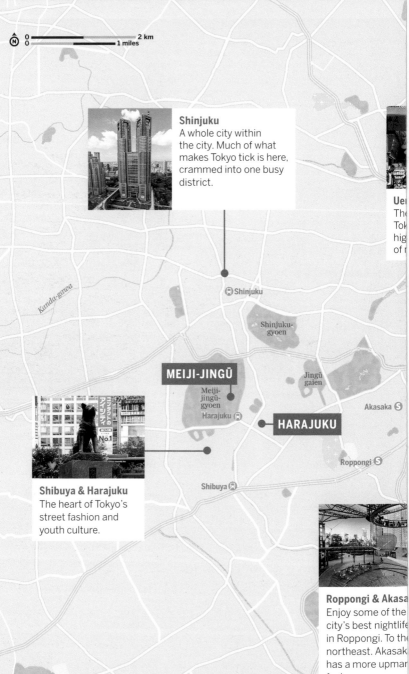

Shinjuku
A whole city within the city. Much of what makes Tokyo tick is here, crammed into one busy district.

Ue
The
Tok
hig
of

🚇 Shinjuku

Shinjuku-gyoen

MEIJI-JINGŪ

Meiji-jingū-gyoen

Harajuku 🚇

Jingū gaien

Akasaka 🆂

HARAJUKU

Roppongi 🆂

Shibuya & Harajuku
The heart of Tokyo's street fashion and youth culture.

Shibuya 🚇

Kanda-gawa

Roppongi & Akas
Enjoy some of the city's best nightlife in Roppongi. To th northeast. Akasak has a more upmar feel.

0 ——————— 2 km
0 ——————— 1 miles

Tokyo Sky Tree (p53)

Arriving in Tokyo

Tokyo is the main gateway to Japan. Most travellers will be arriving from **Narita Airport** (p95) in neighbouring Chiba Prefecture; however, **Haneda Airport** (p95), closer to the city centre, is now seeing an increasing number of international flights. Both airports have smooth, hassle-free entry procedures, and are connected to the city centre by public transport.

Sleeping

The busy western hub of Shinjuku is a traveller favourite; Asakusa, in the east, is the backpacker district. If you're here for the nightlife, consider staying in Shibuya or Roppongi. Ueno and Marunouchi (Tokyo Station) have direct train access to Narita.

For more information on the best neighbourhoods to stay in, see p99.

Kiddyland

MARTIN MOOS / GETTY IMAGES ©

Shopping in Harajuku

Harajuku is the gathering point for Tokyo's eccentric fashion tribes: the teens who hang out on Takeshita-dōri, the polished divas who strut up and down Omote-sandō and the trendsetters and peacocks who haunt the side streets.

Great For...

☑ Don't Miss

The narrow streets on either side of Omote-sandō, known as Ura-Hara ('back' Harajuku).

Takeshita-dōri

Takeshita-dōri (竹下通り; Map p66; 🚇JR Yamanote line to Harajuku, Takeshita exit) is Tokyo's famously outré fashion bazaar and a pilgrimage site for teens from all over Japan. Here trendy duds sit alongside the trappings of decades of fashion subcultures (plaid and safety pins for the punks; colourful tutus for the decora; Victorian dresses for the Gothic Lolitas).

LaForet

Laforet (ラフォーレ; Map p66; www.laforet. ne.jp; 1-11-6 Jingūmae, Shibuya-ku; ⏰11am-8pm; 🚇JR Yamanote line to Harajuku, Omote-sandō exit) has been a beacon of cutting-edge Harajuku style for decades and lots of quirky, cult favourite brands still cut their teeth here (you'll find some examples at the ground floor boutique, Wall).

Takeshita-dōri

❶ Need to Know

The JR Yamanote line stops at Harajuku. Meiji-jingūmae subway station (Chiyoda and Fukutoshin lines) is also convenient.

✕ Take a Break

Grab a bite at Harajuku Gyōza-rō (p83).

★ Top Tip

For serious shopping, avoid weekends when Harajuku gets very crowded; Takeshita-dōri in particular gets packed.

KiddyLand

Multistorey toy emporium **KiddyLand** (キデイランド; Map p66; www.kiddyland. co.jp/en/index.html; 6-1-9 Jingūmae, Shibuya-ku; ⏰10am-9pm; ®JR Yamanote line to Harajuku, Omote-sandō exit) is packed to the rafters with character goods, including all your Studio Ghibli, Sanrio and Disney faves. It's not just for kids either; you'll spot plenty of adults on a nostalgia trip down the Hello Kitty aisle.

Cat Street

Had enough of crowded Harajuku? Exit, stage right, for **Cat Street** (キャット ストリート; Map p66; ®JR Yamanote line to Harajuku, Omote-sandō exit), a windy road closed to cars and lined with a mishmash of boutiques and more room to move.

Dog

Club kids and stylists love the showpiece items at legendary Ura-Hara boutique **Dog** (ドッグ; Map p66; www.dog-hjk.com/index. html; basement fl, 3-23-3 Jingūmae, Shibuya-ku; ⏰noon-8pm; ®JR Yamanote line to Harajuku, Takeshita exit). The store itself, which is decorated to look like a derelict carnival funhouse, is much of the appeal: it looks like an art installation.

6% Doki Doki

Tucked away on an Ura-Hara backstreet in a bubblegum-pink building, **6% Doki Doki** (ロクパーセントドキドキ; Map p66; www.dokidoki6.com; 2nd fl, 4-28-16 Jingūmae, Shibuya-ku; ⏰noon-8pm; ®JR Yamanote line to Harajuku, Omote-sandō exit) sells acid-bright accessories that are part raver, part school-girl and, according to the shop's name, 'six percent exciting'. We wonder what more excitement would look like! Anyway, it's 100% Harajuku.

JAVIER LARREA / AGE FOTOSTOCK ©

Tokyo National Museum

If you visit only one museum, make it this one. Established in 1872, this collection of Japanese art covers ancient pottery, Buddhist sculpture, samurai swords, colourful ukiyo-e (woodblock prints), gorgeous kimonos and more.

Great For...

☑ **Don't Miss**

For a couple of weeks in spring and autumn, the back garden, home to five vintage teahouses, opens to the public.

Allow two hours to take in the highlights, a half-day to do the Honkan in depth or a whole day to take in everything.

Honkan (Japanese Gallery)

The museum is divided into several buildings, the most important of which is the **Honkan** (Japanese Gallery), which houses the collection of Japanese art. Visitors with only an hour or two should hone in on the galleries here. The building itself is in the Imperial Style of the 1930s, with art-deco flourishes throughout.

Gallery of Hōryū-ji Treasures

Next on the priority list is the enchanting **Gallery of Hōryū-ji Treasures**, which displays masks, scrolls and gilt Buddhas from Hōryū-ji (in Nara Prefecture, dating from 607) in a spare, elegant, box-shaped

Exhibit in the Honkan (Japanese Gallery)

ℹ️ Need to Know

東京国立博物館; Tokyo Kokuritsu Hakubu-tsukan; Map p70; ☎03-3822-1111; www.tnm.jp; 13-9 Ueno-kōen, Taitō-ku; adult/child & senior/student ¥620/free/410; ⏰9.30am-5pm Tue-Sun year-round, to 8pm Fri Mar-Dec, to 6pm Sat & Sun Mar-Aug; 🚇JR lines to Ueno, Ueno-kōen exit

✕ Take a Break

There are restaurants in the Gallery of Hōryū-ji Treasures and in the Tōyōkan.

★ Top Tip

Be sure to pick up the brochure Highlights of Japanese Art from room 1-1 on the 2nd floor of the Honkan.

contemporary building (1999) by Taniguchi Yoshio. Nearby, to the west of the main gate, is the **Kuro-mon** (Black Gate), transported from the Edo-era mansion of a feudal lord. On weekends it opens for visitors to pass through.

Tōyōkan & Heiseikan

Visitors with more time can explore the three-storied **Tōyōkan** (Gallery of Asian Art), with its collection of Buddhist sculptures from around Asia and delicate Chinese ceramics. The **Heiseikan**, accessed via a passage on the 1st floor of the Honkan, houses the Japanese Archaeological Gallery, full of pottery, talismans and articles of daily life from Japan's palaeolithic and neolithic periods. Temporary exhibitions (which cost extra) are held on the second floor of the Heiseikan; these can be fantastic, but sometimes lack the English signage found throughout the rest of the museum.

Kuroda Memorial Hall

Kuroda Seiki (1866–1924) is considered the father of modern Western-style painting in Japan. The **Kuroda Memorial Hall** (黒田記念室; Map p70; ☎03-5777-8600; www.tobunken.go.jp/kuroda/index_e.html; 13-9 Ueno-kōen, Taitō-ku; ⏰9.30am-5pm Tue-Sun; 🚇JR lines to Ueno, Ueno-kōen exit) **FREE**, an annexe to the Tokyo National Museum, has some of his works, including key pieces such as *Maiko Girl* and *Wisdom, Impression and Sentiment*, a striking triptych of three nude women on canvases coated with ground gold.

What's Nearby

Nezu-jinja
Shinto Shrine

(根津神社; Map p70; ☎03-3822-0753; www.
nedujinja.or.jp; 1-28-9 Nezu, Bunkyō-ku; ⊗24hr;
ⓈChiyoda line to Nezu, exit 1) Not only is this
one of Japan's oldest shrines, it is also easily the most beautiful in a district packed
with attractive religious buildings. The
opulently decorated structure, which dates
from the early 18th century, is one of the
city's miraculous survivors and is offset by
a long corridor of small red *torii* that makes
for great photos.

Ueno-kōen
Park

(上野公園; Map p70; http://ueno-bunka.
jp; Ueno-kōen, Taitō-ku; ⓇJR lines to Ueno,
Ueno-kōen & Shinobazu exits) Best known for
its profusion of cherry trees that burst
into blossom in spring (making this one

of Tokyo's top *hanami* – blossom viewing
– spots), sprawling Ueno-kōen is also the
location of the city's highest concentration
of museums. At the southern tip is the large
scenic pond, Shinobazu-ike, choked with
lotus flowers.

Ueno Tōshō-gū
Shinto Shrine

(上野東照宮; Map p70; ☎03-3822-3455;
www.uenotoshogu.com; 9-88 Ueno-kōen, Taitō-
ku; ¥500; ⊗9am-5.30pm Mar-Sep, to 4.30pm
Oct-Feb; ⓇJR lines to Ueno, Shinobazu exit) This
shrine inside Ueno-kōen (p42) was built
in honour of Tokugawa Ieyasu, the warlord
who unified Japan. Resplendent in gold
leaf and ornate details, it dates from 1651
(though it has had recent touch-ups). You
can get a pretty good look from outside the
gate, if you want to skip the admission fee.

Ameya-yokochō

Ameya-yokochō
Market

(アメヤ横町; Map p70; www.ameyoko.net; 4 Ueno, Taitō-ku; ⏰10am-7pm, some shops close Wed; 🚉JR lines to Okachimachi, north exit) Step into this partially open-air market paralleling and beneath the JR line tracks, and ritzy, glitzy Tokyo feels like a distant memory. It got its start as a black market, post-WWII, when American goods were sold here. Today, it's packed with vendors selling everything from fresh seafood and exotic cooking spices to jeans, sneakers and elaborately embroidered bomber jackets.

Don't miss the neighbourhood of Yanaka, near the Tokyo National Museum. It's home to dozens of temples; many artists have studios here, too. Start your exploration at the Asakura Museum of Sculpture, Taitō (p43).

Asakura Museum of Sculpture, Taitō
Museum

(朝倉彫塑館; Map p70; www.taitocity.net/ taito/asakura; 7-16-10 Yanaka, Taitō-ku; adult/ student ¥500/250; ⏰9.30am-4.30pm Tue, Wed & Fri-Sun; 🚉JR Yamanote line to Nippori, north exit) Sculptor Asakura Fumio (artist name Chōso; 1883–1964) designed this atmospheric house himself. It combined his original Japanese home and garden with a large studio that incorporated vaulted ceilings, a 'sunrise room' and a rooftop garden with wonderful neighbourhood views. It's now a reverential museum with many of the artist's signature realist works, mostly of people and cats, on display.

Yanaka Ginza
Area

(谷中銀座; Map p70; 🚉JR Yamanote line to Nippori, north exit) Yanaka Ginza is pure, vintage mid-20th-century Tokyo, a pedestrian street lined with butcher shops, vegetable vendors and the like. Most Tokyo neighbourhoods once had stretches like these (until supermarkets took over). It's popular with Tokyoites from all over the city, who come to soak up the nostalgic atmosphere, plus the locals who shop here.

SCAI the Bathhouse
Gallery

(スカイザバスハウス; Map p70; 🎵03-3821-1144; www.scaithebathhouse.com; 6-1-23 Yanaka, Taitō-ku; ⏰noon-6pm Tue-Sat; 🚇Chiyoda line to Nezu, exit 1) **FREE** This 200-year-old bathhouse has for several decades been an avant-garde gallery space, showcasing Japanese and international artists in its austere vaulted space.

Ueno Zoo
Zoo

(上野動物園; Ueno Dōbutsu-en; Map p70; 🎵03-3828-5171; www.tokyo-zoo.net; 9-83 Ueno-kōen, Taitō-ku; adult/child ¥600/free; ⏰9.30am-5pm Tue-Sun; 🚉JR lines to Ueno, Ueno-kōen exit) Japan's oldest zoo, established in 1882, is home to animals from around the globe, but the biggest attractions are two giant pandas that arrived from China in 2011 – Rī Rī and Shin Shin. There's also a whole area devoted to lemurs, which makes sense given Tokyoites' love of all things cute.

PISGAXX / SHUTTERSTOCK ©

Tokyo National Museum

HISTORIC HIGHLIGHTS

It would be a challenge to take in everything the sprawling Tokyo National Museum has to offer in a day. Fortunately, the Honkan (Japanese Gallery) is designed to give visitors a crash course in Japanese art history from the Jōmon era (13,000–300 BC) to the Edo era (AD 1603–1868). The works on display here are rotated regularly, to protect fragile ones and to create seasonal exhibitions, so you're always guaranteed to see something new.

Buy your ticket from outside the main gate then head straight to the Honkan with its sloping tile roof. Stow your coat in a locker and take the central staircase up to the 2nd floor, where the exhibitions are arranged chronologically. Allow two hours for this tour of the highlights.

The first room on your right starts from the beginning with **ancient Japanese art ❶**. Be sure to pick up a copy of the brochure *Highlights of Japanese Art* at the entrance.

Continue to the **National Treasure Gallery ❷**. 'National Treasure' is the highest distinction awarded to a work of art in Japan. Keep an eye out for more National Treasures, labelled in red, on display in other rooms throughout the museum.

Moving on, stop to admire the **courtly art gallery ❸**, the **samurai armour and swords ❹** and the *ukiyo-e* and kimono ❺.

Next, take the stairs down to the 1st floor, where each room is dedicated to a different decorative art, such as lacquerware or ceramics. Don't miss the excellent examples of **religious sculpture ❻** and **folk art ❼**.

Finish your visit with a look inside the enchanting **Gallery of Hōryū-ji Treasures ❽**.

Ukiyo-e & Kimono (Room 10)
Chic silken kimono and lushly coloured *ukiyo-e* (woodblock prints) are two icons of the Edo-era (AD 1603–1868) *ukiyo* – the 'floating world', or world of fleeting beauty and pleasure.

Japanese Sculpture (Room 11)
Many of Japan's most famous sculptures, religious in nature, are locked away in temple reliquaries. This is a rare chance to see them up close.

MUSEUM GARDEN

Don't miss the garden if you visit in spring and autumn during the few weeks it's open to the public.

Heiseikan & Japanese Archaeology Gallery

Research & Information Centre

Hyōkeikan

Kuro-mon

Main Gate

Gallery of Hōryū-ji Treasures
Surround yourself with miniature gilt Buddhas from Hōryū-ji, one of Japan's oldest Buddhist temples, founded in 607. Don't miss the graceful Pitcher with Dragon Head, a National Treasure.

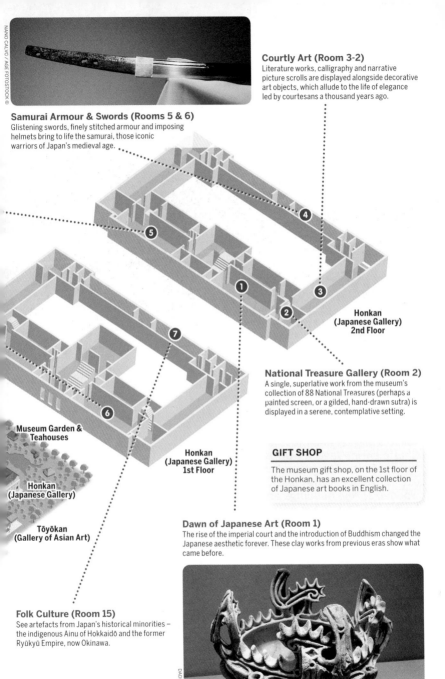

Courtly Art (Room 3-2)
Literature works, calligraphy and narrative picture scrolls are displayed alongside decorative art objects, which allude to the life of elegance led by courtesans a thousand years ago.

Samurai Armour & Swords (Rooms 5 & 6)
Glistening swords, finely stitched armour and imposing helmets bring to life the samurai, those iconic warriors of Japan's medieval age.

Honkan (Japanese Gallery) 2nd Floor

National Treasure Gallery (Room 2)
A single, superlative work from the museum's collection of 88 National Treasures (perhaps a painted screen, or a gilded, hand-drawn sutra) is displayed in a serene, contemplative setting.

Museum Garden & Teahouses

Honkan (Japanese Gallery)

Tōyōkan (Gallery of Asian Art)

Honkan (Japanese Gallery) 1st Floor

GIFT SHOP

The museum gift shop, on the 1st floor of the Honkan, has an excellent collection of Japanese art books in English.

Dawn of Japanese Art (Room 1)
The rise of the imperial court and the introduction of Buddhism changed the Japanese aesthetic forever. These clay works from previous eras show what came before.

Folk Culture (Room 15)
See artefacts from Japan's historical minorities – the indigenous Ainu of Hokkaidō and the former Ryūkyū Empire, now Okinawa.

NANO CALVO / AGE FOTOSTOCK ©

DADEROT / CC0 1.0 ©

COWARDLION / SHUTTERSTOCK ©

Meiji-jingū

Tokyo's largest and most famous Shintō shrine feels a world away from the city. The grounds are vast, enveloping the classic wooden shrine buildings and a landscaped garden in a thick coat of green.

Meiji-jingū is dedicated to the Emperor Meiji and Empress Shōken, whose reign (1868–1912) coincided with Japan's transformation from isolationist, feudal state to modern nation. The shrine is undergoing renovation in preparation for its centennial in 2020; some structures may be under wraps, but as a whole it will remain open.

The Gates

Several wooden *torii* mark the entrance to Meiji-jingū. The largest, created from a 1500-year-old Taiwanese cypress, stands 12m high. It's the custom to bow upon passing through a *torii,* which marks the boundary between the mundane world and the sacred one.

Great For...

☑ **Don't Miss**

Meiji-jingū Gyoen when the irises bloom in June.

Ladles at the *temizuya* (font)

⊙ **Meiji-jingu**

Yoyogi-kōen

Meiji-dōri

Takeshita-dōri

Harajuku Ⓡ

Ⓢ Meiji-jingūmae

ⓘ Need to Know

明治神宮; Map p66; www.meijijingu.
or.jp; 1-1 Yoyogi Kamizono-chō, Shibuya-ku;
⊘dawn-dusk; ®JR Yamanote line to Harajuku, Omote-sandō exit FREE

✕ Take a Break

Coffee shop **Mori no Terrace** (杜の
テラス; Map p66; ☑03-3379-9222; 1-1
Yoyogi Kamizono-chō, Shibuya-ku; ⊘9am-
dusk) is right on the gravel path leading
into the shrine grounds.

★ Top Tip

Time your visit for 8am or 2pm to
catch the twice daily *nikkusai*, the ceremonial offering of food and prayers
to the gods.

The Font

Before approaching the main shrine, visitors purify themselves by pouring water
over their hands at the *temizuya* (font).
Dip the ladle in the water and first rinse
your left hand then your right. Pour some
water into your left hand and rinse your
mouth, then rinse your left hand again.
Make sure none of this water gets back
into the font!

Main Shrine

Constructed in 1920 and destroyed in
WWII air raids, the shrine was rebuilt in
1958; however, unlike so many of Japan's
postwar reconstructions, Meiji-jingū has
an authentic old-world feel. The main
shrine is made of cypress from the Kiso
region of Nagano. To make an offering,
toss a ¥5 coin in the box, bow twice, clap

your hands twice and then bow again. To
the right, you'll see kiosks selling *ema*
(wooden plaques on which prayers are
written) and *omamori* (charms).

Meiji-jingū Gyoen

The shrine itself occupies only a small
fraction of the sprawling forested
grounds, which contain some 120,000
trees collected from all over Japan. Along
the path towards the main shrine, is the
entrance to **Meiji-jingū Gyoen**
(明治神宮御苑; Inner Garden; Map p66;
¥500; ⊘9am-4.30pm, to 4pm Nov-Feb; ®JR
Yamanote line to Harajuku, Omote-Sandō exit), a
landscaped garden. It once belonged to a
feudal estate; however, when the grounds
passed into imperial hands, the emperor
himself designed the iris garden to please
the empress.

Pop Culture in Akihabara

With its neon-bright electronics stores, retro arcades and cosplay (costume play) cafes 'Akiba' – as it's known to locals – is equal parts sensory overload, cultural mind-bender and just plain fun.

Great For...

☑ **Don't Miss**

See anime fans dressed as their favourite characters on Chūō-dōri on Sunday afternoons.

Manga & Anime

When *otaku* (geeks) dream of heaven, it probably looks a lot like **Mandarake Complex** (まんだらけコンプレックス; www. mandarake.co.jp; 3-11-2 Soto-Kanda, Chiyoda-ku; ☻noon-8pm; ℞JR Yamanote line to Akihabara, Electric Town exit). Eight storeys are piled high with comic books and DVDs, action figures and cell art just for starters. The 5th floor, in all its pink splendour, is devoted to women's comics, while the 4th floor is for men.

Retro Arcades

On the 5th floor of **Super Potato Retro-kan** (スーパーポテトレトロ館; www.superpotato. com; 1-11-2 Soto-kanda, Chiyoda-ku; ☻11am-8pm Mon-Fri, from 10am Sat & Sun; ℞JR Yamanote line to Akihabara, Electric Town exit), a store specialising in used video games, there's a retro video arcade where you can get your

Akihabara

ⓘ Need to Know

The JR Yamanote and Sōbu lines and Hibiya subway line stop at Akihabara.

✕ Take a Break

Akihabara is full of restaurants serving comfort food like ramen and curry.

★ Top Tip

Pick up an English map at Akiba Info (☎080-3413-4800; www.animecenter.jp; 2nd fl, Akihabara UDX Bldg, 4-14-1 Soto-Kanda, Chiyoda-ku; ⊙11am-5.30pm Tue, Wed & Fri-Sun; ☎; ⓇJR Yamanote line to Akihabara, Electric Town exit)**; the helpful staff here speak English.**

hands on some old-fashioned consoles at a bargain ¥100 per game.

Go-Karting

We're not sure how this is legal but rest-assured (at least at the time of research) it is: *cosplay* go-karting on city streets. Sign up in advance with **Akiba Kart** (アキバカート; ☎03-6206-4752; http:// akibanavi.net; 2-4-6 Soto-kanda, Chiyoda-ku; 1hr from ¥2700; ⊙10am-8pm; ⓇJR Yamanote line to Akihabara, Electric Town exit); you'll need an international driver's licence.

Maid Cafes

'Maid cafes' with *kawaii* (cute) waitresses, dressed as saucy French or prim Victorian maids, are a stock in trade of Akiba. **@Home** (@ほぉ〜むカフェ; www.cafe-athome. com; 4th-7th fl, 1-11-4 Soto-Kanda, Chiyoda-ku;

drinks from ¥500; ⊙11.30am-10pm Mon-Fri, 10.30am-10pm Sat & Sun; ⓇJR Yamanote line to Akihabara, Electric Town exit) is one of the more 'wholesome' of them. You'll be welcomed as *go-shujinsama* (master) or *o-jōsama* (miss) the minute you enter. The maids serve drinks and dishes, such as curried rice, topped with smiley faces.

Live Performances

Shows by the girl group Kamen Joshi – singing and dancing young women wearing cute outfits and hockey masks – are all the rage at **P.A.R.M.S** (☎012-075-9835; www. pasela.co.jp; 7th fl, Pasela Resorts Akihabara-Den-kigai, 1-13-2 Soto-kanda, Chiyoda-ku; admission incl 1 drink Mon-Fri ¥1500, Sat & Sun ¥3500; ⊙shows 5.30pm & 8.15pm Mon-Fri, 10.30am Sat & Sun; ⓇJR Yamanote line to Akihabara, Electric Town exit), a live-music show in the Pasela Resort's karaoke emporium. It's a chance to swing around a light sabre (handed out to audience members) in a thoroughly Akiba night out.

COWARD_LION · GETTY IMAGES ©

Sensō-ji

Sensō-ji is the capital's oldest temple, far older than Tokyo itself. Today the temple stands out for its old-world atmosphere – a glimpse of a bygone Japan rarely visible in Tokyo today.

Great For...

☑ Don't Miss

All the traditional snack food sold along Nakamise-dōri.

According to legend, in AD 628, two fishermen brothers pulled out a golden image of Kannon (the bodhisattva of compassion) from the nearby Sumida-gawa. Sensō-ji was built to enshrine it.

Kaminari-mon

The temple precinct begins at the majestic **Kaminari-mon**, which means Thunder Gate. An enormous *chōchin* (lantern), which weighs 670kg, hangs from the centre. On either side are a pair of protective deities: Fūjin, the god of wind, on the right; and Raijin, the god of thunder, on the left. Kaminari-mon has burnt down countless times over the centuries; the current gate dates to 1970.

Nakamise-dōri Shopping Street

Beyond Kaminari-mon is the bustling shopping street, Nakamise-dōri. With its lines of

Kaminari-mon lantern

❶ Need to Know

浅草寺; Map p70; ☑03-3842-0181; www.
senso-ji.jp; 2-3-1 Asakusa, Taitō-ku; ⏰24hr;
Ⓢ Ginza line to Asakusa, exit 1 FREE

✕ Take a Break

Stop for ice cream at **Chōchin Monaka**
(ちょうちんもなか; Map p70; 2-3-1
Asakusa, Taitō-ku; ice cream ¥330; ⏰10am-
5pm; Ⓢ Ginza line to Asakusa, exit 1) on
Nakamise-dōri.

> ### ★ Top Tip
> The minutes just before the sun sinks
> make for some of the best pictures of
> this photogenic sanctuary.

souvenir stands it is very touristy, though
that's nothing new: Sensō-ji has been
Tokyo's top tourist sight for centuries, since
travel was restricted to religious pilgrimages during the feudal era. In addition to the
usual T-shirts, you can find Edo-style crafts
and oddities (such as wigs done up in traditional hairstyles). There are also numerous
snack vendors serving up crunchy *sembei*
(rice crackers) and *age-manju* (deep-fried
anko – bean-paste – buns).

Hōzō-mon

At the end of Nakamise-dōri is **Hōzō-mon**
(宝蔵門; Map p70; www.senso-ji.jp/guide/
hozomon_e.html; 2-3-1 Asakusa, Taitō-ku;
Ⓢ Ginza line to Asakusa, exit 1), another gate
with fierce guardians. On the gate's back
side are a pair of 2500kg, 4.5m-tall *waraji*
(straw sandals) crafted for Sensō-ji by

some 800 villagers in northern Yamagata
Prefecture. These are meant to symbolise
the Buddha's power, and it's believed that
evil spirits will be scared off by the giant
footwear.

Hondō (Main Hall)

In front of the grand **Hondō** (Main Hall), with
its dramatic sloping roof, is a large cauldron
with smoking incense. The smoke is said to
bestow health and you'll see people wafting
it over their bodies. The current Hondō was
constructed in 1958, replacing the one destroyed in WWII air raids. The style is similar
to the previous one, though the roof tiles are
made of titanium.

The **Kannon image** (a tiny 6cm) is
cloistered away from view deep inside the
Main Hall (and admittedly may not exist
at all). Nonetheless, a steady stream of
worshippers visits the temple to cast coins,
pray and bow in a gesture of respect. Do
feel free to join in.

Off the courtyard stands a 53m-high **Five-Storey Pagoda**, a 1973 reconstruction of a pagoda built by Tokugawa Iemitsu; the current structure, renovated in 2017, is the second-highest pagoda in Japan.

Omikuji

Don't miss getting your fortune told by an *omikuji* (paper fortune). Drop ¥100 into the slots by the wooden drawers at either side of the approach to the Main Hall, grab a silver canister and shake it. Extract a stick and note its number (in kanji). Replace the stick, find the matching drawer and withdraw a paper fortune (there's English on the back). If you pull out 大凶 (*dai-kyō*, Great Curse), never fear. Just tie the paper on the nearby rack, ask the gods for better luck, and try again!

Asakusa-jinja

On the east side of the temple complex is **Asakusa-jinja** (浅草神社; Map p70; ☎03-3844-1575; www.asakusajinja.jp/english; 2-3-1 Asakusa, Taitō-ku; ◷9am-4.30pm; ⑤Ginza line to Asakusa, exit 1), built in honour of the brothers who discovered the Kannon statue that inspired the construction of Sensō-ji. (Historically, Japan's two religions, Buddhism and Shintō, were intertwined and it was not uncommon for temples to include shrines and vice versa.) This section of Sensō-ji survived WWII and Asakusa-jinja's current structure dates to 1649. Painted a deep shade of red, it is a rare example of early Edo architecture.

Next to the shrine is the temple complex's eastern gate, **Niten-mon**, standing since 1618. Though it appears minor today, this gate was the point of entry for visitors

Nakamise-dōri (p50)

arriving in Asakusa via boat – the main form of transport during the Edo period.

What's Nearby?

Edo-Tokyo Museum Museum

(江戸東京博物館; ☏03-3626-9974; www.edo-to-kyo-museum.or.jp; 1-4-1 Yokoami, Sumida-ku; adult/child ¥600/free; ◷9.30am-5.30pm, to 7.30pm Sat, closed Mon; 🚉JR Sōbu line to Ryō-goku, west exit) This history museum, in a cavernous building, does an excellent job laying out Tokyo's miraculous transformation from feudal city to modern capital, through city models, miniatures of real

> ☑ **Don't Miss**
>
> Sensō-ji is home to many annual traditional festivals, the most famous of which is May's Sanja Matsuri. Ask for a list of events at a TIC.

TAKASHI IMAGES / SHUTTERSTOCK ©

buildings, reproductions of old maps and *ukiyo-e*. It starts with a bang as you cross the life-sized partial replica of the original Nihombashi bridge and gaze down on facades of a kabuki theatre and Meiji-era bank. There is English signage throughout and a free audio guide available (¥1000 deposit).

Sumida Hokusai Museum Museum

(すみだ北斎美術館; ☏03-6658-8931; http://hokusai-museum.jp; 2-7-2 Kamezawa, Sumida-ku; adult/child/student ¥1200/400/900; ◷9.30am-5.30pm Tue-Sun; 🚇Oedo line to Ryōgoku, exit A4) The artist Katsushika Hokusai was born and died close to the location of this new museum, opened in 2016. The striking aluminium-clad building is designed by Pritzker Prize–winning architect Kazuyo Sejima. The museum's collection numbers more than 1500 pieces and includes some of the master's most famous images, such as *The Great Wave off Kanagawa* from his series *Thirty-six Views of Mount Fuji*.

Tokyo Sky Tree Tower

(東京スカイツリー; Map p70; www.tokyo-skytree.jp; 1-1-2 Oshiage, Sumida-ku; 350m/450m observation decks ¥2060/3090; ◷8am-10pm; 🚇Hanzōmon line to Oshiage, Sky Tree exit) Tokyo Sky Tree opened in May 2012 as the world's tallest 'free-standing tower' at 634m. Its silvery exterior of steel mesh morphs from a triangle at the base to a circle at 300m. There are two observation decks, at 350m and 450m. You can see more of the city during daylight hours – at peak visibility you can see up to 100km away, all the way to Mt Fuji – but it is at night that Tokyo appears truly beautiful.

> ★ **Did You Know?**
>
> Tokyo Sky Tree employs an ancient construction technique used in pagodas: a shimbashira column, structurally separate from the exterior truss. It acts as a counterweight when the tower sways, cutting vibrations by 50%.

BORIS B / SHUTTERSTOCK ©

Day Trip to Nikkō

Ancient moss clinging to a stone wall; rows of perfectly aligned stone lanterns; vermilion gates; and towering cedars: this is only a pathway in Nikkō (日光), a sanctuary that enshrines the glories of the Edo period (1600–1868).

Great For...

☑ Don't Miss

While Tōshō-gū is the star attraction, Tai-yūin-byō (p56), built two generations later, is considered more refined.

History

In the middle of the 8th century the Buddhist priest Shōdō Shōnin (735–817) established a hermitage at Nikkō. For centuries the mountains served as a training ground for Buddhist monks, though the area fell gradually into obscurity. Nikkō's enduring fame was sealed, however, when it was chosen as the site for the mausoleum of Tokugawa Ieyasu, the warlord who established the shogunate that ruled Japan for more than 250 years.

Ieyasu was laid to rest among Nikkō's towering cedars at a much less grand Tōshō-gū in 1617. Seventeen years later his grandson, Tokugawa Iemitsu, commenced work on the colossal shrine that can be seen today, using an army of some 15,000 artisans from across Japan, who took two years to complete the project.

Torii in front of Yōmei-mon, Tōshō-gū

Tōshō-gū

A World Heritage Site, **Tōshō-gū** (東照宮; www.toshogu.jp; 2301 Sannai; adult/child ¥1300/450; ⊗8am-4.30pm Apr-Oct, to 3.30pm Nov-Mar) is a brilliantly decorative shrine in a beautiful natural setting. The stone steps of **Omotesandō** lead past the towering stone *torii*, **Ishi-dorii**, and the **Gōjūnotō** (五重塔; Five Storey Pagoda), a 1819 reconstruction of the mid-17th-century original, to **Omote-mon** (表門), Tōshō-gū's main gateway, protected on either side by Deva kings.

In the first courtyard are the **Sanjinko** (三神庫; Three Sacred Storehouses); on the upper storey of the Kamijinko (upper storehouse) are relief carvings of 'imaginary elephants' by an artist who had never seen the real thing. Nearby is the **Shinkyūsha** (神厩舎; Sacred Stable), adorned with relief carvings of monkeys. The allegorical 'hear no evil, see

no evil, speak no evil' simians demonstrate three principles of Tendai Buddhism.

Continuing further, to the left of the drum tower, is **Honji-dō** (本地堂), a hall known for the painting on its ceiling of the Nakiryū (Crying Dragon). Monks demonstrate the hall's acoustical properties by clapping two sticks together. The dragon 'roars' (a bit of a stretch) when the sticks are clapped beneath its mouth, but not elsewhere.

Once the scaffolding comes off in 2018, the **Yōmei-mon** (陽明門; Sunset Gate) will be grander than ever, its gold leaf and intricate, coloured carvings and paintings of flowers, dancing girls, mythical beasts and Chinese sages renewed. Worrying that the gate's perfection might arouse envy in the gods, those responsible for its construction had the final supporting pillar placed upside down as a deliberate error.

Gōhonsha (御本社), the main inner courtyard, includes the **Honden** (本殿; Main Hall) and **Haiden** (拝殿; Hall of Worship). Inside these halls are paintings of the 36 immortal poets of Kyoto, and a ceiling-painting pattern from the Momoyama period; note the 100 dragons, each different. *Fusuma* (sliding door) paintings depict a *kirin* (a mythical beast that's part giraffe and part dragon).

To the right of the Gōhonsha is **Sakashita-mon** (坂下門), into which is carved a tiny wooden sculpture of the **Nemuri-neko** that's famous for its lifelike appearance (though admittedly the attraction is lost on some visitors). From here it's an uphill path through towering cedars to the appropriately solemn **Okumiya** (奥宮), Ieyasu's tomb.

Rinnō-ji

The Tendai-sect temple **Rinnō-ji** (輪王寺; ☎0288-54-0531; http://rinnoji.or.jp; 2300 Yamanouchi; adult/child ¥400/200; ⊗8am-5pm Apr-Oct, to 4pm Nov-Mar) was founded 1200 years ago by Shōdō Shōnin. The main hall houses a trio of 8m gilded wooden Buddha statues: Amida Nyorai (a primal deity in the Mahayana Buddhist canon) flanked by Senjū (deity of mercy and compassion) and Batō (a horse-headed Kannon). Its exterior is under wraps for restoration until 2019, with a life-size graphic adorning the building's scaffolding, *trompe l'œil* style.

Rinnō-ji's **Hōmotsu-den** (宝物殿, Treasure Hall; ¥300; ⊗8am-5pm, to 4pm Nov-Mar) houses some 6000 treasures associated with the temple; the separate admission ticket includes entrance to the lovely Edo-period strolling garden, **Shōyō-en** (逍遥園; in combination with Hōmotsu-den ¥300; ⊗8am-5pm Apr-Oct, to 4pm Nov-Mar).

Taiyūin-byō

Ieyasu's grandson Iemitsu (1604–51) is buried at **Taiyūin-byō** (大猷院廟; adult/child ¥550/250; ⊗8am-4.30pm Apr-Oct, to 3.30pm Nov-Mar). Although the shrine houses many of the same elements as Tōshō-gū (storehouses, drum tower, Chinese-style

Sake barrels, Rinnō-ji

gates etc), the more intimate scale and setting in a cryptomefria forest make it very appealing.

Look for dozens of lanterns donated by *daimyō* (domain lords), and the gate Niō-mon, whose guardian deities have a hand up (to welcome those with pure hearts) and a hand down (to suppress those with impure hearts). Inside the main hall, 140 dragons painted on the ceiling are said to carry prayers to the heavens; those holding

Under Construction

As the shrine gears up for its 400th anniversary, a major restoration program is underway. Until at least 2018, Tōshō-gū's Yōmei-mon and Shimojinko (one of the Three Sacred Storehouses) will be obscured by scaffolding.

BRIAN GUZZETTI / DESIGN PICS / GETTY IMAGES ©

pearls are on their way up, and those without are returning to gather more prayers.

Kanman-ga-Fuchi Abyss

Kanman-ga-Fuchi Abyss (憾満ガ淵) is a wooded path lined with a collection of *Jizō* statues (the small stone effigies of the Buddhist protector of travellers and children). After passing the Shin-kyō bridge, follow the Daiya-gawa west for about 1km, crossing another bridge near Jyoko-ji temple en route. It's said that if you try to count the statues there and again on the way back, you'll end up with a different number, hence the nickname 'Bake-jizō' (ghost Jizō).

Getting There & Away

You can usually get last-minute seats on the Tōbu Nikkō line's hourly reserved *tokkyū* (limited-express) trains (¥2700, 1¾ hours) departing from Tōbu Asakusa Station. *Kaisoku* (rapid) trains (¥1360, 2½ hours, hourly from 6.20am to 5.30pm) require no reservation, but you may have to change at Shimo-imaichi. Be sure to ride in the last two cars to reach Nikkō (some cars may separate at an intermediate stop).

JR Pass holders can take the Tōhoku *shinkansen* (bullet train) from Tokyo to Utsunomiya (¥4930, 54 minutes) and change there for an ordinary train to Nikkō (¥740, 45 minutes).

★ Did you know?

This much-photographed red footbridge, Shin-kyō, is where Shōdō Shōnin is said to have been carried across the Daiya-gawa on the backs of two giant serpents.

Shinjuku After Dark

Shinjuku is Tokyo's largest – and liveliest – nightlife district. The size and depth means there is truly something for everyone, from flashy cabarets to bohemian hole-in-the walls

Start Shinjuku Station (east exit)
Distance 1.5km
Duration one hour

Shokuan-dori

 Seibu Shinjuku

Kabukicho Ichiban-gai

Ome-kaido

2 Bask in the lights of Shinjuku's main drag, **Yasukuni-dōri**, where *izakaya* (Japanese pub-eateries) are stacked several stories high.

Yasukuni-dori

2

Shinjuku-nishiguchi

START **1**

Shinjuku

NISHI-SHINJUKU

 Shinjuku

Shinjuku

1 Start the evening with a round of *yakitori* at the historic cluster of stalls **Omoide-yokochō** (p83).

3 Kabukichō, Tokyo's red-light district, is marked by an electric red *torii* (gate).

4 Don't miss the neighbourhood's newest landmark, **Shinjuku TOHO building**, with its enormous Godzilla statue.

KABUKICHO

KABUKICHO

4

3

Central Rd

5

Kuyakusho-dori

7 Stroll through Golden Gai, a warren of tiny alleys and narrow, two-storey wooden buildings housing hundreds of closet-sized bars.

7

Take a Break Finish with a late night bowl of ramen at **Nagi** (p85).

6

Yasukuni-dori

FINISH

GOLDEN GAI

SHINJUKU

Classic Photo Posing with the buxom robots parked outside the Robot Restaurant.

6 At **Don Quijote** (p78), an out-there, all-night emporium, you can pick up everything from a bottle of wine to a nurse's costume.

5 Kabukichō cabaret **Robot Restaurant** (p93) glows bright enough to light all of Shinjuku.

◉ SIGHTS

◉ Ginza & Marunouchi

Tsukiji Market
Market

(東京都中央卸売市場, Tokyo Metropolitan
Central Wholesale Produce; Map p62; ☎03-
3261-8326; www.tsukiji-market.or.jp; 5-2-1 Tsukiji,
Chūō-ku; ☺5am-1pm, closed Sun, most Wed &
all public holidays; ⑤Hibiya line to Tsukiji, exit 1)
FREE Fruit, vegetables, flowers and meat
are sold here, but it's seafood – around
2000 tonnes of it traded daily – that Tsukiji
is most famous for. The frenetic **inner
market** (*jōnai-shijō*) is slated to move to
Toyosu in 2017 or possibly later; the equally
fascinating **outer market** (場外市場; Jōgai
Shijō; Map p62; 6-chōme Tsukiji, Chūō-ku;
☺5am-2pm; ⑤Hibiya line to Tsukiji, exit 1),
comprising hundreds of food stalls and
restaurants, will stay put.

Before coming here, check the market's
online calendar to make sure it's open,
and for instructions on attending the **tuna
auctions**, which start around 5am.

Imperial Palace
Palace

(皇居; Kōkyo; Map p62; ☎03-5223-8071;
http://sankan.kunaicho.go.jp/english/guide/
koukyo.html; 1 Chiyoda, Chiyoda-ku; tours
usually 10am & 1.30pm Tue-Sat; ⑤Chiyoda line to
Ōtemachi, exits C13b & C10) **FREE** The Imperial
Palace occupies the site of the original
Edo-jō, the Tokugawa shogunate's castle.
In its heyday this was the largest fortress in
the world, though little remains of it today
apart from the moat and stone walls. Most
of the 3.4-sq-km complex is off-limits, as
this is the emperor's home, but you can
join one of the free tours organised by the
Imperial Household Agency to see a small
part of the inner compound.

Intermediatheque
Museum

(Map p62; ☎03-5777-8600; www.intermedia
theque.jp; 2nd & 3rd fl, JP Tower, 2-7-2
Marunouchi, Chiyoda-ku; ☺11am-6pm Sun &
Tue-Thu, to 8pm Fri & Sat; ℝJR Yamanote line
to Tokyo, Marunouchi exit) **FREE** Dedicated to
interdisciplinary experimentation, Interme-
diatheque cherry picks from the vast collection of the University of Tokyo (Tōdai) to
craft a fascinating, contemporary museum

Buyers inspecting tuna, Tsukiji Market

experience. Go from viewing the best ornithological taxidermy collection in Japan to a giant pop-art print or the beautifully encased skeleton of a dinosaur. A handsome Tōdai lecture hall is reconstituted as a forum for events, including the playing of 1920s jazz recordings on a gramophone or old movie screenings.

National Museum of Modern Art (MOMAT) Museum

(国立近代美術館; Kokuritsu Kindai Bijutsukan; Map p62; 03-5777-8600; www.momat.go.jp/english; 3-1 Kitanomaru-kōen, Chiyoda-ku; adult/student ¥430/130, extra for special exhibitions; 10am-5pm Tue-Thu, Sat & Sun, to 8pm Fri; Tōzai line to Takebashi, exit 1b) Regularly changing displays from the museum's superb collection of more than 12,000 works, by both local and international artists, are shown over floors four to two; special exhibitions are mounted on the ground floor. All pieces date from the Meiji period onward and impart a sense of how modern Japan has developed through portraits, photography, contemporary sculptures and video works. Don't miss the 'Room with a View' for a panorama of the Imperial Palace East Garden (p61).

Hama-rikyū Onshi-teien Gardens

(浜離宮恩賜庭園; Detached Palace Garden; Map p62; www.tokyo-park.or.jp/park/format/index028.html; 1-1 Hama-rikyū-teien, Chūō-ku; adult/child ¥300/free; 9am-5pm; Ōedo line to Shiodome, exit A1) This beautiful garden, one of Tokyo's finest, is all that remains of a shogunal palace that once extended into the area now occupied by Tsukiji Market (p60). The main features are a large duck pond with an island that's home to a charming tea pavilion, Nakajima no Ochaya, as well as some wonderfully manicured trees (black pine, Japanese apricot, hydrangeas etc), some of which are hundreds of years old.

Imperial Palace East Garden Gardens

(東御苑; Kōkyo Higashi-gyoen; Map p62; http://sankan.kunaicho.go.jp; 1 Chiyoda, Chiyoda-ku; 9am-4pm Nov-Feb, to 4.30pm Mar–mid-

 Ghibli Museum

Master animator Miyazaki Hayao and his Studio Ghibli (pronounced 'jiburi') have been responsible for some of the best-loved films in Japan – and the world. Miyazaki designed the **Ghibli Museum** (ジブリ美術館; www.ghibli-museum.jp; 1-1-83 Shimo-Renjaku, Mitaka-shi; adult ¥1000, child ¥100-700; 10am-6pm, closed Tue; JR Sōbu-Chūō line to Mitaka, south exit) himself, and it's redolent of the dreamy, vaguely steampunk atmosphere that makes his animations so enchanting. A highlight for children (sorry grown-ups!) is a giant, plush replica of the cat bus from the classic *My Neighbor Totoro* (1988) that kids can climb on. There's also a small theatre where original animated shorts – which can only be seen here – are screened (you'll get a ticket for this when you enter). The film changes monthly to keep fans coming back.

Tickets must be purchased in advance, and you must choose the exact time and date you plan to visit. Get them through a travel agent in your home country up to three months before (the sooner the better). See the website for details. A minibus (round trip/one way ¥320/210) leaves for the museum every 20 minutes from Mitaka Station (bus stop 9).

Apr, Sep & Oct, to 5pm mid-Apr–Aug, closed Mon & Fri year-round; Chiyoda line to Ōtemachi, exit C13b or C10) FREE Crafted from part of the original castle compound, these lovely free

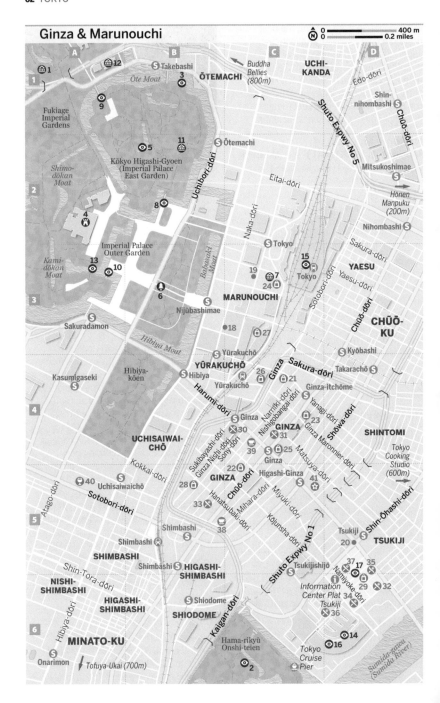

Ginza & Marunouchi

Ginza & Marunouchi

gardens allow you to get close-up views of the massive stones used to build the castle walls, and even climb the ruins of one of the keeps, off the upper lawn. The number of visitors at any one time is limited, so it never feels crowded.

Crafts Gallery   Museum

(東京国立近代美術館 工芸館; Map p62; www.momat.go.jp/english; 1 Kitanomaru-kōen, Chiyoda-ku; adult/child ¥210/70, 1st Sun of month free; ◈10am-5pm Tue-Sun; Ⓢ Tōzai line to Takebashi, exit 1b) Housed in a vintage red-brick building, this annexe of MOMAT (p61) stages excellent changing exhibitions of *mingei* (folk crafts): ceramics, lacquerware, bamboo, textiles, dolls and much more. Artists range from living national treasures to contemporary artisans. The building was once the headquarters of the imperial guards, and was rebuilt after its destruction in WWII.

◎ Roppongi & Akasaka

Mori Art Museum   Museum

(森美術館; Map p66; www.mori.art.museum; 52nd fl, Mori Tower, Roppongi Hills, 6-10-1 Roppongi, Minato-ku; adult/child/student ¥1600/600/1100; ◈10am-10pm Wed-Mon, to 5pm Tue, inside Sky Deck 10am-10pm; Ⓢ Hibiya line to Roppongi, exit 1) Atop Mori Tower this gigantic gallery space sports high ceilings, broad views and thematic programs that continue to live up to all the hype associated with **Roppongi Hills** (六本木ヒルズ; Map p66; www.roppongihills. com/en; 6-chōme Roppongi, Minato-ku; ◈11am-11pm; Ⓢ Hibiya line to Roppongi, exit 1). Contemporary exhibits are beautifully presented and include superstars of the art world from both Japan and abroad.

National Art Center Tokyo   Museum

(国立新美術館; Map p66; ☎03-5777-8600; www.nact.jp; 7-22-1 Roppongi, Minato-ku; admission varies by exhibition; ◈10am-6pm Wed, Thu & Sat-Mon, to 8pm Fri; Ⓢ Chiyoda line to Nogizaka, exit 6)

Designed by Kurokawa Kishō, this architectural beauty has no permanent collection, but boasts the country's largest exhibition space for visiting shows, which have included titans such as Renoir and Modigliani. Apart from exhibitions, a visit here is recommended to admire the building's awesome undulating glass facade, its cafes atop giant inverted cones and the great gift shop Souvenir from Tokyo (p75).

21_21 Design Sight — Museum

(21_21デザインサイト; Map p66; ☑03-3475-2121; www.2121designsight.jp; Tokyo Midtown, 9-7-6 Akasaka, Minato-ku; admission varies; ◎11am-8pm Wed-Mon; ⑤Ōedo line to Roppongi, exit 8) An exhibition and discussion

Omote-sandō Architecture

Omote-sandō (表参道; Map p66; ⑤Ginza line to Omote-sandō, exits A3 & B4, ⊠JR Yamanote line to Harajuku, Omote-sandō exit), the wide boulevard that runs through Harajuku, is like a walk-through showroom of the who's who of contemporary architecture. Here you'll see buildings from several of Japan's Pritzker Prize winners.

Highlights include the **Dior boutique** (2003), designed by SANAA with a filmy exterior that seems to hang like a dress; Itō Toyō's construction for **Tod's** (2004) with criss-crossing strips of concrete that take their inspiration from the zelkova trees below (and are also structural); and the convex glass fishbowl that is the **Prada Aoyama boutique** (2003), created by Herzog and de Meuron.

Prada Aoyama boutique, Omote-sandō

space dedicated to all forms of design, the 21_21 Design Sight acts as a beacon for local art enthusiasts, whether they be designers themselves or simply onlookers. The striking concrete and glass building, bursting out of the ground at sharp angles, was designed by Pritzker Prize–winning architect Andō Tadao.

Suntory Museum of Art — Museum

(サントリー美術館; Map p66; ☑03-3479-8600; www.suntory.com/sma; 4th fl, Tokyo Midtown, 9-7-4 Akasaka, Minato-ku; admission varies, child free; ◎10am-6pm Sun-Wed, to 8pm Fri & Sat; ⑤Ōedo line to Roppongi, exit 8) Since its original 1961 opening, the Suntory Museum of Art has subscribed to an underlying philosophy of lifestyle art. Rotating exhibitions focus on the beauty of useful things: Japanese ceramics, lacquerware, glass, dyeing, weaving and such. Its current Tokyo Midtown digs, designed by architect Kuma Kengō, are both understated and breathtaking.

Complex 665 — Gallery

(Map p66; 6-5-24 Roppongi, Minato-ku; ◎11am-7pm Tue-Sat; ⑤Hibiya line to Roppongi, exit 1) Opened in October 2016, this new three-storey building tucked on a backstreet is the location of three major commercial art galleries: **Taka Ishii** (www.takaishiigallery.com), **ShugoArts** (https://shugoarts.com) and **Tomio Koyama Gallery** (www.tomiokoyamagallery.com). The free shows gather up an eclectic selection of Japanese contemporary works and are generally worth a look.

◉ Ebisu & Meguro

TOP Museum — Museum

(東京都写真美術館; Tokyo Photographic Arts Museum; ☑03-3280-0099; http://topmuseum.jp; 1-13-3 Mita, Meguro-ku; ¥500-1000; ◎10am-6pm Tue, Wed, Sat & Sun, to 8pm Thu & Fri; ⊠JR Yamanote line to Ebisu, east exit) Tokyo's principal photography museum reopened in 2016 after a two-year overhaul. In addition to drawing on its extensive collection, the museum also hosts travelling exhibitions. In the fall, it curates a show of up-and-coming Japanese photographers. Usually several

Suntory Museum of Art

exhibitions happen simultaneously; ticket prices depend on how many you see.

Beer Museum Yebisu Museum

(エビスビール記念館; ☎03-5423-7255; www.sapporoholdings.jp/english/guide/yebisu; 4-20-1 Ebisu, Shibuya-ku; ⏰11am-7pm Tue-Sun; 🚉JR Yamanote line to Ebisu, east exit) **FREE** Photos, vintage bottles and posters document the rise of Yebisu, and beer in general, in Japan at this small museum located where the actual Yebisu brewery stood until 1988. At the 'tasting salon' you can sample four kinds of Yebisu beer (¥400 each). It's behind the Mitsukoshi department store at Yebisu Garden Place.

Shibuya & Harajuku

Shibuya Crossing Street

(渋谷スクランブル交差点; Shibuya Scramble; Map p66; 🚉JR Yamanote line to Shibuya, Hachikō exit) Rumoured to be the busiest intersection in the world (and definitely in Japan), Shibuya Crossing is like a giant beating heart, sending people in all directions with every pulsing light change. Perhaps nowhere else says 'Welcome to Tokyo' better than this. Hundreds of people – and at peak times said to be over 1000 people – cross at a time, coming from all directions at once yet still managing to dodge each other with a practised, nonchalant agility.

Shibuya Center-gai Area

(渋谷センター街; Shibuya Sentā-gai; Map p66; 🚉JR Yamanote line to Shibuya, Hachikō exit) Shibuya's main drag is closed to cars and chock-a-block with fast-food joints and high-street fashion shops. At night, lit bright as day, with a dozen competing soundtracks (coming from who knows where), wares spilling onto the streets, shady touts in sunglasses, and strutting teens, it feels like a block party – or Tokyo's version of a classic Asian night market.

Yoyogi-kōen Park

(代々木公園; Map p66; www.yoyogipark.info; 🚉JR Yamanote line to Harajuku, Omote-sandō exit) If it's a sunny and warm weekend afternoon, you can count on there being a crowd lazing around the large grassy expanse that is Yoyogi-kōen. You can also

Roppongi, Harajuku & Shibuya

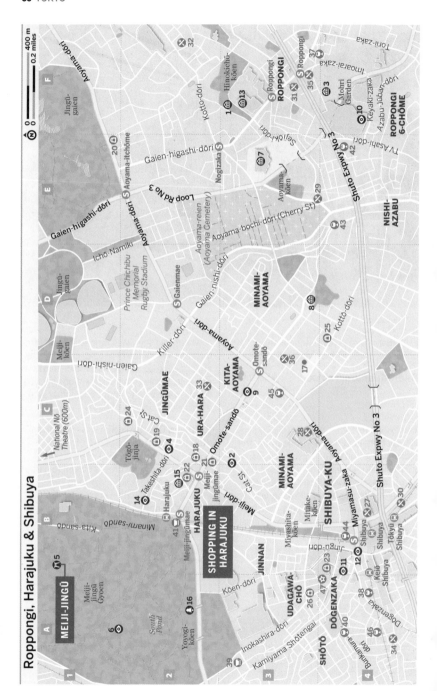

0 400 m
0 0.2 miles

MEIJI-JINGŪ

MEIJI-JINGŪ

Meiji-jingū Gyoen

South Pond

Yoyogi-kōen

SHOPPING IN HARAJUKU

JINNAN

UDAGAWA-CHŌ

DŌGENZAKA

SHŌTŌ

SHIBUYA-KU

MINAMI-AOYAMA

JINGŪMAE

URA-HARA

KITA-AOYAMA

MINAMI-AOYAMA

NISHI-AZABU

ROPPONGI

ROPPONGI 6-CHŌME

Jingū-gaien

Jingū-gaien

Prince Chichibu Memorial Rugby Stadium

Meiji-kōen

Tōgō-jinja

Aoyama-reien (Aoyama Cemetery)

Aoyama-kōen

Hinokichō-kōen

Mōhri Garden

Miyashita-kōen

Mitake-kōen

Aoyama-dōri

Aoyama-dōri

Aoyama-dōri

Aoyama-chōme

Aoyama-dōri

Gaien-higashi-dōri

Gaien-higashi-dōri

Gaien-higashi-dōri

Gaien-nishi-dōri

Gaien-nishi-dōri

Killer-dōri

Ichō Namiki

Kōtō-dōri

Kōtō-dōri

Kōtō-dōri

Seijō-dōri

Aoyama-bochi-dōri (Cherry St)

Loop Rd No 3

Loop Rd No 3

Nogizaka

Omote-sandō

Omote-sandō

Omote-sandō

Cat St

Cat St

Cat St

Takeshita-dōri

Meiji-dōri

Meiji-dōri

Meiji-jingūmae

Meiji-jingūmae

Minami-sandō

Kita-sandō

Kōen-dōri

Inokashira-dōri

Kamiyama Shōtengai

Bunkamura-dōri

Dōgenzaka

Jingū-dōri

Miyamasu-zaka

Shuto Expwy No 3

Shuto Expwy No 3

Shuto Expwy No 3

TV Asahi-dōri

Azabu-Jūban-dōri

Keyaki-zaka

Imoarai-zaka

Tōrii-zaka

Tōrii-zaka

Harajuku

Gaienmae

National/Nō Theatre (600m)

Aoyama-itchōme

Roppongi

Roppongi

Roppongi

Tōkyū Shibuya

Keiō Shibuya

Shibuya

1
5
6
2
3
4
7
8
9
10
11
12
13
14
15
16
17
18
19
20
21
22
23
24
25
26
27
28
29
30
31
32
33
34
35
36
37
38
39
40
41
42
43
44
45
46
47

Roppongi, Harajuku & Shibuya

usually find revellers and noisemakers of all stripes, from hula-hoopers to African drum circles to a group of retro greasers dancing around a boom box. It's an excellent place for a picnic and probably the only place in the city where you can reasonably toss a frisbee without fear of hitting someone.

Nezu Museum
Museum

(根津美術館; Map p66; ☎03-3400-2536; www.nezu-muse.or.jp; 6-5-1 Minami-Aoyama, Minato-ku; adult/student/child ¥1100/800/free, special exhibitions extra ¥200; ⏰10am-5pm Tue-Sun; Ⓢ Ginza line to Omote-sandō, exit A5) Nezu Museum offers a striking blend of old and new: a renowned collection of Japanese, Chinese and Korean antiquities in a gallery space designed by contemporary architect Kuma Kengo. Select items from the extensive collection are displayed in seasonal

exhibitions. The English explanations are usually pretty good. Behind the galleries is a woodsy strolling garden laced with stone paths and studded with teahouses and sculptures.

Ukiyo-e Ōta Memorial Museum of Art
Museum

(浮世絵太田記念美術館; Map p66; ☎03-5777-8600; www.ukiyoe-ota-muse.jp; 1-10-10 Jingūmae, Shibuya-ku; adult ¥700-1000, child free; ⏰10.30am-5.30pm Tue-Sun; Ⓡ JR Yamanote line to Harajuku, Omote-sandō exit) Change into slippers to enter the peaceful, hushed museum that houses the excellent *ukiyo-e* collection of Ōta Seizo, the former head of the Toho Life Insurance Company. Seasonal, thematic exhibitions are easily digested in an hour and usually include a few works by masters such

Best Free Sights

Tokyo Metropolitan Government Building (p68)

Shibuya Crossing (p65)

Meiji-jingū (p46)

Sensō-ji (p50)

From left: Sensō-ji (p50); Meiji-jingū (p46); Shibuya Crossing (p65)

as Hokusai and Hiroshige. It's often closed the last few days of the month.

Kawaii Monster Cafe Notable Building
(Map p66; ☎03-5413-6142; http://kawaii-monster.jp/pc/; 4th fl, YM Bldg, 4-31-10 Jingūmae, Shibuya-ku; cover charge ¥500, drinks from ¥800; ⏰11.30am-4.30pm & 6-10.30pm Mon-Sat, 11am-8pm Sun; ☒JR Yamanote line to Harajuku, Omote-sandō exit) Lurid colours, surrealist installations and out-of-this world costumes – this is the vision of Sebastian Masuda, stylist to pop star Kyary Pamyu Pamyu, who designed this new cafe. It's an embodiment of the now-reigning aesthetic of *guro-kawaii* (somewhat grotesque cuteness). Food and drink (not what you're here for, but you have to order something) are coloured to match the decor.

◉ Shinjuku

Tokyo Metropolitan Government Building Notable Building
(東京都庁; Tokyo Tochō; www.metro.tokyo.jp/ENGLISH/OFFICES/observat.htm; 2-8-1 Nishi-Shinjuku, Shinjuku-ku; ⏰observatories 9.30am-11pm; ☒Ōedo line to Tochōmae, exit A4)

FREE Tokyo's seat of power, designed by Tange Kenzō and completed in 1991, looms large and looks somewhat like a pixelated cathedral (or the lair of an animated villain). Take an elevator from the ground floor of Building 1 to one of the twin 202m-high observatories for panoramic views over the never-ending cityscape (the views are virtually the same from either tower). On a clear day (morning is best), you may catch a glimpse of Mt Fuji to the west.

Shinjuku-gyoen Park
(新宿御苑; ☎03-3350-0151; www.env.go.jp/garden/shinjukugyoen; 11 Naito-chō, Shinjuku-ku; adult/child ¥200/50; ⏰9am-4.30pm Tue-Sun; ☒Marunouchi line to Shinjuku-gyoenmae, exit 1) Though Shinjuku-gyoen was designed as an imperial retreat (completed 1906), it's now definitely a park for everyone. The wide lawns make it a favourite for urbanites in need of a quick escape from the hurly-burly of city life. Don't miss the greenhouse, with its giant lily pads and perfectly formed orchids, and the cherry blossoms in spring.

SEAN PAVONE / SHUTTERSTOCK ©

⊕ ACTIVITIES

⊕ Onsen

Ōedo Onsen Monogatari   Onsen

(大江戸温泉物語; www.ooedoonsen.jp; 2-6-3
Aomi, Kōtō-ku; adult/child ¥2280/980, surcharge
Sat & Sun ¥200; ⊙11am-9am, last entry 7am;
⊞Yurikamome line to Telecom Center, Rinkai line
to Tokyo Teleport with free shuttle bus) Just to
experience the truly Japanese phenome-
non that is an amusement park centred on
bathing is reason enough to visit. The baths
here, which include gender-divided indoor
tubs and *rotemburo* (outdoor baths), are
filled with real hot-spring water, pumped
from 1400m below Tokyo Bay. Come after
6pm for a ¥500 discount. Visitors with
tattoos will be denied admission.

Spa LaQua   Onsen

(スパ　ラクーア; ⍾03-5800-9999; www.laqua.jp;
5th-9th fl, Tokyo Dome City, 1-1-1 Kasuga, Bunkyō-
ku; weekday/weekend ¥2635/2960; ⊙11am-9am;
⑤Marunouchi line to Kōrakuen, exit 2) One of
Tokyo's few true onsen, this chic complex re-
lies on natural hot-spring water from 1700m
below ground. There are indoor and outdoor

baths, saunas and a bunch of add-on options, such as *akasuri* (Korean-style whole-
body exfoliation). A fascinating introduction
to Japanese health and beauty rituals.

Jakotsu-yu   Bathhouse

(蛇骨湯; Map p70; ⍾03-3841-8645; www.
jakotsuyu.co.jp; 1-11-11 Asakusa, Taitō-ku; adult/
child ¥460/180; ⊙1pm-midnight Wed-Mon;
⑤Ginza line to Tawaramachi, exit 3) Unlike most
sentō (public baths), tubs here are filled with
pure hot-spring water, naturally the colour
of weak tea. Another treat is the lantern-lit,
rock-framed *rotemburo*. Jakotsu-yu is a welcoming place; it has English signage and has
no policy against tattoos. It's an extra ¥200
for the sauna, ¥140 for a small towel.

⊕ Amusement Parks

Tokyo Disney Resort Amusement Park

(東京ディズニーリゾート; ⍾domestic calls
0570-00-8632, from overseas +81-45-330-5211;
www.tokyodisneyresort.co.jp; 1-1 Maihama,
Urayasu-shi, Chiba-ken; 1-day ticket for 1 park
adult/child ¥7400/4800, after 6pm ¥4200;
⊙varies by season; ⊞JR Keiyō line to Maihama)
Here you'll find not only Tokyo Disneyland,

Ueno & Asakusa

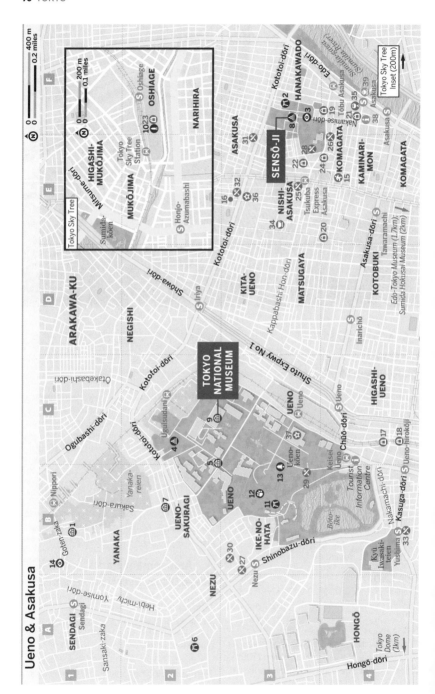

ARAKAWA-KU

SENDAGI Ⓢ Sendagi

Sansaki-zaka

Hebi-michi/Yomise-dōri

YANAKA

Gōten-zaka

Ⓚ Nippori

Yanaka-dōri

Otakebashi-dōri

Ogubashi-dōri

Sakura-dōri

Yanaka-reien

NEGISHI

Kototoi-dōri

Showa-dōri

Ⓢ Iriya

KITA-UENO

MATSUGAYA

Kappabashi Hon-dōri

Ⓢ Inarichō

HIGASHI-UENO

Shuto Expwy No 1

TOKYO NATIONAL MUSEUM

Uguisudani Ⓚ

UENO-SAKURAGI

Kototoi-dōri

UENO

UENO
Ueno-kōen

Ⓚ Ⓢ Ueno

Ⓚ Ⓢ Ueno

Chūō-dōri

Tourist Information Centre

Ⓚ Keisei Ueno

Nakamachi-dōri

Kasuga-dōri Ⓢ Ueno-hirokōji

NEZU
Nezu Ⓢ

IKE-NO-HATA

Shinobazu-dōri

Bentō-ike

Kyū Iwasaki-teien

Yushima Ⓢ

HONGŌ

Tokyo Dome (1km)

Hongō-dōri

ASAKUSA

NISHI-ASAKUSA

Tsukuba Express Asakusa

Asakusa-dōri

Kototoi-dōri

Edo-Tokyo Museum (1.7km)/Sumida Hokusai Museum (2km)

KOTOBUKI

Tawaramachi Ⓢ

SENSŌ-JI

Nakamise-dōri

Ⓚ Tōbu Asakusa

Asakusa Ⓢ

KAMINARI-MON

KOMAGATA

KOMAGATA

HANAKAWADO

Kototoi-dōri

Edo-dōri

(Sumida-gawa/Sumida River)

Inset

Tokyo Sky Tree Inset (200m)

Tokyo Sky Tree

Mitsume-dōri

HIGASHI-MUKŌJIMA

MUKŌJIMA

Sumida-kōen

Honjo-Azumabashi Ⓢ

Tokyo Sky Tree Station Ⓚ

Ⓢ Oshiage

OSHIAGE

NARIHIRA

N

0 · · · 200 m
0 · · · 0.1 miles

N

0 · · · 400 m
0 · · · 0.2 miles

Ueno & Asakusa

modelled after the one in California, but also Tokyo DisneySea, an original theme park with seven 'ports' evoking locales real and imagined (the Mediterranean and 'Mermaid Lagoon', for example). DisneySea targets a more grown-up crowd, but still has many attractions for kids. Both resorts get extremely crowded, especially on weekends and during summer holidays; you'll have to be strategic with your fast passes. Book admission tickets online to save time.

Tokyo Joypolis   Amusement Park

(東京ジョイポリス; http://tokyo-joypolis.com; 3rd-5th fl, DECKS Tokyo Beach, 1-6-1 Daiba, Minato-ku; adult/child ¥800/300, all-rides passport ¥4300/3300, passport after 5pm ¥3300/2300; ⊙10am-10pm; ⊠Yurikamome line to Odaiba Kaihin-kōen) This indoor amusement park is stacked with virtual-reality attractions and adult thrill rides, such as the video-enhanced Halfpipe Canyon; there are rides for little ones, too. Separate admission and individual

ride tickets (¥500 to ¥800) are available, but if you plan to go on more than half a dozen attractions, the unlimited 'passport' makes sense.

⦿ Cooking Courses

Tokyo Cooking Studio   Cooking

(東京クッキングスタジオ; http://tokyo.cook ingstudio.org; Hins Minato #004, 3-18-14 Minato, Chūō-ku; classes for up to 3 people from ¥30,000; ⊠Yūrakuchō line to Shintomichō, exit 7) Genial English-speaking chef Inoue Akira is a master of soba – noodles made from nutty buckwheat flour. He's taught how to make and eat this classic Tokyo dish to chefs who have gone on to win Michelin stars for their cooking. Classes are held in a compact kitchen overlooking the Sumida River.

Buddha Bellies   Cooking

(http://buddhabelliestokyo.jimdo.com; 2nd fl, Uekuri Bldg, 22-4-3 Kanda-Jimbōchō, Chiyoda-ku;

Bathers at Ōedo Onsen Monogatari (p69)

courses from ¥7500; S Shinjuku line to Jimbōchō, exit A2) Professional sushi chef and sake sommelier Ayuko leads small hands-on classes in sushi, *bentō* (boxed lunch) and udon making. Prices start at ¥7500 per person for a 2½-hour course.

Tokyo Sushi Academy   Cooking
(Map p62; ☑ 03-3362-2789; http://sushimaking. tokyo; 2nd fl, Tsukiji KY Bldg, 4-7-5 Tsukiji, Chūō-ku; per person ¥5400; ☺ 9am-3pm Sat; S Hibiya line to Tsukiji, exit 1) English-speaking sushi chefs will give you a 30-minute crash course in making the vinegared rice speciality, after which you'll have an hour in which to make (and eat) as much of your favourite type of sushi as you like. Classes are held on Saturday (and sometimes Sunday) in a modern kitchen a stone's throw from the Tsukiji Outer Market (p60).

🎨 Arts & Crafts

Wanariya   Traditional Craft
(和なり屋; Map p70; ☑ 03-5603-9169; www. wanariya.jp; 1-8-10 Senzoku, Taitō-ku; indigo dyeing/weaving from ¥1920/1980; ☺ 10am-5pm Thu-Tue; S Hibiya line to Iriya, exit 1) A team

of young and friendly Japanese runs this indigo dyeing and traditional hand-loom-weaving workshop where you can learn the crafts and have a go yourself in under an hour or so. It's a fantastic way to make your own unique souvenir, with a whole range of items you can dye, from *tenugui* (thin cotton towels) to canvas sneakers.

Mokuhankan   Traditional Craft
(木版館; Map p70; ☑ 070-5011-1418; http:// mokuhankan.com/parties; 2nd fl, 1-41-8 Asakusa, Taitō-ku; per person ¥2000; ☺ 10am-5.30pm Wed-Mon; 🚊 Tsukuba Express to Asakusa, exit 5) Try your hand at making *ukiyo-e* at this studio run by expat David Bull. Hour-long 'print parties' are great fun and take place daily; sign up online. There's a shop here too, where you can see Bull's and Jed Henry's *Ukiyo-e Heroes* series – prints featuring video-game characters in traditional settings.

Ohara School of Ikebana   Ikebana
(小原流いけばな; Map p66; ☑ 03-5774-5097; www.ohararyu.or.jp; 5-7-17 Minami-Aoyama, Minato-ku; per class ¥4000; S Ginza line to Omote-sandō, exit B1) Every Thursday, from

10.30am to 12.30pm, this well-regarded, modern ikebana school teaches introductory flower-arrangement classes in English. Sign up via email by 3pm the Tuesday before.

TOURS

Bus tours are convenient for travellers who want to cover a lot of ground in one day (or want some respite from navigating).

Gray Line (☎03-3595-5948; www.jgl.co.jp/inbound/index.htm; per person ¥4000-13,000) Offers half-day and full-day tours with stops, covering key downtown sights and also day trips to Mt Fuji. Pick-up service from major hotels is available, otherwise most tours leave from in front of the Dai-Ichi Hotel in Shimbashi (near Ginza).

Hato Bus Tours (☎03-3435-6081; www.hatobus.com; per person ¥1500-12,000; ⓡJR Yamanote line to Hamamatsuchō, south exit) Tokyo's most well-known bus-tour company offers hour-long, half-day and full-day bus tours of the city. Shorter tours cruise by the sights in an open-air double-decker bus; longer ones make stops. Tours leave from Hato Bus terminals in the annexe to the World Trade Centre in Hamamatsuchō, and Shinjuku and Tokyo stations.

SkyBus (Map p62; ☎03-3215-0008; www.skybus.jp; 2-5-2 Marunouchi, Chiyoda-ku; tours adult/child from ¥1600/700, Sky Hop Bus ¥2500/1200; ⊗ticket office 9am-6pm; ⓡJR Yamanote line to Tokyo, Marunouchi south exit) Open-top double-decker buses cruise through different neighbourhoods of the city (for roughly 50 to 80 minutes); most have English-language audio guidance aboard. The Sky Hop Bus plan allows you to hop on and off buses on any of the three routes.

🔒 SHOPPING

Ginza, home to high-end department stores and boutiques, has long been the premier shopping district. Though Harajuku – popular with younger shoppers – puts up a good fight for claim to that title. Shibuya is another trendy district. Asakusa, meanwhile, is good for traditional crafts.

🔒 Ginza & Marunouchi

Itōya Arts & Crafts
(伊東屋; Map p62; www.ito-ya.co.jp; 2-7-15 Ginza, Chūō-ku; ⊗10.30am-8pm Mon-Sat, to 7pm Sun; ⓢGinza line to Ginza, exit A13) Nine floors (plus several more in the nearby annexe) of stationery-shop love await visual-art professionals and seekers of office accessories

⛵ Bay & River Cruises

Standing among the skyscrapers of downtown, it's easy to forget that Tokyo is a city on the water. The Sumida-gawa, is the city's principal river, which flows into Tokyo Bay. One unique way to travel is by river bus. **Tokyo Cruise** (水上バス, Suijō Bus; ☎0120-977-311; http://suijobus.co.jp) runs boats up and down the Sumida-gawa (Sumida River), roughly twice an hour between 10am and 6pm, connecting Asakusa with Hama-rikyū Onshi-teien (¥980, 35 minutes) and Odaiba (¥1260, 70 minutes). Tickets can be purchased immediately before departure, if available, at any pier.

If you're lucky, you might wind up on Hotoluna or Himiko, two futuristic cruise boats, designed by manga and anime artist Leiji Matsumoto. In the evening they morph into **Jicoo the Floating Bar** (ジークザフローティングバー; ☎0120-049-490; www.jicoofloatingbar.com; cover from ¥2600; ⊗8-10.30pm Thu-Sat; ⓡYurikamome line to Hinode or Odaiba Kaihin-kōen), which cruises around Tokyo Bay. The evening-long 'floating pass' usually includes some sort of live music; check the schedule online. Board on the hour at Hinode pier and the half-hour at Odaiba Kaihin-kōen.

Tokyo Cruise boat

with both everyday items and luxury such as fountain pens and Italian leather agendas. You'll also find *washi* (fine Japanese handmade paper), *tenugui* (beautifully hand-dyed thin cotton towels) and *furoshiki* (wrapping cloths).

Akomeya
Food

(Map p62; ☎03-6758-0271; www.akomeya. jp; 2-2-6 Ginza, Chūō-ku; ⊗shop 11am-9pm, restaurant 11.30am-10pm; ⓈYūrakuchō line to Ginza-itchōme, exit 4) Rice is at the core of Japanese cuisine and drink. This stylish store sells not only many types of the grain but also products made from it (such as sake), a vast range of quality cooking ingredients and a choice collection of kitchen, home and bath items.

Dover Street Market Ginza
Fashion & Accessories

(DSM; Map p62; ☎03-6228-5080; http:// ginza.doverstreetmarket.com; 6-9-5 Ginza, Chūō-ku; ⊗11am-8pm; ⓈGinza line to Ginza, exit A2) A department store as envisioned by Kawakubo Rei (of Comme des Garçons), DSM has seven floors of avant-garde

brands, including several Japanese labels and everything in the Comme des Garçons line-up. The quirky art installations alone make it worth the visit.

Takumi
Arts & Crafts

(たくみ; Map p62; ☎03-3571-2017; www.ginza-takumi.co.jp; 8-4-2 Ginza, Chūō-ku; ⊗11am-7pm Mon-Sat; ⓈGinza line to Shimbashi, exit 5) You're unlikely to find a more elegant selection of traditional folk crafts, including toys, textiles and ceramics from around Japan. Ever thoughtful, this shop also encloses information detailing the origin and background of the pieces if you make a purchase.

Muji
Homewares

(無印良品; Map p62; ☎03-5208-8241; www. muji.com; 3-8-3 Marunouchi, Chiyoda-ku; ⊗10am-9pm; ⓇJR Yamanote line to Yūrakuchō, Kyōbashi exit) The flagship store of the famously understated brand sells elegant, simple clothing, accessories and homewares. There are scores of other outlets across Tokyo, including a good one in Tokyo Midtown, but the Yūrakuchō store is the largest with the biggest range. It also offers tax-free

KITTE

shopping, bicycle rental (¥1080 a day from 10am to 8pm) and a great cafeteria.

KITTE — Mall

(Map p62; https://jptower-kitte.jp/en; 2-7-2 Marunouchi, Chiyoda-ku; ⏰11am-9pm Mon-Sat, to 8pm Sun; ℝJR lines to Tokyo, Marunouchi south exit) This well-designed shopping mall at the foot of JP Tower incorporates the restored facade of the former Tokyo Central Post Office. It is notable for its atrium, around which is arrayed a quality selection of craft-orientated Japanese brand shops selling homewares, fashion, accessories and lifestyle goods.

Tsukiji Hitachiya — Homewares

(つきじ常陸屋; Map p62; 4-14-18 Tsukiji, Chūō-ku; ⏰8am-3pm Mon-Sat, 10am-2pm Sun; ⓢHibiya line to Tsukiji, exit 1) Tokyo chefs and cooks seek out Hitachiya for hand-forged knives, sturdy bamboo baskets and other great kitchen and cooking tools.

Mitsukoshi — Department Store

(三越; Map p62; www.mitsukoshi.co.jp; 4-6-16 Ginza, Chūō-ku; ⏰10am-8pm; ⓢGinza line to Ginza, exits A7 & A11) One of Ginza's grande dames, Mitsukoshi embodies the essence of the Tokyo department store. Don't miss the basement food hall.

🏛 Roppongi & Akasaka

Japan Traditional Crafts Aoyama Square — Arts & Crafts

(伝統工芸 青山スクエア; Map p66; ☎03-5785-1301; http://kougeihin.jp/home.shtml; 8-1-22 Akasaka, Minato-ku; ⏰11am-7pm; ⓢGinza line to Aoyama-itchōme, exit 4) Supported by the Japanese Ministry of Economy, Trade and Industry, this is as much a showroom as a shop exhibiting a broad range of traditional crafts, including lacquerwork boxes, woodwork, cut glass, paper, textiles and earthy pottery. The emphasis is on high-end pieces, but you can find beautiful things in all price ranges here.

Souvenir from Tokyo — Gifts & Souvenirs

(スーベニアフロムトーキョー; Map p66; ☎03-6812 9933; www.souvenirfromtokyo.jp; basement fl, National Art Center Tokyo, 7-22-2

Markets

On weekends a **farmers' market** (Map p66; www.farmersmarkets.jp; 5-53-7 Jingūmae, Shibuya-ku; ⏰10am-4pm Sat & Sun; ⓢGinza line to Omote-sandō, exit B2), with colourful produce and a dozen food trucks, sets up on the plaza in front of the United Nations University on Aoyama-dōri. It's as much a social event as a shopping stop. Events pop up, too, including the hipster flea market **Raw Tokyo** (www.rawtokyo.jp) – with DJs and live painting – which takes place over the first weekend of the month.

Quality vendors gather twice a month at Tokyo International Forum for the excellent **Ōedo Antique Market** (大江戸骨董市; Map p62; ☎03-6407-6011; www.antique-market.jp; 3-5-1 Marunouchi, Chiyoda-ku; ⏰9am-4pm 1st & 3rd Sun of month; ℝJR Yamanote line to Yūrakuchō, Kokusai Forum exit).

For an updated schedule of all the city's flea markets, see www.frma.jp (in Japanese).

Ōedo Antique Market
STEVE VIDLER / ALAMY STOCK PHOTO ©

Roppongi, Minato-ku; ⏰10am-6pm Sat-Mon, Wed & Thu, to 8pm Fri; ⓢChiyoda line to Nogizaka, exit 6) This shop, in the basement of the National Art Center Tokyo (p63), sells an expert selection of home-grown design bits and bobs that make for perfect, unique souvenirs: a mobile by Tempo, a bag made from fabric dyed using the *shibori* technique or a fun face pack with a kabuki design.

Ebisu & Meguro

Okura Fashion & Accessories

(オクラ; www.hrm.co.jp/okura; 20-11 Sarugaku-chō, Shibuya-ku; ⊙11.30am-8pm Mon Fri, 11am-8.30pm Sat & Sun; 🚉Tōkyū Tōyoko line to Daikanyama) Almost everything in this

 Breakfast at Tsukiji

For over 80 years, Tsukiji Market has been the place for top chefs, fishmongers, department stores and hotels to source their ingredients. The **Outer Market** (p60) sprang up organically, with vendors gathering to sell ingredients – like seaweed and dried fish – that chefs might need. Small restaurants, too, were established to feed the market workers. It's an excellent place to visit for breakfast. Here are some of our favourite stalls:

Yamachō (山長; Map p62; 🖉03-3248-6002; 4-16-1 Tsukiji; omlette slices ¥100; ⊙6am-3.30pm; 🚇Hibiya line to Tsukiji, exit 1) Venerable purveyor of *tamago-yaki* (Japanese rolled-egg omelettes).

Tsukugon (つくごん; Map p62; www.tsukugon.co.jp; 4-12-5 Tsukiji, Chūō-ku; snacks from ¥210; ⊙6.30am-2pm Tue-Sun; 🚇Hibiya line to Tsukiji, exit 1) Five generation seafood paste specialist; try their delicious specialty *chiyoda* (a bacon-wrapped onion with fish paste) warm from the frying pan.

Kimagure-ya (気まぐれ屋; Map p62; 6-21-6 Tsukiji, Chūō-ku; sandwiches from ¥140; ⊙5am-10am; 🚇Hibiya line to Tsukiji, exit 1) Sandwich shop in an old barber's shop, with the cheapest coffee in town.

Preparing *tamago-yaki* at Tsukiji Market
NIRAD / SHUTTERSTOCK ©

enchanting shop is dyed a deep indigo blue – from contemporary tees and sweatshirts to classic work shirts. There are some beautiful, original items (though unfortunately most aren't cheap). The shop itself looks like a rural house, with worn, wooden floorboards and whitewashed walls. Note: there's no sign out the front, but the building stands out.

Kapital Fashion & Accessories

(キャピタル; 🖉03-5725-3923; http://kapital.jp; 2-20-2 Ebisu, Shibuya-ku; ⊙11am-8pm; 🚉JR Yamanote line to Ebisu, west exit) Cult brand Kapital is hard to pin down, but perhaps a deconstructed mash-up of the American West and the centuries-old Japanese aesthetic of *boro* (tatty) chic comes close. Almost no two items are alike; most are unisex. The shop itself is like an art installation. The staff, not snobby at all, can point you towards the other two shops nearby.

Daikanyama T-Site Books

(代官山T-SITE; http://tsite.jp/daikanyama; 17-5 Sarugaku-chō, Shibuya-ku; ⊙7am-2am; 🚉Tōkyū Tōyoko line to Daikanyama) Locals love this stylish shrine to the printed word, which has a fantastic collection of books on travel, art, design and food (and some of them in English). The best part is that you can sit at the in-house Starbucks and read all afternoon – if you can get a seat that is.

Shibuya & Harajuku

Tokyu Hands Department Store

(東急ハンズ; Map p66; http://shibuya.tokyu-hands.co.jp; 12-18 Udagawa-chō, Shibuya-ku; ⊙10am-8.30pm; 🚉JR Yamanote line to Shibuya, Hachikō exit) This DIY and *zakka* (miscellaneous goods) store has eight fascinating floors of everything you didn't know you needed. Like reflexology slippers, bee-venom face masks and cartoon-character-shaped rice-ball moulds. Most stuff is inexpensive, making it perfect for souvenir- and gift-hunting. Warning: you could lose hours in here.

Loft

Sou-Sou   Fashion & Accessories

(そうそう; Map p66; ☏03-3407-7877; http://
sousounetshop.jp; 5-3-10 Minami-Aoyama,
Minato-ku; ⏰11am-8pm; Ⓢ Ginza line to Omote-
sandō, exit A5) Kyoto brand Sou-Sou gives
traditional Japanese clothing items – such
as split-toed *tabi* socks and *haori* (coats
with kimono-like sleeves) – a contemporary
spin. It is best known for producing the
steel-toed, rubber-soled *tabi* shoes worn
by Japanese construction workers in fun,
playful designs, but it also carries bags, tees
and super-adorable children's clothing.

Musubi   Arts & Crafts

(むす美; Map p66; http://kyoto-musubi.com;
2-31-8 Jingūmae, Shibuya-ku; ⏰11am-7pm Thu-
Tue; ⓇJR Yamanote line to Harajuku, Takeshita
exit) *Furoshiki* are versatile squares of cloth
that can be folded and knotted to make
shopping bags and gift wrap. This shop
sells pretty ones in both traditional and
contemporary patterns. There is usually
an English-speaking clerk who can show
you how to tie them, or pick up one of the
English-language books sold here.

Loft   Department Store

(ロフト; Map p66; ☏03-3462-3807; www.
loft.co.jp; 18-2 Udagawa-chō, Shibuya-ku;
⏰10am-9pm; ⓇJR Yamanote line to Shibuya,
Hachikō exit) This emporium of homewares,
stationery and accessories specialises in
all that is cute and covetable. The 1st floor,
which stocks seasonal stuff and gifts, is
particularly ripe for souvenir-hunting.

🅐 Shinjuku

Isetan   Department Store

(伊勢丹; www.isetan.co.jp; 3-14-1 Shinjuku,
Shinjuku-ku; ⏰10am-8pm; Ⓢ Marunouchi line
to Shinjuku-sanchōme, exits B3, B4 & B5) Most
department stores play to conservative
tastes, but this one doesn't. For an always
changing line-up of up-and-coming Japanese womenswear designers, check out the
Tokyo Closet (2nd floor) and Re-Style (3rd
floor) boutiques. Men get a whole building
of their own (connected by a passageway).
Don't miss the basement food hall, featuring
famous purveyors of sweet and savoury
goodies.

Beams — Fashion & Accessories

(ビームス; www.beams.co.jp; 3-32-6 Shinjuku, Shinjuku-ku; ⏰11am-8pm; ⓡJR Yamanote line to Shinjuku, east exit) Beams, a national chain of boutiques, is a cultural force in Japan. This multistorey Shinjuku shop is particularly good for the latest Japanese streetwear labels and work from designers giving traditional looks a modern twist (including men, women and unisex fashions). Also sometimes available: crafts, housewares and original artwork (the line-up is always changing).

Don Quijote — Gifts & Souvenirs

(ドン・キホーテ; ☎03-5291-9211; www.donki. com; 1-16-5 Kabukichō, Shinjuku-ku; ⏰24hr; ⓡJR Yamanote line to Shinjuku, east exit) This fluorescent-lit bargain castle is filled to the brink with weird loot. Chaotic piles of electronics and designer goods sit alongside sex toys, fetish costumes and packaged foods. Though it's now a national chain, it started as a rare (at the time) 24-hour store for the city's night workers.

🔒 Asakusa & Ryōgoku

Kakimori — Stationery

(カキモリ; ☎03-3864-3898; www.kakimori. com; 4-20-12 Kuramae, Taitō-ku; ⓢAsakusa line to Kuramae, exit 3) Stationery lovers flock from far and wide to this shop that allows you to custom build your own notebooks (from around ¥1000), choosing the paper, covers, binding and other bits and pieces to make a unique keepsake. It also stocks pens, pencils and 24 colours of ink by Japanese brand Pilot.

Marugoto Nippon — Food & Drinks

(まるごとにっぽん; Map p70; ☎03-3845-0510; www.marugotonippon.com; 2-6-7 Asakusa, Taitō-ku; ⏰10am-8pm; ⓢGinza line to Tawaramachi, exit 3) Think of this as a modern mini department store, showcasing the best of Japan's best in terms of speciality food and drink (ground floor) and arts and crafts (2nd floor). There are also plenty of tasting samples, and cafes and restaurants on the 3rd and 4th floors should you want something more substantial.

From left: Beams; Kappabashi-dōri; ramen at Kagari

TAKAMEX / SHUTTERSTOCK ©

W1BOW0 RUSLI / GETTY IMAGES ©

Tokyo Hotarudo
Vintage

(東京蛍堂; Map p70; ☑03-3845-7563; http://
tokyohotarudo.com; 1-41-8 Asakusa, Taitō-ku;
⊙11am-8pm Wed-Sun; ◉Tsukuba Express to
Asakusa, exit 5) This curio shop is run by an
eccentric young man who prefers to dress
as if the 20th century hasn't come and gone
already. If you think that sounds marvellous,
then you'll want to check out his collection
of vintage dresses and bags, antique lamps,
watches and decorative *objet*.

Fujiya
Arts & Crafts

(ふじ屋; Map p70; ☑03-3841-2283; www.
asakusa-noren.ne.jp/tenugui-fujiya/sp.html; 2-2-15
Asakusa, Taitō-ku; ⊙10am-6pm Wed-Mon; ⑤Ginza line to Asakusa, exit 1) Fujiya specialises in
tenugui: dyed cloths of thin cotton that can
be used as tea towels, handkerchiefs, gift
wrapping (the list goes on – they're surprisingly versatile). Here they come in traditional
designs and humorous modern ones.

Kappabashi-dōri
Homewares

(合羽橋通り; Map p70; ⑤Ginza line to Tawaramachi, exit 3) Kappabashi-dōri is the country's
largest wholesale restaurant-supply and
kitchenware district. Gourmet accessories

include bamboo steamer baskets, lacquer
trays, neon signs and *chōchin* (paper lanterns). It's also where restaurants get their
freakishly realistic plastic food models.

Kurodaya
Stationery

(黒田屋; Map p70; ☑03-3844-7511; 1-2-5
Asakusa, Taitō-ku; ⊙10am-6pm; ⑤Ginza line to
Asakusa, exit 3) Since 1856, Kurodaya has
been specialising in *washi* and products
made from paper such as cards, kites and
papier-mâché folk-art figures. It sells its own
designs and many others from across Japan.

✖ EATING

Tokyo has a vibrant and cosmopolitan
dining scene and a strong culture of eating
out – popular restaurants are packed most
nights of the week.

🍴 Ginza & Marunouchi

Kagari
Ramen ¥

(篝; Map p62; 4-4-1 Ginza; small/large ramen
¥950/1050; ⊙11am-3.30pm & 5.30-10.30pm;
⑤Ginza line to Ginza, exit A10 or B1) Don't get
confused – even though the English sign

View over Tsukiji Outer Market (p60)

outside Kagari says 'Soba', this stands for *chūka soba*, meaning Chinese noodles, ie ramen. Kagari's luscious, flavoursome chicken broth makes all the difference here and has earned the shop a cult following; there's sure to be a long queue trailing from its tucked-away location on a Ginza alley.

Kyūbey   Sushi ¥¥¥

(久兵衛; Map p62; ☎03-3571-6523; www. kyubey.jp; 8-7-6 Ginza, Chūō-ku; lunch/dinner from ¥4000/10,000; ⏰11.30am-2pm & 5-10pm Mon-Sat; ⑤Ginza line to Shimbashi, exit 3) Since 1936, Kyūbey's quality and presentation has won it a moneyed and celebrity clientele. Even so, this is a supremely foreigner-friendly and relaxed restaurant. The friendly owner Imada-san speaks excellent English as do some of his team of talented chefs, who will make and serve your sushi, piece by piece.

Trattoria Tsukiji Paradiso! Italian ¥¥

(Map p62; ☎03-3545-5550; www.tsukiji-paradiso.com; 6-27-3 Tsukiji, Chūō-ku; mains ¥1500-3600; ⏰11am-2pm & 6-10pm; ⑤Hibiya line to Tsukiji, exit 2) Paradise for food lovers, indeed. This charming, aqua-painted trattoria

serves seafood pasta dishes that will make you want to lick the plate clean. Its signature linguine is packed with shellfish in a scrumptious tomato, chilli and garlic sauce. Lunch (from ¥980) is a bargain, but you may well need to wait in line; book for dinner.

Apollo   Greek ¥¥

(Map p62; ☎03-6264-5220; www.theapollo.jp; 11th fl, Tōkyū Plaza Ginza, 5-2-1 Ginza, Chūō-ku; mains ¥1800-5800; ⏰11.30am-10pm; ⑤Ginza line to Ginza, exits C2 & C3) Ginza's glittering lights are the dazzling backdrop to this ace import from Sydney with its delicious take on modern Greek cuisine. The Mediterranean flavours come through strongly in dishes such as grilled octopus and fennel salad, taramasalata, and Kefalograviera cheese fried in a saganaki pan with honey, oregano and lemon juice. Portions are large and meant for sharing.

Hōnen Manpuku   Japanese ¥

(豊年萬福; ☎03-3277-3330; www.hounenman puku.jp; 1-8-16 Nihombashi-Muromachi, Chūō-ku; mains ¥1280-1850; ⏰11.30am-2.30pm & 5-11pm Mon-Sat, 5-10pm Sun; ⑤Ginza line to Mitsukoshi-mae, exit A1) Hōnen Manpuku's interior is dominated by giant *washi* lanterns, beneath which patrons tuck into bargain-priced beef or pork sukiyaki and other traditional dishes. Ingredients are sourced from gourmet retailers in Nihombashi. Lunchtime set menus are great value, and there's a riverside terrace in the warmer months.

Roppongi & Akasaka

Kikunoi   Kaiseki ¥¥¥

(菊乃井; Map p66; ☑03-3568-6055; http://kikunoi.jp; 6-13-8 Akasaka, Minato-ku; lunch/dinner set menu from ¥5940/17,820; ⊘noon-1pm Tue-Sat, 5-8pm Mon-Sat; ⓢChiyoda line to Akasaka, exit 7) Exquisitely prepared seasonal dishes are as beautiful as they are delicious at this Michelin–starred Tokyo outpost of a three-generation-old Kyoto-based *kaiseki* (Japanese haute cuisine) restaurant. Kikunoi's chef Murata has written a book translated into English on *kaiseki* that the staff helpfully use to explain the dishes you are served, if you don't speak Japanese. Reservations are necessary.

Sougo   Vegetarian ¥

(宗胡; Map p66; ☑03-5414-1133; www.sougo.tokyo; 3rd fl, Roppongi Green Bldg, 6-1-8 Roppongi, Minato-ku; mains ¥600-2000, set lunch/dinner from ¥1500/5000; ☑; ⓢHibiya line to Roppongi, exit 3) Sit at the long counter beside the open kitchen or in booths and watch the expert chefs prepare delicious and beautifully presented *shōjin-ryōri* (vegetarian cuisine as served at Buddhist temples). Reserve at least one day in advance if you want them to prepare a vegan meal. Look for it in the building opposite the APA Hotel.

Tofuya-Ukai   Kaiseki ¥¥¥

(とうふ屋うかい; ☑03-3436-1028; www.ukai.co.jp/english/shiba; 4-4-13 Shiba-kōen, Minato-ku; lunch/dinner set menu from ¥5500/8400; ⊘11am-10pm, last order 8pm; ☑; ⓢŌedo line to Akabanebashi, exit 8) One of Tokyo's most gracious restaurants is located in a former sake brewery (moved from northern Japan), with an exquisite traditional garden, in the shadow of Tokyo Tower. Seasonal preparations of tofu and accompanying

dishes are served in the refined *kaiseki* style. Make reservations well in advance.

Honmura-An   Soba ¥

(本むら庵; Map p66; ☑03-5772-6657; www.honmuraantokyo.com; 7-14-18 Roppongi, Minato-ku; soba from ¥900, set lunch/dinner ¥1600/7400; ⊘noon-2.30pm & 5.30-10pm Tue-Sun, closed 1st & 3rd Tue of month; ☎; ⓢHibiya line to Roppongi, exit 4) This fabled soba shop, once located in Manhattan, now serves its handmade buckwheat noodles at this contemporary noodle shop on a Roppongi side street. The delicate flavour of these noodles is best appreciated when served on a bamboo mat, with tempura or with dainty slices of *kamo* (duck).

Gogyō   Ramen ¥

(五行; Map p66; ☑03-5775-5566; www.ramendining-gogyo.com; 1-4-36 Nish-Azabu, Minato-ku; ramen from ¥1290; ⊘11.30am-4pm & 5pm-3am, to midnight Sun; ⓢHibiya line to Roppongi, exit 2) Keep an eye on the open kitchen: no, that's not your dinner going up in flames but the cooking of *kogashi* (burnt) ramen, which this dark and stylish *izakaya* (Japanese pub-eatery) specialises in. It's the burnt lard that gives the broth its dark and intense flavour. There are plenty of other dishes on the menu, and a good range of drinks too.

Ebisu & Meguro

Afuri   Ramen ¥

(あふり; 1-1-7 Ebisu, Shibuya-ku; noodles from ¥880; ⊘11am-5am; ⓡJR Yamanote line to Ebisu, east exit) Hardly your typical, surly *rāmen-ya*, Afuri has upbeat young cooks and a hip industrial interior. The unorthodox menu might draw eye-rolls from purists, but house specialities such as *yuzu-shio* (a

---

Foodie Hotspots

Tsukiji Market (p60)

Tokyo Cooking Studio (p71)

Akomeya (p74)

Cha Ginza (p88)

Kappabashi-dōri (p79)

light, salty broth flavoured with yuzu, a type of citrus) draw lines at lunchtime. Order from the vending machine.

Tonki
Tonkatsu ¥

(とんき; 1-2-1 Shimo-Meguro, Meguro-ku; meals ¥1900; ☺4-10.45pm Wed-Mon, closed 3rd Mon of month; 🚃JR Yamanote line to Meguro, west exit) Tonki is a Tokyo *tonkatsu* (crumbed pork cutlet) legend, deep-frying pork cutlets, recipe unchanged, for nearly 80 years. The seats at the counter – where you can watch the perfectly choreographed chefs – are the most coveted, though there is usually a queue. There are tables upstairs.

Ouca
Ice Cream ¥

(櫻花; www.ice-ouca.com; 1-6-6 Ebisu, Shibuya-ku; ice cream from ¥400; ☺11am-11.30pm Mar-Oct, noon-11pm Nov-Feb; 🚃JR Yamanote line to Ebisu, east exit) Green tea isn't the only flavour Japan has contributed to the ice-cream playbook; other delicious innovations available (seasonally) at Ouca include *kuro-goma* (black sesame), *kinako kurosato* (roasted soy-bean flour and black sugar) and *beni imo* (purple sweet potato).

Yakiniku Champion
Barbecue ¥¥

(焼肉チャンピオン; ☎03-5768-6922; www.yakiniku-champion.com; 1-2-8 Ebisu, Shibuya-ku; dishes ¥780-3300, course from ¥5250; ☺5pm-12.30am Mon-Fri, to 1am Sat, 4.30pm-midnight Sun; 🚃JR Yamanote line to Ebisu, west exit) Ready for an introduction into the Japanese cult of *yakiniku* (Korean barbecue)? Champion's sprawling menu includes everything from sweetbreads to the choicest cuts of grade A5 *wagyu* (Japanese beef); the menu even has a diagram of the cuts. You can't go wrong with popular dishes such as *kalbi* (short ribs, ¥980). It's very popular, best to reserve ahead.

Higashi-Yama
Japanese ¥¥¥

(ヒガシヤマ; ☎03-5720-1300; www.higashiyama-tokyo.jp; 1-21-25 Higashiyama, Meguro-ku; lunch/dinner from ¥1650/4950; ☺11.30am-2pm Tue-Sat, 6pm-1am Mon-Sat; 🚇Hibiya line to Naka-Meguro) Higashi-Yama serves scrumptious modern Japanese cuisine paired with gorgeous crockery. The interior, a rustic take on minimalism, is stunning too. The restaurant is all but hidden, on a side street with little signage; see the website

Beer Museum Yebisu (p65)

JOINTSTAR / SHUTTERSTOCK ©

for a map. Tasting courses make ordering easy; the 'chef's recommendation' course (¥9020) is a worthwhile splurge. Best to book ahead.

⊗ Shibuya & Harajuku

Harajuku Gyōza-rō　　Dumplings ¥

(原宿餃子楼; Map p66; 6-4-2 Jingūmae, Shibuya-ku; 6 gyōza ¥290; ⊙11.30am-4.30am; ⊠JR Yamanote line to Harajuku, Omote-sandō exit) *Gyōza* (dumplings) are the only thing on the menu here, but you won't hear any complaints from the regulars who queue up to get their fix. Have them *sui* (boiled) or *yaki* (pan-fried), with or without *niniku* (garlic) or *nira* (chives) – they're all delicious. Expect to wait on weekends, but the line moves quickly.

Maisen　　Tonkatsu ¥

(まい泉; Map p66; http://mai-sen.com; 4-8-5 Jingūmae, Shibuya-ku; lunch/dinner from ¥995/1680; ⊙11am-10pm; ⒮Ginza line to Omote-sandō, exit A2) You could order something else (maybe fried shrimp), but everyone else will be ordering the famous *tonkatsu* (breaded, deep-fried pork cutlets). There are different grades of pork on the menu, including prized *kurobuta* (black pig), but even the cheapest is melt-in-your-mouth divine. The restaurant is housed in an old public bathhouse. A takeaway window serves delicious *tonkatsu sando* (sandwich).

d47 Shokudō　　Japanese ¥

(d47食堂; Map p66; www.hikarie8.com/d47shokudo/about.shtml; 8th fl, Shibuya Hikarie, 2-21-1 Shibuya, Shibuya-ku; meals ¥1200-1780; ⊙11am-2.30pm & 6-10.30pm; ⊠JR Yamanote line to Shibuya, east exit) There are 47 prefectures in Japan and d47 serves a changing line-up of *teishoku* (set meals) that evoke the specialities of each, from the fermented tofu of Okinawa to the stuffed squid of Hokkaido. A larger menu of small plates is available in the evening. Picture windows offer bird's-eye views over the trains coming and going at Shibuya Station.

🍽️ Food Alleys

Food alleys – often called *yokochō* – are a popular post-work gathering spot for Tokyoites. These narrow strips are lined with teeny-tiny bars and restaurants; some offer seating outside on stools or over-turned beer carts. Some favourites include the following:

Ebisu-yokochō (恵比寿横町; www.ebisu-yokocho.com; 1-7-4 Ebisu, Shibuya-ku; dishes ¥500-1500; ⊙5pm-late; ⊠JR Yamanote line to Ebisu, east exit) Retro arcade chock-a-block with food stalls dishing up everything from humble *yaki soba* (fried buckwheat noodles) to decadent *hotate-yaki* (grilled scallops). It's a loud, lively (and smoky) place, especially on a Friday night; go early to get a table.

Omoide-yokochō (思い出横丁; Nishi-Shinjuku 1-chōme, Shinjuku-ku; skewers from ¥150; ⊙noon-midnight, vary by shop; ⊠JR Yamanote line to Shinjuku, west exit) A collection of rickety, wooden *yakitori* (skewers of grilled meat or vegetables) joints along the train tracks in Shinjuku. It dates to the post-war days: the name literally means 'Memory Lane'. Several stalls have English menus.

Hoppy-dōri (ホッピー通り; Map p70; 2-5 Asakusa, Taitō-ku; skewers from ¥120; ⊠Tsukuba Express to Asakusa, exit 4) Asakusa strip (nicknamed after 'hoppy', a cheap malt beverage) with outdoor tables and *yakitori* from noon until late.

An *izakaya* on Hoppy-dōri

👍 Golden Gai

Golden Gai, a warren of tiny alleys and narrow, two-storey wooden buildings, began as a black market following WWII. It later functioned as a licensed quarter, until prostitution was outlawed in 1958. Now those same buildings are filled with more than a hundred closet-sized bars. Each is as unique and eccentric as the 'master' or 'mama' who runs it. That Golden Gai – prime real estate – has so far resisted the kind of development seen elsewhere in Shinjuku is a credit to these stubbornly bohemian characters.

The best way to experience Golden Gai is to stroll the lanes and pick a place that suits your mood. Bars here usually have a theme – from punk rock to photography – and draw customers with matching expertise and obsessions (many of whom work in the media and entertainment industries).

Since regular customers are their bread and butter, some establishments are likely to give tourists a cool reception. Don't take it personally. Japanese visitors unaccompanied by a regular get the same treatment; this is Golden Gai's peculiar, invisible velvet rope. However, there are also an increasing number of bars that expressly welcome tourists (with English signs posted on their doors). Note that many bars have a cover charge (usually ¥500 to ¥1500).

Matsukiya   Hotpot ¥¥¥

(松木家; Map p66; ☎03-3461-2651; 6-8 Maruyama-chō, Shibuya-ku; sukiyaki from ¥5400; ⏱5-11pm Mon-Sat; 🚉JR Yamanote line to Shibuya, Hachikō exit) Matsukiya has been making sukiyaki (thinly sliced beef, simmered and then dipped in raw egg) since 1890, and the chefs really, really know what they're doing. It's worth upgrading to the premium course (¥7500) for even meltier meat. Prices are per person and for a full course that includes veggies and finishes with noodles cooked in the broth.

Yanmo   Seafood ¥¥¥

(やんも; Map p66; ☎03-5466-0636; www.yanmo.co.jp/aoyama/index.html; basement fl, T Place bldg, 5-5-25 Minami-Aoyama, Minato-ku; lunch/dinner set menu from ¥1100/7560; ⏱11.30am-2pm & 6-10.30pm Mon-Sat; 🚇Ginza line to Omotesandō, exit A5) Freshly caught seafood from the nearby Izu Peninsula is the speciality at this upscale, yet unpretentious restaurant. If you're looking to splash out on a seafood dinner, this is a great place to do so. The reasonably priced set menus include sashimi and steamed and grilled fish. Reservations are essential for dinner. Lunch is a bargain, but you might have to queue.

Gyūkatsu Motomura   Tonkatsu ¥

(牛かつ もと村; Map p66; 03-3797-3735; basement fl, 3-18-10 Shibuya, Shibuya-ku; set meal ¥1200; ⏱10.30am-10.30pm Mon-Sat, 10.30am-8.30pm Sun; 🚉JR Yamanote line to Shibuya, east exit) You know *tonkatsu*, the deep-fried breaded pork cutlet that is a Japanese staple; meet *gyūkatsu*, the deep-fried breaded beef cutlet that is Tokyo's latest food-craze. At Motomura, the beef is super-crisp on the outside and still very rare on the inside; diners get a small individual grill to finish the job to their liking. Set meals include cabbage, rice and soup.

✖ Shinjuku

Donjaca   Izakaya ¥

(呑者家; ☎03-3341-2497; 3-9-10 Shinjuku, Shinjuku-ku; dishes ¥350-850; ⏱5pm-7am; 🚇Marunouchi line to Shinjuku-sanchōme, exit C6) The platonic ideal of a Shōwa-era (1926–89)

Gyukatsu (deep-fried beef cutlet)

izakaya, Donjaca, in business since 1979, has red pleather stools, paper-lantern lighting and hand-written menus on the wall. The food is equal parts classic (grilled fish and fried chicken) and inventive: house specialities include *natto gyoza* (dumplings stuffed with fermented soy beans) and *mochi* gratin. Excellent sake is served in convenient tasting sets.

Nagi   Ramen ¥

(凪; www.n-nagi.com; 2nd fl, Golden Gai G2, 1-1-10 Kabukichō, Shinjuku-ku; ramen from ¥850; 24hr; R JR Yamanote line to Shinjuku, east exit) Nagi, once an upstart, has done well and now has branches around the city – and around Asia. This tiny shop, one of the originals, up a treacherous stairway in Golden Gai, is still our favourite. (It's many people's favourite and often has a line.) The house speciality is *niboshi* ramen (egg noodles in a broth flavoured with dried sardines).

Nakajima   Kaiseki ¥

(中嶋; 03-3356-4534; www.shinjyuku-nakajima. com; basement fl, 3-32-5 Shinjuku, Shinjuku-ku; lunch/dinner from ¥800/8640; 11.30am-2pm & 5.30-10pm Mon-Sat; S Marunouchi line to Shinjuku-sanchōme, exit A1) In the evening, this Michelin-starred restaurant serves exquisite *kaiseki* dinners. On weekdays, it also serves a set lunch of humble *iwashi* (sardines) for one-tenth the price; in the hands of Nakajima's chefs they're divine. The line for lunch starts to form shortly before the restaurant opens at 11.30am. Look for the white sign at the top of the stairs.

Kozue   Japanese ¥¥¥

(梢; 03-5323-3460; http://tokyo.park.hyatt.jp/ en/hotel/dining/Kozue.html; 40th fl, Park Hyatt, 3-7-1-2 Nishi-Shinjuku, Shinjuku-ku; lunch set menu ¥2850-12,400, dinner set menu ¥12,400-27,300; 11.30am-2.30pm & 5.30-9.30pm; S Ōedo line to Tochōmae, exit A4) It's hard to beat Kozue's combination of well-executed, seasonal Japanese cuisine, artisan crockery and soaring views over Shinjuku from the floor-to-ceiling windows. As the (kimono-clad) staff speak English and the restaurant caters well to allergies and personal preferences, this is a good splurge spot for diners who don't want to give up complete control. Reservations are essential.

⊗ Ueno & Yanesen

Hantei
Japanese ¥¥

(はん亭; Map p70; ☑03-3828-1440; http://hantei.co.jp; 2 12 15 Nezu, Bunkyō-ku; meals from ¥3000; ⊙noon-3pm & 5-10pm Tue-Sun; ⑤Chiyoda line to Nezu, exit 2) Housed in a beautifully maintained, century-old traditional wooden building, Hantei is a local landmark. Delectable skewers of seasonal *kushiage* (fried meat, fish and vegetables) are served

 Shinjuku-nichōme

Shinjuku-nichōme (nicknamed 'Nichōme') is the city's gay and lesbian enclave, where hundreds of establishments are crammed into a space of a few blocks, including bars, dance clubs, saunas and love hotels.

Aiiro Cafe (アイイロ カフェ; http://aliving.net/aiirocafe/; 2-18-1 Shinjuku, Shinjuku-ku; ⊙6pm-2am Mon-Thu, 6pm-5am Fri & Sat, 6pm-midnight Sun; ⑤Marunouchi line to Shinjuku-sanchōme, exit C8) is the best place to start any night out in the neighbourhood (thanks to the all-you can-drink beer for ¥1000 happy-hour special). Aiiro is a welcoming place and staff speak excellent English; it's a good place to meet people and find out about events.

A fixture on Tokyo's gay scene for many a moon, **Arty Farty** (アーティファーティ; www.arty-farty.net; 2nd fl, 2-11-7 Shinjuku, Shinjuku-ku; ⊙6pm-1am; ⑤Marunouchi line to Shinjuku-sanchōme, exit C8) welcomes all in the community to come shake a tail feather on the dancefloor here. It usually gets going later in the evening.

with small, refreshing side dishes. Lunch includes eight or 12 sticks and dinner starts with six, after which you'll continue to receive additional rounds (¥210 per skewer) until you say stop.

Innsyoutei
Japanese ¥

(韻松亭; Map p70; ☑03-3821-8126; www.innsyoutei.jp; 4-59 Ueno-kōen, Taitō-ku; lunch/dinner from ¥1680/5500; ⊙restaurant 11am-3pm & 5-9.30pm, tearoom 11am-5pm; ℝJR lines to Ueno, Ueno-kōen exit) In a gorgeous wooden building dating back to 1875, Innsyoutei (pronounced 'inshotei' and meaning 'rhyme of the pine cottage') has long been a favourite spot for fancy *kaiseki*-style meals while visiting Ueno-kōen (p42). Without a booking (essential for dinner) you'll have a long wait but it's worth it. Lunchtime *bentō* (boxed meals) offer beautifully presented morsels and are great value.

Shinsuke
Izakaya ¥¥

(シンスケ; Map p70; ☑03-3832-0469; 3-31-5 Yushima, Bunkyō-ku; ⊙5-9.30pm Mon-Fri, to 9pm Sat; ⑤Chiyoda line to Yushima, exit 3) In business since 1925, Shinsuke has honed the concept of an ideal *izakaya* to perfection: long cedar counter, 'master' in *happi* (traditional short coat) and *hachimaki* (traditional headband), and smooth-as-silk *dai-ginjo* (premium-grade sake). The food – contemporary updates of classics – is fantastic. Don't miss the *kitsune raclette* – deep-fried tofu stuffed with raclette cheese.

Kamachiku
Udon ¥

(釜竹; Map p70; ☑03-5815-4675; http://kamachiku.com/top_en; 2-14-18 Nezu, Bunkyō-ku; noodles from ¥850, small dishes ¥350-850; ⊙11.30am-2pm Tue-Sun, 5.30-9pm Tue-Sat; ⑤Chiyoda line to Nezu, exit 1) Udon (thick wheat noodles) made fresh daily is the speciality at this popular restaurant, in a beautifully restored brick warehouse from 1910 with a view onto a garden. In addition to noodles, the menu includes lots of *izakaya*-style small dishes (such as grilled fish and vegies). Expect to queue on weekends.

🍴 Asakusa & Ryōgoku

Otafuku — Japanese ¥¥

(大多福; Map p70; ☎03-3871-2521; www. otafuku.ne.jp; 1-6-2 Senzoku, Taitō-ku; oden ¥110-550; ⊗5-11pm Tue-Sat, to 10pm Sun; 圓Tsukuba Express to Asakusa, exit 1) Over a century old, Otafuku specialises in *oden* (a classic Japanese stew). It's simmered at the counter and diners pick what they want from the pot. You can dine cheaply on radishes and kelp, or splash out on scallops and tuna or a full-course menu for ¥5400 – whichever way you go, you get to soak up Otafuku's convivial, old-time atmosphere.

Asakusa Imahan — Japanese ¥¥¥

(浅草今半; Map p70; ☎03-3841-1114; www. asakusaimahan.co.jp; 3-1-12 Nishi-Asakusa, Taitō-ku; lunch/dinner set menu from ¥3800/10,000; ⊗11.30am-9.30pm; 圓Tsukuba Express to Asakusa, exit 4) For a meal to remember, swing by this famous beef restaurant, in business since 1895. Choose between courses of sukiyaki and *shabu-shabu* (beef blanched in broth); prices rise according to the grade of meat. For diners on a budget, Imahan sells a limited number of cheaper lunch sets (from ¥1500).

Onigiri Yadoroku — Japanese ¥

(おにぎり 浅草 宿六; Map p70; ☎03-3874-1615; http://onigiriyadoroku.com; 3-9-10 Asakusa, Taitō-ku; set lunch ¥660 & ¥900, onigiri ¥200-600; ⊗11.30am-5pm Mon-Sat, 6pm-2am Thu-Tue; 圓Tsukuba Express to Asakusa, exit 1) *Onigiri* (rice-ball snacks), usually wrapped in crispy sheets of *nori* (seaweed) are a great Japanese culinary invention and this humbly decorated and friendly place specialises in them. The set lunches, including a choice of two or three *onigiri*, are a great deal. At night there's a large range of flavours to choose from along with alcohol.

Kappō Yoshiba — Japanese ¥¥

(割烹吉葉; ☎03-3623-4480; www.kapou-yoshiba.jp/english/index.html; 2-14-5 Yokoami, Sumida-ku; dishes ¥600-6600; ⊗11.30am-2pm & 5-10pm Mon-Sat; ⑤Ōedo line to Ryōgoku Station, exit 1) The former Miyagino sumo stable is the location for this one-of-a-kind restaurant that has preserved the *dōyo* (practice ring) as its centrepiece. Playing

Yaki onigiri (grilled rice-ball snacks)

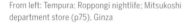

From left: Tempura; Roppongi nightlife; Mitsukoshi department store (p75), Ginza

up to its sumo roots, you can order the protein-packed stew *chanko-nabe* (for two people from ¥4600), but Yoshiba's real strength is its sushi, which is freshly prepared in jumbo portions.

Daikokuya   Tempura ¥
(大黒家; Map p70; ☎03-3844-1111; www.tempura.co.jp/english/index.html; 1-38-10 Asakusa, Taitō-ku; meals ¥1550-2100; ⊙11am-8.30pm Sun-Fri, to 9pm Sat; ⑤Ginza line to Asakusa, exit 1) Near Nakamise-dōri, this is the place to get old-fashioned tempura fried in pure sesame oil, an Asakusa speciality. It's in a white building with a tile roof. If there's a queue (and there often is), you can try your luck at the annexe one block over, where they also serve set-course meals.

🍸 DRINKING & NIGHTLIFE

Shinjuku, Shibuya and Roppongi are the biggest nightlife districts. Roppongi is particularly known as an expat haunt; Shibuya has the best nightclubs, which really get going on Fridays and Saturdays after midnight (be sure to bring picture ID for entry).

🍵 Marunouchi & Ginza
Cafe de l'Ambre   Cafe
(カフェ・ド・ランブル; Map p62; ☎03-3571-1551; www.h6.dion.ne.jp/~lambre; 8-10-15 Ginza, Chūō-ku; coffee from ¥650; ⊙noon-10pm Mon-Sat, to 7pm Sun; ⑨Ginza line to Ginza, exit A4) The sign over the door here reads 'Coffee Only' but, oh, what a selection. Sekiguchi Ichiro started the business in 1948 and – remarkably at the age of 100 – still runs it himself, sourcing and roasting aged beans from all over the world. It's dark, retro and classic Ginza.

Cha Ginza   Teahouse
(茶・銀座; Map p62; ☎03-3571-1211; www.uogashi-meicha.co.jp/shop/ginza; 5-5-6 Ginza, Chūō-ku; ⊙11am-5pm, shop to 6pm Tue-Sun; ⑤Ginza line to Ginza, exit B3) At this slick contemporary tea room, it costs ¥800 for either a cup of perfectly prepared *matcha* (green tea) and a small cake or two, or for a choice of *sencha* (premium green tea). Buy your token for tea at the shop on the ground floor, which sells top-quality teas from various growing regions in Japan.

KIRKUSUNG / SHUTTERSTOCK ©

🍶 Roppongi & Akasaka

SuperDeluxe   Club
(スーパー・デラックス; Map p66; ☏03-5412-0515; www.super-deluxe.com; B1 fl, 3-1-25 Nishi-Azabu, Minato-ku; admission varies; ⑤Hibiya line to Roppongi, exit 1B) This groovy basement performance space, also a cocktail lounge and club of sorts, stages everything from electronic music to literary evenings and creative presentations in the 20 x 20 Pecha-Kucha (20 slides x 20 seconds) format. Check the website for event details. It's in a brown-brick building by a shoe-repair shop.

These   Lounge
(テーゼ; Map p66; ☏03-5466-7331; www.these-jp.com; 2-15-12 Nishi-Azabu, Minato-ku; cover charge ¥500; ⊙7pm-4am, to 2am Sun; ⑤Hibiya line to Roppongi, exit 3) Pronounced *teh*-zeh, this delightfully quirky, nook-ridden 'library lounge' overflows with armchairs, sofas, and books on the shelves and on the bar. Imbibe champagne by the glass, whiskies or seasonal-fruit cocktails. Bites include escargot garlic toast, which goes down very nicely with a drink in the secret room on the 2nd floor. Look for the flaming torches outside.

Brewdog   Craft Beer
(Map p66; ☏03-6447-4160; www.brewdog.com/bars/worldwide/roppongi; 5-3-2 Roppongi, Minato-ku; ⊙5pm-midnight Mon-Fri, 3pm-midnight Sat & Sun; 🛜; ⑤Hibiya line to Roppongi, exit 3) This Scottish craft brewery's Tokyo outpost is nestled off the main drag. Apart from its own brews, there's a great selection of other beers, including Japanese ones on tap, mostly all served in small, regular or large (a full pint) portions. Tasty food and computer and board games to while away the evening round out a class operation.

Sake Plaza   Sake
(日本酒造会館; Map p62; www.japansake.or.jp; 1-6-15 Nishi-Shimbashi, Minato-ku; ⊙10am-6pm Mon-Fri; ⑤Ginza line to Toranomon, exit 9) Sake Plaza isn't a bar, but who cares when you can get 30mL thimbles of regionally brewed sake (some 36 types) or *shōchū* (16 types) for as little as ¥100 a shot. There are four tasting sets of three glasses from ¥200 to ¥500. This showroom and tasting space is an ideal place to learn about the national drink.

🍸 Ebisu & Meguro

Nakame Takkyū Lounge   Lounge

(中目卓球ラウンジ; 2nd fl, Lion House
Naka-Meguro, 1-3-13 Kami-Meguro, Meguro-ku;
cover before/after 10pm ¥500/800; ⊘6pm-2am
Mon-Sat; S Hibiya line to Naka-Meguro) *Takkyū*
means table tennis and it's a serious sport
in Japan. This hilarious bar looks like a
university table-tennis clubhouse – right
down to the tatty furniture and posters of
star players on the wall. It's in an apartment
building next to a parking garage (go all the
way down the corridor past the bikes); ring
the doorbell for entry.

Bar Trench   Cocktail Bar

(バートレンチ; ☑03-3780-5291; http://small-
axe.net/bar-trench/; 1-5-8 Ebisu-Nishi, Shibuya-ku;
cover ¥500; ⊘7pm-2am Mon-Sat, 6pm-1am Sun;
R JR Yamanote line to Ebisu, west exit) One of
the pioneers in Tokyo's new cocktail scene,
Trench (named for the trench-like alley in
which it is nestled) is a tiny place with the air
of old-world bohemianism. It has a short but
sweet menu of original tipples. Highlights
include the 'Shady Samurai' (green-tea-
infused gin with elderflower liquor, egg white
and lime; ¥1620). Cover charge ¥500.

Buri   Bar

(ぶり; ☑03-3496-7744; 1-14-1 Ebisu-nishi,
Shibuya-ku; ⊘5pm-3am; R JR Yamanote line
to Ebisu, west exit) Buri – the name means
'super' in Hiroshima dialect – is one
of Ebisu's most popular *tachinomi-ya*
(standing bars). On almost any night you
can find a lively crowd packed in around the
horseshoe-shaped counter here. Generous
quantities of sake (more than 40 varieties;
¥770) are served semifrozen, like slushies
in colourful jars.

🍸 Shibuya & Harajuku

Good Beer Faucets   Craft Beer

(グッドビアフォウセッツ; Map p66; http://
shibuya.goodbeerfaucets.jp; 2nd fl, 1-29-1 Shōtō,
Shibuya-ku; pints from ¥800; ⊘5pm-midnight
Mon-Thu & Sat, to 3am Fri, 4-11pm Sun; 🛜; R JR
Yamanote line to Shibuya, Hachikō exit) With 40
shiny taps, Good Beer Faucets has one of the
city's best selections of Japanese craft brews
and regularly draws a full house of locals and

Pouring a craft beer

expats. The interior is chrome and concrete (and not at all grungy). Come for happy hour (5pm to 8pm Monday to Thursday, 1pm to 7pm Sunday) and get ¥200 off any pint.

Womb   Club

(ウーム; Map p66; ✆03-5459-0039; www. womb.co.jp; 2-16 Maruyama-chō, Shibuya-ku; cover ¥1500-4000; ⊙11pm-late Fri & Sat, 4-10pm Sun; ⬚JR Yamanote line to Shibuya, Hachikō exit) A long-time (in club years, at least) club-scene fixture, Womb gets a lot of big-name international DJs playing mostly house and techno on Friday and Saturday nights. Frenetic lasers and strobes splash across the heaving crowds, which usually jam all four floors. Weekdays are quieter, with local DJs playing EDM mix and ladies getting free entry (with flyer).

Two Rooms   Bar

(トゥールームス; Map p66; ✆03-3498-0002; www.tworooms.jp; 5th fl, AO bldg, 3-11-7 Kita-Aoyama, Minato-ku; ⊙11.30am-2am Mon-Sat, to 10pm Sun; ⑤Ginza line to Omote-sandō, exit B2) Expect a crowd dressed like they don't care that wine by the glass starts at ¥1600. You can eat here too, but the real scene is at night by the bar. Call ahead (staff speak English) on Friday or Saturday night to reserve a table on the terrace, which has sweeping views towards the Shinjuku skyline.

Contact   Club

(コンタクト; Map p66; ✆03-6427-8107; www.contacttokyo.com; basement, 2-10-12 Dōgenzaka, Shibuya-ku; ¥2000-3500; ⬚JR Yamanote line to Shibuya, Hachikō exit) This is Tokyo's newest hot spot, a stylish underground club that's keen on keeping up with the times (even if that means it's a little heavy on rules): the dance floor is no smoking and no photos (so you can dance with abandon). Weekends see big international names and a young, fashionable crowd. Under-23s get in for ¥2000. ID required.

Tight   Bar

(タイト; Map p66; 2nd fl, 1-25-10 Shibuya, Shibuya-ku; ⊙6pm-2am Mon-Sat, to midnight Sun; ⬚JR Yamanote line to Shibuya, Hachikō exit) This teeny-tiny bar is wedged among

the wooden shanties of Nonbei-yokochō, a narrow nightlife strip along the elevated JR tracks. Like the name suggests, it's a tight fit, but the lack of seats doesn't keep regulars away: on a busy night, they line the stairs. Look for the big picture window. No cover charge; drinks around ¥700.

Fuglen Tokyo   Cafe

(Map p66; www.fuglen.com; 1-16-11 Tomigaya, Shibuya-ku; coffee from ¥360; ⊙8am-10pm Mon & Tue, to 1am Wed-Sun; ☎; ⑤Chiyoda line to Yoyogi-kōen, exit 2) This outpost of a long-running Oslo coffee shop serves Aeropress coffee by day and some of the city's most creative cocktails (from ¥1000) by night. It's Tomigaya's principal gathering spot.

Shinjuku

BenFiddich   Cocktail Bar 58-59

(ベンフィディック; ✆03-6279-4223; 9th fl, 1-13-7 Nishi-Shinjuku, Shinjuku-ku; ⊙6pm-3am Mon-Sat; ⬚JR Yamanote line to Shinjuku, west exit) Step into the magical space that is BenFiddich. It's dark, it's tiny, and vials of infusions line the shelves, while herbs hang drying from the ceiling. Classical music simmers and soars. The barman, Kayama Hiroyasu, in a white suit, moves like a magician. There's no menu, but cocktails run about ¥1500; service charge is 10%.

Zoetrope   Bar

(ゾートロープ; http://homepage2.nifty.com/zoetrope; 3rd fl, 7-10-14 Nishi-Shinjuku, Shinjuku-ku; ⊙7pm-4am Mon-Sat; ⬚JR Yamanote line to Shinjuku, west exit) A must-visit for whisky fans, Zoetrope has some 300 varieties of Japanese whisky behind its small counter – including hard-to-find bottles from cult favourite Chichibu Distillery. The owner speaks English and can help you pick from the daunting menu. Cover charge ¥1000; whisky by the glass from ¥400 to ¥19,000, though most are reasonable.

New York Bar   Bar

(ニューヨークバー; ✆03-5323-3458; http://tokyo.park.hyatt.com; 52nd fl, Park Hyatt, 3-7-1-2 Nishi-Shinjuku, Shinjuku-ku; ⊙5pm-midnight Sun-Wed, to 1am Thu-Sat; ⬚Ōedo line to Tochōmae,

Sumo wrestlers at Ryōgoku Kokugikan

exit A4) Head to the Park Hyatt's 52nd floor to swoon over the sweeping nightscape from the floor-to-ceiling windows at this bar (of *Lost in Translation* fame). There's a cover charge of ¥2400 if you visit or stay past 8pm (7pm Sunday); go earlier and watch the sky fade to black. Cocktails start at ¥2000. Note: dress code enforced and 20% service charge levied.

Asakusa & Ryōgoku

Popeye   Pub

(ポパイ; ☑03-3633-2120; www.70beersontap. com; 2-18-7 Ryōgoku, Sumida-ku; ☺5-11.30pm Mon-Sat; ℝJR Sōbu line to Ryōgoku, west exit) Popeye boasts an astounding 70 beers on tap, including the world's largest selection of Japanese beers – from Echigo Weizen to Hitachino Nest Espresso Stout. The happy-hour deal (5pm to 8pm) offers select brews with free plates of pizza, sausages and other munchables. It's extremely popular and fills up fast; get here early to grab a seat.

Café Otonova   Cafe

(カフェ・オトノヴァ; Map p70; ☑03-5830-7663; www.cafeotonova.net/#3eme; 3-10-4 Nishi-Asakusa; ☺noon-11pm, to 9pm Sun; ⑤) Tucked away on an alley running parallel to Kappabashi-dōri (p79), this charming cafe occupies an old house. Exposed beams are whitewashed and an atrium has been created, with cosy booths upstairs and a big communal table downstairs in front of the DJ booth. It's a stylish cafe by day and a romantic bolthole for drinks at night, with no table charge.

Kamiya Bar   Bar

(神谷バー; Map p70; ☑03-3841-5400; www.kamiya-bar.com; 1-1-1 Asakusa, Taitō-ku; ☺11.30am-10pm Wed-Mon; ⑤Ginza line to Asakusa, exit 3) One of Tokyo's oldest Western-style bars, Kamiya opened in 1880 and is still hugely popular – though probably more so today for its enormous, cheap draught beer (¥1050 for a litre). Its real speciality, however, is Denki Bran (¥270), a herbal liquor that's been produced in-house for over a century. Order at the counter, then give your tickets to the server.

⭐ ENTERTAINMENT

The easiest way to get tickets for many live shows and events is at one of the **Ticket Pia** (チケットぴあ; ☑0570-02-9111; http://t.pia.jp; ⊙10am-8pm) kiosks scattered across Tokyo. Its online booking site is in Japanese only. See **Tokyo Time Out** (http://www.timeout.com/tokyo) for event listings and **Tokyo Dross** (http://tokyodross.blogspot.co.uk) for live gig info.

⭐ Spectator Sports

Ryōgoku Kokugikan Spectator Sport

(両国国技館; Ryōgoku Sumo Stadium; ☑03-3623-5111; www.sumo.or.jp; 1-3-28 Yokoami, Sumida-ku; ¥2200-14,800; ⊛JR Sōbu line to Ryōgoku, west exit) If you're in town when a tournament is on – for 15 days each January, May and September – catch the big boys in action at Japan's largest sumo stadium. Doors open at 8am, but the action doesn't heat up until the senior wrestlers hit the ring around 2pm. Tickets can be bought online one month before the start of the tournament.

Tokyo Dome Baseball

(東京ドーム; www.tokyo-dome.co.jp/e; 1-3 Kōraku, Bunkyō-ku; tickets ¥2200-6100; ⊛JR Chūō line to Suidōbashi, west exit) Tokyo Dome (aka 'Big Egg') is home to the Yomiuri Giants. Love 'em or hate 'em, they're the most consistently successful team in Japanese baseball. If you're looking to see the Giants in action, the baseball season runs from the end of March to the end of October. Tickets sell out in advance; get them early at www.giants.jp/en.

Arashio Stable Spectator Sport

(荒汐部屋, Arashio-beya; ☑03-3666-7646; www.arashio.net/tour_e.html; 2-47-2 Hama-chō, Nihombashi, Chūō-ku; ⑤Toei Shinjuku line to Hamachō, exit A2) **FREE** Catch morning sumo practice between 7.30am and 10am at this friendly stable. Call the day before to double-check that practice (*keiko*) is on; more info is on the English website.

⭐ Performing Arts

Kabukiza Theatre

(歌舞伎座; Map p62; ☑03-3545-6800; www.kabuki-bito.jp/eng; 4-12-15 Ginza, Chūō-ku; tickets ¥4000-21,000, single-act tickets ¥800-2000; ⊛Hibiya line to Higashi-Ginza, exit 3) The flamboyant facade of this venerable theatre, which was completely reconstructed in 2013 to incorporate a tower block, makes a strong impression. It is a good indication of the extravagant dramatic flourishes that are integral to the traditional performing art of kabuki. Check the website for performance details and to book tickets; you'll also find an explanation about cheaper one-act, day seats.

National Nō Theatre Theatre

(国立能楽堂; Kokuritsu Nō-gakudō; ☑03-3230-3000; www.ntj.jac.go.jp/english; 4-18-1 Sendagaya, Shibuya-ku; adult ¥2600-4900, student ¥1900-2200; ⊛JR Sōbu line to Sendagaya) The traditional music, poetry and dances that *nō* (stylised dance-drama peformed on a bare stage) is famous for unfold here on an elegant cypress stage. Each seat has a small screen displaying an English translation of the dialogue. Shows take place only a few times a month and can sell out fast; purchase tickets one month in advance through the Japan Arts Council website.

Robot Restaurant Cabaret

(ロボットレストラン; ☑03-3200-5500; www.shinjuku-robot.com; 1-7-1 Kabukichō, Shinjuku-ku; tickets ¥8000; ⊙shows at 4pm, 5.55pm, 7.50pm & 9.45pm; ⊛JR Yamanote line to Shinjuku, east exit) This Kabukichō spectacle is wacky Japan at its finest, with giant robots operated by bikini-clad women and enough neon to light all of Shinjuku – though it's become more family-friendly in recent years. Reservations aren't necessary but are recommended: the show's popularity is evinced by the ever-creeping ticket price. Look for discount tickets at hotels around town.

⭐ Live Music

Unit
Live Music

(ユニット; ☏03-5459-8630; www.unit-tokyo. com; 1-34-17 Ebisu-nishi, Shibuya-ku; ¥2500-5000; 🚉Tōkyū Tōyoko line to Daikanyama) On weekends, this subterranean club has two shows: live music in the evening and a DJ-hosted event from around midnight. The solid line-up includes Japanese indie bands, veterans playing to a smaller crowd and overseas artists making their Japan debut. Unit is less grungy than other Tokyo live houses and, with high ceilings, doesn't get as smoky.

WWW
Live Music

(Map p66; www-shibuya.jp/index.html; 13-17 Udagawa-chō, Shibuya-ku; tickets ¥2000-5000; 🚉JR Yamanote line to Shibuya, Hachikō exit) In a former arthouse cinema (with the tell-tale tiered floor still intact), this is one of those rare venues where you could turn up just about any night and hear something good. The line-up varies from indie pop to punk to electronica. Upstairs is the new WWW X, with more space.

Shinjuku Pit Inn
Jazz

(新宿ピットイン; ☏03-3354-2024; www.pit-inn. com; basement, 2-12-4 Shinjuku, Shinjuku-ku; from ¥3000; ⊙matinee 2.30pm, evening show 7.30pm; ⑤Marunouchi line to Shinjuku-sanchōme, exit C5) This is not the place you come to talk over the music. It's the kind of place you come to sit in thrall of Japan's best jazz performers (as Tokyoites have been doing for half a century now). Weekday matinees feature up-and-coming artists and cost only ¥1300.

Tokyo Bunka Kaikan
Classical Music

(東京文化会館; Map p70; www.t-bunka.jp/en; 5-45 Ueno-kōen, Taitō-ku; ⊙library 1-8pm Tue-Sat, to 5pm Sun; 🚉JR lines to Ueno, Ueno-kōen exit) The Tokyo Metropolitan Symphony Orchestra and the Tokyo Ballet both make regular appearances at this concrete bunker of a building designed by Maekawa Kunio, an apprentice of Le Corbusier. Prices vary wildly; look out for monthly morning classical-music performances that cost only ¥500. The gorgeously decorated auditorium has superb acoustics.

Oiwake
Traditional Music

(追分; Map p70; ☏03-3844-6283; www. oiwake.info; 3-28-11 Nishi-Asakusa, Taitō-ku; admission ¥2000 plus 1 food item & 1 drink; ⊙5.30pm-midnight; 🚉Tsukuba Express to Asakusa, exit 1) Oiwake is one of Tokyo's few *minyō izakaya,* pubs where traditional folk music is performed. It's a homey place, where the waitstaff and the musicians – who play *tsugaru-jamisen* (a banjo-like instrument), hand drums and bamboo flute – are one and the same. Sets start at 7pm and 9pm; children are welcome for the early show. Seating is on tatami.

ℹ️ INFORMATION

DANGERS & ANNOYANCES

Of note are reports that drink-spiking continues to be a problem in Roppongi (resulting in robbery, extortion and, in extreme cases, physical assault). Be wary of following touts into bars there and in Kabukichō; men are also likely to be solicited in both neighbourhoods. Women, especially those alone, walking through Kabukichō and Dōgenzaka (both red-light districts) risk being harassed. Note that many budget hotels in Shinjuku targeting foreign tourists are in fact in Kabukichō.

INTERNET ACCESS

Free wi-fi can be found on subway platforms, on the streets of some districts and at many convenience stores, major attractions and shopping centres – though signals are often weak. Look for the sticker that says 'Japan Wi-Fi'.

TOURIST INFORMATION

Tokyo Metropolitan Government Building Tourist Information Center (☏03-5321-3077; 1st fl, Tokyo Metropolitan Government bldg 1, 2-8-1 Nishi-Shinjuku, Shinjuku-ku; ⊙9.30am-6.30pm; ⑤Ōedo line to Tochōmae, exit A4) Has English-language information and publications. Additional branches in Keisei Ueno Station, Haneda Airport and Shinjuku Bus Terminal.

JR East Travel Service Center (JR東日本訪日旅行センター; Map p62; www.jreast.co.jp/e/customer_support/service_center_tokyo.html; Tokyo Station, 1-9-1 Marunouchi, Chiyoda-ku;

Kabukiza (p93), Tokyo's principal kabuki theatre

⏰7.30am-8.30pm; 📶; 🚇JR Yamanote line to Tokyo, Marunouchi north exit) Tourist information, money exchange, and bookings for ski and onsen getaways. There are branches in the two airports, too.

ℹ️ GETTING THERE & AWAY

AIR

The excellent, modern **Narita Airport** (NRT; 成田 空港; 📞0476-34-8000; www.narita-airport.jp) is inconveniently located 66km east of Tokyo. There are three terminals (the new Terminal 3 handles low-cost carriers). Note that only Terminals 1 and 2 have train stations. Free shuttle buses run between all the terminals every 15 to 30 minutes (from 7am to 9.30pm). Another free shuttle runs between Terminal 2 and Terminal 3 every five to 12 minutes (4.30am to 11.20pm); otherwise it is a 15-minute walk between the two terminals.

Closer to central Tokyo, **Haneda Airport** (HND; 羽 田空港; 📞international terminal 03-6428-0888; www.tokyo-airport-bldg.co.jp/en) has two domestic terminals and one international terminal. Note that some international flights arrive at awkward night-time hours, between midnight and 5am, when public transportation is sporadic.

BUS

Travellers coming by bus from other parts of Japan will likely arrive at **Shinjuku Bus Terminal** (バスタ新宿; Busuta Shinjuku; 📞03-6380-4794; http://shinjuku-busterminal.co.jp; 5-24-55 Sendagaya, Shibuya-ku; 📶; 🚇JR Yamanote line to Shinjuku, new south exit), part of the JR Shinjuku train station complex. There is direct access to JR rail lines on the 2nd floor.

CAR & MOTORCYCLE

Driving on the *shutokō*, the convoluted Tokyo city expressway, is not for the faint of heart. If you're arriving by rental car from other parts of Japan, it's advisable to return it on the outskirts of the city and take the train in the rest of the way.

TRAIN

Tokyo Station (東京駅; Map p62; www.tokyostationcity.com/en; 1-9 Marunouchi, Chiyoda-ku; 🚇JR lines to Tokyo Station) is the main point of entry for travellers coming via *shinkansen* from other parts of Japan. From

Tokyo Station you can transfer to the JR Chūō and JR Yamanote lines as well as the Marunouchi subway line.

Coming from points west, if you're staying on the west side of the city, you can choose to get off one stop early, at Shinagawa, where you can connect to the JR Yamanote line. From points east, and if you're staying on the east side of the city, you can choose to get off one stop early, at Ueno; from Ueno you can transfer to the JR Yamanote line and the Ginza and Hibiya subway lines.

 GETTING AROUND

TO/FROM NARITA

BUS

Purchase tickets from kiosks in the arrivals hall (no advance reservations necessary). From Tokyo, there's a ticket counter inside the Shinjuku Bus Terminal (p95).

Friendly Airport Limousine (www.limousine bus.co.jp/en) Scheduled, direct, reserved-seat buses (¥3100) depart from all Narita Airport terminals for major hotels and train stations in Tokyo. The journey takes 1½ to two hours depending on traffic. At the time of research, discount round-trip 'Welcome to Tokyo Limousine Bus Return Voucher' tickets (¥4500) were available for foreign tourists; ask at the ticket counter at the airport.

Keisei Tokyo Shuttle (www.keiseibus.co.jp) Discount buses connect all Narita Airport terminals and Tokyo Station (¥1000, approximately 90 minutes, every 20 minutes from 6am to 11pm). There are less frequent departures from Tokyo Station for Narita Airport terminals 2 and 3 between 11pm and 6am (¥2000), which are handy for budget flights at odd hours.

TRAIN

Both Japan Railways (JR) and the independent Keisei line run between central Tokyo and Narita Airport Terminals 1 and 2. For Terminal 3, take a train to Terminal 2 and then walk or take the free shuttle bus to Terminal 3 (and budget an extra 15 minutes). Tickets can be purchased in the basement of either terminal, where the entrances to the train stations are located.

Keisei Skyliner (www.keisei.co.jp/keisei/tetudou/skyliner/us) The quickest service into Tokyo runs nonstop to Nippori (¥2470, 36 minutes) and Ueno (¥2470, 41 minutes) stations, on the city's northeast side, where you can connect to the JR Yamanote line or the subway (Ueno Station only). Trains run twice an hour, 8am to 10pm. Foreign nationals can purchase advanced tickets online for slightly less (¥2200). The **Skyliner & Tokyo Subway Ticket**, which combines a one-way or round-trip ticket on the Skyliner and a one-, two- or three-day subway pass, is a good deal.

Keisei Main Line Limited-express trains (*kaisoku kyūkō*; ¥1030, 71 minutes to Ueno) follow the same route as the Skyliner but make stops. This is a good budget option. Trains run every 20 minutes during peak hours.

Narita Express (www.jreast.co.jp/e/nex) A swift and smooth option, especially if you're staying on the west side of the city, N'EX trains depart Narita approximately every half-hour between 7am and 10pm for Tokyo Station (¥3020, 53 minutes) and Shinjuku (¥3190, 80 minutes); the latter also stops at Shibuya (¥3190; 75 minutes). At the time of research, foreign tourists could purchase return N'EX tickets for ¥4000 (valid for 14 days; ¥2000 for under 12s). Check online or enquire at the JR East Travel Service centres at Narita Airport for the latest deals. Long-haul JR passes are valid on N'EX trains, but you must obtain a seat reservation (no extra charge) from a JR ticket office.

TAXI

Fixed-fare taxis run ¥20,000 to ¥22,000 for most destinations in central Tokyo. There's a 20% surcharge between 10pm and 5am. Credit cards accepted.

TO/FROM HANEDA

BUS

Purchase tickets at the kiosks at the arrivals hall. In Tokyo, there's a ticket counter inside the **Shinjuku Bus Terminal** (p95).

Friendly Airport Limousine (www.limousine bus.co.jp/en) Coaches connect Haneda with major train stations and hotels in Shibuya (¥1030), Shinjuku (¥1230), Roppongi (¥1130), Ginza (¥930) and others; fares double between midnight and 5am. Travel times vary wildly, taking anywhere from 30 to 90 minutes depending on traffic. Night buses depart for Shibuya Station at 12.15am, 12.50am and 2.20am and Shinjuku Bus Terminal at 12.20am and 1am; for Haneda, there is a bus from Shibuya Station at 3.30am and one from Shinjuku Bus Terminal at 4am. Regular service resumes at 5am.

Haneda Airport Express (http://hnd-bus.com) Though more useful for suburban destinations than downtown ones, coaches do travel to handy places such as Shibuya Station (¥1030) and To-kyo Station (¥930) in about an hour, depending on traffic, from 5am to midnight. Night buses depart for Shibuya Station (¥2600) via Roppongi Hills at 12.50am and 2.20am.

TRAIN & MONORAIL

Note that the international and domestic terminals have their own stations; when traveling to the airport, the international terminal is the second to last stop.

Keikyū Airport Express (www.haneda-tokyo-access.com/en) Trains depart several times an hour (5.30am to midnight) for Shinagawa (¥410, 12 minutes), where you can connect to the JR Yamanote line. From Shinagawa, some trains continue along the Asakusa subway line, which runs to Asakusa.

Tokyo Monorail (www.tokyo-monorail.co.jp/english) Leaves approximately every 10 minutes (5am to midnight) for Hamamatsuchō Station (¥490, 15 minutes), which is a stop on the JR Yamanote line.

TAXI

Fixed fares include Ginza (¥5600), Shibuya (¥6400), Shinjuku (¥6800) and Asakusa (¥6900). There's a 20% surcharge between 10pm and 5am. Credit cards accepted.

BICYCLE

Tokyo is by no means a bicycle-friendly city. Bike lanes are almost nonexistent and you'll see no-parking signs for bicycles everywhere (ignore these at your peril: your bike could get impounded, requiring a half-day excursion to the pound and a ¥3000 fee). Still, you'll see people cycling everywhere and it can be a really fun way to get around the city. Some hostels and ryokan have bikes to lend. See **Rentabike** (http://rentabike.jp) for places around town that rent bicycles.

21_21 Design Sight (p64)

Interior of Tokyo Station, Marunouchi

TRAIN & SUBWAY

Tokyo's train and subway system should get you everywhere you need to go. Trains run roughly 5am to midnight. There are JR (Japan Rail) lines and 13 subway lines, nine operated by Tokyo Metro and four by Toei. The lines are colour-coded, making navigation fairly simple. Major transit hubs include Tokyo, Shinagawa, Shibuya, Shinjuku, Ikebukuro and Ueno stations.

Fares run ¥133 to ¥220 on JR, ¥170 to ¥240 on Tokyo Metro and ¥180 to ¥320 on Toei lines, depending on how far you travel. Unfortunately a transfer ticket is required to change between lines run by different operators; a Pasmo or Suica card makes this process seamless, but either way a journey involving more than one operator comes out costing more.

Tokyo Metro's **One-Day Open Ticket** (adult/child ¥600/300) gives you unlimited rides over a 24-hour period on Tokyo Metro subway lines; it's an excellent deal, though you'll have to be mindful of only riding Tokyo Metro lines. Purchase at Tokyo Metro stations.

Otherwise purchase a Suica card from any JR train station; for more on IC cards, see p312.

KEY ROUTES

Ginza subway line Shibuya to Asakusa, via Ginza and Ueno. Colour-coded orange.

Hibiya subway line Connects Roppongi, Ginza, Akihabara and Ueno. Colour-coded grey.

JR Yamanote line Loop line stopping at many sightseeing destinations, such as Shibuya, Harajuku, Shinjuku, Marunouchi (Tokyo Station) and Ueno. Colour-coded light green.

JR Chūō line Marunouchi (Tokyo Station) to points in west Tokyo, via Shinjuku. Colour-coded reddish-orange.

JR Sōbu line Runs across the city centre, connecting Shinjuku with Suidōbashi, Ryōgoku and Akihabara. Colour-coded yellow.

Yurikamome line Elevated train running from Shimbashi to points around Tokyo Bay.

TAXI

Fares start at ¥730 for the first 2km, then rise by ¥90 for every 280m you travel (or for every 105 seconds spent in traffic). There's a surcharge of 20% between 10pm and 5am.

Where to Stay

Tokyo is known for being expensive; however, more budget and midrange options are popping up every year. As Tokyo is huge, it's smart to zero in on an area in which you want to spend significant time.

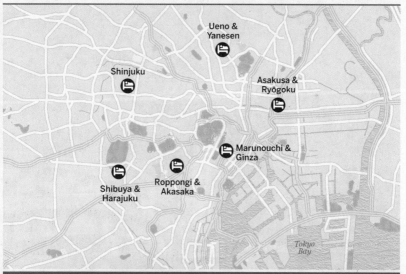

Neighbourhood	Atmosphere
Marunouchi & Ginza	Convenient for all sights and for travel out of the city; a major business and commercial district with sky-high prices and relatively quiet weekends.
Roppongi & Akasaka	Nightlife district with lots of eating and drinking options, plus art museums; mix of midrange to high-end hotels; noisy and hectic at night with some seedy pockets.
Shibuya & Harajuku	Convenient transport links and plenty of nightlife in Shibuya, with mostly midrange options. Can get extremely crowded with a chance of possible sensory overload.
Shinjuku	Superb transport links, food and nightlife options; very crowded around station areas and cheaper options are clustered around the red-light district.
Ueno & Yanesen	Ryokans abound, lots of greenery and museums and easy airport access; good for families; the best ryokan here tend to be isolated in residential neighbourhoods.
Asakusa & Ryōgoku	Atmospheric old city feel, great budget options and backpacker vibe; can feel quiet at night and far from more central areas.

KYOTO

In This Chapter

Kyoto

Kyoto is old Japan writ large: quiet temples, sublime gardens, colourful shrines and geisha scurrying to secret liaisons. With 17 Unesco World Heritage Sites, more than a thousand Buddhist temples and over 400 Shintō shrines it is one of the world's most culturally rich cities. But Kyoto is not just about sightseeing. While the rest of Japan has adopted modernity with abandon, the old ways are still clinging on in Kyoto. Visit an old shōtengai (market street) and admire the ancient speciality shops: tofu sellers, washi (Japanese handmade paper) stores and tea merchants.

Kyoto in Two Days

Start your Kyoto experience in Southern Higashiyama, home to famous temples **Kiyomizu-dera** (p117) and **Chion-in** (p118). In the afternoon follow the **Path of Philosophy** (p122) to **Ginka-ku-ji** (p121) in Northern Higashiyama. On the second day, visit stunning **Kinkaku-ji** (p110) and the Zen garden at **Ryōan-ji** (p111), then hop in a taxi for Arashiyama. End with an evening stroll through the historic geisha district, **Gion** (p107).

Kyoto in Four Days

With four days, we recommend doing the two-day itinerary in three days to give yourself more time to explore smaller sights en route and soak up the atmosphere. On the fourth day, take a break from temples to stroll around downtown, hitting the excellent **Nishiki Market** (p114), craft shops and department stores and having a picnic in **Kyoto Imperial Palace Park** (p114).

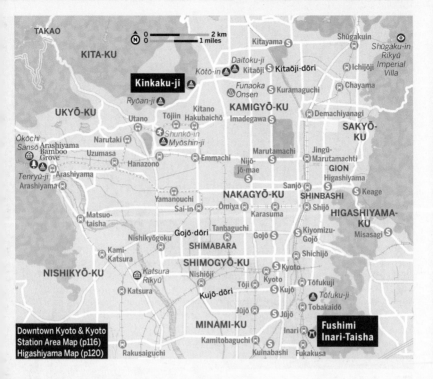

TAKAO

KITA-KU

N 0 ____ 2 km
0 ____ 1 miles

Kitayama Ⓢ

Shūgakuin Ⓡ

Shūgaku-in Rikyū Imperial Villa ◉

Daitoku-ji ⛩
Kōtō-in ⛩ Kitaōji Ⓢ **Kitaōji-dōri**

Ⓡ Ichijōji

Kinkaku-ji ⛩

Funaoka Ⓢ Kuramaguchi
⨀ Onsen

Ⓡ Chayama

Ryōan-ji ⛩

UKYŌ-KU

Kitano **KAMIGYŌ-KU**
Utano Tōjiin Hakubaichō Imadegawa Ⓢ

Ⓡ Demachiyanagi

SAKYŌ-KU

Ōkōchi
Sansō Arashiyama ⛩ Narutaki Ⓡ
⛩ Bamboo
⛩ ⛩ Grove Uzumasa

🔘 Shunkō-in
⛩ Myōshin-ji

Ⓡ Hanazono

Emmachi Ⓡ Nijō- Ⓢ
Ⓡ jō-mae

Marutamachi
Ⓡ Marutamachti

Jingū- GION

Tenryū-ji ⛩ Arashiyama
Arashiyama Ⓡ

Higashiyama

Sanjō Ⓢ

Ⓡ Keage

Matsuo-
taisha ⛩

Yamanouchi Ⓡ **NAKAGYŌ-KU** SHINBASHI
Sai-in Ⓡ Ōmiya Ⓡ Ⓡ Shijō
Karasuma

HIGASHIYAMA-
KU

Kami-
Katsura ⛩

Nishikyōgoku Ⓡ **Gojō-dōri**
SHIMABARA

Tanbaguchi
Ⓡ Gojō Ⓢ

Ⓡ Kiyomizu-
Gojō

Misasagi Ⓢ

NISHIKYŌ-KU

Katsura ⛩
Rikyū Nishiōji Ⓡ

SHIMOGYŌ-KU

Ⓡ Shichijō

Ⓢ Kyoto

Ⓡ Katsura

Kyoto
Tōji Ⓡ Ⓢ Kujō
Kujō-dōri

Ⓡ Tōfukuji

Tōfuku-ji ⛩

Jūjō Ⓡ

Ⓡ Tobakaidō

**Downtown Kyoto & Kyoto
Station Area Map (p116)**
Higashiyama Map (p120)

Rakusaiguchi Ⓡ

MINAMI-KU
Kamitobaguchi Ⓡ

Jūjō Ⓢ

Inari Ⓡ Ⓢ

**Fushimi
Inari-Taisha**

Kuinabashi Fukakusa

Arriving in Kyoto

The closest major airport is Kansai International Airport, about 75 minutes away from Kyoto by direct express train. Kyoto Station, in the south of the city, is served by the Tōkaidō Shinkansen (bullet train), several JR main lines and a few private rail lines. The easiest way to get downtown from this station is to hop on the Karasuma subway line.

Sleeping

Downtown Kyoto, which has the largest mix of options, is the most convenient place to stay. Beware that accommodation in Kyoto can get fully booked; reserve as soon as you know your travel dates. Osaka is a great Plan B if Kyoto is full.

For more information on the best neighbourhoods to stay in, see p139.

Fushimi Inari-Taisha

With seemingly endless arcades of vermilion torii *(shrine gates) spread across a thickly wooded mountain, this vast shrine complex is a world unto its own. It is, quite simply, one of the most impressive and memorable sights in all of Kyoto.*

Great For...

☑ Don't Miss

The classic photo op from inside the tunnel of *torii* gates.

History

Fushimi Inari-Taisha was dedicated to the gods of rice and sake by the Hata family in the 8th century. As the role of agriculture diminished, deities were enrolled to ensure prosperity in business. Nowadays the shrine is one of Japan's most popular, and is the head shrine for some 40,000 Inari shrines scattered the length and breadth of the country.

Messenger of Inari

As you explore the shrine, you will come across hundreds of stone foxes. The fox is considered the messenger of Inari, the god of cereals, and the stone foxes, too, are often referred to as Inari. The key often seen in the fox's mouth is for the rice granary. On an incidental note, the Japanese tradition-ally see the fox as a sacred, somewhat

Fushimi Inari-Taisha's vermilion *torii*

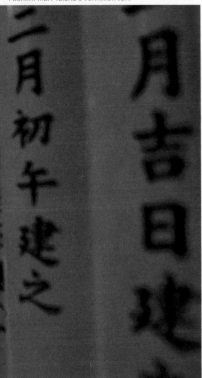

❶ Need to Know

(伏見稲荷大社; Map p103; 68 Yabunouchi-chō, Fukakusa, Fushimi-ku; ◷dawn-dusk; ℝJR Nara line to Inari or Keihan line to Fushimi-Inari) **FREE**

✕ Take a Break

Vermillion (バーミリオン; 85 Fukakusa-inari, Onmae-chō, Fushimi-ku; ◷10am-5.30pm Mon-Wed & Fri, 9am-5.30pm Sat & Sun; ℝJR Nara line to Inari) serves excellent coffee and cakes.

★ Top Tip

Don't be afraid to get lost – that's part of the fun at Fushimi.

---

mysterious figure capable of 'possessing' humans – the favoured point of entry is under the fingernails.

Hiking the Grounds

A pathway wanders 4km up the mountain and is lined with dozens of atmospheric sub-shrines. The walk around the upper precincts is a pleasant day hike. It also makes for a very eerie stroll in the late afternoon and early evening, when the various graveyards and miniature shrines along the path take on a mysterious air. It's best to go with a friend at this time.

What's Nearby?

Tōfuku-ji Buddhist Temple

(東福寺; Map p103; ℐ075-561-0087; 15-778 Honmahi, Higashiyama-ku; Hōjō garden ¥400, Tsūten-kyō bridge ¥400; ◷9am-4pm;

ℝKeihan line to Tōfukuji or JR Nara line to Tōfukuji) Home to a spectacular garden, several superb structures and beautiful precincts, Tōfuku-ji is one of the best temples in Kyoto. It's well worth a visit and can easily be paired with a trip to Fushimi Inari-Taisha (the temples are linked by the Keihan and JR train lines). The present temple complex includes 24 subtemples. The huge **San-mon** is the oldest Zen main gate in Japan, the **Hōjō** (Abbot's Hall) was reconstructed in 1890, and the gardens were laid out in 1938.

The northern garden has stones and moss neatly arranged in a chequerboard pattern. From a viewing platform at the back of the gardens you can observe the **Tsūten-kyō** (Bridge to Heaven), which spans a valley filled with maples.

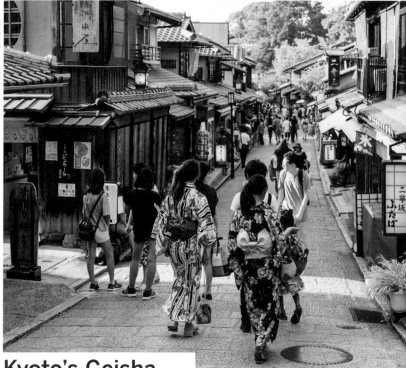

ASIATRAVEL / SHUTTERSTOCK ©

Kyoto's Geisha Culture

Though dressed in the finest silks and often astonishingly beautiful, geisha are first and foremost accomplished musicians and dancers. These now-rare creatures – who seem lifted from another world – continue to entertain in Kyoto today.

Great For...

☑ Don't Miss

A stroll through Gion at night (p112).

Geiko & Maiko

The word geisha literally means 'arts person'; in Kyoto the term used is *geiko* – 'child of the arts'. It is the *maiko* (apprentice *geiko*) who are spotted on city streets in ornate dress, long trailing obi and towering wooden clogs, their faces painted with thick white make-up, leaving only a suggestive forked tongue of bare flesh on the nape of the neck. As geisha grow older their make-up becomes increasingly natural; by then their artistic accomplishments need no fine-casing. At their peak in the 1920s there were around 80,000 geisha in Japan. Today there are approximately 1000 (including apprentices), with nearly half working in Kyoto.

Life of a Geisha Then & Now

Prior to the mid-20th century, a young girl might arrive at an *okiya* (geisha living

JURI POZZI / SHUTTERSTOCK ©

❶ Need to Know

Gion, on the east bank of the Kamo-gawa, is Kyoto's most famous geisha district.

✖ Take a Break

Stop at Gion institution Kagizen Yoshifusa (p131) for tea and sweets.

★ Top Tip

Geisha sometimes work with local tourism boards to create experiences for visitors; check with the Kyoto Tourist Information Center (p136) for events.

quarters) to work as a maid. Should she show promise, the owner of the *okiya* would send her to begin training at the *kaburenjo* (school for geisha arts) at around age six. She would continue maid duty, waiting on the senior geisha of the house, while honing her skills and eventually specialising in one of the arts, such as playing the *shamisen* (three-stringed instrument resembling a lute or a banjo) or dance.

Geisha were often indebted to the *okiya* who covered their board and training. Given the lack of bargaining chips that have been afforded women in history, there is no doubt that many geisha of the past, at some point in their careers, engaged in compensated relationships; this would be with a *danna* (a patron) with whom the geisha would enter a contractual relationship not unlike a marriage (and one that could

be terminated). A wealthy *danna* could help a woman fulfil her debt to the *okiya* or help her start her own. Other geisha married, which required them to leave the profession; some were adopted by the *okiya* and inherited the role of house mother; still others worked until old age.

Today's geisha begin their training no earlier than in their teens – perhaps after being inspired by a school trip to Kyoto – while completing their compulsory education (in Japan, until age 15). Then they'll leave home for an *okiya* (they do still exist) and start work as an apprentice. While in the past a *maiko* would never be seen out and about in anything but finery, today's apprentices act much like ordinary teens in their downtime. For some, the magic is in the *maiko* stage and they never proceed to become geisha; those who do live largely normal lives, free to live where they choose, date as they like and change professions when they please.

Hanamachi

Traditionally, the districts where geisha were licensed to entertain in *ochaya* (teahouses) were called *hanamachi*, which means 'flower town'. Of the five that remain in Kyoto, **Gion** (祇園周辺; Map p120; Higashiyama-ku; ⑤ Tōzai line to Sanjō, ⑭ Keihan line to Gion-Shijō), is the grandest. Many of Kyoto's most upmarket restaurants and exclusive hostess bars are here.

On the other side of the river, **Ponto-chō** (先斗町; Map p116; Ponto-chō, Nakagyō-ku; ⓢ Tōzai line to Sanjo-Keihan or Kyoto-Shiyakusho-mae, ⓡ Keihan line to Sanjo, Hankyū line to Kawara machi) has a different feel, with very narrow lanes. Not much to look at by day, the street comes alive at night, with wonderful lanterns, traditional wooden exteriors, and elegant Kyotoites disappearing into the doorways of elite old restaurants and bars.

Experiencing Geisha Culture

Modern *maiko* and geisha entertain their clients in exclusive restaurants, banquet halls and traditional *ochaya* much like they did a century ago. This world is largely off limits to travellers, as a personal connection is required to get a foot in the door, though some tour operators can act as mediators.

Of course, these experiences can cost hundreds of dollars (if not more).

Ryokan Gion Hatanaka offers a rare chance to witness geisha perform and then interact with them. The inn's **Kyoto Cuisine & Maiko Evening** (ぎおん畑中; Map p120; ☎075-541-5315; www.kyoto-maiko.jp; Hatanaka Ryokan, 505 Minamigawa, Gion-machi, Yasaka-jinja Minamimon-mae, Higashiyama-ku; per person ¥19,000; ⊘6-8pm Mon, Wed, Fri & Sat; ☒Kyoto City bus 206 to Gion or Chionin-mae, ⓡKeihan line to Gion-Shijō), is a regularly scheduled evening of elegant Kyoto *kaiseki* (haute cuisine) food and personal entertainment by real Kyoto *geiko* (fully fledged geisha) as well as *maiko*.

Geisha Dances

An excellent way to experience geisha culture is to see one of Kyoto's annual public dance performances (known as *odori*), a

Geisha performing in Gion

city tradition for over a century. Get tickets as early as you can; your accommodation might be able to help.

Gion Odori (祇園をどり; Map p120; 📞075-561-0224; Gion, Higashiyama-ku; ¥4000, with tea ¥4500; ⊙shows 1.30pm & 4pm; 🚌Kyoto City bus 206 to Gion) From 1 to 10 November, at the Gion Kaikan Theatre (祇園会館).

Kyō Odori (京おどり; Map p120; 📞075-561-1151; Miyagawachō Kaburenjo, 4-306 Miyagawasuji, Higashiyama-ku; nonreserved seat with/without tea ¥2800/2200, reserved seat ¥4800/4200; ⊙shows 1pm, 2.45pm & 4.30pm; 🚃Keihan line to Gion-Shijō) From the first to the third Sunday in April at the Miyagawa-chō Kaburen-jō Theatre (宮川町歌舞練場).

Miyako Odori (都をどり; Map p120; 📞075-541-3391; www.miyako-odori.jp; Gionkobu Kaburenjo, 570-2 Gion-machi minamigawa, Higashiyama-ku; nonreserved/reserved seat ¥2500/4200, reserved seat with tea ¥4800; ⊙shows 12.30pm, 2pm, 3.30pm & 4.50pm; 🚌Kyoto City bus 206 to Gion, 🚃Keihan line to Gion-Shijō) Throughout April usually at the Gion Kōbu Kaburen-jō Theatre. As of late 2016, the building was under renovation and performances are held at Kyoto Art Theater Shunjuza in the meantime.

Kamogawa Odori (鴨川をどり; Map p116; 📞075-221-2025; Ponto-chō, Sanjō-sagaru, Nakagyō-ku; normal/special seat ¥2300/4200, special seat with tea ¥4800; ⊙shows 12.30pm, 2.20pm & 4.10pm; 🚇Tōzai line to Kyoto-Shiyakusho-mae) From 1 to 24 May at Ponto-chō Kaburen-jō Theatre.

Maiko Makeover

Ever wondered how you might look as a *maiko*? Give it a try at **Maika** (舞香; Map p120; 📞075-551-1661; www.maica.tv; 297 Miyagawa suji 4-chōme, Higashiyama-ku; maiko/geisha from ¥7500/9000; ⊙shop 9am-9pm; 🚃Keihan line to Gion-Shijo or Kiyomizu-Gojo) in the Gion. Prices begin at ¥7500 for the basic treatment, which includes full make-up and formal kimono. If you don't mind spending some extra yen, it's possible to head out in costume for a stroll through Gion – and be stared at like never before! The process takes about an hour. Call to reserve at least one day in advance.

Photographing Geisha

A photo of a *maiko* is a much-coveted Kyoto souvenir; however bear in mind that these are young women – many of whom are minors – trying to get to work. Be respectful and let them pass.

FRANK CARTER / GETTY IMAGES ©

Kinkaku-ji

Kyoto's famed 'Golden Pavilion', Kinkaku-ji is one of Japan's best-known sights. The main hall, covered in brilliant gold leaf, shining above its reflecting pond is truly spectacular.

Great For...

☑ Don't Miss

The mirror-like reflection of the temple in the Kyō-ko pond is extremely photogenic.

History

Originally built in 1397 as a retirement villa for shogun Ashikaga Yoshi-mitsu, Kinkaku-ji was converted into a Buddhist temple by his son, in compliance with his wishes. In 1950 a young monk consummated his obsession with the temple by burning it to the ground. The monk's story is fictionalised in Mishima Yukio's 1956 novel *The Temple of the Golden Pavilion*. In 1955 a full reconstruction was completed, following the original design exactly, but the gold-foil covering was extended to the lower floors.

The Pavilion & Grounds

The three-storey pavilion, covered in bright gold leaf with a bronze phoenix on top of the roof, is naturally the highlight. But there's more to this temple than its shiny main hall. Don't miss the Ryūmon-taki

Below right: Kinkaku-ji's tea garden

Kinkaku-ji 🏯

🏯 *Ryōan-ji*

Utano   Ryōanji   Tōjiin   🏯 Kitano
    🏯   🏯 🏯   Hakubaichō
Narutaki   ᐧᐧᐧ Myōshinji
   🏯   Omura-   🏯 *Myōshin-ji*
     Ninnaji

❶ Need to Know

金閣寺; Map p103; 1 Kinkakuji-chō, Kita-ku;
¥400; ⊘9am-5pm; 🚍Kyoto City bus 205
from Kyoto Station to Kinkakuji-michi, Kyoto
City bus 101 or 205 from Kyoto Station to
Kinkakuji-mae

✗ Take a Break

There is a small tea garden near the
entrance that serves *matcha* (green
powdered tea) and sweets.

★ Top Tip

Kinkaku-ji is on everyone's 'must-see'
list: it's best to go early in the day
or just before closing, ideally on a
weekday.

waterfall and Rigyo-seki stone, which looks
like a carp attempting to swim up the falls.
Nearby, there is a small gathering of stone
Jizō figures onto which people throw coins
and make wishes. The quaint teahouse
Sekka-tei embodies the spirit of *wabi sabi*
(rustic simplicity) that defines the Japanese tea-ceremony ethic. It's at the top of
the hill shortly before the exit of the temple.

What's Nearby?

Ryōan-ji   Buddhist Temple

(龍安寺; Map p103; 13 Goryōnoshitamachi,
Ryōan-ji, Ukyō-ku; adult/child ¥500/300; ⊘8am-
5pm Mar-Nov, 8.30am-4.30pm Dec-Feb; 🚍Kyoto
City bus 59 from Sanjō-Keihan to Ryoanji-mae)
You've probably seen a picture of the rock
garden here – it's one of the symbols of
Kyoto and one of Japan's better-known
sights. Ryōan-ji belongs to the Rinzai school

and was founded in 1450. The garden, an
oblong of sand with an austere collection of
15 carefully placed rocks, apparently adrift
in a sea of sand, is enclosed by an earthen
wall. The designer, who remains unknown
to this day, provided no explanation.

Myōshin-ji   Buddhist Temple

(妙心寺; Map p103; www.myoshinji.or.jp;
1 Myoshin-ji-chō, Hanazono, Ukyō-ku; main
temple free, other areas of complex adult/child
¥500/100; ⊘9.10-11.40am & 1-4.40pm; 🚍Kyoto
City bus 10 from Sanjo-Keihan to Myoshinji
Kita-mon-mae) Myōshin-ji is a separate
world within Kyoto, a walled-off complex of
temples and subtemples that invites lazy
strolling. The subtemple of **Taizō-in** here
contains one of the city's more interesting
gardens. Myōshin-ji dates from 1342 and
belongs to the Rinzai school. There are 47
subtemples, but only a few are open to the
public.

Walk Through the Floating World

Gion is Kyoto's famous entertainment and geisha quarter. See it with an evening stroll around the atmospheric streets lined with 17th-century traditional restaurants and teahouses lit up with lanterns.

Start Yasaka-jinja
Distance 3km
Duration Two hours

Classic Photo The cherry blossoms hanging over the Shirakawa Canal.

4 At the fork in the road is the small Tatsumi shrine; take a left and walk west along **Shirakawa Canal**.

SHIMBASHI

GION

7 End with a stroll through Kyoto's cosiest entertainment strip, **Pontochō** (p108).

6 Cross Kyoto's principle river, **Kamo-gawa**, which runs through the heart of the city.

5 Back on Shijō-dōri, you'll pass Kyoto's grand old kabuki theatre, **Minami-za** (p135).

Ⓝ 0 ———— 200 m
0 ———— 0.1 miles

3 Tatsumi-bashi bridge marks the entrance to **Shimbashi**, with some of Kyoto's finest traditional architecture.

Ⓢ Higashiyama

Shinmonzen-dori

Hanami-kōji

Higashioji-dori

Kiri-doshi

❸

❷

Tominagacho-dori

2 Walk up Shijō-dōri and head to **Hanami-kōji**, a picturesque street of *ryōtei* (traditional, high-class restaurants).

HIGASHIYAMA-KU

START ❶

Hanami-kōji

Higashioji-dori

1 Start on the steps of **Yasaka-jinja** (p121), the guardian shrine of Gion.

Take a Break... Gion Finlandia Bar (p134) is in an old Gion geisha house.

Yasaka-dori

⊙ SIGHTS

⊙ Downtown Kyoto

Nijō-jō   Castle

(二条城, Map p116; 541 Nijōjō-chō, Nijō-dōri, Horikawa nishi-iru, Nakagyō-ku; adult/child ¥600/200; ⊙8.45am-5pm, Ninomaru Palace 9am-4pm, closed Tue Dec, Jan, Jul & Aug; ⑤Tōzai line to Nijō-jō-mae, ⓇJR line to Nijō Station) The military might of Japan's great warlord generals, the Tokugawa shoguns, is amply demonstrated by the imposing stone walls and ramparts of their great castle, Nijō-jō, which dominates a large part of Northwest Kyoto. Hidden behind these you will find a superb palace surrounded by beautiful gardens. As you might expect, a sight of this grandeur attracts a lot of crowds, so it's best to visit just after opening or shortly before closing.

Nishiki Market   Market

(錦市場; Map p116; Nishikikōji-dōri, btwn Teramachi & Takakura, Nakagyō-ku; ⊙9am-5pm; ⑤Karasuma line to Shijō, ⓇHankyū line to Karasuma or Kawaramachi) Head to the covered Nishiki Market to check out the weird and wonderful foods that go into Kyoto cuisine.

It's in the centre of town, one block north of (and parallel to) Shijō-dōri, running west off the Teramachi covered arcade. Wander past stalls selling everything from barrels of *tsukemono* (pickled vegetables) and cute Japanese sweets to wasabi salt and *yakitori* (chicken, and other meats or vegetables, grilled on skewers). Drop into Aritsugu (p127) here for some of the best Japanese chef's knives money can buy.

Kyoto Imperial Palace Park   Park

(京都御苑; Map p116; Kyoto Gyōen, Nakagyō-ku; ⊙dawn-dusk; ⑤Karasuma line to Marutamachi or Imadegawa) FREE The Kyoto Imperial Palace (p115) (Kyoto Gosho) and Sentō Gosho (p115) are surrounded by the spacious Kyoto Imperial Palace Park, which is planted with a huge variety of flowering trees and open fields. It's perfect for picnics, strolls and just about any sport you can think of. Take some time to visit the pond at the park's southern end, which contains gorgeous carp. The park is most beautiful in the plum- and cherry-blossom seasons (late February and late March, respectively).

Nijō-jō

PÅL TERAVAGIMOV / SHUTTERSTOCK ©

Kyoto
Imperial Palace   Historic Building
(京都御所 , Kyoto Gosho; Map p116; 🕽075-
211-1215; www.kunaicho.go.jp; Kyoto Gosho,
Nakagyō-ku; ⊗9am-5pm Apr-Aug, 9am-4.30pm
Sep & Mar, 9am-4pm Oct-Feb, last entry 40min
before closing, closed Mon; ⓢKarasuma line to
Marutamachi or Imadegawa) **FREE** The Kyoto
Imperial Palace, known as Gosho in Japanese, is a walled complex that sits in the
middle of the Kyoto Imperial Palace Park
(p114). Although no longer the official
residence of the Japanese emperor, it's
still a grand edifice, though it doesn't rate
highly in comparison with other attractions
in Kyoto. Visitors can wander around the
marked route in the grounds where English
signs explain the history of the buildings.
Entrance is via the main Seishomon Gate
where you'll be given a map.

Sentō Gosho Palace Historic Building
(仙洞御所; Map p116; 🕽075-211-1215; www.
kunaicho.go.jp; Kyoto Gyōen, Nakagyō-ku; ⊗tours
9.30am, 11am, 1.30pm & 3pm; ⓢKarasuma line
to Marutamachi or Imadegawa) **FREE** The Sentō
Gosho is the second imperial property
located within the Kyoto Imperial Palace Park
(the other one is the Imperial Palace itself).
The structures are not particularly grand, but
the gardens, laid out in 1630 by renowned
landscape designer Kobori Enshū, are
excellent. Admission is by one-hour tour only
(in Japanese; English audio guides are free of
charge). You must be over 18 years old and
you will need to bring your passport for ID.

Daitoku-ji   Buddhist Temple
(大徳寺; Map p103; 53 Daitokuji-chō, Murasakino, Kita-ku; admission varies; ⊗hours vary;
ⓢKarasuma line to Kitaōji) Daitoku-ji is a
separate world within Kyoto – a world
of Zen temples, perfectly raked gardens
and wandering lanes. It's one of the most
rewarding destinations in this part of the
city, particularly for those with an interest
in Japanese gardens. The eponymous
Daitoku-ji temple (usually not open to the
public) serves as the headquarters of the
Rinzai Daitoku-ji school of Zen Buddhism.
The highlights among the subtemples

🎟 Admission to Kyoto's Imperial Properties

As of mid-2016, visitors no longer have
to apply for permission to visit the **Kyoto
Imperial Palace**. The palace, situated
inside the Imperial Palace Park, is open
to the public from Tuesday to Sunday
and you just need to go straight to the
main gate for entry. Children are permit-
ted with an accompanying adult.

Permission to visit the **Sentō Gosho**,
Katsura Rikyū (p124) and **Shūgaku-in
Rikyū** (p123) is granted by the Kuna-
ichō, the **Imperial Household Agency**
(宮内庁京都事務所; 🕽075-211-1215; www.
kunaicho.go.jp; ⊗8.45am-5pm, closed Mon;
ⓢKarasuma line to Imadegawa), which is inside the **Imperial Palace Park** (p114).
For morning tours, fill out an application
form and show your passport, or you can
apply via its website. You must be over
18 to enter each property. For afternoon
tours, you can book tickets on the same
day at the properties themselves from
11am. Only a certain number of tickets
is issued each day, so it's first-come
first-served. Sentō Gosho and Shūgaku-in Rikyū tours last 60 minutes, while
the Katsura Rikyū runs for 80 minutes.
All tours are free and in Japanese, with
English audio guides available.

generally open to the public include **Dais-
en-in**, Kōtō-in (p117), **Ōbai-in**, **Ryō-
gen-in** and **Zuihō-in**.

Downtown Kyoto & Kyoto Station Area

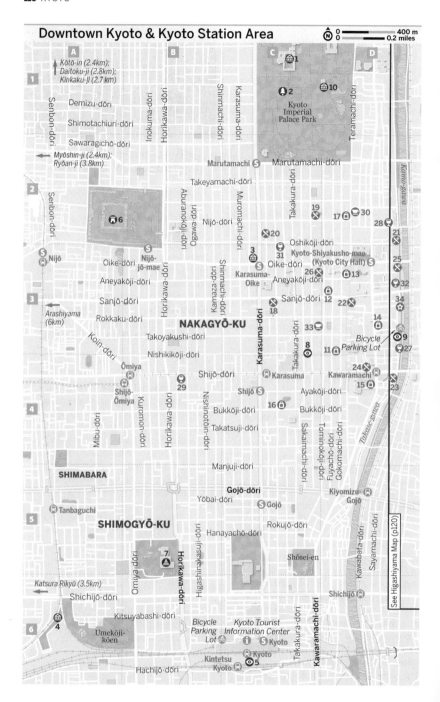

Ⓝ 0 ———— 400 m
0 ———— 0.2 miles

Kōtō-in (2.4km);
Daitoku-ji (2.8km);
Kinkaku-JI (2.7km)

Senbon-dōri

Demizu-dōri

Shimotachiuri-dōri

Sawaragichō-dōri

Myōshin-ji (2.4km);
Ryōan-ji (3.8km)

Inokuma-dōri

Horikawa-dōri

Shinmachi-dōri

Karasuma-dōri

Teramachi-dōri

🏛1

Ⓘ2   🏛10

Kyoto
Imperial
Palace Park

Marutamachi Ⓢ   Marutamachi-dōri

Takeyamachi-dōri

Aburanokōji-dōri

Ōmiya-dōri

Muromachi-dōri

Takakura-dōri

Kamo-gawa

19
✗   17 🔒 Ⓡ30
                    28 Ⓡ

Senbon-dōri

🏯6

✗20

21
✗

Nijō Ⓢ
Ⓡ Nijō

Oike-dōri

Nijō-
jō-mae Ⓢ

Aneyakōji-dōri

Horikawa-dōri

Karasuma-dōri

Shinmachi-dōri

3
🏛
Ⓢ

31
Ⓡ

Oshikōji-dōri

Oike-dōri

Kyoto-Shiyakusho-mae
(Kyoto City Hall) Ⓢ

25
✗

Karasuma-
Oike

26✗
Aneyakōji-dōri

🔒13

Ⓡ32

Sanjō-dōri

Rokkaku-dōri

Koin-dōri

Sanjō-dōri
18 ✗

🏛
12   22✗

34
✗

NAKAGYŌ-KU

Arashiyama
(6km)

Takoyakushi-dōri

33Ⓡ

14
🔒

⊙⊙9

Nishikikōji-dōri

8
⊙

11 🔒

Bicycle
Parking Lot

Ⓡ27

Ōmiya
Ⓡ

Karasuma-dōri

Shijō-dōri

✗Karasuma

24✗
Kawaramachi

Shijō-
Ōmiya

Mibu-dōri

Kuromon-dōri

Horikawa-dōri

Nishinotōin-dōri

Ⓡ
29

Shijō Ⓢ

16 🔒

Ayakōji-dōri

15 🔒

23

Bukkōji-dōri

Bukkōji-dōri

Takatsuji-dōri

Sakaimachi-dōri

Tominokōji-dōri

Fuyachō-dōri

Gokomachi-dōri

Takase-gawa

SHIMABARA

Manjuji-dōri

Gojō-dōri

Kiyomizu-
Gojō

Tanbaguchi

Yōbai-dōri

Ⓢ Gojō

SHIMOGYŌ-KU

Hanayachō-dōri

Rokujō-dōri

Shōsei-en

Kawabata-dōri

Sayamachi-dōri

See Higashiyama Map (p120)

Katsura Rikyū (3.5km)

Omiya-dōri

7
⛩

Horikawa-dōri

Higashinakasuji-dōri

Shichijō-dōri

Shichijō Ⓢ

Kitsuyabashi-dōri

🏛4

Umekōji-
kōen

Bicycle
Parking
Lot

Kyoto Tourist
Information Center
ⓘ Ⓢ Kyoto

Takakura-dōri

Kawaramachi-dōri

Hachijō-dōri

Kintetsu
Kyoto Ⓡ

Kyoto
⊙5

Downtown Kyoto & Kyoto Station Area

Kōtō-in · Buddhist Temple

(高桐院; Map p103; 73-1 Daitokuji-chō, Murasakino, Kita-ku; ¥400; ⊙9am-4.30pm; ⑤Karasuma line to Kitaōji) On the far western edge of the Daitoku-ji complex, the sublime garden of this subtemple is one of the best in all Kyoto and it's worth a special trip. It's located within a fine bamboo grove that you traverse via a moss-lined path. Once inside there is a small stroll garden that leads to the centrepiece: a rectangle of moss and maple trees, backed by bamboo. Take some time on the verandah to soak it all up.

Kyoto International Manga Museum · Museum

(京都国際マンガミュージアム; Map p116; www.kyotomm.jp; Karasuma-dōri, Oike-agaru, Nakagyō-ku; adult/child ¥800/100; ⊙10am-6pm, closed Wed; ⊡; ⑤Karasuma or Tōzai lines to Karasuma-Oike) Located in an old elementary school building, this museum is the perfect introduction to the art of manga (Japanese comics). It has 300,000 manga in its collection, 50,000 of which are on display in the Wall of Manga exhibit. While most of the manga and displays are in Japanese, the collection of translated works is growing. In addition to the galleries that show both the historical development of manga and original artwork done in manga style, there are beginners' workshops and portrait drawings on weekends.

> *... this museum is the perfect introduction to the art of manga*

◉ Southern Higashiyama

Kiyomizu-dera · Buddhist Temple

(清水寺; Map p120; ☎075-551-1234; www.kiyomizudera.or.jp; 1-294 Kiyomizu, Higashiyama-ku; ¥400; ⊙6am-6pm, closing times vary seasonally; ⊡Kyoto City bus 206 to Kiyōmizu-michi or Gojō-zaka, ⊡Keihan line to Kiyomizu-Gojō) A buzzing hive of activity perched on a hill overlooking the basin of Kyoto, Kiyomizudera is one of Kyoto's most popular and most enjoyable temples. It may not be a tranquil refuge, but it represents the favoured expression of faith in Japan. The excellent website is a great first port of call for information on the temple, plus a how-to guide to praying here. Note that the Main

Kyoto's Traditional Townhouses

One of the city's most notable architectural features are its *machiya*, long and narrow wooden row houses that functioned as both homes and workplaces. The shop area was located in the front of the house, while the rooms lined up behind it formed the family's private living quarters. Although well suited to Kyoto's humid, mildew-prone summers, a wooden *machiya* has a limited lifespan of about 50 years. In modern times, they've also been up against the increasing costs of traditional materials and workmanship and the siren call of low-maintenance concrete. Many owners have replaced their *machiya* with seven-storey apartment buildings; occupying the ground floor, they can live off the rent of their tenants. The result is that Kyoto's urban landscape – once a harmonious sea of clay-tiled two-storey wooden townhouses – is now a jumble of ferro-concrete offices and apartment buildings.

However, *machiya* are making a comeback. After their numbers drastically declined, the old townhouses began to acquire an almost exotic appeal. Astute developers began to convert them into restaurants, clothing boutiques and even hair salons. Today such shops are a major draw for the city's tourist trade, and not only foreign visitors – the Japanese themselves (especially Tokyoites) – love their old-fashioned charm.

Hall is undergoing renovations and may be covered, though is still accessible. This ancient temple was first built in 798, but the present buildings are reconstructions dating from 1633. The Hondō (Main Hall) has a huge verandah that is supported by pillars and juts out over the hillside. Just below this hall is the waterfall Otowa-no-taki, where visitors drink sacred waters believed to bestow health and longevity.

Shōren-in   Buddhist Temple
(青蓮院; Map p120; 69-1 Sanjōbō-chō, Awataguchi, Higashiyama-ku; ¥500; ⊙9am-5pm; ⑤Tōzai line to Higashiyama) This temple is hard to miss, with its giant camphor trees growing just outside the walls. Fortunately, most tourists march right on past, heading to the area's more famous temples. That is their loss, because this intimate sanctuary contains a superb landscape garden, which you can enjoy while drinking a cup of green tea (¥400, 9am to 4pm; ask at the reception).

Chion-in   Buddhist Temple
(知恩院; Map p120; www.chion-in.or.jp; 400 Rinka-chō, Higashiyama-ku; inner buildings & garden adult/child ¥500/250, grounds free; ⊙9am-4.30pm; ⑤Tōzai line to Higashiyama) A collection of soaring buildings and spacious courtyards, Chion-in serves as the headquarters of the Jōdo sect, the largest school of Buddhism in Japan. It's the most popular pilgrimage temple in Kyoto and it's always a hive of activity. For visitors with a taste for the grand, this temple is sure to satisfy.

Kōdai-ji   Buddhist Temple
(高台寺; Map p120; ☎075-561-9966; www.kodaiji.com; 526 Shimokawara-chō, Kōdai-ji, Higashiyama-ku; ¥600; ⊙9am-5.30pm; ☒Kyoto City bus 206 to Yasui, ⑤Tōzai line to Higashiyama) This exquisite temple was founded in 1605 by Kita-no-Mandokoro in memory of her late husband, Toyotomi Hideyoshi. The extensive grounds include gardens designed by the famed landscape architect Kobori Enshū, and teahouses designed by

the renowned master of the tea ceremony, Sen no Rikyū.

The temple holds three annual special night-time illuminations, when the gardens are lit by multicoloured spotlights. The illuminations are held from mid-March to early May, 1 to 18 August, and late October to early December.

Kyoto National Museum   Museum

(京都国立博物館; Map p120; www.kyohaku. go.jp; 527 Chaya-machi, Higashiyama-ku; ¥520; ◉9.30am-5pm, to 6pm during special exhibitions, to 8pm Fri, closed Mon; 🚌Kyoto City bus 206 or 208 to Sanjūsangen-dō-mae, 🚃Keihan line to Shichijō) The Kyoto National Museum is the city's premier art museum and plays host to the highest-level exhibitions in the city. It was founded in 1895 as an imperial repository for art and treasures from local temples and shrines. In the original **main hall** there are rooms with displays of over 1000 artworks, historical artefacts and handicrafts. The **Heisei Chishinkan**, designed by Taniguchi Yoshio and opened in 2014, is a brilliant modern counterpoint to the original building.

Ninen-zaka & Sannen-zaka Area   Area

(二年坂・三年坂; Map p120; Higashiyama-ku; 🚌Kyoto City bus 206 to Kiyomizu-michi or Gojō-zaka, 🚃Keihan line to Kiyomizu-Gojō) Just downhill from and slightly to the north of Kiyomizu-dera, you will find one of Kyoto's loveliest restored neighbourhoods, the Ninen-zaka–Sannen-zaka area. The name refers to the two main streets of the area: Ninen-zaka and Sannen-zaka, literally 'Two-Year Hill' and 'Three-Year Hill' (the years referring to the ancient imperial years when they were first laid out). These two charming streets are lined with old wooden houses, traditional shops and restaurants.

Kennin-ji   Buddhist Temple

(建仁寺; Map p120; www.kenninji.jp; 584 Komatsu-chō, Yamatoōji-dōri, Shijo-sagaru, Higashiyama-ku; ¥500; ◉10am-5pm Mar-Oct, to 4.30pm Nov-Feb; 🚃Keihan line to Gion-Shijō) Founded in 1202 by the monk Eisai, Kennin-ji is the oldest Zen temple in Kyoto. It is an island of peace and calm on the border of the boisterous Gion nightlife district and it makes a fine counterpoint to the worldly pleasures of that

Rodin's *The Thinker,* Kyoto National Museum

Higashiyama

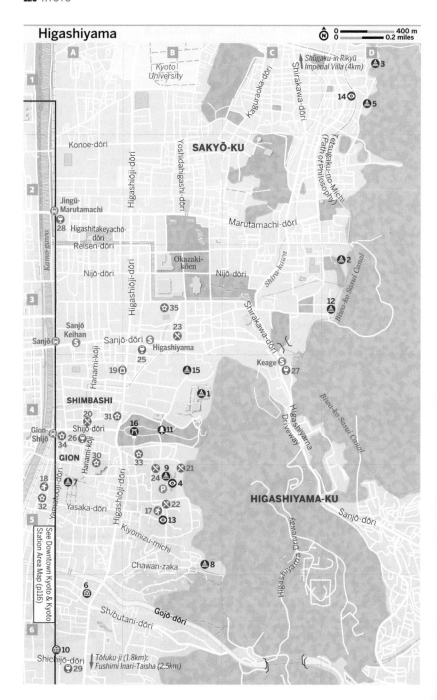

N 0 ——————— 400 m
   0 ——————— 0.2 miles

Shūgaku-in Rikyū
Imperial Villa (4km) ⚱3

14 ◉ ⚱5

Kaguraoka-dōri

Shirakawa-dōri

Konoe-dōri

SAKYŌ-KU

Yoshidanigashi-dōri

Tetsugaku-no-Michi
(Path of Philosophy)

Higashiōji-dōri

Jingū-
Marutamachi
28

Higashitakeyachō-
dōri
Reisen-dōri

Marutamachi-dōri

Nijō-dōri

Okazaki-
kōen

Nijō-dōri

Higashiōji-dōri

⚱2

Shira-kawa

Biwa-ko Sosui Canal

12 ⚱

Shirakawa-dōri

⭐35

23
❌

Sanjō
Keihan

Sanjō Ⓢ

Sanjō-dōri Ⓢ
Higashiyama

25

Keage Ⓢ
27

⚱15

Hanami-kōji

19 🏛

⚱1

SHIMBASHI

20

31 ⭐

Shijō-dōri

16
🏛

🌳11

Higashiyama
Driveway

Biwa-ko Sosui Canal

Gion-
Shijō

26 🌳

34

GION

30 ⭐

33 ⭐

9
❌

❌21

24 ⚱
◉4

HIGASHIYAMA-KU

Sanjō-dōri

18 🌳

🌳7

Yasaka-dōri

17
❌

❌22

◉13

Kiyomizu-michi

32

See Downtown Kyoto & Kyoto
Station Area Map (p116)

⚱8

Chawan-zaka

6
🏛

Higashiyama Driveway

Shibutani-dōri

Gojō-dōri

🏛10

Shichijō-dōri

29

↓ Tōfuku-ji (1.8km);
Fushimi Inari-Taisha (2.5km)

Higashiyama

area. The highlight at Kennin-ji is the fine and expansive *kare-sansui* (dry landscape). The painting of the twin dragons on the roof of the **Hōdō** hall is also fantastic.

Kawai Kanjirō Memorial Hall
Museum

(河井寛次郎記念館; Map p120; 075-561-3585; 569 Kanei-chō, Gojō-zaka, Higashiyama-ku; ¥900; ⊙10am-5pm Tue-Sun; ➡Kyoto City bus 206 or 207 to Umamachi) This small memorial hall is one of Kyoto's most commonly overlooked little gems. The hall was the home and workshop of one of Japan's most famous potters, Kawai Kanjirō (1890–1966). The 1937 house is built in rural style and contains examples of Kanjirō's work, his collection of folk art and ceramics, his workshop and a fascinating *nobori-gama* (stepped kiln). The museum is near the intersection of Gojō-dōri and Higashiōji-dōri.

Maruyama-kōen
Park

(円山公園; Map p120; Maruyama-chō, Higashiyama-ku; ⓢTōzai line to Higashiyama) Maruyama-kōen is a favourite of locals and visitors alike. This park is the place to escape the bustle of the city centre and amble around gardens, ponds, souvenir shops and restaurants. Peaceful paths meander through the trees, and carp glide through the waters of a small pond in the park's centre.

Yasaka-jinja
Shinto Shrine

(八坂神社; Map p120; ✆075-561-6155; www.yasaka-jinja.or.jp; 625 Gion-machi, Kita-gawa, Higashiyama-ku; ⊙24hr; ⓢTōzai line to Higashiyama) FREE This colourful and spacious shrine is considered the guardian shrine of the Gion entertainment district. It's a bustling place that is well worth a visit while exploring Southern Higashiyama; it can easily be paired with Maruyama-kōen, the park just up the hill.

◉ Northern Higashiyama

Ginkaku-ji
Buddhist Temple

(銀閣寺; Map p120; 2 Ginkaku-ji-chō, Sakyō-ku; adult/child ¥500/300; ⊙8.30am-5pm Mar-Nov, 9am-4.30pm Dec-Feb; ➡Kyoto City bus 5 to Ginkakuji-michi stop) Home to a sumptuous garden and elegant structures, Ginkaku-ji is one of Kyoto's premier sites. The temple started its life in 1482 as a retirement villa for Shogun Ashikaga Yoshimasa, who desired a place to retreat from the turmoil of a civil war. While the name Ginkaku-ji literally translates as 'Silver Pavilion', the shogun's ambition to cover the building with silver was never realised. After Yoshimasa's death, the villa was converted into a temple.

Walkways lead through the gardens, which include meticulously raked cones of white sand (said to be symbolic of a mountain and a lake), tall pines and a pond in front of the temple. A path also leads up the mountainside through the trees.

Note that Ginkaku-ji is one of the city's most popular sites, and it is almost always crowded, especially during spring and autumn. We strongly recommend visiting right after it opens or just before it closes.

Nanzen-ji — Buddhist Temple

(南禅寺; Map p120; www.nanzenji.com; 86 Fukuchi-chō, Nanzen-ji, Sakyō-ku; Nanzen-in ¥300, Hōjō garden ¥500, San-mon gate ¥500, grounds free; ⏰8.40am-5pm Mar-Nov, to 4.30pm Dec-Feb; 🚌Kyoto City bus 5 to Eikandō-michi, Ⓢ Tōzai line to Keage) This is one of the most rewarding

temples in Kyoto, with its expansive grounds and numerous subtemples. At its entrance stands the massive **San-mon**. Steps lead up to the 2nd storey, which has a great view over the city. Beyond the gate is the main hall of the temple, above which you will find the **Hōjō**, where the Leaping Tiger Garden, a classic Zen garden, is well worth a look.

Eikan-dō — Buddhist Temple

(永観堂; Map p120; 📞075-761-0007; www.eikando.or.jp; 48 Eikandō-chō, Sakyō-ku; adult/child ¥1000/400; ⏰9am-5pm; 🚌Kyoto City bus 5 to Eikandō-michi, Ⓢ Tōzai line to Keage) Perhaps Kyoto's most famous (and crowded) autumn destination, Eikan-dō is a superb temple just a short walk south of the famous Path of Philosophy. Eikan-dō is made interesting by its varied architecture, its gardens and its works of art. It was founded as Zenrin-ji in 855 by the priest Shinshō, but the name was changed to Eikan-dō in the 11th century to honour the philanthropic priest Eikan.

Path of Philosophy (Tetsugaku-no-Michi) — Area

(哲学の道; Map p120; Sakyō-ku; 🚌Kyoto City bus 5 to Eikandō-michi or Ginkakuji-michi, Ⓢ Tōzai

SEAN PAVONE / SHUTTERSTOCK ©

line to Keage) Tetsugaku-no-Michi is one of the most pleasant walks in all of Kyoto. Lined with a great variety of flowering plants, bushes and trees, it is a corridor of colour throughout most of the year. Follow the traffic-free route along a canal lined with cherry trees that come into spectacular bloom in early April. It only takes 30 minutes to do the walk, which starts at Nyakuōji-bashi, above Eikan-dō, and leads to Ginkaku-ji.

Hōnen-in   Buddhist Temple

(法然院; Map p120; 30 Goshonodan-chō, Shishigatani, Sakyō-ku; ☺6am-4pm; ☒Kyoto City bus 5 to Ginkakuji-michi) FREE One of Kyoto's hidden pleasures, this temple was founded in 1680 to honour the priest Hōnen. It's a lovely, secluded temple with carefully raked gardens set back in the woods. The temple buildings include a small gallery where frequent exhibitions featuring local and international artists are held. If you need to escape the crowds that positively plague nearby Ginkaku-ji, come to this serene refuge.

Shūgaku-in Rikyū
Imperial Villa   Notable Building

(修学院離宮; Map p103; ☎075-211-1215; www.kunaicho.go.jp; Shūgaku-in, Yabusoe, Sakyō-ku; ☺tours 9am, 10am, 11am, 1.30pm & 3pm Tue-Sun; ☒Kyoto City bus 5 from Kyoto Station to Shūgakuinrikyū-michi) FREE One of the highlights of northeast Kyoto, this superb imperial villa was designed as a lavish summer retreat for the imperial family. Its gardens, with their views down over the city, are worth the trouble it takes to visit. The 80-minute tours are held in Japanese, with English audio guides free of charge; try to arrive early. You must be over 18 years to enter and you will need to bring your passport for ID.

◎ Arashiyama

Arashiyama Bamboo Grove   Park

(嵐山竹林; Map p103; Ogurayama, Saga, Ukyō-ku; ☺dawn-dusk; ☒Kyoto City bus 28 from Kyoto Station to Arashiyama-Tenryuji-mae, ☒JR Sagano/San-in line to Saga-Arashiyama or Hankyū line to Arashiyama, change at Katsura) FREE Walking into this extensive bamboo grove is like entering another world – the thick green

ROLLING ROCK / SHUTTERSTOCK ©

Kyoto's Best Gardens

Ryōan-ji (p111)

Tōfuku-ji (p105)

Sentō Gosho Palace (p115)

Katsura Rikyū (p124)

Ōkōchi Sansō (p124)

From left: Ryōan-ji (p111); Tōfuku-ji (p105); gardens at Ōkōchi Sansō (p124)

ELEANOR SCRIVEN / GETTY IMAGES ©

 Hozu-gawa River Trip

The **Hozu-gawa river trip** (☎0771-22-5846; www.hozugawakudari.jp; Hozu-chō, Kameoka-shi; adult/child 4-12yr ¥4100/2700; 👶) is a great way to enjoy the beauty of Kyoto's western mountains without any strain on the legs. With long bamboo poles, boatmen steer flat-bottom boats down the Hozu-gawa from Kameoka, 30km west of Kyoto Station, through steep, forested mountain canyons, before arriving at Arashiyama.

Between 10 March and 30 November there are seven daily trips leaving on the hour from 9am to 3pm. During winter the number of trips is reduced to four per day (10am, 11.30am, 1pm and 2.30pm) and the boats are heated.

The ride lasts two hours and covers 16km through occasional sections of choppy water – a scenic jaunt with minimal danger. The scenery is especially breathtaking during cherry-blossom season in April and maple-foliage season in autumn.

The boats depart from a dock that is eight minutes' walk from Kameoka Station. Kameoka is accessible by rail from Kyoto Station or Nijō Station on the JR Sagano-San-in line. The Kyoto Tourist Information Center provides an English-language leaflet and timetable for rail connections. The fare from Kyoto to Kameoka is ¥400 one way by regular train (don't spend the extra for the express; it makes little difference in travel time).

bamboo stalks seem to continue endlessly in every direction and there's a strange quality to the light. You'll be unable to resist trying to take a few photos, but you might be disappointed with the results: photos just can't capture the magic of this place. The grove runs from outside the north gate of Tenryū-ji to just below Ōkōchi Sansō villa.

Tenryū-ji — Buddhist Temple

(天龍寺; Map p103; ☎075-881-1235; www.tenryuji.com; 68 Susukinobaba-chō, Saga-Tenryū-ji, Ukyō-ku; garden only ¥500, temple buildings & garden ¥800; ⊙8.30am-5.30pm, to 5pm mid-Oct–mid-Mar; 🚌Kyoto City bus 28 from Kyoto Station to Arashiyama-Tenryuji-mae, 🚉JR Sagano/San-in line to Saga-Arashiyama or Hankyū line to Arashiyama, change at Katsura) A major temple of the Rinzai school, Tenryū-ji has one of the most attractive gardens in Kyoto, particularly during the spring cherry-blossom and autumn-foliage seasons. The main 14th-century Zen garden, with its Arashiyama mountain backdrop, is a good example of *shakkei* (borrowed scenery). Unfortunately, it's no secret that the garden here is world class, so it pays to visit early in the morning or on a weekday.

Ōkōchi Sansō — Historic Building

(大河内山荘; Map p103; 8 Tabuchiyama-chō, Sagaogurayama, Ukyō-ku; ¥1000; ⊙9am-5pm; 🚌Kyoto City bus 28 from Kyoto Station to Arashiyama-Tenryuji-mae, 🚉JR Sagano/San-in line to Saga-Arashiyama or Hankyū line to Arashiyama, change at Katsura) This is the lavish estate of Ōkōchi Denjirō, an actor famous for his samurai films. The sprawling gardens may well be the most lovely in all of Kyoto, particularly when you consider the brilliant views eastwards across the city. The house and teahouse are also sublime. Be sure to follow all the trails around the gardens. Hold onto the tea ticket you were given upon entry to claim the *matcha* and sweet that comes with admission.

Katsura Rikyū — Historic Building

(桂離宮; Map p103; ☎075-211-1215; www.kunaicho.go.jp; Katsura Detached Palace, Katsura Misono, Nishikyō-ku; ⊙tours 9am, 10am, 11am, 1.30pm, 2.30pm & 3.30pm; 🚌Kyoto City bus 33

Nishi Hongan-ji

to Katsura Rikyū-mae, 🚃Hankyū line to Katsura)
FREE Katsura Rikyū, one of Kyoto's imperial
properties, is widely considered to be the
pinnacle of Japanese traditional architecture
and garden design. Set amid an otherwise
drab neighbourhood, it is (very literally) an
island of incredible beauty. One-hour tours
are in Japanese, with English audio guides
free of charge. You must be over 18 years and
you will need to bring your passport for ID.

⊙ Kyoto Station Area

Kyoto Station   Notable Building
(京都駅; Map p116; www.kyoto-station-building.
co.jp; Karasuma-dōri, Higashishiokōji-chō,
Shiokōji-sagaru, Shimogyō-ku; 🚃Kyoto Station)
The Kyoto Station building is a striking steel-
and-glass structure – a kind of futuristic
cathedral for the transport age – with a
tremendous space that arches above you
as you enter the main concourse. Be sure to
take the escalator from the 7th floor on the
east side of the building up to the 11th-floor
glass corridor, Skyway (open 10am to 10pm),
that runs high above the main concourse of

the station, and catch some views from the
15th-floor Sky Garden terrace.

Nishi Hongan-ji   Buddhist Temple
(西本願寺; Map p116; Horikawa-dōri, Hanaya-
chō-sagaru, Shimogyō-ku; ⊙5.30am-5pm
Nov-Feb, to 5.30pm Mar, Apr, Sep & Oct, to 6pm
May-Aug; 🚃Kyoto Station) **FREE** A vast temple
complex located about 15 minutes' walk
northwest of Kyoto Station, Nishi Hongan-ji comprises five buildings that feature
some of the finest examples of architecture and artistic achievement from the
Azuchi-Momoyama period (1568–1603).
The **Goei-dō** (Main Hall) is a marvellous
sight. Another must-see is the **Daisho-in**
hall, which has sumptuous paintings, carvings and metal ornamentation. A small
garden and two stages for *nō* (stylised
Japanese dance-drama) are connected
with the hall. The dazzling **Kara-mon** has
intricate ornamental carvings.

Kyoto Railway Museum   Museum
(梅小路蒸気機関車館; Map p116; www.kyoto
railwaymuseum.jp; Kankiji-chō, Shimogyō-ku;
adult/child ¥1200/200, train ride ¥300/100;

Funaoka Onsen

⏱10am-5.30pm, closed Wed; 👪; 🚌Kyoto City bus 103, 104 or 105 from Kyoto Station to Umekō-ji Kōen-mae) The Umekoji Steam Locomotive Museum underwent a massive expansion in 2016 to reopen as the Kyoto Railway Museum. This superb museum is spread over three floors showcasing 53 trains, from vintage steam locomotives in the outside Roundhouse Shed to commuter trains and the first *shinkansen* (bullet train) from 1964. Kids will love the interactive displays and impressive railroad diorama with miniature trains zipping through the intricate landscape. You can also take a 10-minute ride on one of the smoke-spewing choo-choos.

🌀 ACTIVITIES

Uzuki   Cooking
(www.kyotouzuki.com; 2hr class per person ¥4500) If you want to learn how to cook some of the delightful foods you've tried in Kyoto, we highly recommend Uzuki, a small cooking class conducted in a Japanese home for groups of two to four people. You will learn

how to cook a variety of dishes and then sit down and enjoy the fruits of your labour.

Funaoka Onsen   Onsen
(船岡温泉; Map p103; https://funaokaonsen. info; 82-1 Minami-Funaoka-chō-Murasakino, Kita-ku; ¥430; ⏱3pm-1am Mon-Sat, 8am-1am Sun & holidays; 🚌Kyoto City Bus 9 from Kyoto Station to Horikawa-Kuramaguchi) This old onsen on Kuramaguchi-dōri is Kyoto's best. It boasts an outdoor bath, a sauna, a cypress-wood tub, an electric bath, a herbal bath and a few more for good measure. To get here, head west about 400m on Kuramaguchi-dōri from the Kuramaguchi and Horiikawa intersection. It's on the left, not far past Lawson convenience store. Look for the large rocks.

Shunkō-in   Meditation
(春光院; Map p103; ☏075-462-5488; www. shunkoin.com; meditation class ¥1500, class & guided tour ¥2500) A subtemple of Myōshin-ji (p111), Shunkō-in is run by a monk who has studied abroad and made it his mission to introduce foreigners to his temple and Zen Buddhism. Regular introductory meditation classes are held in English and there

is the option of a guided tour of the temple; check website for class schedule.

Arashiyama Station Foot Onsen
Onsen

(Keifuku Arashiyama Randen Station; ¥200; ☺9am-8pm, to 6pm in winter; ⓡKeifuku Arashiyama, Randen, line to Keifuku Arashiyama) Give your feet a soak after all the temple-hopping at this foot onsen located at the end of the Keifuku Arashiyama Randen Station platform. Price includes a souvenir towel.

SHOPPING

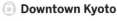 Downtown Kyoto

Aritsugu
Homewares

(有次; Map p116; ☎075-221-1091; 219 Kajiya-chō, Nishikikōji-dōri, Gokomachi nishi-iru, Nakagyō-ku; ☺9am-5.30pm; ⓡHankyū line to Kawaramachi) While you're in Nishiki Market, have a look at this store – it has some of the best kitchen knives in the world. Choose your knife – all-rounder, sushi, vegetable – and the staff will show you how to care for it before sharpening and boxing it up. You can also have your name engraved in English or Japanese. Knives start at around ¥10,000.

Ippōdō Tea
Tea

(一保堂茶舗; Map p116; ☎075-211-3421; www.ippodo-tea.co.jp; Teramachi-dōri, Nijō-agaru, Nakagyō-ku; ☺9am-6pm; ⓢTōzai line to Kyoto-Shiyakusho-mae) This old-style tea shop sells some of the best Japanese tea in Kyoto, and you'll be given an English leaflet with prices and descriptions of each one. Its *matcha* makes an excellent and lightweight souvenir; 40g containers start at ¥500. Ippōdō is north of the city hall, on Teramachi-dōri. It has an adjoining teahouse, Kaboku Tearoom (p134); last order 5.30pm.

Zōhiko
Arts & Crafts

(象彦; Map p116; ☎075-229-6625; www.zohiko.co.jp; 719-1 Yohojimae-chō, Teramachi-dōri, Nijō-agaru, Nakagyō-ku; ☺10am-6pm; ⓢTōzai line to Kyoto-Shiyakusho-mae) Zōhiko is the best place in Kyoto to buy one of Japan's most beguiling art and craft forms: lacquerware. If you aren't familiar with just how beautiful

🍴 Kaiseki

Kyoto is famed for *kaiseki ryōri*, Japan's haute cuisine. Dinner at one of the city's top restaurants, such as **Kikunoi** (p130) or **Kitcho Arashiyama** (p132) definitely qualifies for meal-of-a-lifetime status. But you don't have to spend a week's travel budget on dinner to get a taste of *kaiseki*.

Kiyamachi Sakuragawa (木屋町 櫻川; Map p116; ☎075-255-4477; Kiyamachi-dōri, Nijō-saguru, Nakagyō-ku; lunch/dinner sets from ¥5000/10,000; ☺11.30am-2pm & 5-9pm, closed Sun; ⓢTōzai line to Kyoto-Shiyakusho-mae) This elegant restaurant, on a scenic stretch of Kiyamachi-dōri, serves modest but fully satisfying food, beautifully presented. It's a joy to watch the chef in action and the warmth of the reception adds to the quality of the food. Reservations are recommended and smart casual is the way to go here.

Tagoto Honten (田ごと本店; Map p116; ☎075-221-1811; www.kyoto-tagoto.co.jp; 34 Otabi-chō, Shijō-dōri, Kawaramachi nishi-iru, Nakagyō-ku; lunch/dinner from ¥1850/4000; ☺11am-8.30pm; ⓡKeihan line to Shijō or Hankyū line to Kawaramachi) This long-standing Kyoto restaurant serves approachable *kaiseki* fare in a variety of rooms, both private and common. The *kiku* set (¥1850) includes some sashimi, tempura and a variety of other nibblies. *Kaiseki* dinner courses start at ¥6500 and you must make reservations in advance. Otherwise, try the cheaper mini *kaiseki* dinner as a sampler (¥4000).

Kaiseki dishes on display

these products can be, you owe it to yourself to make the pilgrimage to Zōhiko. You'll find a great selection of cups, bowls, trays and various kinds of boxes.

Takashimaya   Department Store

(高島屋; Map p116; ☑075-221-8811; Shijō-Kawaramachi Kado, Shimogyō-ku; ☺10am-8pm, restaurants to 9.30pm; ⓇHankyū line to Kawaramachi) The *grande dame* of Kyoto department stores, Takashimaya is almost a tourist attraction in its own right, from the mind-boggling riches of the basement food floor to the wonderful selection of lacquerware and ceramics on the 6th floor. And don't miss the kimono display.

Maruzen   Books

(丸善; Map p116; basement, BAL, 251 Yamazaki-chō, Kawaramachi-sanjo sagaru, Nakagyō-ku; ☺11am-9pm; ⓇHankyū line to Kawaramachi) Kyoto's most beloved bookshop closed in 2005 and finally reopened after 10 years in 2015. Occupying two basement floors of the BAL department store, this excellent bookshop has a massive range of English-language books across all subjects on basement level 2, plenty of titles on Kyoto and Japan, a great selection of Japanese literature, magazines from around the globe and travel guides.

Wagami no Mise   Arts & Crafts

(倭紙の店; Map p116; ☑075-341-1419; 1st fl, Kajinoha Bldg, 298 Ōgisakaya-chō, Higashinotōin-dōri, Bukkōji-agaru, Shimogyō-ku; ☺9.30am-5.30pm Mon-Fri, to 4.30pm Sat; ⓈKarasuma line to Shijō) This place sells a fabulous variety of *washi* for reasonable prices and is a great spot to pick up a gift or souvenir. Look for the Morita Japanese Paper Company sign on the wall out the front.

Kyoto Design House   Arts & Crafts

(Map p116; ☑075-221-0200; www.kyoto-dh.com; 1F Nikawa Bldg, Tominokōji-dōri, 105 Fukanaga-chō, Nakagyō-ku; ☺11am-8pm; ⓈKarasuma or Tōzai lines to Karasuma-Oike) The Tadao Ando–designed Nikawa building is the perfect home for this design store, which stocks arts and crafts mainly designed by local Kyoto artists melding traditional with modern

design. From handmade ceramics and *ohako* candy boxes to beautiful cushions using silk from the Nishijin textile district, this is another great place to pick up gifts and souvenirs.

Kyūkyo-dō   Arts & Crafts

(鳩居堂; Map p116; ☑075-231-0510; 520 Shimo-honnōjimae-chō, Teramachi-dōri, Aneyakōji-agaru, Nakagyō-ku; ☺10am-6pm Mon-Sat, closed Sun; ⓈTōzai line to Kyoto-Shiyakusho-mae) This old shop in the Teramachi covered arcade sells a selection of incense, *shodō* (calligraphy) goods, tea-ceremony supplies and *washi*. Prices are on the high side but the quality is good.

ⓐ Southern Higashiyama

Ichizawa Shinzaburo Hanpu   Fashion & Accessories

(一澤信三郎帆布; Map p120; ☑075-541-0436; www.ichizawa.co.jp; 602 Takabatake-chō, Higashiyama-ku; ☺9am-6pm; ⓈTōzai line to Higashiyama) This company has been making its canvas bags for over 110 years and the store is often crammed with those in the know picking up a skilfully crafted Kyoto product. They were originally designed as 'tool' bags for workers to carry sake bottles, milk and ice blocks, and current designs still reflect this idea. Choose from a range of styles and colours.

⊗ EATING

Downtown Kyoto

Roan Kikunoi   Kaiseki ¥¥¥

(露庵菊乃井; Map p116; ☑075-361-5580; www.kikunoi.jp; 118 Saito-chō, Kiyamachi-dōri, Shijō-sagaru, Shimogyō-ku; lunch/dinner from ¥4000/13,000; ☺11.30am-1.30pm & 5-8.30pm; ⓇHankyū line to Kawaramachi or Keihan line to Gion-Shijō) Roan Kikunoi is a fantastic place to experience the wonders of *kaiseki* (Japanese haute cuisine). It's a clean, intimate space located downtown. The chef takes an experimental and creative approach to *kaiseki* and the results are a wonder for the eyes and the palate. Highly recommended. Reserve through your hotel or ryokan.

Honke Owariya   Soba ¥

(本家尾張屋; Map p116; ☏075-231-3446; www.honke-owariya.co.jp; 322 Kurumaya-chō, Nijō, Nakagyō-ku; soba from ¥760; ⏱11am-7pm; ⓢKarasuma or Tōzai lines to Karasuma-Oike) Set in an old sweets shop in a traditional Japanese building on a quiet downtown street, this is where locals come for excellent soba (buckwheat noodle) dishes. The highly recommended house speciality, *hourai soba* (¥2160), comes with a stack of five small plates of soba with a selection of toppings, including shiitake mushrooms, shrimp tempura, thin slices of omelette and sesame seeds.

Yoshikawa   Tempura ¥¥¥

(吉川; Map p116; ☏075-221-5544; www.kyoto-yoshikawa.co.jp; 135 Matsushita-chō, Tominokōji, Oike-sagaru, Nakagyō-ku; lunch ¥3000-25,000; dinner ¥8000-25,000; ⏱11am-2pm & 5-8.30pm; ⓢTōzai line to Karasuma-Oike or Kyoto-Shiyakusho-mae) This is the place to go for delectable tempura. Attached to the Yoshikawa ryokan, it offers table seating, but it's much more interesting to sit and eat around the small counter and observe the chefs at work. It's near Oike-dōri in a fine traditional Japanese-style building. Reservation is required for tatami room; counter and table seating is unavailable on Sunday.

Café Bibliotec Hello!   Cafe ¥

(カフェビブリオティックハロー！; Map p116; ☏075-231-8625; 650 Seimei-chō, Nijō-dōri, Yanaginobanba higashi-iru, Nakagyō-ku; meals from ¥1000, coffee ¥450; ⏱11.30am-midnight; ❄⏣; ⓢTōzai line to Kyoto-Shiyakusho-mae) As the name suggests, books line the walls of this cool cafe located in a converted *machiya* (traditional Japanese townhouse) attracting a mix of locals and tourists. It's a great place to relax with a book or to tap away at your laptop over a coffee or light lunch. Look for the huge banana plants out the front.

Mishima-tei   Japanese ¥¥¥

(三嶋亭; Map p116; ☏075-221-0003; 405 Sakurano-chō, Teramachi-dōri, Sanjō-sagaru, Nakagyō-ku; sukiyaki lunch/dinner from ¥7128/13,662; ⏱11.30am-9pm; ⓢTōzai line to Kyoto-Shiyakusho-mae) Mishima-tei is a good place to sample sukiyaki (thin slices of beef cooked in sake, soy and vinegar broth, and

Tempura soba set

The Way of Tea

In the 16th century, a distinct culture emerged that elevated the preparation, serving and consumption of *matcha* (powdered green tea) to an elaborate ritual – and *sadō* (the way of tea) was born. Above all, *sadō* is a celebration of the aesthetic principle of *wabi-sabi*, reached when naturalness, spontaneity and humility come together. Many Japanese art forms, including pottery, ikebana (the art of flower arranging), calligraphy and garden design, developed in tandem with the tea ceremony. Tea ceremonies could be short and spontaneous or long and extremely formal. They might be held to mark an anniversary, the changing of the seasons or just as an opportunity to see old friends.

Camellia Tea Experience (茶道体験カメリア; Map p120; ☑075-525-3238; www.tea-kyoto.com; 349 Masuya-chō, Higashiyama-ku; per person ¥2000; 🚌Kyoto City bus 206 to Yasui) is a superb place to try a simple Japanese tea ceremony. It's located in a beautiful old Japanese house just off Ninen-zaka. The host speaks fluent English and explains the ceremony simply and clearly, while managing to perform an elegant ceremony. The price includes a bowl of *matcha* and a sweet. The 45-minute ceremonies are held on the hour from 10am to 5pm.

Whisking *matcha*
NISHIHAMA / SHUTTERSTOCK ©

dipped in raw egg) as the quality of the meat is very high, which is hardly surprising when there is a butcher right downstairs. It's at the intersection of the Sanjō and Teramachi covered arcades. Note that you'll need your hotel to make a booking for you as it doesn't accept reservations without a Japanese telephone number.

Tōsuirō Tofu ¥¥
(豆水楼; Map p116; ☑075-251-1600; www.tousuiro.com; Kiyamachi-dōri, Sanjō-agaru, Nakagyō-ku; lunch/dinner from ¥2494/3969; 🕙11.30am-2pm & 5-9.30pm Mon-Sat, noon-3pm & 5-8.30pm Sun; Ⓢ Tōzai line to Kyoto-Shiyakusho-mae) You will be amazed by the incredible variety of dishes that can be created with tofu at this specialist tofu restaurant. It has great traditional Japanese decor and in summer you can sit on the *yuka* (dining platform) outside and take in a view of the river. You'll find it at the end of an alley on the north side off Kiyamachi-dōri.

Biotei Vegetarian ¥
(びお亭; Map p116; ☑075-255-0086; 2nd fl, M&I Bldg, 28 Umetada-chō, Sanjō-dōri, Higashi-notōin nishi-iru, Nakagyō-ku; lunch/dinner sets from ¥840/1300; 🕙lunch 11.30am-2pm Sun-Fri, dinner 5-8.30pm Tue, Thu, Fri & Sat; 🥢; Ⓢ Tōzai or Karasuma lines to Karasuma-Oike) Located diagonally across from Nakagyō post office, this is a favourite of Kyoto vegetarians, serving daily sets of Japanese food with dishes such as deep-fried crumbed tofu and black seaweed salad with rice, miso and pickles. The seating is rather cramped but the food is excellent, beautifully presented and carefully made from quality ingredients.

✗ Southern Higashiyama

Kikunoi Kaiseki ¥¥¥
(菊乃井; Map p120; ☑075-561-0015; www.kikunoi.jp; 459 Shimokawara-chō, Yasaka-toriimae-sagaru, Shimokawara-dōri, Higashi-yama-ku; lunch/dinner from ¥8000/15,000; 🕙noon-1pm & 5-8pm; 🚌Keihan line to Gion-Shijō) This is one of Kyoto's true culinary temples, serving some of the finest *kaiseki* in the city by famous Michelin-starred chef Mutara. Located in a hidden nook

Ippōdō Tea (p127)

near Maruyama-kōen, this restaurant has everything necessary for the full over-the-top *kaiseki* experience, from setting to service to exquisitely executed cuisine, often with a creative twist. Reserve through your hotel or ryokan concierge.

Omen Kodai-ji · Noodles ¥

(おめん 高台寺店; Map p120; 075-541-5007; 358 Masuya-chō, Kōdaiji-dōri, Shimokawara higashi-iru, Higashiyama-ku; noodles from ¥1150, set menu ¥1850; 11am-9pm; Kyoto City bus 206 to Higashiyama-Yasui) Housed in a remodelled Japanese building with a light, airy feeling, this branch of Kyoto's famed Omen noodle chain is the best place to stop while exploring the Southern Higashiyama district. The signature udon (thick, white wheat noodles) served in broth with a selection of fresh vegetables is delicious, and there are many other à la carte offerings.

Kagizen Yoshifusa · Teahouse ¥

(鍵善良房; Map p120; 075-561-1818; www. kagizen.co.jp; 264 Gion machi, Kita-gawa, Higashiyama-ku; kuzukiri ¥900; 9.30am-6pm, closed Mon; Hankyū line to Kawaramachi, Keihan line to Gion-Shijō) This Gion institution is one of Kyoto's oldest and best-known *okashi-ya* (sweet shops). It sells a variety of traditional sweets and has a lovely tearoom out the back where you can sample cold *kuzukiri* (transparent arrowroot noodles) served with a *kuro-mitsu* (sweet black sugar) dipping sauce, or just a nice cup of *matcha* and a sweet.

Rakushō · Cafe ¥

(洛匠; Map p120; 075-561-6892; 516 Washio-chō, Kodaijikitamon-dōri, Shimogawara higashi-iru, Higashiyama-ku; tea from ¥600; 9.30am-6pm, closed irregularly; Kyoto City bus 204 to Higashiyama-Yasui) This casual Japanese-style tearoom on Nene-no-Michi in the Southern Higashiyama sightseeing district is well placed for a break while doing the area's main tourist route. The real attraction is the small koi (Japanese carp) pond adjoining the tearoom. The owner is a champion koi breeder and his fish are superb!

Oshokujidokoro Asuka · Shokudo ¥

(お食事処明日香; Map p120; 075-751-1941; 144 Nishi-machi, Sanjō-dōri, Jingū-michi nishi-iru, Higashiyama-ku; meals from ¥800; 11am-11pm,

Kyoto's Top Temples

Nanzen-ji (p122)

Ginkaku-ji (p121)

Kinkaku-ji (p110)

Kiyomizu-dera (p117)

Shōren-in (p118)

From left: Dharma hall at Nanzen-ji (p122); Ginkaku-ji (p121); Kiyomizu-dera (p117)

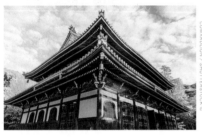

closed Mon; 🚇Tōzai line to Higashiyama) With an English menu and convivial atmosphere, this is a great place for a cheap lunch or dinner while sightseeing in the Higashiyama area. The assorted tempura set is excellent value at ¥1000. Look for the red lantern and pictures of the set meals.

✖ Arashiyama

Shigetsu Vegetarian, Japanese ¥¥

(篩月; ☑075-882-9725; 68 Susukinobaba-chō, Saga-Tenryū-ji, Ukyō-ku; lunch sets incl temple admission ¥3500, ¥5500 & ¥7500; ☺11am-2pm; 🅿; 🚌Kyoto City bus 28 from Kyoto Station to Arashiyama-Tenryuji-mae, 🚇JR Sagano/San-in line to Saga-Arashiyama or Hankyū line to Arashiyama, change at Katsura) To sample *shōjin-ryōri* (Buddhist vegetarian cuisine), try Shigetsu in the precincts of Tenryū-ji. This healthy fare has been sustaining monks for more than a thousand years in Japan, so it will probably get you through an afternoon of sightseeing, although carnivores may be left craving. Shigetsu has beautiful garden views.

Kitcho Arashiyama Kaiseki ¥¥¥

(吉兆嵐山本店; ☑075-881-1101; www.kitcho. com/kyoto/shoplist_en/arashiyama; 58 Susuki-

nobaba-chō, Saga-Tenryūji, Ukyō-ku; lunch/ dinner from ¥43,200/48,600; ☺11.30am-3pm & 5-9pm, closed Wed; 🚇JR Sagano/San-in line to Saga-Arashiyama) Considered one of the best *kaiseki* restaurants in Kyoto (and Japan, for that matter), Kitcho Arashiyama is the place to sample the full *kaiseki* experience. Meals are served in private rooms overlooking gardens. The food, service, explanations and atmosphere are all first rate. We suggest having a Japanese person call to reserve, or make a booking online via its website.

Arashiyama Yoshimura Noodles ¥

(嵐山よしむら; ☑075-863-5700; Togetsu-kyo kita, Saga-Tenryū-ji, Ukyō-ku; soba from ¥1080, meals from ¥1600; ☺11am-5pm; 🚌Kyoto City bus 28 from Kyoto Station to Arashiyama-Tenryuji-mae, 🚇JR Sagano/San-in line to Saga-Arashiyama or Hankyū line to Arashiyama, change at Katsura) For a tasty bowl of soba noodles and a million-dollar view over the Arashiyama mountains and the Togetsu-kyō bridge, head to this extremely popular eatery just north of the famous bridge, overlooking the Katsura-gawa. There's an English menu

EVERYTHING / SHUTTERSTOCK ©

but no English sign; look for the big glass windows and the stone wall.

🍷 DRINKING & NIGHTLIFE

For a night out, your best bet is to head to Kiyamachi-dōri and the surrounding streets where you'll find bars and clubs around the Shijō-dōri end, and a great selection of restaurants and nightlife around the Sanjo-dōri end.

🔵 Downtown Kyoto

Bungalow   Craft Beer

(バンガロー; Map p116; ☑075-256-8205; www. bungalow.jp; Shijō-dōri, Shimoji-ku, Nakagyō-ku; ◷3pm-2am Tue-Sat, noon-11pm Sun; ℝŌmiya) Spread over two floors, Bungalow serves a great range of Japanese craft beer in a cool industrial space. The menu changes regularly but generally you'll find 10 beers on tap from all over Japan, from a Baird Brewery Scotch ale to a peach Weizen from Minoh. It also does excellent food, most of which is organic.

Weekenders Coffee
Tominoko-ji   Coffee

(ウィークエンダーズ コーヒー; Map p116; ☑075-746-2206; www.weekenderscoffee.com; 560 Honeyana-chō, Nakagyo-ku; ◷7.30am-6pm, closed Wed; ℝHankyū line to Kawaramachi) Weekenders is a standing-room-only coffee bar tucked away at the back of a parking lot in Downtown Kyoto. Sure, it's a strange location but it's where you'll find some of the city's best coffee being brewed by roaster-owner, Masahiro Kaneko.

Sama Sama   Bar

(サマサマ; Map p116; ☑075-241-4100; 532-16 Kamiōsaka-chō, Kiyamachi, Sanjō-agaru, Nakagyō-ku; ◷6pm-2am, closed Mon; ⑤Tōzai line to Kyoto-Shiyakusho-mae) Sama Sama is an Indonesian-owned bar that feels like a very comfortable cave somewhere near the Mediterranean. Scoot up to the counter or make yourself at home on the floor cushions and enjoy a wide variety of drinks paired with food, including Indonesian classics like nasi goreng (¥800). It's down an alley just north of Sanjō; look for the signboard.

Sake Bar Yoramu   Bar

(酒バー よらむ; Map p116; ☑075-213-1512;
www.sakebar-yoramu.com; 35-1 Matsuya-chō,
Nijō-dōri, Higashinotoin, higashi-iru, Nakagyō-ku;
🕑6pm-midnight Wed-Sat; ⑤Karasuma or Tōzai
lines to Karasuma-Oike) Named for Yoramu,
the Israeli sake expert who runs Sake Bar
Yoramu, this bar is highly recommended for
anyone looking for an education in sake. It's
very small and can only accommodate a
handful of people. Sake tasting sets start at
around ¥1600 for a set of three. By day, it's
a soba restaurant called Toru Soba.

Atlantis   Bar

(アトランティス; Map p116; ☑075-241-1621;
161 Matsumoto-chō, Ponto-chō-Shijō-agaru,
Nakagyō-ku; 🕑6pm-2am, to 1am Sun; ☒Hankyū
line to Kawaramachi) This is one of the few bars
on Ponto-chō that foreigners can walk into
without a Japanese friend. It's a slick, trendy
place that draws a fair smattering of Kyoto's
beautiful people, and wannabe beautiful
people. In summer you can sit outside on a
platform looking over the Kamo-gawa.

Kaboku Tearoom   Teahouse

(喫茶室嘉木; Map p116; Teramachi-dōri,
Nijō-agaru, Nakagyō-ku; 🕑10am-6pm; ⑤Tōzai
line to Kyoto-Shiyakusho-mae) A casual
lovely tearoom attached to the Ippōdō
Tea (p127) store, Kaboku serves a range
of tea including *sencha, genmaicha* and
matcha, and provides a great break while
exploring the shops around the Teramachi
covered arcade. Try the thicker *koicha*-style
matcha and grab a counter seat to watch it
being prepared.

Bar K6   Bar

(バーK6; Map p116; ☑075-255-5009; 2nd fl,
Le Valls Bldg, Nijō-dōri, Kiyamachi higashi-iru,
Nakagyō-ku; 🕑6pm-3am, until 5am Fri & Sat;
⑤Tōzai line to Kyoto-Shiyakusho-mae, ☒Keihan
line to Jingu-Marutamachi) Overlooking one of
the prettiest stretches of Kiyamachi-dōri,
this upscale modern Japanese bar has a
great selection of single malts and some
of the best cocktails in town. There's even
a local craft brew on offer. It's popular with

well-heeled locals and travellers staying at
some of the top-flight hotels nearby.

🍴 Southern Higashiyama

Beer Komachi   Craft Beer

(ビア小町; Map p120; ☑075-746-6152; www.
beerkomachi.com; 444 Hachiken-chō, Higashiyama-ku; 🕑5-11pm Mon & Wed-Fri, 3-11pm Sat &
Sun, closed Tue; 🛜; ⑤Tōzai line to Higashiyama)
Located in the Furokawa-chō covered shopping arcade close to Higashiyama Station,
this tiny casual bar is dedicated to promot-
ing Japanese craft beer. There are usually
seven Japanese beers on tap, which rotate
on an almost daily basis. The excellent
bar-food menu tempts with delights, such
as fried chicken in beer batter and even a
stout chocolate gateau for dessert.

Tōzan Bar   Bar

(Map p120; ☑075-541-3201; www.kyoto.
regency.hyatt.com; Hyatt Regency Kyoto,
644-2 Sanjūsangendō-mawari, Higashiyama-ku;
🕑5pm-midnight; ☒Keihan line to Shichijō)
Even if you're not spending the night at the
Hyatt Regency, drop by the cool and cosy
underground bar for a tipple. Kitted out by
renowned design firm Super Potato, the
dimly lit atmospheric space features interesting touches, such as old locks, wooden
beams, an antique-book library space and a
wall feature made from traditional wooden
sweet moulds.

Gion Finlandia Bar   Bar

(ぎをん フィンランディアバー; Map p120;
☑075-541-3482; www.finlandiabar.com; 570-
123 Gion-machi minamigawa, Higashiyama-ku;
cover ¥500; 🕑6pm-3am; ☒Keihan line to
Gion-Shijō) This stylish, minimalist Gion bar
in an old geisha house is a great place for
a civilised drink. There's no menu, so just
prop up at the bar and let the bow-tied
bartender know what you like, whether it's
an expertly crafted cocktail or a high-end
Japanese single malt. Friday and Saturday
nights can get busy, so you may have to
queue.

Northern Higashiyama

Kick Up   Bar
(キックアップ; Map p120; ☑075-761-5604;
331 Higashikomonoza-chō, Higashiyama-ku;
⊗7pm-midnight, closed Wed; ⑤Tōzai line to
Keage) Located just across the street from
the Westin Miyako Kyoto, this wonderful bar
attracts a regular crowd of Kyoto expats,
local Japanese and guests from the Westin.
It's subdued, relaxing and friendly.

Metro   Club
(メトロ; Map p120; ☑075-752-4765; www.
metro.ne.jp; BF Ebisu Bldg, Kawabata-dōri,
Marutamachi-sagaru, Sakyō-ku; ⊗about
8pm-3am; ᴿKeihan line to Jingū-Marutamachi)
Metro is part disco, part live house and it
even hosts the occasional art exhibition.
It attracts an eclectic mix of creative
types and has a different theme nightly,
so check ahead in *Kansai Scene* to see
what's going on. Metro is inside exit 2 of
the Jingū-Marutamachi Station on the
Keihan line.

Arashiyama

% Arabica   Coffee
(☑075-748-0057; www.arabica.coffee; 3-47
Susukinobaba-chō, Saga-Tenryūji, Ukyō-ku;
⊗8am-6pm; ᴿJR Sagano/San-in line to Saga-
Arashiyama) Peer through the floor-to-ceiling
windows that look across the Hozu-gawa
and mountain backdrop as you order your
coffee at this tiny cafe bringing excellent
brew to Arashiyama. There are just a few
seats that can be 'rented', but your best bet
is to grab a takeaway and stroll along the
river or nab a bench out front to take in the
views.

⭐ ENTERTAINMENT

Minami-za   Theatre
(南座; Map p120; ☑075-561-0160; www.
kabuki-bito.jp; Shijō-Ōhashi, Higashiyama-ku;
performances ¥5000-27,000; ᴿKeihan line to
Gion-Shijō) The oldest kabuki theatre in Japan
is the Minami-za in Gion. The major event of
the year is the **Kaomise festival** (30 November to 25 December), which features Japan's
finest kabuki actors. Other performances

A highly decorated Kyoto bar

take place on an irregular basis – check the website for the schedule or enquire at the Kyoto Tourist Information Center.

ROHM Theatre Kyoto   Theatre
(京都観世会館; Map p120; ☑075-771-6051; www.rohmtheatrekyoto.jp; 44 Okazaki Enshōji-chō, Sakyō-ku; tickets from ¥3000; ⊗box office 10am-7pm; Ⓢ Tōzai line to Higashiyama) The Kyoto Kaikan Theatre underwent a renovation early in 2016 and transformed into the ROHM Theatre Kyoto. Housed in a striking modernist building, it holds three multi-purpose halls with a 2000-seater main hall hosting everything from international ballet and opera performances to comedy shows, music concerts and nō.

Gion Corner   Theatre
(ギオンコーナー; Map p120; ☑075-561-1119; www.kyoto-gioncorner.com; Yasaka Kaikan, 570-2 Gionmachi Minamigawa, Higashiyama-ku; adult/child ¥3150/1900; ⊗performances 6pm & 7pm daily mid-Mar–Nov, Fri-Sun Dec–mid-Mar; ⓑKyoto City bus 206 to Gion, ⓡKeihan line to Gion-Shijō) Gion Corner presents regularly scheduled one-hour shows that include a bit of tea ceremony, koto (Japanese zither) music, ikebana (art of flower arranging), gagaku (court music), kyōgen (ancient comic plays), kyōmai (Kyoto-style dance) and bunraku (classical puppet theatre). It's geared to a tourist market and is fairly pricey for what you get. Try to arrive early for front-row seats.

ⓘ INFORMATION

INTERNET ACCESS

Kyoto launched a free wi-fi access program for foreign travellers, with hotspots across the city, mainly at bus and train stations. As it requires you to email for an access code and is limited to 30 minutes it is not terribly useful.

TOURIST INFORMATION

Kyoto Tourist Information Center (京都総合観光案内所, TIC; Map p116; ☑075-343-0548; 2F Kyoto Station Bldg, Shimogyō-ku; ⊗8.30am-7pm; Ⓢ Karasuma line to Kyoto) Stocks bus and city maps, has plenty of transport info and English speakers are available to answer your questions.

You'll find other small tourist offices dotted around the downtown area along Kawaramachi-

Minami-za (p135), Japan's oldest kabuki theatre

dōri, such as **Kawaramachi Sanjo Tourist Information Center** (Map p116; ☑075-213-1717; 1F Kyoto Asahi Kaikan Bldg, 427 Ebisu-cho, Kawaramachi-dōri, Sanjo-agaru; ☺10am-6pm; ⑤Tōzai line to Kyoto-Shiyakusho-mae).

ℹ️ GETTING THERE & AWAY

If Kyoto is your first destination, it makes sense to fly into nearby Kansai International Airport (KIX; Kyoto's main international entry point), though flights to Tokyo are often cheaper.

Kyoto Station is on the Tōkaidō Shinkansen, with service to Tokyo (¥13,910, 2½ hours) and Shin-Osaka (¥3020, 15 minutes) stations. Some westward trains continue on the San-yō shinkansen line for Okayama (¥7850, one hour; for Naoshima) and Hiroshima (¥11410; 1¾ hours).

Both JR and private lines connect Kyoto with nearby Osaka and Nara.

ℹ️ GETTING AROUND

TO/FROM THE AIRPORT

The fastest and most convenient way to move between KIX and Kyoto is the special JR Haruka airport express (reserved/unreserved ¥3370/2850, 75 minutes) to Kyoto Station. First and last departures from KIX to Kyoto are at 6.30am and 10.16pm Monday to Friday (6.40am on weekends); first and last departures from Kyoto to KIX are at 5.45am and 8.30pm.

When it comes time to depart, those travelling on Japanese airlines (JAL and ANA) can make use of an advance check-in counter inside the JR ticket office in Kyoto Station. This service allows you to check in with your luggage at the station, which is a real bonus for those with heavy bags.

Another convenient option is the **MK Taxi Sky Gate Shuttle limousine van service** (☑075-778-5489; www.mktaxi-japan.com; one-way to Kansai airport ¥3600, to Itami airport ¥2400), which will drop you off anywhere in Kyoto for ¥3600 – simply go to the staff counter at the south end of the KIX arrivals hall and they will do the rest. From Kyoto to the airport it is necessary to make reservations two days in advance, staff will pick you up anywhere in Kyoto and take

Discount Passes

You can purchase a *shi-basu Kyoto-bus ichinichi jōshaken kādo* (one-day card) valid for unlimited travel on Kyoto City buses and Kyoto buses (different companies) for ¥500.

A similar pass (*Kyoto kankō ichinichi jōsha-ken*) that allows unlimited use of the bus and subway costs ¥1200. A *Kyoto kankō futsuka jōsha-ken* (two-day bus/subway pass) costs ¥2000.

Purchase any of the above at major bus terminals, at the bus information centre at Kyoto Station or at the Kyoto Tourist Information Center (p136).

The **Kansai Thru Pass** (p314) is useful if you're planning to do some exploring in the Kansai area.

you to the airport. Keep in mind that these are shared taxis (actually vans), so you may be delayed by the driver picking up or dropping off other passengers.

BICYCLE

Kyoto is a great city to explore on a bicycle. It is mostly flat and there is a useful bike path running the length of the Kamo-gawa. Many guesthouses hire or lend bicycles to their guests and there are also hire shops around Kyoto Station, in Arashiyama and in Downtown Kyoto.

The downside is that you'll have to be mindful of where you park. In order to keep pavements clear, bicycle parking is prohibited in many areas except designated lots (which require a fee of ¥100 to ¥200 to use). Park illegally at your peril: your bike could get impounded.

A great place to hire a bicycle is the **Kyoto Cycling Tour Project** (京都サイクリングツアープロジェクト, KCTP; Map p116; 075-354-3636; www.kctp.net; 552-13 Higashi-Aburanokoji-cho, Aburanokoji-dori, Shiokoji-sagaru, Shimogyo-ku; 9am-7pm; S Karasuma line to Kyoto, R JR line to Kyoto). These folk hire bikes (¥1000 per day) that are perfect for getting around the city. KCTP also conducts a variety of bicycle city tours with English-speaking guides, which are an excellent way to see Kyoto (check the website for details). Most hire outfits require you to leave a deposit and ID such as a passport.

BUS

Kyoto has an intricate network of bus routes, which you will need to ride to get to some sights. Many of the routes used by visitors have announcements in English. Most buses run between 7am and 9pm, though a few run earlier or later. In addition to the regular city buses, Kyoto now has a hop-on, hop-off sightseeing bus, K'Loop, travelling around the city's World Heritage Sites.

Bus entry is usually through the back door and exit is via the front door. Inner-city buses charge a flat fare (¥230 for adults, ¥120 for children aged six to 12, free for those younger), which you drop into the clear plastic receptacle on top of the machine next to the driver on your way out. A separate machine gives change for ¥100 and ¥500 coins or ¥1000 notes.

To save time and money you can buy a *kaisu-ken* (book of five tickets) for ¥1000 from the driver.

Kyoto's main bus terminals are also train stations: Kyoto Station, Sanjo Station, Karasuma-Shijo Station and Kitaoji Station. The bus terminal at Kyoto Station is on the north side and has three main departure bays (departure points are indicated by the letter of the bay and number of the stop within that bay).

The main bus information centre is located in front of Kyoto Station. Here you can pick up bus maps, purchase bus tickets and passes (on all lines, including highway buses), and get additional information. The Kyoto Tourist Information Center (TIC) stocks the *Bus Navi: Kyoto City Bus Sightseeing Map,* which shows the city's main bus lines.

TAXI

Flagfall in Kyoto is around ¥600 (there is some variation among operators). While not the most economical way to get around, taxis save time, especially if there is no direct bus route to where you need to go.

TRAIN & SUBWAY

The main train station in Kyoto is Kyoto Station, which is actually two stations under one roof: JR Kyoto Station and Kintetsu Kyoto Station. In addition to the private Kintetsu line that operates from Kyoto Station, there are two other private train lines in Kyoto: the Hankyu line that operates from Downtown Kyoto along Shijo-dori and the Keihan line that operates from stops along the Kamo-gawa.

Kyoto has two efficient subway lines, operating from 5.30am to 11.30pm. Minimum adult fare is ¥210 (child ¥110). The quickest way to travel between the north and south of the city is the Karasuma subway line, which passes through Kyoto Station. The east–west Tozai subway line meets the Karasuma subway line at Karasuma-Oike Station.

Where to Stay

Kyoto has many lodgings (in all price ranges) in beautiful old buildings (though be mindful that this will mean stairs and possibly thin walls). For modern convenience, there are plenty of hotels.

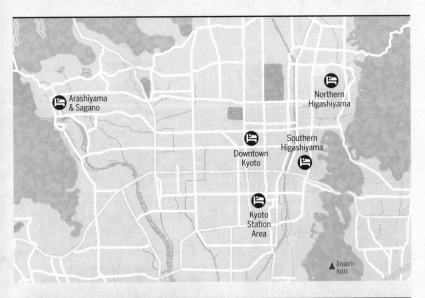

Neighbourhood	Atmosphere
Kyoto Station Area	Lots of choices in all price ranges; convenient for travel in and out of the city; plenty of easy dining options. Far from most sightseeing districts; not particularly attractive area.
Downtown Kyoto	In the heart of everything – shops, restaurants and nightlife. Though it can feel rather hectic, with crowded pavements and fairly high ambient noise on street level. Good transit links.
Southern Higashiyama	The city's main sightseeing district, with beautiful walks in every direction. Fewer dining options than downtown; crowded in the cherry-blossom season.
Northern Higashiyama	Lots of sights nearby; peaceful and green; nice day and evening strolls. Just not many places to stay or eat out this way.
Arashiyama & Sagano	One of the main sightseeing districts with some truly beautiful ryokan; magical at night. Inconvenient for other parts of the city; quiet at night and lacking budget options.

NARA

Nara

Japan's first permanent capital, Nara (奈良) is one of the country's most rewarding destinations. With eight Unesco World Heritage Sites, it's second only to Kyoto as a repository of Japan's cultural legacy. The centrepiece is the Daibutsu (Great Buddha), which is one of the largest bronze figures in the world and rivals Mt Fuji and Kyoto's Golden Pavilion (Kinkaku-ji) as Japan's single most impressive sight. The Great Buddha is housed in Tōdai-ji, a soaring temple that presides over Nara-kōen, a park that is home to about 1200 deer. In pre-Buddhist times the deer were considered messengers of the gods and today enjoy the status of National Treasures.

Nara in One Day

Nara is compact: it's quite possible to pack the highlights – the temples, shrines and museums of Nara-kōen – into one full day. Many travellers visit Nara as a side trip from Kyoto.

Nara in Two Days

Overnighting in Nara gives you time to take it slower, and also to get a head start in the morning – before the day trippers arrive. You'll be able to take more time in the museums and less-famous (and less-crowded) temples, and to explore other quarters such as the historic Nara-machi district. There are also excellent lodgings and restaurants here.

Kyoto
(40km)
**KYOTO
PREFECTURE**

0 ——————— 1 km
0 ——————— 0.5 miles

Yamato-
Saidaiji

Daibutsu-
den Hall

Nigatsu-dō &
Sangatsu-dō

Kintetsu
Nara

Tōdai-ji

Nobori-
Ōji

Tōdai-ji
Nandai-mon

Osaka
(30km)

Nara

Nara-
kōen

Nishinokyō

Kintetsu-
kōriyama

Kōriyama

Nara Map (p152)

Arriving in Nara

Nara is most often visited as part of a journey to the Kansai region that includes Kyoto (40km to the north) and Osaka (30km to the west). Given the excellent train links between the three cities, it's better to use public transport than to drive (parking and traffic in Nara can be a challenge). For travellers coming from elsewhere via *shinkansen* (bullet train), transit via Kyoto.

Sleeping

There are several budget guesthouses and easily accessed hotels within the vicinity of Nara's train stations. Though not as convenient to the sights, the guesthouses and ryokan in Naramachi, south of the the town centre, are an attractive alternative. Many are in heritage structures.

Tōdai-ji's Daibutsu (Great Buddha)

GRANT DIXON / GETTY IMAGES ©

Tōdai-ji

Nara's star attraction is the famous Daibutsu (Great Buddha), centrepiece of this grand temple on the Unesco World Heritage List, with origins going back to AD 728. The Daibutsu-den (大仏殿, Great Buddha Hall) is the largest wooden building in the world.

Great For...

☑ Don't Miss

Standing in awe at the 15m-tall gilt-bronze Daibutsu, first created in the 8th century.

Except for the Daibutsu-den, which houses the Daibutsu, most of Tōdai-ji's grounds can be visited free of charge.

Daibutsu

The Daibutsu is an image of Dainichi Nyorai (also known as Vairocana Buddha), the cosmic Buddha believed to give rise to all worlds and their respective Buddhas. Historians believe that Emperor Shōmu ordered the building of the Buddha as a charm against smallpox, which had ravaged Japan in preceding years. Originally cast in 746, the present statue was recast in the Edo period. It stands just over 16m high and consists of 437 tonnes of bronze and 130kg of gold. Over the centuries the statue took quite a beating from earthquakes and fires, losing its head a couple of times (note the slight difference in colour between the head and the body).

Statue of Tamonten, one of Japan's Seven Gods of Fortune

COWARDLION / SHUTTERSTOCK ©

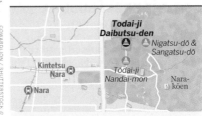

Todai-ji
Daibutsu-den

Nigatsu-dō &
Sangatsu-dō

Kintetsu
Nara

Tōdai-ji
Nandai-mon

Nara-
kōen

Nara

❶ Need to Know

東大寺; Map p143; 406-1 Zōshi-chō; Daibutsu-den admission ¥500, combination ticket with Tōdai-ji Museum ¥800; ☺Daibutsu-den 8am-4.30pm Nov-Feb, to 5pm Mar & Oct, 7.30am-5.30pm Apr-Sep

✗ Take a Break

Go for tea at Mizuya-chaya (p153) near Nigatsu-dō.

★ Top Tip

Everyone makes a beeline for the Daibutsu-den; budget some time to get away from the crowds and visit some subtemples.

As you circle the statue towards the back, you'll see a wooden column with a hole through its base. Popular belief maintains that those who can squeeze through the hole, which is exactly the same size as one of the Great Buddha's nostrils, are ensured of enlightenment. There's usually a line of children waiting to give it a try and parents waiting to snap their pictures. A hint for bigger 'kids': try going through with one or both arms above your head – someone on either end to push and pull helps too.

Nandai-mon

The great **Nandai-mon** (東大寺南大門, South Gate; Map p143) contains two fierce-looking Niō guardians. These recently restored wooden images, carved in the 13th century by the famed sculptor Unkei,

are some of the finest wooden statues in all of Japan, if not the world. They are truly dramatic works of art and seem ready to spring to life at any moment. The gate is about 200m south of the Tōdai-ji temple enclosure.

Nigatsu-dō & Sangatsu-dō

Nigatsu-dō & Sangatsu-dō (二月堂 · 三月堂; Map p143; Nigatsu-dō free, Sangatsu-dō ¥500; ☺Nigatsu-dō 24hr, Sangatsu-dō 8am-4.30pm Nov-Feb, to 5pm Mar & Oct, 7.30am-5.30pm Apr-Sep), two subtemples of Tōdai-ji uphill from the Daibutsu-den, and far less clamorous. Nigatsu-dō, a national treasure from 1669 (originally built c 750), has a verandah with sweeping views across town. Sangatsu-dō is the oldest building in the Tōdai-ji complex and home to a small collection of fine Nara-period statues.

Tōdai-ji

VISIT THE GREAT BUDDHA

The Daibutsu (Great Buddha) at Nara's Tōdai-ji is one of the most arresting sights in Japan. The awe-inspiring physical presence of the vast image is striking. It's one of the largest bronze Buddha images in the world and it's contained in an equally huge building, the Daibutsu-den Hall, which is among the largest wooden buildings on earth.

Tōdai-ji was built by order of Emperor Shōmu during the Nara period (710–784) and the complex was finally completed in 798, after the capital had been moved from Nara to Kyoto. Most historians agree the temple was built to consolidate the country and serve as its spiritual focus. Legend has it that over two million labourers worked on the temple, but this is probably apocryphal. What's certain is that its construction brought the country to the brink of bankruptcy.

The original Daibutsu was cast in bronze in eight castings over a period of three years. It has been recast several times over the centuries. The original Daibutsu was covered in gold leaf and one can only imagine its impact on Japanese visitors during the eighth century AD.

The temple belongs to the Kegon school of Buddhism, one of the six schools of Buddhism popular in Japan during the Nara period. Kegon Buddhism, which comes from the Chinese Huayan Buddhist sect, is based on the Flower Garland Sutra. This sutra expresses the idea of worlds within worlds, all manifested by the Cosmic Buddha (Vairocana or Dainichi Nyorai). The Great Buddha and the figures that surround him in the Daibutsu-den Hall are the perfect physical symbol of this cosmological map.

Kokuzo Bosatsu
Seated to the left of the Daibutsu is Kokuzo Bosatsu, the bodhisattva of memory and wisdom, to whom students pray for help in their studies and the faithful pray for help on the path to enlightenment.

The Daibutsu (Great Buddha)
Known in Sanskrit as 'Vairocana' and in Japanese as the 'Daibutsu', this is the Cosmic Buddha that gives rise to all other Buddhas, according to Kegon doctrine. The Buddha's hands send the messages 'fear not' and 'welcome'.

FACT FILE

THE DAIBUTSU
Height 14.98m
Weight 500 tonnes
Nostril width 50cm

THE DAIBUTSU-DEN HALL
Height 48.74m
Length 57m
Number of roof tiles 112,589

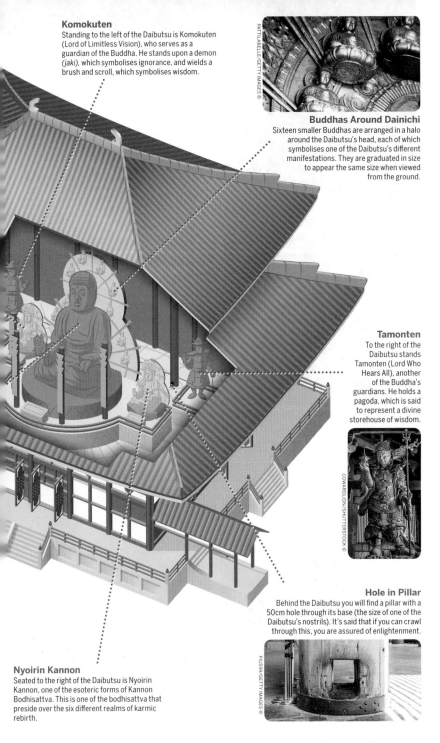

Komokuten
Standing to the left of the Daibutsu is Komokuten (Lord of Limitless Vision), who serves as a guardian of the Buddha. He stands upon a demon *(jaki)*, which symbolises ignorance, and wields a brush and scroll, which symbolises wisdom.

Buddhas Around Dainichi
Sixteen smaller Buddhas are arranged in a halo around the Daibutsu's head, each of which symbolises one of the Daibutsu's different manifestations. They are graduated in size to appear the same size when viewed from the ground.

Tamonten
To the right of the Daibutsu stands Tamonten (Lord Who Hears All), another of the Buddha's guardians. He holds a pagoda, which is said to represent a divine storehouse of wisdom.

Hole in Pillar
Behind the Daibutsu you will find a pillar with a 50cm hole through its base (the size of one of the Daibutsu's nostrils). It's said that if you can crawl through this, you are assured of enlightenment.

Nyoirin Kannon
Seated to the right of the Daibutsu is Nyoirin Kannon, one of the esoteric forms of Kannon Bodhisattva. This is one of the bodhisattva that preside over the six different realms of karmic rebirth.

Sights of Nara-kōen

Many of Nara's most important sites are located around Nara-kōen (奈良公園), a fine park that occupies much of the eastern side of the city.

Start Kintetsu Nara Station
Distance 5km
Duration Half a day

2 Isui-en (p151), Nara's prettiest strolling garden, offers some peaceful respite.

7 Stroll through the grounds of **Kō-fuku-ji** (p150), passing between the Nanen-dō and Hokuen-dō halls.

Kintetsu Nara

Nobori-Oji

FINISH

7

6

Sanjo-dori

Sarusawa-ike

Nara

NARAMACHI

6 Admire the heights of **Five-storey pagoda**, Japan's second-tallest, dating from 1426.

Take a Break... Stop for tea in the garden at Isui-en.

3 Admire the Niō guardians at the massively impressive southern gate of **Tōdai-ji Nandai-mon** (p145) before exploring Tōdai-ji.

4 Climb the steps to **Nigatsu-dō & Sangatsu-dō** (p145) to enjoy the view, taking in the graceful curves of Daibutsu-den and the Nara plain.

Nara-kōen

START

Classic Photo A close-up of one of Nara-kōen's famously tame deer.

1 Upon entering the park you'll be greeted by **Nara-kōen's deer** hoping for a handout of *shika-sembei* (deer biscuits; ¥150), sold by vendors.

5 Explore **Kasuga Taisha** (p150), Nara's grandest Shintō shrine, with many smaller sub-shrines within.

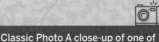

◉ SIGHTS

Kasuga Taisha   Shinto Shrine
(春日大社; 160 Kasugano-chō; ⊘dawn-dusk)
FREE Founded in the 8th century, this
sprawling shrine on the Unesco World
Heritage List lies at the foot of a deeply
forested hill, where herds of sacred deer
await handouts. Until the end of the 19th
century, Kasuga Taisha was completely
rebuilt every 20 years, according to Shintō
tradition. Pathways are lined with hundreds
of lanterns, with many hundreds more in
the shrine itself. They're illuminated during
the twice-yearly **Mantōrō** (Lantern Festival;
⊘early Feb & mid-Aug) festivals, held in early
February and mid-August.

Kōfuku-ji   Buddhist Temple
(興福寺; www.kohfukuji.com; grounds free,
Tōkondō ¥300, National Treasure Museum
¥600, combined ticket ¥800; ⊘grounds 24hr,
Tōkondō 9am-5pm) Another of Nara's sights
on the Unesco World Heritage List, this
temple was founded in Kyoto in AD 669
and relocated here in 710. The original
Nara temple complex had 175 buildings,
and although only a dozen remain after
fires and destruction due to power struggles, many of those are national treasures.
Two pagodas – one of three and the other
of five storeys – date from 1143 and 1426
respectively. The taller one is Japan's
second tallest, outclassed by the one at
Kyoto's Tō-ji by a few centimetres.

Nara National Museum   Museum
(奈良国立博物館, Nara Kokuritsu Hakubutsu-
kan; ☑050-5542-8600; www.narahaku.go.jp;
50 Noboriōji-chō; ¥520, special exhibitions
¥1120-1420; ⊘9.30am-5pm, closed Mon) This
world-class museum of Buddhist art is
divided into two sections. Built in 1894
and strikingly renovated in 2016, the Nara
Buddhist Sculpture Hall & Ritual Bronzes
Gallery displays a rotating selection of
about 100 *butsu-zō* (statues of Buddhas
and bodhisattvas) at any one time, about
half of which are national treasures or
important cultural properties. Each image
has detailed English explanations; the
excellent booklet *Viewing Buddhist Sculptures* provides even more detail and is well
worth the additional ¥500 donation.

From left: Kasuga Taisha; fountain at Kōfuku-ji; Nara
National Museum

BOHISTOCK / GETTY IMAGES ©

COWARDLION / SHUTTERSTOCK ©

Isui-en & Neiraku
Art Museum   Gardens
(依水園・寧楽美術館; 74 Suimon-chō; museum
& garden ¥900; ⏰9.30am-4.30pm Wed-Mon,
daily Apr, May, Oct & Nov) This exquisite,
contemplative Meiji-era garden features
abundant greenery, ponds and walkways
with stepping stones designed for each
to be observed as you walk, to appreciate
their individual beauty. For ¥850 you can
enjoy a cup of tea on tatami mats overlooking the garden. Admission covers the
adjoining **Neiraku Art Museum**, displaying
Chinese and Korean ceramics and bronzes
in a quiet setting.

🎧 TOURS

Nara Walk   Tours
(奈良ウォーク; 📞090-9708-0036; www.
narawalk.com; Nara Park ¥3000, Old Town
¥2000; ⏰Mar-Nov or by appointment) Nara
Walk offers well-regarded walking tours in
English, including a morning tour around
Nara Park (Tōdai-ji, Kasuga Taisha etc)
and an afternoon Old Town stroll (through
Naramachi). Other tours to Tōshōdai-ji,

👍 Naramachi

South of Sanjō-dōri and Sarusawa-ike
pond, Naramachi (奈良町) is a
traditional neighbourhood with many
well-preserved *machiya* (shophouses)
and *kura* (storehouses). It's a mellow
place for a stroll away from the busier
sights around Nara-kōen, and has good
restaurants, shops and cafes.

Yakushi-ji, Hōryū-ji and Tōdai-ji are available
by appointment.

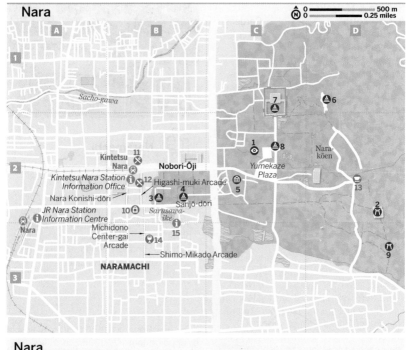

Nara

🔒 SHOPPING

Nipponichi   Arts & Crafts

(日本市; ☏0742-23-5650; 1-1 Tsunofuri-shin-yamachi; ⏱10am-7pm) From humble beginnings as a linen merchant in 1716, this retailer has evolved to repurpose traditional craft-making (clothing, towels, housewares and accessories) for the 21st century in Japan's sweet spot of cool, adorable, fun and quietly chic. Because this is Nara, look for deer motifs: paper clips, handkerchiefs and *shika-sembei* (crackers for deer), though these are for human consumption.

🍴 EATING & DRINKING

Washokuya Happoh   Izakaya ¥¥

(和食屋八寶; ☏0742-26-4834; 22 Higashi-muki-nakamachi; dishes ¥360-1380, lunch menus ¥750-1050; ⏱11.30am-10.30pm Mon-Sat, to 10pm Sun) This large, cheery, modern farmhouse-style spot salutes Nara as the birthplace of sake, in both drink and food. Alongside *izakaya* (Japanese pub-eatery) standards such as sashimi and *karaage* (fried chicken pieces), we loved the dishes marinated in sake lees (especially pork) and seared *wagyū* sushi. The wide-ranging, fastidiously detailed menu gets props for cute pictures of ingredients, for diners with allergies or dietary restrictions.

Sakura Burger
Burgers ¥¥

(さくらバーガー; ☑0742-31-3813; http://sakuraburger.com; 6 Higashimuki-kitamachi; burgers & sandwiches ¥490-1230; ☺11am-4pm & 5-9pm Thu-Tue) This unassumingly gourmet burger joint is steps north of Kintetsu Nara Station. Expect a lunchtime queue for burgers, sandwiches and hot dogs with your choice of toppings. The namesake Sakura burger comes piled with veggies and a thick slice of house-smoked bacon. They even make their own ketchup. Dessert (while it lasts) is homemade apple pie or caramel walnut tart.

Nara Izumi Yūsai
Bar

(なら泉勇斎; ☑0742-26-6078; 22 Nishi-Tera-bayashi-chō; ☺11am-8pm Fri-Wed) Drop in on this small standing bar in Naramachi for tastings (¥200 to ¥600) of sakes produced in Nara Prefecture (120 varieties from 29 makers, also available for purchase). There is a useful English explanation sheet.

Mizuya-chaya
Teahouse

(水谷茶屋; ☑07542-22-0627; 30 Kasugano-chō; ☺10am-4pm Thu-Tue) In a small wooded, brookside clearing between Nigatsu-dō and Kasuga Taisha, this quaint thatched-roof teahouse is one of Nara's most atmospheric spots. Stop for a cup of *matcha* (powdered green tea; ¥700 including a sweet), *onigiri* (rice balls; ¥350 to ¥400) or a bowl of udon (¥580 to ¥850) for a pick-me-up.

ℹ️ INFORMATION

There are Tourist Information Centers just outside **JR Nara Station** (☑0742-22-9821; www.narashikanko.or.jp; ☺9am-9pm; 🛜) and **Kintetsu Nara Station** (☑0742-24-4858; ☺9am-9pm; 🛜) that stock maps and can assist with same-day hotel reservations; you can store luggage in the former (¥500 per piece per day). **Nara Visitor Center & Inn** (奈良県猿沢イン; Nara-ken Sarusawa Inn; ☑0742-81-7461; www.sarusawa.nara.jp; 3 Ikeno-chō; ☺8am-9pm) has a daily roster of cultural happenings, including tea-ceremony and kimono experiences.

ℹ️ GETTING THERE & AROUND

The comfortable Kintetsu Nara line runs from Kyoto Station (¥620, 45 minutes) and Osaka's Namba Station (¥560, 40 minutes) to Kintetsu Nara Station. Japan Rail Pass holders can take the JR Nara line from Kyoto Station (45 minutes) or the JR Yamatoji line from Osaka's Tennōji Station (50 minutes) to JR Nara Station.

Nara is a very walkable town. It's a 15-minute walk from JR Nara Station to Nara-kōen (about five minutes from Kintetsu Nara). A bus (¥210) also makes the trip.

JAPAN ALPS

Japan Alps

The awesome Japan Alps rise sharply near the border of Gifu and Nagano Prefectures before rolling north to the dramatic Sea of Japan coast. All but one of Japan's 30 highest peaks (Mt Fuji) are here. There are opportunities for challenging treks, but also gentle ones like the trail through the Kiso Valley between the well-preserved villages of Magome and Tsumago. North of the Kiso Mountains, the Hida Mountains are home to the World Heritage–listed villages of Ogimachi and Ainokura, famed for their signature thatch-roofed gasshō-zukuri architecture; and its centrepiece, Takayama, one of Japan's most likeable cities. East of Takayama, Matsumoto has a magnificent castle and alpine scenery.

Japan Alps in Two Days

From Nagoya, take the train to the village of Magome in the morning and spend the afternoon hiking the old Nakasendō postal road to Tsumago, another historic village, where you can spend the night in a ryokan. The next day, continue by train to the castle town of Matsumoto.

Japan Alps in Four Days

On the morning of your third day, pick up a rental car in Matsumoto and drive over to Shiragawa-gō (about a three-hour drive) to explore the historic architecture for which the region is famed. End up in charming Takayama (where you can reconnect with the train network).

Caption

Arriving in the Japan Alps

Nagoya is a convenient hub, a stop on the Tōkaidō Shinkansen line between Tokyo (¥10,360, 1¾ hours) and Kansai (Kyoto: ¥5070, 35 minutes; Shin-Osaka: ¥5830, 50 minutes), from where you can transfer for trains to destinations in the Alps or pick up a car (the easiest way to get around here, if you don't mind narrow, windy roads). Convenient local airports include Central Japan International Airport (in Nagoya) and Shinshū Matsumoto Airport.

Sleeping

While you'll find hotels in larger cities, the Alps are an excellent place to sample more traditional accommodation. Villages in the Kiso Valley have beautiful ryokan; in Shirakawa-gō you can stay in a (minimally modernised) old farmhouse. Onsen (hot springs) resorts are scattered around Takayama and Matsumoto.

Shirakawa-gō

The remote, mountainous districts of Shirakawa-gō (白川郷) are best known for farmhouses in the thatched gasshō-zukuri style. They're rustic and lovely whether set against the vibrant colours of spring, draped with the gentle mists of autumn, or peeking through a carpet of snow.

Great For...

☑ **Don't Miss**

Sleeping in a thatch-roofed house in Ainokura, a World Heritage–listed village.

Passionate debate continues around the impact tour buses have upon these unique communities, and how best to mitigate disruption to daily life. To avoid the crowds, steer clear of weekends, holidays, and cherry-blossom and autumn-foliage seasons.

Ogimachi

Ogimachi (荻町), the Shirakawa-gō region's central and most accessible settlement, has some 600 residents and the largest concentration of *gasshō-zukuri* buildings – more than 110. There are a few houses in town, including Shirakawa-gō's largest *gasshō* house (a designated National Treasure), **Wada-ke** (和田家; ☎05769-6-1058; adult/child ¥300/150; ◷9am-5pm). It once belonged to a wealthy silk-trading family and dates back to the mid-Edo period. Upstairs you'll find

ⓘ Need to Know

Most of Shirakawa-gō's sights are in Ogimachi, linked by expressway to Takayama; a car is necessary for getting around.

✖ Take a Break

The Gasshō-zukuri Folk Village is a nice place for a picnic.

★ Top Tip

For a lovely view of Ogimachi, climb the path (five minutes) from near the intersection of Rtes 156 and 360 to the Shiroyama Tenbōdai (Observation Point).

silk harvesting equipment and a valuable lacquerware collection.

Gasshō-zukuri Folk Village

Over two dozen *gasshō-zukuri* buildings have been relocated to the **Gasshō-zukuri Folk Village** (合掌造り民家園, Gasshō-zukuri Minka-en; ☑05769-6-1231; www.shirakawago-minkaen.jp; 2499 Ogimachi; adult/child ¥600/400; ⊙8.40am-5pm Apr-Nov, 9am-6pm Fri-Wed Dec-Mar) in Ogimachi. While great for getting to see a variety of structures, the arrangement can feel contrived. Several houses are used for demonstrating regional crafts such as woodwork, straw handicrafts and ceramics (in Japanese only, reservations required). Pick up free multilingual maps at the **Tourist Information Center** (白川後観光案内所; ☑05769-6-1013; 2495-3 Ogimachi; ⊙9am-5pm) by the main bus stop in front.

Ainokura & Suganuma

Stroll through the Ainokira to **Ainokura Minzoku-kan** (相倉民族館, ☑0763-66-2732; 352 Ainokura; ¥210; ⊙8.30am-5pm), a folklore museum with displays of local crafts and paper. It's divided into two buildings, the former Ozaki and Nakaya residences (prominent local families).

Between Suganuma and Ainokura, in the hamlet of Kaminashi, you'll find **Murakami-ke** (村上家; ☑0763-66-2711; www.murakamike.jp; 742 Kaminashi; adult/child ¥300/150; ⊙8.30am-5pm Apr-Nov, 9am-4pm Dec-Mar), one of the oldest *gasshō* houses in the region (dating from 1578). It's now a small museum; the proud owner delights in showing visitors around and might sing you some local folk songs. Close by, the main hall of Hakusan-gū shrine dates from 1502.

Tsumago

Tsumago-Magome Hike

This rewarding hike, along a twisty, craggy old post road, connects two of the most attractive towns along the Nakasendō (中仙道), one of the five highways of the Edo period connecting Edo (now Tokyo) with Kyoto.

Great For...

☑ Don't Miss

Staying overnight in a *minshuku* or ryokan here; there are lovely, inexpensive options.

From Magome (elevation 600m), the 7.8km hike to Tsumago (elevation 420m) follows a steep, largely paved road until it reaches its peak at the top of Magome-tōge (pass) – elevation 801m. After the pass, the trail meanders by waterfalls, forest and farmland. The route is easiest in this direction and is clearly signposted in English; allow three to six hours to enjoy it.

Magome-juku

Pretty Magome-juku (馬篭) is the furthest south of the Kiso Valley post villages. Its buildings line a steep, cobblestone pedestrian road (unfriendly to wheelie suitcases); the rustic shopfronts and mountain views will keep your finger on the shutter. Magome's **Tourist Information Center** (観光案内館; ☏0264-59-2336; 4300-1 Magome; ⊙9am-5pm) is located halfway up the hill, to the right.

Hiking along the Nakasendō

JENNY JONES / GETTY IMAGES ©

ⓘ **Need to Know**

Magome and Tsumago are in the Kiso Valley northeast of Nagoya, the nearest transit hub.

✕ **Take a Break**

Both towns have a smattering of lunch spots and snack vendors but are quiet after dark.

★ **Top Tip**

The towns offer a baggage forwarding service from either Tourist Information Center to the other. Deposit your bags between 8.30am and 11.30am, for delivery by 1pm.

Tsumago

Tsumago (妻籠) feels like an open-air museum, and is about 15 minutes' walk from end to end. It was designated by the government as a protected area for the preservation of traditional buildings, where modern developments such as telephone poles aren't allowed to mar the scene. The dark-wood glory of its lattice-fronted buildings is particularly beautiful at dawn and dusk. Among the most impressive structures is the re-stored **waki-honjin** (脇本陣（奥谷）・歴史資料館, Rekishi Shiryōkan; 2159-2 Azuma; adult/child ¥600/300; ⊙9am-5pm), a former rest stop for the retainers of *daimyōs* (domain lords). The adjacent Local History Museum houses elegant exhibitions about Kiso and the Nakasendō, with some English signage.

Tsumago's **Tourist Information Center** (観光案内館; ☑0264-57-3123; www.tumago.jp/english; 2159-2 Azuma; ⊙8.30am-5pm) is in the centre of town. Some English is spoken and there's English-language literature.

Getting There & Away

Catch a *tokkyū* (limited express) Shinano train on the JR Chūō line from Nagoya to Nakatsugawa (for Magome; ¥2500, 55 minutes) or Nagiso (for Tsumago; ¥2840, one hour); getting to Nagiso may require a transfer in Nakatsugawa.

Buses run approximately once an hour between Nakatsugawa Station and Magome-juku (¥540, 30 minutes) and between Nagiso Station and Tsumago (¥270, 10 minutes, eight daily). There's infrequent bus service between Magome and Tsumago (¥600, 25 minutes), via Magome-tōge.

Takayama

SIGHTS

This original district of three main streets of merchants (Ichino-machi, Nino-machi and Sanno-machi) has been immaculately preserved. Sake breweries are designated by spheres of cedar fronds hanging above their doors; some are open to the public in January and early February, but most sell their brews year-round. You'll find artisans, antiques, clothiers and cafes. Day and night, photographic opportunities abound.

Karakuri Museum   Museum

(飛騨高山獅子会館·からくりミュージアム; ☑0577-32-0881; www.takayamakarakuri.jp; 53-1 Sakura-machi; adult/child ¥600/400; ☺9am-4.30pm) On display here are over 300 *shishi* (lion) masks, instruments and drums related to festival dances. The main draw is the twice-hourly puppet show where you can see the mechanical *karakuri ningyō* in action.

Takayama Shōwa-kan   Museum

(高山昭和館, ☑0577-33-7836; www.takayama-showakan.com; 6 Shimoichino-machi; adult/child ¥500/300; ☺9am-5pm) This nostalgia bonanza from the Shōwa period (1926–89) concentrates on the years between 1955 and 1965, a time of great optimism between Japan's postwar malaise and pre-Titan boom. Lose yourself among the delightful mishmash of endless objects, from movie posters to cars and everything in-between, lovingly presented in a series of themed rooms.

Yoshijima
Heritage House   Historic Building

(吉島家, Yoshijima-ke; ☑0577-32-0038; 1-51 Ōjin-machi; adult/child ¥500/300; ☺9am-5pm Mar-Nov, 9am-4.30pm Wed-Sun Dec-Feb) Design buffs shouldn't miss Yoshijima-ke, which is well covered in architectural publications. Its lack of ornamentation allows you to focus on the spare lines, soaring roof and skylight. Admission includes a cup of delicious shiitake tea, which you can also purchase for ¥600 per can.

Kusakabe
Folk Crafts Museum   Museum

(日下部民藝館, Kusakabe Mingeikan; ☑0577-32-0072; www.kusakabe-mingeikan.com; 1-52 Ōjin-machi; adult/child ¥500/300; ☺9am-4.30pm Mar-Nov, 9am-4pm Wed-Mon Dec-Feb) This building dating from the 1890s showcases the striking craftsmanship of traditional Takayama carpenters. Inside is a collection of folk art.

SHOPPING

Takayama is renowned for arts and crafts. Look for *ichi ittobori* (woodcarvings), *shunkei* lacquerware, and the rustic *yamada-yaki* and decorative *shibukusa-yaki* styles of pottery.

Miya-gawa Asa-ichi   Market

(宮川朝市; www.asaichi.net; ☺7am-noon) Stalls here are primarily produce-centric with seasonal fruits (autumnal apples are out of this world!), vegetables and traditional snacks. A number of permanent storefronts offer handicrafts and souvenirs.

✖ EATING

Takayama specialities include soba (buckwheat noodles), *hoba-miso* (sweet miso paste grilled on a magnolia leaf), *sansai* (mountain vegetables) and *Hida-gyū* (Hida beef). Street foods include *mitarashi-dango* (soy-seasoned grilled rice-ball skewers) and *shio-sembei* (salty rice crackers). *Hida-gyū* turns up on *kushiyaki* (skewers), and in *korokke* (croquettes) and *niku-man* (steamed buns).

Kyōya   Shokudo ¥¥

(京や; ☑0577-34-7660; www.kyoya-hida.jp; 1-77 Ōjin-machi; mains ¥750-5200; ☺11am-10pm Wed-Mon) This traditional eatery specialises in regional dishes such as *hoba-miso* and *Hida-gyū* soba. Seating is on tatami mats around long charcoal grills, under a cathedral ceiling supported by dark timbers. It's on a corner, by a bridge over the canal. Look for the sacks of rice over the door.

Takayama

Sakurajaya   Fusion ¥¥

(さくら茶屋; ☑0577-57-7565; www.sakurajaya.
jimdo.com; 3-8-14 Sowa-machi; dinner courses
from ¥3000; ⏱11.30am-2.30pm & 6-11pm
Thu-Tue) Sakurajaya is what you get when
you take a Japanese man to Germany, introduce him to the European culinary arts,
hone his craft over years then plonk him
down in the quiet back lanes of Takayama.
His wonderful artisanal creations draw
from both German and Japanese lines.
There's something here for all palates, including vegetarians. It's well worth the walk.

Ebisu-Honten   Noodles ¥

(恵比寿本店; ☑0577-32-0209; www.takayama-
ebisu.jp; 46 Kamini-no-machi; noodle bowls from
¥880; ⏱10am-5pm Thu-Tue; ☑) These folks
have been making *teuchi* (handmade) soba
since 1898. Try their cold *zaru soba* to strip
it bare and taste the flavour of the noodles.
The *tororo nameko soba* is also very good:
noodles in a hot soup with boiled mush-
room and grated mountain potato. The
building has an interesting red-glass sign
with white characters and a little roof on it.

INFORMATION

The **Tourist Information Center** (飛騨高山観
光案内所; ☑0577-32-5328; www.hida.jp/english;
⊙8.30am-5pm Nov-Mar, 8.30am-6.30pm Apr-
Oct) is directly in front of JR Takayama Station,
where knowledgeable English-speaking staff
dispense maps and pamphlets on sights, accommodation, special events and regional transport.
Staff are unable to assist with accommodation
reservations.

GETTING THERE & AROUND

From Tokyo or cities to the south (Kyoto, Osaka,
Hiroshima, Fukuoka), Takayama can be reached
by catching a frequent *shinkansen* (bullet train)
service to Nagoya, then connecting with the JR
Takayama line (*tokkyū* ¥5510, 2½ hours).

Most sights in Takayama can be covered
easily on foot. Takayama is bicycle-friendly but
rentals can be expensive. Try **Hara Cycle** (ハラ
サイクル; ☑0577-32-1657; 61 Suehiro-chō; 1st
hour ¥300, additional hour ¥200, per day ¥1300;
⊙9am-8pm Wed-Mon).

Matsumoto

⊙ SIGHTS

Matsumoto-jō   Castle
(松本城; ☑0263-32-9202; www.matsumoto-
castle.jp; 4-1 Marunōchi; adult/child ¥610/420;
⊙8.30am-5pm early Sep–mid-Jul, to 6pm mid-
Jul–early Sep) Must-see Matsumoto-jō is
Japan's oldest wooden castle and one of
four castles designated National Treasures –
the others are Hikone, Himeji and Inuyama.
The striking black-and-white three-turreted
donjon (main keep) was completed around
1595, earning the nickname Karasu-jō
(Crow Castle). You can climb steep steps
all the way to the top, with impressive views
and historical displays on each level. Don't
miss the recently restored *tsukimi yagura*
(moon-viewing pavilion). The **Goodwill
Guide Group** (☑0263-32-7140) offers free
one-hour tours by reservation.

Nawate-dōri   Area
(縄手道り) Nawate-dōri, a few blocks from
the castle, is a popular place for a stroll.
Vendors along this riverside walk sell

Matsumoto-jō

PHATTANA STOCK / SHUTTERSTOCK ©

antiques, souvenirs and delicious *tai-yaki* (filled waffles in the shape of a carp) of varying flavours. Look for the big frog statue by the bridge.

Japan Ukiyo-e Museum   Museum

(日本浮世絵美術館; ☑0263-47-4440; www. japan-ukiyoe-museum.com; 2206-1 Koshiba; adult/child ¥1200/600; ☺10am-5pm Tue-Sun) Housing more than 100,000 woodblock prints, paintings, screens and old books, this renowned museum exhibits but a fraction of its collection. The museum is approximately 3km from JR Matsumoto Station (about ¥1600 by taxi) or 15 minutes' walk from Ōniwa Station on the Matsumoto Dentetsu line (¥180, six minutes).

❶ INFORMATION

Online, visit http://welcome.city.matsumoto. nagano.jp.

The excellent **Matsumoto Tourist Information Center** (松本市観光案内所; ☑0263-32-2814; 1-1-1 Fukashi; ☺9.30am-5.45pm) inside JR Matsumoto Station has friendly English-speaking staff and a wide range of well-produced English language materials on the area.

❶ GETTING THERE & AWAY

Shinshū Matsumoto Airport (MMJ; www.matsumoto-airport.co.jp) has daily flights to Fukuoka, Osaka and Sapporo. An airport shuttle bus runs to downtown (¥600, 25 minutes); a taxi costs around ¥5000.

Train connections include Tokyo's Shinjuku Station (*tokkyū* ¥6380, 2¾ hours, hourly), Nagoya (*tokkyū* ¥5510, two hours) and Nagano (Shinano *tokkyū* ¥2320, 50 minutes; Chūō *futsū* ¥1140, 1¼ hours).

Nōhi Bus (濃飛バス; ☑0577-32-1688; www. nouhibus.co.jp/english) services Takayama (¥3900, 2½ hours, at least six daily). Reservations are advised.

 **Hida Cycling Tours**

The fantastic crew at **Satoyama Experience** (☑0577-73-5715; www.satoyama-experience.com; 8-8 Nino-machi; half-day tours from ¥4700; ☺9am-6pm Fri-Wed) is eager to introduce you to its beloved region, culture and people. Small-group cycling tours include a friendly, English-speaking guide, mountain-bike rental and insurance. A variety of tours (including walking) cater to different levels of fitness, but all capture the spirit and scenery of Hida – highly recommended. The team can also connect you with some unique, traditional accommodation (for longer stays) in town and around – just ask.

❶ GETTING AROUND

Matsumoto-jō and the city centre are easily covered on foot and free bicycles are available for loan – enquire at the Tourist Information Center. Three 'Town Sneaker' loop bus routes operate between 9am and 5.30pm for ¥200 per ride (¥500 per day).

FUJI FIVE LAKES

Fuji Five Lakes

Japan's highest and most famous peak is the natural draw of the Fuji Five Lakes (富士五湖) region, but even if you don't intend to climb Fuji-san, it's still worth coming to enjoy the visual and natural delights around the volcano's northern foothills; the five lakes here act as natural reflecting pools for the mountain's perfect cone. Kawaguchi-ko is the most popular lake, with plenty of accommodation, eating and hiking options around it. The other lakes are Yamanaka-ko, Sai-ko, Shōji-ko and Motosu-ko. The nearby town of Fuji-Yoshida (富士吉田) was the original starting point for pilgrims ascending Fuji.

The Fuji Five Lakes Region in One Day

Travellers who have climbing Fuji on their bucket list but have little time tend to take the bus in from Tokyo, climb through the night and take the bus back in the morning. Outside the climbing season, you can also visit as a day trip from Tokyo, either to visit the Fifth Station or to enjoy views from Kawaguchi-ko.

The Fuji Five Lakes Region in Two Days

Climbing over two days (and overnighting in a mountain hut) allows for a more leisurely pace, and is also a strategy for beating the crowds. If you're not climbing, spending the night in one of the lake towns gives you more opportunities to hunt for Fuji views, often best first thing in the morning.

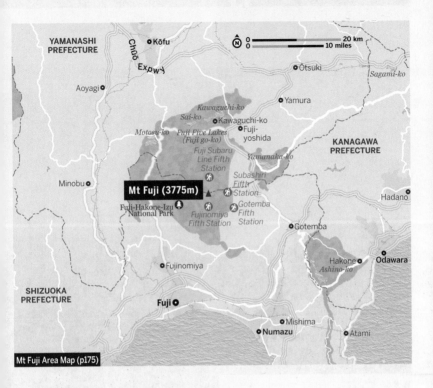

Mt Fuji Area Map (p175)

Map labels:

YAMANASHI PREFECTURE

Kōfu

Chūō Expwy

20 km
10 miles

Ōtsuki

Sagami-ko

Aoyagi

Yamura

Kawaguchi-ko

Sai-ko

Motosu-ko

Kawaguchi-ko

Fuji Five Lakes (Fuji go-ko)

Fuji-yoshida

KANAGAWA PREFECTURE

Fuji Subaru Line Fifth Station

Yamanaka-ko

Subashiri Fifth Station

Minobu

Mt Fuji (3775m)

Fuji-Hakone-Izu National Park

Fujinomiya Fifth Station

Gotemba Fifth Station

Hadano

Gotemba

Fujinomiya

Hakone

Ashino-ko

Odawara

SHIZUOKA PREFECTURE

Fuji

Mishima

Numazu

Atami

Arriving in the Fuji Five Lakes Region

The Fuji Five Lakes area is most easily reached from Tokyo by bus or train, with Fuji-Yoshida and Kawaguchi-ko being the principal gateways. It's also possible to bus in from Tokyo straight to the Fuji Subaru Line Fifth Station on the mountain during the official climbing season. Coming from western Japan (Kyoto, Osaka), you can take an overnight bus to Kawaguchi-ko.

Sleeping

If you're not overnighting in a mountain hut, Fuji-Yoshida and Kawaguchi-ko make good bases. Upscale options in Kawaguchi-ko have onsen, often with Fuji-views. Hostels here are good for meeting other hikers and picking up climbing info. Campgrounds and small inns dot the perimeters of the other lakes.

Sunrise from Mt Fuji's summit

NONCHANON / SHUTTERSTOCK ©

Mt Fuji

Catching a glimpse of Mt Fuji (富士山; 3776m), Japan's highest and most famous peak, will take your breath away. Climbing it and watching the sunrise from the summit is one of Japan's superlative experiences (though it's often cloudy).

Great For...

☑ Don't Miss

Watching the sunrise from the summit is a profound, once-in-a-lifetime experience.

Climbing Mt Fuji

The mountain is divided into 10 'stations' from base (First Station) to summit (Tenth), but most hikers start from one of the four Fifth Stations. The vast majority of visitors hike the **Kawaguchi-ko Trail** from the **Fuji Subaru Line Fifth Station** (aka Kawaguchi-ko Fifth Station), as it has the most modern facilities and it's easy to reach from Tokyo. From here, allow five to six hours to reach the top (though some climb it in half the time) and about three hours to descend, plus 1½ hours for circling the crater at the top. Descending the mountain is much harder on the knees than ascending; hiking poles will help.

The less trodden, but more scenic, forested **Subashiri Trail** is a good alternative; it merges with the Kawaguchi-ko Trail at the Eighth Station. Other Fifth Stations

SOPON SETH / SHUTTERSTOCK ©

Fuji Subaru Line Fifth Station

Taishikan Fujisan Hotel

Mt Fuji

Fuji-Hakone-Izu National Park

Subashiri Fifth Station

Gotemba Fifth Station

Fujinomiya Fifth Station Hōei-san (2693m)

ⓘ Need to Know

The official climbing season runs from 1 July to 31 August.

✕ Take a Break

Mountain huts offer hikers simple hot meals in addition to a place to sleep. Most huts allow you to rest inside as long as you order something.

★ Top Tip

Check summit weather conditions before planning a climb at www. snow-forecast.com/resorts/ Mount-Fuji/6day/top.

are **Fujinomiya**, which is best for climbers coming from the west (Nagoya, Kyoto and beyond) and the seldom-used and neglected **Gotemba Trail**, a tough 7½-hour climb to the summit.

Fuji Subaru Line Fifth Station

During the climbing season, Keiō Dentetsu Bus runs direct buses (¥2700, 2½ hours; reservations necessary) from the Shinjuku Bus Station to Fuji Subaru Line Fifth Station. Buses also run from both Kawaguchi-ko Station and Fujisan Station to the Fuji Subaru Line Fifth Station (one way/return ¥1540/2100, one hour) from roughly mid-April to early December; in the trekking season, buses depart hourly from around 6.30am until 7pm (ideal for climbers intending to make an overnight ascent). Returning from Fifth Station, buses head

back to town from 8am to 8.30pm. Even when summiting is off-limits, so long as the road isn't snowed under, it's possible to take the bus to the Fifth Station, just to stand in awesome proximity to the snow-capped peak.

Know Before You Go

Make no mistake: Mt Fuji is a serious mountain, high enough for altitude sickness, and on the summit it can go from sunny and warm to wet, windy and cold remarkably quickly. Even if conditions are fine, you can count on it being close to freezing in the morning, even in summer. Also be aware that visibility can rapidly disappear with a blanket of mist rolling in suddenly. To avoid altitude sickness, be sure to take it slowly and take regular breaks. If you're suffering severe symptoms, you'll need to make an immediate descent. At a minimum, bring clothing appropriate for cold and wet weather, including a hat and gloves. Also bring at least 2L of water (you can buy more on the mountain during the climbing season) and cash for other necessities (like toilets; ¥200); if you're climbing at night, bring a torch (flashlight) or headlamp, and spare batteries.

When To Climb

To time your arrival for dawn you can either start up in the afternoon, stay overnight in a mountain hut and continue early in the morning, or climb the whole way at night. You do not want to arrive on the top too long before dawn, as it will be very cold and windy, even at the height of summer. It's a very busy mountain during the two-month climbing season. To avoid the worst of the crush, head up on a weekday, or start earlier during the day.

Authorities strongly caution against climbing outside the regular season, when the weather is highly unpredictable and first-aid stations on the mountain are closed. Once snow or ice is on the mountain, Fuji becomes a very serious and dangerous undertaking and should only be attempted by those with winter mountaineering equipment and plenty of experience. Do not climb alone; a guide will be invaluable.

Mountain Huts

Conditions in mountain huts are spartan (a blanket on the floor sandwiched between other climbers), but reservations are recommended and are essential on weekends. It's also important to let huts know if you decide to cancel at the last minute; be prepared to pay to cover the cost of your no show. These two at the Eighth Station usually have English-speaking staff:

Fuji Subaru Line Fifth Station (p170)

Taishikan (太子館; Map p175; ☎0555-22-1947; www.mfi.or.jp/w3/home0/taisikan; per person incl 2 meals from ¥8500) Vegetarian or halal meals possible with advance request.

Fujisan Hotel (富士山ホテル; Map p175; ☎0555-22-0237; www.fujisanhotel.com; per person from ¥5950, incl 2 meals ¥8350) One of the largest and most popular huts.

Resources

Climbing Mt Fuji (www17.plala.or.jp/climb_fujiyama) and the Official Web Site for Mt Fuji Climbing (www.fujisan-climb.jp) are good online resources. The *Climbing Mt Fuji* brochure and maps for other area hikes are available at the Kawaguchi-ko Tourist Information Center.

Tours

There are several reliable companies offering private tours with English-speaking guides.

Discover Japan Tours (www.discover-japan-tours.com/en; 2-day Mt Fuji tours per person ¥10,000) Reputable company offering guided tours from Tokyo for groups of two or more, and specialising in less-frequented routes.

Fuji Mountain Guides (☎042-445-0798; www.fujimountainguides.com; 2-day Mt Fuji tours per person ¥44,000) Aimed at foreign visitors, these excellent tours are run both in and out of season by highly experienced and very professional American bilingual guides.

Fuji-Spotting

Mt Fuji has many different personalities depending on the season. Winter and spring months are your best bet for seeing it in all its clichéd glory; however, even during these times the snowcapped peak may be visible only in the morning before it retreats behind its cloud curtain. Its elusiveness, however, is part of the appeal, making sightings all the more special. Here are some of our top spots for viewing around Fuji Five Lakes:

Kawaguchi-ko On the north side of the lake, where Fuji looms large over its shimmering reflection.

Motosu-ko The famous view depicted on the ¥1000 bill can be seen from the northwest side of the lake.

Panorama-dai The end of this hiking trail (p177), which starts near Motosu-ko, rewards you with a magnificent front-on view of the mountain.

Kōyō-dai Mt Fuji can be seen from this lookout (Map p175) on the western edge of Sai-ko, particularly stunning in the autumn colours.

★ Did you know?

The Japanese have a proverb 'He who climbs Mt Fuji once is a wise man, he who climbs it twice is a fool'.

Kawaguchi-ko

⊙ SIGHTS

Kubota Itchiku Art Museum   Museum
(久保田一竹美術館; Map p175; ☎0555-76-8811; www.itchiku-museum.com; 2255 Kawaguchi; adult/child ¥1300/400; ⊗9.30am-5.30pm Wed-Mon Apr-Nov, 10am-4.30pm Wed-Mon Dec-Mar) In an attractive Gaudí-influenced building, this excellent museum exhibits the kimono art of Kubota Itchiku (1917–2003). A small number of lavishly dyed kimonos from his life's work of continuous landscapes are displayed at any one time, in a grand hall of cypress. You might see Mt Fuji in the wintertime, or the cherry blossoms of spring spread across oversized kimonos that have been painstakingly and intricately dyed, embroidered and hand-painted. Take the bus to the Kubota Itchiku Bijyutsukan-mae stop.

Ide Sake Brewery   Brewery
(Map p175; ☎0555-72-0006; www.kainokaiun.jp; 8 Funatsu; tours ¥500) Using the spring waters from Mt Fuji, this small-scale sake brewery has been producing Japan's favourite tipple for 21 generations. Tours (9.30am and 3pm; around 40 minutes) provide a fascinating insight into the production process and include tastings of various sakes with a souvenir glass. Tours can be given in English, but reservations are essential.

Fujisan World Heritage Center   Museum
(富士ビジターセンター; Map p175; ☎72-0259; www.fujisan-whc.jp; 6663-1 Funatsu; adult/child ¥420/free; ⊗8.30am-5pm, to 6pm or 7pm in peak season) Get up to speed on Mt Fuji at the new South Hall of this visitor centre. Its circular, beautifully designed exhibition hall features interpretive displays detailing the spiritual and geological history of the mountain (most accompanied by excellent English-language translations). Upstairs, you can view a gorgeously shot, eight-minute video (with sparse English subtitles), complete with mood lighting from the fabric Fuji suspended across the exhibition hall. An observation deck at the North Hall (free) affords great views of Mt Fuji.

Fuji Viewing Platform   Viewpoint
(Map p175) If you're a Fuji admirer but not a hiker, consider this viewing platform. Weather permitting, your ride up the **Kachi Kachi Yama Ropeway** (カチカチ山ロープウェイ; Map p175; www.kachikachiyama-ropeway.com; 1163-1 Azagawa; one way/return adult ¥450/800, child ¥230/400; ⊗9am-5pm) will reward you with dramatic views from the platform at the top (1104m).

⊗ EATING & DRINKING

Hōtō Fudō   Noodles ¥¥
(ほうとう不動; Map p175; ☎0555-72-8511; www.houtou-fudou.jp; 707 Kawaguchi; hōtō ¥1080; ⊗11am-7pm) Hōtō are Kawaguchi-ko's noodles, hand-cut and served in a miso stew with pumpkin, sweet potato and other vegetables. It's a hearty meal best sampled at this chain with five branches around town. This is the most architecturally interesting, an igloo-like building in which you can also sample basashi – horsemeat sashimi (¥1080).

Idaten   Tempura ¥¥
(いだ天; Map p175; ☎0555-73-9218; 3486-4 Funatsu; meals from ¥800; ⊗11am-10pm) Load up on some delicious, deep-fried goodness pre- or post-hike at the Idaten counter, where you can watch the chefs prepare your tempura to order. Aside from Fujisan-themed lunch and dinner sets, you can also order à la carte (various vegetables are ¥90 to ¥180 a piece; a crab leg is ¥1000).

Sanrokuen   Japanese ¥¥
(山麓園; Map p175; ☎0555-73-1000; 3370-1 Funatsu; set meals ¥2100-4200; ⊗11am-7.30pm Fri-Wed) Diners sit on the floor around traditional irori charcoal pits grilling their meals – skewers of fish, meat, tofu and veggies. From Kawaguchi-ko Station, turn left, then left again after the 7-Eleven and after 600m you'll see the thatched roof on the right.

Zero Station   Bar
(Map p175; ☎0555-72-9525; 6713-120 Funatsu; ⊗6pm-midnight) This small bar is a good spot to meet fellow travellers.

ⓘ INFORMATION

Kawaguchi-ko Tourist Information Center
(Map p175; ☎0555-72-6700; ⊗8.30am-5.30pm Sun-Fri, to 7pm Sat), to the right as you

Mt Fuji Area

Mt Fuji Area

◉ Sights
1 Fuji Sengen-jinja	B3
2 Fuji Viewing Platform	A2
3 Fujisan World Heritage Center	A3
4 Ide Sake Brewery	A2
5 Kōyō-dai	B2
6 Kubota Itchiku Art Museum	C1
7 Togawa-ke Oshi-no-ie Restored Pilgrim's Inn	B3

✪ Activities, Courses & Tours
8 Benifuji-no-yu	D2
9 Fuji-Q Highland	A3
10 Kachi Kachi Yama Ropeway	A2
11 Kōan Motosu	A2
12 Panorama-dai	A2

✗ Eating
13 Hōtō Fudō	A3
14 Idaten	A2
15 Sanrokuen	A3

◉ Drinking & Nightlife
16 Zero Station	A2

ℹ Information
17 Fuji-Yoshida Tourist Information Center	B3
18 Kawaguchi-ko Tourist Information Center	A3

ℹ Transport
19 Sazanami	A2

exit Kawaguchi-ko Station, has English speakers as well as maps and brochures; ask about local hikes.

ℹ GETTING THERE & AWAY

JR Chūō line trains go from Shinjuku to Ōtsuki (*tokkyū* ¥2770, one hour; *futsū* ¥1320, 1½ hours), where you transfer to the Fuji Kyūkō line for Kawaguchi-ko (¥1140, one hour and five minutes).

Buses run year-round to Kawaguchi-ko (¥1750, 1¾ hours) from the Shinjuku Bus Terminal in Tokyo. Coming from western Japan, the overnight bus departs from Osaka's Higashi-Umeda Subway Station (¥8700, 10.15pm) via Kyoto Station (¥8200, 11.18pm) to Kawaguchi-ko Station (arrives 8.32am).

Beyond Kawaguchi-ko

Kawaguchi-ko is the most popular lake, but the others have their charms. **Sai-ko** (紅葉台) is a quiet lake area that's good for hiking, fishing and boating. Mt Fuji is mostly obstructed but there are great views from the Kōyō-dai lookout, near the main road, and from the western end of the lake. On the south side of the lake there are several interesting lava caves to explore. Further west from Sai-ko, low-key and tiny **Shōji-ko** (精進湖) is said to be the prettiest of the Fuji lakes and offers Mt Fuji views, fishing and boating. Further west still, **Motosu-ko** is the deepest and has excellent Fuji views.

The region's largest lake, **Yamanaka-ko** (山中湖村), is popular with locals. The southern shore is overdeveloped and has a tourist-trap feel but the northern side is more appealing and has a sleepier vibe. One reason to visit here is **Benifuji-no-yu** (山中湖温泉紅富士の湯; Map p175; ☎0555-20-2700; www.benifuji.co.jp; adult/child ¥800/300, face/bath towel rental ¥220/100; ⊕10am-9pm), an admittedly somewhat faded onsen that has dramatic views of Mt Fuji from the outdoor stone and *hinoki* (cypress) baths.

A car is the best way to get around these parts, as buses can be infrequent.

Canoes at Shōji-ko.
STRUCTURESxx / SHUTTERSTOCK ©

🛈 GETTING AROUND

A rental car is best for getting around; there are a couple of agencies in front of Kawaguchi-ko Station. There is also the **Kawaguchiko-Saiko Sightseeing Bus** (two-day passes adult/child

¥1200/600), which has hop-on hop-off service from Kawaguchi-ko Station to all of the sightseeing spots around the western lakes.

Sazanami (さざなみ; Map p175; ☎0555-72-0041; ⊕7am-5pm summer, 9am-5pm winter), on Kawaguchi-ko's southeast shore, rents regular bicycles (¥400/1500 per hour/day), electric pedal-assisted bicycles (¥600/2600) and rowing boats (¥1000/2500).

Fuji-Yoshida

◉ SIGHTS & ACTIVITIES

Fuji Sengen-jinja   Shinto Shrine

(富士浅間神社; Map p175; ☎0555-22-0221; http://sengenjinja.jp; 5558 Kami-Yoshida, Fuji-Yoshida; ⊕grounds 24hr, staffed 9am-5pm) **FREE**
A necessary preliminary to the Mt Fuji ascent is a visit to this wooded, atmospheric temple, which has been here since the 8th century. Notable points include a 1000-year-old cedar; its main gate, which is rebuilt every 60 years (larger each time); and its two 1-tonne *mikoshi* (portable shrines) used in the annual festival **Yoshida no Himatsuri** (Yoshida Fire Festival; ⊕26-27 Aug). From Fujisan Station it's a 20-minute uphill walk, or take a bus to Sengen-jinja-mae (¥150, five minutes).

Togawa-ke Oshi-no-ie Restored Pilgrim's Inn   Historic Building

(御師旧外川家住宅; Map p175; 3-14-8 Kami-Yoshida; adult/child ¥100/50; ⊕9.30am-4.30pm Wed-Mon) *Oshi-no-ie* (pilgrims' inns) have served visitors since the days when climbing Mt Fuji was a pilgrimage. Very few still function as inns but Togawa-ke Oshi-no-ie offers some insight into the fascinating Edo-era practice of Mt Fuji worship.

Fuji-Q Highland   Amusement Park

(Map p175; www.fujiq.jp/en; 5-6-1 Shin-Nishihara; admission only adult/child ¥1500/900, day passes ¥5700/4300; ⊕9am-5pm Mon-Fri, to 8pm Sat & Sun) As well as a high-octane amusement park with spectacular roller coasters providing a memorable way to bag Fuji views, Fuji-Q's compound is home to Thomas Land (a theme park based on Thomas the Tank Engine), a resort hotel,

Fuji-Q Highland (p176)

onsen and shops. Fun for all the family, one stop west of Fujisan Station.

EATING & DRINKING

Fuji-Yoshida is known for its *te-uchi udon* (handmade wheat-flour noodles); some 60 shops sell them! The Tourist Information Center has a map and a list of restaurants.

INFORMATION

The staff at **Fuji-Yoshida Tourist Information Center** (Map p175; ☑0555-22-7000; ⏰9am-5pm) next to Fujisan train station can provide climbing info, and brochures and maps of the area.

GETTING THERE & AROUND

JR Chūō line trains go from Shinjuku to Ōtsuki (*tokkyū* ¥2770, one hour; *futsū* ¥1320, 1½ hours), where you transfer to the Fuji Kyūkō line for Fujisan (the station for Fuji-Yoshida; ¥1020, one hour). Buses run year-round to Fujisan Station in Fuji-Yoshida (¥1750, 1¾ hours) from the Shinjuku Bus Terminal in Tokyo. From Fujisan Station it's an eight-minute bus ride (¥240) or a five-minute train ride (¥220) to Kawaguchi-ko Station.

Motosu-ko

ACTIVITIES

Panorama-dai   Hiking

(パノラマ台; Map p175) This trail ends in a spectacular view of Mt Fuji and panoramic views of the surrounding lakes and mountains. Midway through, stop at the signed viewpoint to spot Fuji-san between the trees. It's a one-hour hike through the woods from the trailhead, which starts at the Panorama-dai-shita bus stop. Take a blue-line bus (38 minutes from Kawaguchi-ko).

Kōan Motosu   Water Sports

(Map p175; ☑0556-38-0117; www6.nns.ne.jp/~kouan; 2926 Nakanokura; ⏰8am-4pm) Kōan Motosu offers paddleboarding (¥1500/4000 per hour/day), kayaking (¥2000 per person, one hour) and even scuba diving in the lake.

GETTING THERE & AWAY

If you don't have a car, blue-line buses from Kawaguchi-ko Station go as far as the east shore of Motosu-ko before heading back to the station.

HIROSHIMA

Hiroshima

To most people, Hiroshima (広島) means just one thing. The city's name will forever evoke thoughts of 6 August 1945, when Hiroshima became the target of the world's first atomic-bomb attack. Peace Memorial Park is a constant reminder of that day, and it attracts visitors from all over the world with its moving message of peace. Present-day Hiroshima, meanwhile, is far from a depressing place; with its wide, tree-lined boulevards, laid-back friendliness and vibrant eating and drinking scene, the city is an attractive destination in its own right. It's also the jumping-off point for visits to Miyajima, an island in Hiroshima Bay with a captivating seaside shrine.

Hiroshima in One Day

It is possible to do Hiroshima in a day. Spend the morning at the Peace Memorial Park sights and then, after lunch, make your way to Miyajima – sunset is a pretty time to be here. Keep in mind though, that the Peace Memorial Museum will be upsetting to many; you may not want to rush off to the next attraction.

Hiroshima in Two Days

With two days, you can give a full day each to Hiroshima and Miyajima. In Hiroshima, be sure to spend time sampling the city's local specialities, which include *Hiroshima-yaki* (a kind of savoury pancake) and sake. With a whole day for Miyajima you're guaranteed to catch the island's floating *torii* gate at high tide, and have time to spare to ascend Misen for views over Hiroshima Bay.

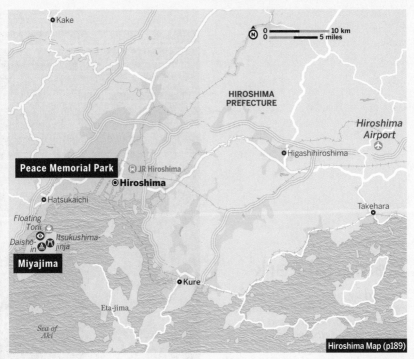

Peace Memorial Park

Miyajima

Hiroshima Map (p189)

Caption

Arriving in Hiroshima

Hiroshima is in western Honshu, on the coast of the Seto Inland Sea. Most travellers arrive via *shinkansen* (bullet train), as part of the classic itinerary that runs westward from Tokyo via Kyoto and Osaka. Hiroshima's *shinkansen* station is conveniently located near downtown. You can also fly from major cities around Japan to Hiroshima Airport, 40km east of the city.

Sleeping

Hiroshima's accommodation is clustered around the station, near Peace Memorial Park, and along the main thoroughfares of Aioi-dōri and Heiwa-Ōdōri (lots of bars and restaurants are here), but the city is compact enough that wherever you base yourself you're never more than a short walk or tram ride away from the main sights. For an atmospheric alternative, spend a night in a ryokan (traditional inn) on Miyajima.

Peace Memorial Park

Hugged by rivers on both sides, Peace Memorial Park is a large, leafy space criss-crossed by walkways and dotted with memorials – many of them designed by Japan's pre-eminent modern architect Tange Kenzō – to the victims of the 1945 atomic bomb. While not an easy place to visit, emotionally-speaking, it is a must-see when visiting Hiroshima.

Genbaku-dōmu-mae (A-Bomb Dome)
Atomic Bomb Dome
Aioi-dōri
Kamiya-chō-nishi

Children's Peace Monument
Flame of Peace

Cenotaph
Peace Memorial Park (Heiwa-kōen)
Hon-dōri
Hiroshima Peace Memorial Museum

Great For...

❶ Need to Know

平和記念公園; Map p189; Heiwa-kinen-kōen; Genbaku-dōmu-mae

★ **Top Tip**

Return to the Atomic Dome at night. It's particularly evocative when it's quiet and the propped-up ruins are floodlit.

The Bombing of Hiroshima

On 6 August 1945, the US B-29 bomber *Enola Gay* released the 'Little Boy' atomic bomb over Hiroshima. The 2000°C (3630°F) blast obliterated 90% of the city and instantly killed 80,000 people. The bomb exploded over the centre of Hiroshima, which was filled with wooden homes and shops. This created intense firestorms that raced through the city for three days and destroyed 92% of the structures, fuelled by broken gas pipes and electrical lines. Toxic black rain fell 30 minutes after the blast, carrying 200 different types of radioactive isotopes, contaminating the thirsty wounded who drank it.

Around 350,000 people were present that day. In the following months, 130,000 more died of radiation exposure and other secondary effects, including intensive burns. Most casualties were civilians, including firefighters and 90% of the city's doctors who came to help; 20,000 forced Korean labourers; and 6000 junior-high-school students who had been working in the city clearing fire breaks in anticipation of a regular attack.

The Japanese government says there were around 187,000 atomic bomb survivors still alive in 2015, many living through the mental trauma, cancers, and other effects of radiation. (No residual radiation remains today.) *Hiroshima* (1946), the book of the article (available on newyorker.com) by Pulitzer Prize–winning writer John Hersey, tells the story of six survivors.

Atomic Bomb Dome

The starkest reminder of the destruction visited upon Hiroshima in WWII is the **Atomic Bomb Dome** (原爆ドーム, Genbaku

Children's Peace Monument

Dome; Map p189; 🚋Genbaku-dōmu-mae)
FREE. Built by a Czech architect in 1915, it
was the Industrial Promotion Hall until the
bomb exploded almost directly above it.
Everyone inside was killed, but the building
was one of very few left standing near the
epicentre. A decision was taken after the
war to preserve the shell as a memorial.

Hiroshima Peace Memorial Museum

The main building, **Hiroshima Peace
Memorial Museum** (広島平和記念資料
館; Map p189; www.pcf.city.hiroshima.jp; 1-2

> ☑ **Don't Miss**
>
> **The Flame of Peace** (平和の灯; Map
> p189), on the pond. It will be ex-
> tinguished only once every nuclear
> weapon on earth has been destroyed.

Nakajima-chō, Naka-ku; adult/child ¥200/free;
⏱8.30am-7pm Aug, to 6pm Mar-Jul & Sep-Nov, to
5pm Dec-Feb; 🚋Genbaku-dōmu-mae or Chūden-
mae), houses a collection of items salvaged
from the aftermath of the atomic bomb.
The displays are confronting and personal – ragged clothes, a child's melted lunch
box, a watch stopped at 8.15am – and there
are some grim photographs. The east building presents a history of Hiroshima and of
the development and destructive power of
nuclear weapons.

The main building is undergoing major
renovations and is closed until summer
2018. During its closure, some items from
the main building will be on display in the
east building. Check the website for the
latest developments as there have been
delays.

Children's Peace Monument

The **Children's Peace Monument** (Map
p189) **FREE** was inspired by Sadako Sasaki,
who was just two years old at the time of
the atomic bomb. At age 11 she developed
leukaemia, and decided to fold 1000 paper
cranes. In Japan, the crane is a symbol of
longevity and happiness, and she believed
if she folded 1000 she would recover. Sadly
she died before reaching her goal, but her
classmates folded the rest. Surrounding
the monument are strings of thousands of
colourful paper cranes sent here by school
children from around the country and all
over the world.

Cenotaph

The curved concrete **cenotaph** (原爆死没
者慰霊碑; Map p189) houses a list of the
names of all the known victims of the atomic
bomb. It stands at one end of the pond at
the centre of the park, framing the Flame of
Peace.

> ✕ **Take a Break**
>
> There are lots of benches in the park, in-
> cluding some along the riverside looking
> across to the Atomic Bomb Dome.

FLIPHOTO / SHUTTERSTOCK ©

Itsukushima-jinja's floating *torii*

KORKUSUNG / GETTY IMAGES ©

Day Trip to Miyajima

The small island of Miyajima (宮島) is one of Japan's most visited tourist spots. Its star attraction is the oft-photographed vermilion torii (shrine gate) of Itsukushima-jinja, which seems to float on the waves at high tide.

Great For...

☑ **Don't Miss**

The *torii* gate is at its evocative best at sunset, or when lit up after dark.

Floating Torii

This 16m-tall **floating torii** (大鳥居; Map p181) is a symbol of Miyajima, standing out in the bay and serving as the watery entrance to World Heritage–listed Itsukushima-jinja. There has been a *torii* at this site since 1168, with the current gate dating from the late 1800s.

Itsukushima-jinja

Itsukushima-jinja (厳島神社; Map p181; 1-1 Miyajima-chō; ¥300; ☺6.30am-6pm Jan-Nov, to 5pm Dec) traces its origins as far back as the late 6th century. The shrine's present form dates from 1168, when it was rebuilt under the patronage of Taira no Kiyomori, head of the doomed Heike clan.

Its pier-like construction is a result of the island's sacred status: commoners were not allowed to set foot on the island and had

Statues of Buddhist disciples line the pathways at Daishō-in

MILOSZ MASLANKA / SHUTTERSTOCK ©

Hiroshima-wan

Floating Torii ◎

Itsukushima-jinja 🏯

Miyajima Ropeway
Momiji-dani Station ◉

Daishō-in ♨

❶ Need to Know

Miyajima is less than an hour away
from Hiroshima and is accessible via a
combination of train and ferry; for more
details see p191.

✖ Take a Break

Stalls along Omote-sandō, one block
back from the waterfront, serve grilled
local oysters and other snacks.

★ Top Tip

Much of the time, the shrine and
torii are surrounded by mud: to get
the classic view of the 'floating' *torii*,
come at high tide.

to approach by boat through the *torii* in the
bay. On one side of the shrine is a floating
stage for *nō* (stylised dance-drama), built by
local lord Asano Tsunanaga in 1680 and still
used for *nō* performances every year from
16 to 18 April as part of the Toka-sai Festival.

Misen

Covered with primeval forest, the sacred,
peaceful Misen is Miyajima's highest mountain (530m), and its ascent is the island's
finest walk. You can avoid most of the uphill
climb by taking the two-stage **ropeway** (弥
山; www.miyajima-ropeway.info; ropeway one-way/
return adult ¥1000/1800, child ¥500/900; ⊗rope-
way 9am-5pm) with its giddying sea views,
which leaves you with a 30-minute walk to
the top. At the summit observatory, you
can kick off your shoes and laze on wooden
platforms while enjoying 360-degree views.

The descent takes a little over an hour, or you
can take the ropeway back down.

Close to the summit is a temple where
Kōbō Daishi meditated for 100 days
following his return from China in the 9th
century. Next to the main temple hall is
a flame that's been burning continually
since Kōbō Daishi lit it 1200 years ago.
From the temple, a path leads down the
hillside to **Daishō-in** (大聖院; Map p181; 210
Miyajima-chō; ⊗8am-5pm) **FREE**. The Shingon
temple is crowded with Buddhist images,
prayer wheels and sharp-beaked *tengu*
(bird-like demons) and a cave containing
images from each of the 88 Shikoku pilgrimage temples. The path continues down
to Itsukushima-jinja.

The ropeway station (Momiji-dani
Station) is about a 10-minute walk on from
Momiji-dani-kōen, or a few minutes on
the free shuttle bus, which runs every 20
minutes from a stop near Iwasō Ryokan.

⊙ SIGHTS

Shukkei-en   Gardens

(縮景園; Map p189; 2-11 Kami-nobori-chō, Naka-ku; ¥260; ⊙9am-6pm Apr-Sep, to 5pm Oct-Mar; ⋒Shukkei-en-mae) Modelled after West Lake in Hangzhou, China, Shukkei-en was built in 1620 for *daimyō* (domain lord) Asano Nagaakira. The garden's name means 'contracted view', and it attempts to recreate grand vistas in miniature. Pathways lead through a series of 'landscapes' and views around an island-dotted pond.

✖ EATING & DRINKING

Hiroshima's main entertainment district is made up of hundreds of bars, restaurants and karaoke joints crowding the lanes between Aioi-dōri and Heiwa-Ōdōri in the city centre.

Okonomi-mura   Okonomiyaki ¥

(お好み村; Map p189; www.okonomimura.jp; 2nd-4th fl, 5-13 Shintenchi; dishes ¥800-1300; ⊙11am-2am; ⋒Ebisu-chō) This Hiroshima institution is a touristy but fun place to get acquainted with *okonomiyaki* (savoury pancakes) and chat with the cooks over a hot griddle. There are 25 stalls spread over three floors, each serving up hearty variations of the local speciality. Pick a floor and find an empty stool at whichever counter takes your fancy.

Hassei   Okonomiyaki ¥

(八誠; Map p189; ☎082-242-8123; 4-17 Fujimi-chō; dishes ¥600-1300; ⊙11.30am-2pm & 5.30-11pm Tue-Sat, 5.30-11pm Sun; ⋒Chūden-mae) The walls of this popular *okonomiyaki* specialist are covered with the signatures and messages of famous and not-so-famous satisfied customers. The tasty, generous servings are indeed satisfying – a half-order is probably more than enough at lunchtime.

Tōshō   Tofu ¥¥

(豆匠; Map p189; ☎082-506-1028; www.toufu-tosho.jp; 6-24 Hijiyama-chō; sets ¥1620-3240; ⊙11am-3pm & 5-10pm Mon-Sat, to 9pm Sun; ✐; ⋒Danbara-1-chōme) In a traditional wooden building overlooking a large garden with a pond and waterfall, Tōshō specialises

Preparing *Hiroshima-yaki* (Hiroshima-style savoury pancakes)

CHRISTIAN KOBER / GETTY IMAGES ©

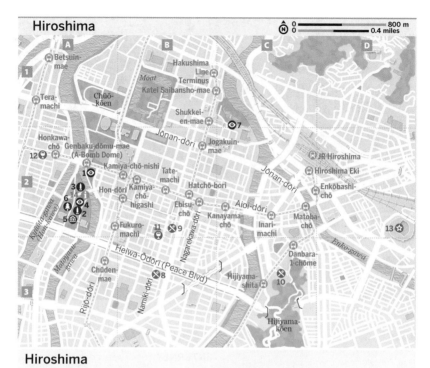

Hiroshima

⊙ Sights

1 Atomic Bomb Dome	A2
2 Cenotaph	A2
3 Children's Peace Monument	A2
4 Flame of Peace	A2
5 Hiroshima Peace Memorial Museum	A2
6 Peace Memorial Park	A2
7 Shukkei-en	C1
9 Okonomi-mura	B2
10 Tōshō	C3

⊗ Eating

8 Hassei	B3

🍷 Drinking & Nightlife

11 Koba	B2
12 Organza	A2

🎭 Entertainment

13 Mazda Zoom Zoom Stadium	D2

ℹ️ Information

14 Hiroshima Rest House	A2

in homemade tofu, served in a variety of tasty and beautifully presented forms by kimono-clad staff. Even the sweets are tofu based. There is a range of set courses, with some pictures and basic English on the menu. Vegetarians can be accommodated.

Organza   Bar

(ヲルガン座; Map p189; ☎082-295-1553; www.organ-za.com; 2nd fl, Morimoto Bldg, Tōka-ichi-machi; ⊗5.30pm-2am Tue-Fri, 11.30am-2am Sat, 11.30am-midnight Sun; 🚃Honkawa-chō) Bookshelves, old-fashioned furniture, a piano and a stuffed deer head all add to the busy surrounds at this smoky lounge-bar. Organza hosts an eclectic schedule of live events (from acoustic guitar to cabaret), some with a cover charge, and food is also served. Lunch on weekends only.

Shukkei-en (p188)

Koba
Bar

(コバ; Map p189; ☎082-249-6556; 3rd fl Rego Bldg, 1-4 Naka-machi; ☺6pm-2am Thu-Tue; 🚋Ebisu-chō) It's bound to be a good night if you drop into this laid-back place, where the friendly metal-loving musician owner 'Bom-san' can be found serving drinks and cooking up small tasty meals. There is occasional live music.

> It's bound to be a good night if you drop into this laid-back place

🟢 ENTERTAINMENT

Mazda Zoom Zoom Stadium
Stadium

(Hiroshima Municipal Stadium; Map p189; 2-3-1 Minami-Kaniya) This stadium in Hiroshima is a good place to catch a baseball game and see the beloved local team, the Carp. It's a short walk southeast of the Hiroshima Station – follow the signs and the red-marked pathways.

ℹ️ INFORMATION

INTERNET

Hiroshima has a free (sometimes patchy) wi-fi service accessible in a number of spots around the city, including at the Peace Park; look for 'Hiroshima Free Wi-fi' to connect.

TOURIST INFORMATION

Check out the Hiroshima Navigator website (www.hcvb.city.hiroshima.jp) for tourism and practical information and downloadable audio guides to the sights. *Get Hiroshima* (www. gethiroshima.com), an expat-run website and magazine, has an events calendar.

Hiroshima Rest House (広島市平和記念公園レストハウス; Map p189; ☎082-247-6738; www.mk-kousan.co.jp/rest-house; 1-1 Nakajima-machi; ☺8.30am-7pm Aug, to 6pm Mar-Jul & Sep-Nov, to 5pm Dec-Feb; 🚋Genba-ku-dōmu-mae) is in Peace Memorial Park next to Motoyasu-bashi bridge, with comprehensive information and English-speaking staff.

A **Tourist Information Office** (観光案内所; Map p189; ☎082-261-1877; ☺9am-5.30pm) is inside the station near the south exit, with

ALARICO / SHUTTERSTOCK ©

English-speaking staff. There is another branch at the **north (shinkansen) exit** (Map p189; ☑082-263-6822; ⊙9am-5.30pm).

ℹ GETTING THERE & AWAY

Hiroshima is a stop on the San-yō Shinkansen from Osaka (¥10,440, 1½ hours); some Tokaidō Shinkansen trains from Tokyo (¥19,080, four hours) via Kyoto continue as far as Hiroshima; otherwise you may need to change trains at Osaka or Okayama en route.

If you're flying into **Hiroshima Airport** (☑082-231-5171; www.hij.airport.jp), you can catch a bus to Hiroshima Station (¥1340, 45 minutes, every 15 to 30 minutes).

ℹ GETTING AROUND

Hiroshima's city centre, Peace Memorial Park, tram terminus and most sights are on the south side of the train station. The *shinkansen* entrance is on the north side of the station; this is also where you board the **Hiroshima Sightseeing Loop Bus** (www.chugoku-jrbus.co.jp; single/day pass ¥200/400). An underground passageway links the two sides of the station.

The tram (¥160) is a convenient way to get around. The three-day **Visit Hiroshima Tourist Pass** (Small Area) is a good deal at ¥1000, covering tram rides, the sightseeing loop bus and Miyajima ferry. Buy passes from the tram terminal or at various hotels and hostels.

TO/FROM MIYAJIMA

JR San-yō line trains run west from Hiroshima to Miyajima-guchi (¥410, 30 minutes). Tram 2

⊙ Hiroshima-yaki

Hiroshima is famous for *okonomiyaki* (savoury pancakes; batter and cabbage, with vegetables and seafood or meat cooked on a griddle). The local version, *Hiroshima-yaki,* comes topped with noodles and a fried egg. The fillings are layered on, rather than mixed, a delicate process that is almost always done by a pro behind the counter.

VICHIE81 / SHUTTERSTOCK ©

(¥260, 70 minutes), which runs from Hiroshima Station via the Atomic Bomb Dome, also runs there. The **ferry terminal** (Map p181) is a brief walk from Miyajima-guchi Station. Ferries (¥180, 10 minutes) operated by two companies shuttle regularly across to the island. JR Pass holders can travel on the JR ferry for free.

The **Aqua Net ferry** (Map p189; ☑082-240-5955; www.aqua-net-h.co.jp/en) travels directly from Peace Memorial Park (one way/return ¥2000/3600, 45 minutes, 10 to 15 daily) to Miyajima. No reservation is required.

Osaka

If Kyoto was the city of the courtly nobility and Tokyo the city of the samurai, then Osaka (大阪) was the city of the merchant class. Japan's third-largest city is a place where things have always moved a bit faster, where people are a bit brasher and interactions are peppered with playful jabs – and locals take pride in this. Osaka is not a pretty city in the conventional sense – though it does have a lovely river cutting through the centre – but it packs more colour than most. The acres of concrete are cloaked in dazzling neon; shopfronts are vivid, unabashed cries for attention.

Osaka in Two Days

Start your first morning with a visit to Osaka-jō then spend the afternoon exploring Osaka's Minami shopping and dining district. Come dusk, join the nightly throngs in neon-lit Dōtombori. On day two, take a day trip to the castle, Himeji-jō, and cap it off with a visit to the Umeda Sky Building for views over the city.

Osaka in Four Days

On day three, take a cycling tour of the city with Cycle Osaka (we love the food route). In the late afternoon, rest your weary legs at Spa World and then go for *kushikatsu* (deep fried skewers) in Shin-Sekai. Spend your last morning at the National Museum of Ethnology or at the bay-front Osaka Aquarium Kaiyūkan, then catch a bunraku (puppet theatre) performance.

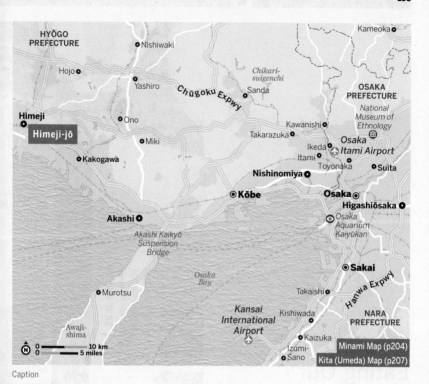

HYŌGO
PREFECTURE

Nishiwaki

Hojo

Yashiro

Chūgoku Expwy

*Chikari-
suigenchi*

Sanda

Kameoka

OSAKA
PREFECTURE

*National
Museum of
Ethnology*

Himeji

Ono

Himeji-jō

Miki

Kakogawa

Takarazuka

Kawanishi

Ikeda
Itami

Osaka
Itami Airport

Toyonaka

Suita

Nishinomiya

Osaka

◉ **Kōbe**

Osaka ◉

Higashiōsaka

Akashi ○

*Osaka
Aquarium
Kaiyūkan*

*Akashi Kaikyō
Suspension
Bridge*

◉ **Sakai**

Hanwa Expwy

*Osaka
Bay*

Takaishi

Murotsu

NARA
PREFECTURE

*Awaji-
shima*

○ N   0 ——— 10 km
        0 ——— 5 miles

*Kansai
International
Airport*

Kishiwada

Kaizuka

Izumi-
Sano

Minami Map (p204)

Kita (Umeda) Map (p207)

Caption

Arriving in Osaka

International and some domestic flights
go to Kansai International Airport
(KIX), 50km south of Osaka. KIX is well
connected to the city with direct train
lines and buses. Shin-Osaka Station is
served by the Tōkaidō-Sanyō Shinkansen
(running between Tokyo and Hakata in
Fukuoka) and the eastern terminus of
the Kyūshū Shinkansen to Kagoshima.
Departures are frequent.

Sleeping

Osaka has plenty of accommodation
in all budgets, including some stylish
new hostels and guesthouses; for
midrange, your best bet is a chain hotel.
Base yourself in Minami for access to
a larger selection of bars, restaurants
and shops, or in Kita for fast access to
long-distance transport.

Restaurant in Osaka's Shinsekai district

Eating Out in Osaka

Above all, Osaka is a city that loves to eat: its unofficial slogan is kuidaore ('eat until you drop'). It really shines in the evening, when it seems that everyone is out for a good meal – and a good time. It's most famous for its comfort food – dishes that are deep-fried or grilled and stuffed with delicacies like octopus and squid.

Great For...

ℹ Need to Know

The Minami district is the centre of Osaka's eating and drinking scene, but you'll find excellent food all over the city.

★ **Top Tip**

Surprisingly good restaurants can be found in mall and train station food courts.

Okonomiyaki

Thick, savoury pancakes filled with shredded cabbage and your choice of meat, seafood, vegetables and more (the name means 'cook as you like'). Often prepared on a *teppan* (steel plate) set into your table, the cooked pancake is brushed with a savoury Worcestershire-style sauce, decoratively striped with mayonnaise and topped with dried bonito flakes, which seem to dance in the rising steam. Slice off a wedge using tiny trowels called *kote*, and – warning – allow it to cool a bit before taking that first bite.

Chibō (千房; Map p204; ☑06-6212-2211; www.chibo.com; 1-5-5 Dōtombori, Chūō-ku; mains ¥885-1675; ☺11am-1am Mon-Sat, to midnight Sun; ⓢMidō-suji line to Namba, exit 14) is one of Osaka's most famous *okonomiyaki* restaurants. It almost always has a line, but

it moves fast because there is seating on multiple floors (though you might want to hold out for the coveted tables overlooking Dōtombori canal).

Tako-yaki

These doughy dumplings stuffed with octopus (*tako* in Japanese) are grilled in specially made moulds. They're often sold as street food, served with pickled ginger, topped with savoury sauce, powdered *aonori* (seaweed), mayonnaise and bonito flakes and eaten with toothpicks. Nibble carefully at first, as the centre can be molten hot!

Try them at **Wanaka Honten** (わなか本店; Map p204; ☑06-6631-0127; http://takoyaki-wanaka.com; 11-19 Sennichi-mae, Chūō-ku; tako-yaki per 8 from ¥450; ☺10am-10pm Mon-Fri, 8.30am-10pm Sat & Sun; ⓢMidō-suji line to Namba, exit 4), which uses custom copper

Tako-yaki (octopus dumplings)

hotplates (instead of cast iron) to make dumplings that are crisper on the outside than usual (but still runny inside).

Kushikatsu

Yakitori refers to skewers of grilled meat, seafood and/or vegetables; *kushikatsu* is the same ingredients crumbed, deep fried and served with a savoury dipping sauce (double-dipping is a serious no-no). For many Japanese, a pilgrimage to **Ganso Kushikatsu Daruma Honten** (元祖串かつ だるま本店; Map p204; ☏06-6645-7056; www. kushikatu-daruma.com; 2-3-9 Ebisu-Higashi,

> ☑ **Don't Miss**
> Dōtombori is Osaka's biggest street food destination, though bear in mind that it gets awfully crowded in the evening.

Naniwa-ku; skewers ¥110-220; ◷11am-10.30pm; Ⓢ Midōsuji line to Dōbutsuen-mae, exit 5) is a necessary part of any visit to Osaka. Opened in 1929, it's said to be the birth-place of *kushikatsu*.

Kaiten-sushi

This Osaka invention (from the 1950s) goes by many names in English: conveyor-belt sushi, sushi-go-round or sushi train. It's all the same – plates of sushi that run past you along a belt built into the counter (you can also order off the menu). **Kaiten Sushi Ganko** (回転寿司がんこ; Map p207; ☏06-4799-6811; Eki Maré, Osaka Station City, Kita-ku; plates ¥130-735; ◷11am-11pm; ® JR Osaka, Sakurabashi exit), inside JR Osaka's Eki Marché food court, is a popular choice – meaning the two whirring tracks of plates are continu-ously restocked with fresh options.

Kappō-ryōri

Osaka's take on Japanese haute cuisine is casual: the dishes are similar to what you might find at a Kyoto *ryōtei* (a formal res-taurant with tatami seating) – incorporating intensely seasonal ingredients and elaborate presentation – but at *kappō* restaurants, diners sit at the counter, chatting with the chef who hands over the dishes as they're finished. Despite the laid-back vibe these restaurants can be frightfully expensive.

    Shoubentango-tei (正弁丹吾亭; Map p204; ☏06-6211-3208; 1-7-12 Dōtombori, Chūō-ku; dinner course ¥3780-10,800; ◷5-10pm; Ⓢ Midō-suji line to Namba, exit 14) isn't, despite its pedigree: established over 100 years ago, it was a literati hangout in the early 20th century. Even the cheapest course, which includes five dishes decided that day by the chef, tastes – and looks! – like a luxurious treat; reservations are necessary for all but the cheapest course.

> ✕ **Take a Break**
> You needn't always stand and eat food sold from street counters; many have tables and chairs out the back.

PISAPHOTOGRAPHY / SHUTTERSTOCK ©

Himeji-jō

ALEKSANDAR TODOROVIC / SHUTTERSTOCK ©

Day Trip to Himeji-jō

Japan's most magnificent castle, Himeji-jō, is a Unesco World Heritage Site, a national treasure and one of only a handful of original castles remaining (most are modern concrete reconstructions).

Great For...

☑ **Don't Miss**

See Himeji-jō on film in the James Bond flick *You Only Live Twice* (1967) and in Kurosawa Akira's *Ran* (1985).

The castle is a 15-minute walk from Himeji Station. The **Himeji Tourist Information Office** (姫路市観光案内所[姫路観光なびポート]; ☑079-287-0003; Ground Fl, Himeji Station; ☺9am-7pm) in the station has English maps and bicycles to lend – first come, first served.

History

Although there have been fortifications in Himeji since 1333, today's castle was built in 1580 by Toyotomi Hideyoshi and was enlarged some 30 years later by Ikeda Terumasa. Ikeda was awarded the castle by Tokugawa Ieyasu when the latter's forces defeated the Toyotomi armies. In the following centuries it was home to 48 successive lords. The castle reopened in 2015 after an extensive five-year renovation.

Kōkō-en

ℹ Need to Know

The San-yō Shinkansen connects Shin-Osaka and Himeji (¥3240, 35 minutes), in neighbouring Hyōgo prefecture.

✕ Take a Break

Kōkō-en has a teahouse and restaurant.

★ Top Tip
Himeji-jō can get crowded during peak travel times, check the website's daily 'congestion forecast'.

and inside the keep. (Note that the keep is inaccessible to wheelchairs and strollers.) Last entry is an hour before closing.

Kōkō-en

Across Himeji Castle's western moat is **Kōkō-en** (好古園; 68 Honmachi; adult/child ¥300/150, combination ticket with Himeji Castle ¥1040/360; ◎9am-6pm May-Aug, to 5pm Sep-Apr), a stunning reconstruction of the former samurai quarters. Nine Edo period–style homes boast garden with various combinations of waterfalls, koi ponds, intricately pruned trees, bamboo, flowering shrubs and a wisteria-covered arbour. If it feels like you're on a movie set amid the stone and plaster walls lining the paths, you would be right; many Japanese historical dramas have been shot here. The teahouse serves *matcha* (powdered green tea; ¥500); the restaurant **Kassui-ken** (活水軒) serves a *bentō* (boxed meal) of *anago* (conger eel, a local speciality; ¥2080).

Himeji-jō

Himeji-jō (姫路城, Himeji Castle; 68 Honmachi; adult/child ¥1000/300, combination ticket with Kōkō-en ¥1040/360; ◎9am-5pm Sep-May, to 6pm Jun-Aug) is nicknamed Shirasagi-jō ('White Egret Castle') for its lustrous white plaster exterior and stately form on a hill rising from the plain. There's a five-storey main *tenshū* (keep) and three smaller keeps, all surrounded by moats and defensive walls punctuated with rectangular, circular and triangular openings for firing guns and shooting arrows. The main keep's walls also feature *ishiotoshi* – narrow openings that allowed defenders to pour boiling water or oil onto anyone trying to scale the walls after making it past the other defences.

It takes about 1½ hours to follow the arrow-marked route around the castle

⊙ SIGHTS

Dōtombori
Area

(道頓堀; Map p204; www.dotonbori.or.jp; [S]Midō-suji line to Namba, exit 14) Highly photogenic Dōtombori is the city's liveliest night spot and centre of the Minami (south) part of town. Its name comes from the 400-year-old canal, Dōtombori-gawa, now lined with pedestrian walkways and a riot of illuminated billboards glittering off its waters. Don't miss the famous **Glico running man** sign. South of the canal is a pedestrianised street that has dozens of restaurants vying for attention with the flashiest of signage.

> *Dōtombori is the city's liveliest night spot*

Amerika-Mura
Area

(アメリカ村, America Village, Ame-Mura; Map p204; Nishi-Shinsaibashi, Chūō-ku; [S]Midō-suji line to Shinsaibashi, exit 7) West of Midō-suji,

Amerika-Mura is a compact enclave of hip, youth-focused and offbeat shops, plus cafes, bars, tattoo and piercing parlours, nightclubs, hair salons and a few discreet love hotels. In the middle is **Triangle Park**, an all-concrete 'park' with benches for sitting and watching the fashion parade. Come night, it's a popular gathering spot.

National Museum of Ethnology
Museum

(国立民族学博物館; Map p195; ☎06-6876-2151; www.minpaku.ac.jp; 10-1 Senri Expo Park, Suita; adult/child ¥420/110; ⊙10am-5pm, closed Wed; ◉Osaka Monorail to Banpaku-kinen-kōen) This ambitious museum showcases the world's cultures, showing them to be the continuous (and tangled) strings that they are. There are plenty of traditional masks, textiles and pottery but also Ghanaian barbershop signboards, Bollywood movie posters and even a Filipino jeepney. Don't miss the music room, where you can summon street performances from around the globe via a touch panel. There are also exhibits on Okinawan history and Japan's indigenous Ainu culture. There's English

Glico running man sign, Dōtombori

signage but the audio guide gives more detail.

Osaka-jō Castle

(大阪城; Osaka Castle; Map p207; www.osaka castle.net; 1-1 Osaka-jō, Chūō-ku; grounds/castle keep free/¥600, combined with Osaka Museum of History ¥900; ⊙9am-5pm, to 7pm Aug; Ⓢ Chūō line to Tanimachi 4-chōme, exit 9, Ⓡ JR Loop line to Osaka-jō-kōen) After unifying Japan in the late 16th century, General Toyotomi Hideyoshi (p277) built this castle (1583) as a display of power, using, it's said, the labour of 100,000 workers. Although the present structure is a 1931 concrete reconstruction (refurbished in 1997), it's nonetheless quite a sight, looming dramatically over the surrounding park and moat. Inside is an excellent collection of art, armour, and day-to-day implements related to the castle, Hideyoshi and Osaka. An 8th-floor observation deck has 360-degree views.

Osaka Aquarium Kaiyūkan Aquarium

(海遊館; Map p195; ☎06-6576-5501; www.kaiyukan.com; 1-1-10 Kaigan-dōri, Minato-ku; adult/child ¥2300/1200; ⊙10am-8pm; Ⓢ Chūō line to Osaka-kō, exit 1) Kaiyūkan is among Japan's best aquariums. An 800m-plus walkway winds past displays of sea life from around the Pacific 'ring of fire': Antarctic penguins, coral-reef butterflyfish, unreasonably cute Arctic otters, Monterey Bay seals and unearthly jellyfish. Most impressive is the enormous central tank, housing a whale shark, manta and thousands of other fish. Note there are also captive dolphins here, which some visitors may not appreciate; there is growing evidence that keeping cetaceans in captivity is harmful for the animals.

Umeda Sky Building Notable Building

(梅田スカイビル; Map p207; www.kuchu-teien.com; 1-1-88 Ōyodonaka, Kita-ku; ¥700; ⊙observation decks 10am-10.30pm, last entry 10pm; Ⓡ JR Osaka, north central exit) Osaka's landmark Sky Building (1993) resembles a 40-storey, space-age Arc de Triomphe. Twin towers are connected

Navigating Osaka

Osaka is roughly divided into Kita (Japanese for 'north'), also known as Umeda, the straight-laced business district encircling Osaka Station; Minami ('south') contains the bustling shopping and nightlife zones of Namba, Shinsaibashi, Amerika-mura and Dōtombori near Namba Station.

Fair warning: Osaka's larger stations can be disorienting, particularly Osaka Station. Exits are often confusingly labelled, even for Japanese. Adding to the confusion, *shinkansen* (bullet trains) stop at Shin-Osaka Station, three subway stops (about five minutes) north of Umeda and JR Osaka Station on the Midō-suji line.

Hankyū Umeda Department Store (p206)
ESCHCOLLECTION / GETTY IMAGES ©

at the top by a 'floating garden' (really a garden-free observation deck), which was constructed on the ground and then hoisted up. The 360-degree city views from here are breathtaking day or night. Getting there is half the fun – an escalator in a see-through tube takes you up the last five storeys (not for vertigo sufferers). The architect, Hara Hiroshi, also designed Kyoto Station.

Kuromon Ichiba Market

(黒門市場, Kuromon Market; Map p204; www.kuromon.com; Nipponbashi, Chūō-ku; ⊙most shops 10am-5pm, closed Sun; Ⓢ Sakai-suji line to Nipponbashi, exit 10) An Osaka landmark for over a century, this 600m-long market is equal parts functioning market and

Minami

0 — 400 m
0 — 0.2 miles

NISHI-KU

CHŪŌ-KU

Daihōji-dōri

Shimizu-dōri

Suomachi-dōri

HIGASHI-SHINSAIBASHI

Hachiman-dōri

AMERIKA-MURA

Orange St

HORIE

Mitsudera-dōri

Tombori River Walk

Souemon-chō-dōri

Dōtombori-gawa

DŌTOMBORI

Namba

Nipponbashi

Namba

Namba

Kintetsu Namba

Kintetsu Nipponbashi

JR Namba

NAMBA

URA-NAMBA

Nansan-dōri

Midō-suji

Nankai Namba

Osaka Visitors Information Center Namba

Kuromon Ichiba

Tanimachi-suji

NANIWA-KU

Nansan-dōri

Ota Rd

Daikoku-chō

Ebisu-chō

Hanshin Expwy

TENNŌJI-KU

SHIN-SEKAI

Sakai-suji

Hanshin Expwy

Tennō-ji-kōen

Abiko-suji

Shin-Imamiya

Yotsubashi-suji

Hanshin Expwy

Shinsaibashi-suji Arcade

Ebisu-bashi-suji Arcade

Sennichi-mae Arcade

Hanshin Expwy

Minami

tourist attraction. Vendors selling fresh fish, meat, produce and pickles attract chefs and local home cooks; shops offering takeaway sushi or with grills set up (to cook the steaks, oysters etc that they sell) cater to visitors – making the market excellent for grazing *and* photo ops.

⊕ ACTIVITIES

Spa World   Onsen
(スパワールド; Map p204; ☑06-6631-0001; www.spaworld.co.jp; 3-4-24 Ebisu-higashi, Naniwa-ku; 3hr/day pass Mon-Fri ¥2400/2700, Sat & Sun ¥2700/3000, additional ¥1300 midnight-5am; ☉10am-8.45am; ⑤Midō-suji line to Dōbutsu-en-mae, exit 5, ⑧JR Loop line to Shin-Imamiya) 'Spa World' isn't a mere euphemism: this huge, seven-storey onsen (hot spring) complex contains dozens of options from saunas to salt baths, styled after a mini-UN's worth of nations including Japan, Finland, Canada, ancient Rome and, er, Atlantis. 'Asian' and 'European' bathing zones are separated by gender (bathe in the buff, towels provided) and switch monthly. Swimsuits (rental ¥600, or bring your own) or special outfits (provided) are worn in swimming pools, eateries and *ganbanyoku* (stone baths; additional ¥800 to ¥1000).

'Spa World' isn't a mere euphemism...

Tombori River Cruise   Cruise
(とんぼりリバークルーズ; Map p204; ☑06-6441-0532; www.ipponmatsu.co.jp/cruise/tombori.html; Don Quijote Bldg, 7-13 Sōemon-chō, Chūō-ku; adult/child ¥900/400; ☉1-9pm Mon-Fri, 11am-9pm Sat & Sun; ⑤Midō-suji line to Namba, exit 14) One way to beat the crowds in Dōtombori is to hop on a boat. Tombori's short, 20-minute trips past the neon signs run on the hour and the half-hour. Night time is best, though slots fill up quickly; tickets go on sale at the pier an hour before the first cruise of the day starts. Osaka Amazing Pass holders ride free.

⊕ TOURS

Cycle Osaka   Cycling
(Map p207; ☑080-5325-8975; www.cycleosaka.com; 2-12-1 Sagisu, Fukushima-ku; half-/full-day ¥5000/10,000; ⑧JR Loop line to Fukushima) English-speaking guides lead well-organised tours to sights both well-known and less-well-known, along the river banks and through the markets. The food route (¥8000) is particularly

recommended. Fees include bicycle and helmet rental, water and food.

🔓 SHOPPING

Hankyū Umeda Department Store   Department Store

(阪急梅田本店; Map p207; www.hankyu-dept. co.jp/honten; 8-7 Kakuda-chō, Kita-ku; ⊙10am-8pm Sun-Thu, to 9pm Fri & Sat; Ⓢ Midō-suji line

👍 Bunraku

In bunraku (Japanese traditional puppet theatre) almost-life-sized puppets are manipulated by black-clad, on-stage puppeteers, to evoke dramatic tales of love, duty and politics. Bunraku's most famous playwright, Chikamatsu Monzaemon (1653–1724), wrote plays about Osaka's merchants and the denizens of the pleasure quarters, social classes otherwise generally ignored in the Japanese arts at the time. Not surprisingly, the art form found a wide audience among them, and a theatre was established to stage Chikamatsu's plays in Dōtombori. Bunraku has been recognised on the Unesco World Intangible Cultural Heritage list. See it at the **National Bunraku Theatre** (国立文楽劇場; Map p204; ☑06-6212-2531, ticket centre 0570-07-9900; www. ntj.jac.go.jp; 1-12-10 Nipponbashi, Chūō-ku; full performance ¥2400-6000, single act ¥500-1500; ⊙opening months vary, check the website; Ⓢ Sakai-suji line to Nipponbashi, exit 7). Learn more at the Japan Arts Council's website, www2.ntj.jac.go.jp/unesco/bunraku/en.

to Umeda, exit 6, 🚇 Hankyū Umeda) Hankyū, which first opened in 1929, pioneered the now ubiquitous concept of the train-station department store. One of Japan's largest department stores, 'Ume-Han' is also among the most fashion-forward, with a good selection of edgy Japanese designers on the 3rd floor. Head to the 7th floor for artisan homewares and to the basement for a cornucopia of gourmet food items.

Standard Books   Books

(スタンダードブックストア; Map p204; ☑06-6484-2239; www.standardbookstore.com; 2-2-12 Nishi-Shinsaibashi, Chūō-ku; ⊙11am-10.30pm; Ⓢ Midō-suji line to Shinsaibashi, exit 7) This cult-fave Osaka bookstore prides itself on not stocking any best sellers. Instead, it's stocked with small-press finds, art books, indie comics and the like, plus CDs and quirky fashion items and accessories.

Tower Knives   Homewares

(タワーナイブズ; Map p204; ☑06-4395-5218; www.towerknives.com; 1-4-1 Ebisu-higashi, Naniwa-ku; ⊙10am-6pm; Ⓢ Midō-suji line to Dōbutsuen-mae, exit 5) Tower Knives has a fantastic selection of kitchen knives – both carbon steel and stainless steel; some are hand-forged by Osaka artisans. Best of all, the English-speaking staff will walk you through the different styles, let you try them out on some veggies (at your own risk: these knives are sharp!) and show you how to care for them. Duty-free shopping available.

Dōguya-suji Arcade   Market

(道具屋筋; Map p204; www.doguyasuji.or.jp/map_eng.html; Sennichi-mae, Chūō-ku; ⊙10am-6pm; Ⓢ Midō-suji line to Namba, exit 4) This long arcade sells just about anything related to the preparation, consumption and selling of Osaka's principal passion: food. There's everything from bamboo steamers and lacquer miso soup bowls to shopfront lanterns and, of course, moulded hotplates for making *tako-yaki* (octopus dumplings). Hours vary per store.

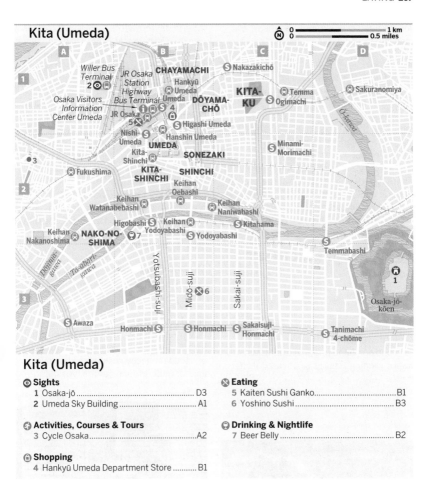

Kita (Umeda)

◈ EATING

Yoshino Sushi   Sushi ¥¥¥
(吉野鮨; Map p207; ☑06-6231-7181; www.
yoshino-sushi.co.jp; 3-4-14 Awaji-machi, Chūō-
ku; lunch/dinner from ¥3200/6500; ⊙11am-
1.30pm & 5.30-9.30pm Mon-Fri; ⑤Midō-suji line
to Honmachi, exit 1) In business since 1841,
Yoshino specialises in Osaka-style sushi,
which is *hako-sushi* ('pressed sushi').
This older version of the dish (compared
to the newer, hand-pressed Tokyo-style
nigiri-sushi) is formed by a wooden
mould, resulting in Mondrian-esque
cubes of spongy omelette, soy-braised

shiitake mushrooms, smoky eel and
vinegar-marinated fish on rice. Reservations are required for dinner.

Imai Honten   Udon ¥¥
(今井本店; Map p204; ☑06-6211-0319; www.
d-imai.com; 1-7-22 Dōtombori, Chūō-ku; dishes
from ¥765; ⊙11am-10pm Thu-Tue; ⑤Midō-suji
line to Namba, exit 14) Step into an oasis of
calm amid Dōtombori's chaos to be welcomed by kimono-clad staff at one of the
area's oldest and most revered udon spe-
cialists. Try *kitsune udon* – noodles topped
with soup-soaked slices of fried tofu. Look

for the traditional exterior and the willow tree outside.

Za Ikaga
Street Food ¥

(ザ・イカが; Map p204; ☎06-6212-0147; www.ikayaki.jp; 2-12-8 Nishi-Shinsaibashi, Chūō-ku; dishes from ¥300; ☺6pm-4am Thu-Tue; ⓢMidō-suji line to Shinsaibashi, exit 7) The signature dish at this small food stand is *ika-yaki* – grilled squid, served here in a thin crêpe splattered with egg, mayonnaise and savoury, *okonomiyaki*-style sauce. There are a few seats inside at the counter and a few folding chairs on the street (perfect for watching the comings and goings in Amerika-Mura). There's a picture menu.

🍺 DRINKING & NIGHTLIFE

Beer Belly
Craft Beer

(Map p207; www.beerbelly.jp/tosabori; 1-1-31 Tosabori, Nishi-ku; ☺5pm-2am Mon-Fri, 3-11pm Sat, 3-9pm Sun; ⓢYotsubashi line to Higobashi, exit 3) Beer Belly is run by Osaka's best microbrewery, Minoh Beer. There are 10 taps and one hand pump featuring Minoh's award-winning classics and seasonal offerings (pints from ¥1000). Pick up a copy of Osaka's *Craft Beer Map* here to further your local beer adventures. From the subway exit, double back and take the road that curves behind the APA Hotel.

Circus
Club

(Map p204; ☎06-6241-3822; http://circus-osaka.com; 2nd fl, 1-8-16 Nishi-Shinsaibashi, Chūō-ku; entry ¥2000-2500; ☺11pm-late; ⓢMidō-suji line to Shinsaibashi, exit 7) This small club is the heart of Osaka's underground electronic scene, drawing a crowd more for the music than a pick-up scene. The dance floor is nonsmoking. It's open on Friday and Saturday nights and sometimes during the week. Look up for the small sign in English and bring a picture ID.

Misono Building
Bar

(味園ビル; Map p204; 2nd fl, Misono Bldg, 2-3-9 Sennichi-mae, Chūō-ku; ☺6pm-late; ⓢSakai-suji line to Nipponbashi, exit 5) With a waterfall and grand, spiralling staircase out front, the Misono Building was once a symbol of the high life (c 1956). It's now fallen into a kind of decadent decay, making the building a lure for underground culture types, who

From left: Umeda Sky Building (p203); Osaka-jō (p203); Dōguya-suji Arcade (p206)

have turned the 2nd floor into a strip of tiny, eccentric bars.

A lure for underground culture types

 ENTERTAINMENT

Namba Bears
Live Music

(難波ベアーズ; Map p204; ☎06-6649-5564; http://namba-bears.main.jp; 3-14-5 Namba-naka, Naniwa-ku; Ⓢ Midō-suji line to Namba, exit 4) For going on three decades this has been the place to hear underground music live in Osaka. It's a small, bare-concrete, smoky space – well suited to the punk, rock and indie bands that play here. In keeping with the alternative spirit, you can bring in your own beer. Most shows start at 7pm; tickets usually cost ¥2000 to ¥2500.

Sumo Spring Tournament
Spectator Sport

(Haru Bashō; www.sumo.or.jp; ◷Mar) The big fellas rumble into Osaka in March for this major tournament, held in the Prefectural Gymnasium (府立体育会館, Fu-ritsu Taiiku-kan) in Namba. Tickets (from ¥3800) go on sale in early February and can be purchased online.

ⓘ INFORMATION

DANGERS & ANNOYANCES

Osaka has a rough image in Japan, with the highest number of reported crimes per capita of any city in the country – though it remains significantly safer than most cities of comparable size. Nishinari-ku (also called Airin-chiku), south of Shinimamiya Station (just below Shin-Sekai), has a sizeable vagrant population and an organised-crime presence. There are a number of budget accommodations here targeting foreign travellers; while it's unlikely you'd encounter any real danger, female travellers, particularly solo female travellers, do risk drawing unwanted attention, especially at night.

INTERNET

Osaka has free wi-fi in some areas (details at www.osaka-info.jp/en/wifi).

TOURIST INFORMATION

Osaka Visitors Information Center Umeda
(大阪市ビジターズインフォメーションセ
ンター・梅田; Map p207; ☎06-6345-2189;
www.osaka-info.jp; JR Osaka Station, ☺8am-
8pm; ℝJR Osaka, north central exit) is on the 1st

 Discount Passes

Enjoy Eco Card (エンジョイエコカード;
weekday/weekend ¥800/600, child ¥300)
One-day unlimited travel on subways, plus
some admission discounts. Purchase at
subway ticket machines.

ICOCA & Haruka One-way fare on the JR Haruka Kansai-Airport Express includes travel
from KIX to Shin-Osaka Station (¥3300) or
Tennōji (¥3100) and an ICOCA card pre-load-
ed with ¥1500 (and the ¥500 deposit).

Osaka Amazing Pass (大阪周遊パス;
www.osaka-info.jp/osp) One-day passes
(¥2300), good for travel on city subways and
trains and admission to 28 sights (including
Osaka-jō and the Umeda Sky Building); or
two-day passes (¥3000) that cover the same
sights but only travel on city subways. Passes
are sold at tourist information centres and
city subway stations.

Yokoso Osaka Ticket (www.howto-osaka.
com/en/ticket/ticket/yokoso.html; ¥1500)
One-way fare on the Nankai Express Rapit
from KIX to Nankai Namba Station and
one-day travel on city subways, plus some
admission discounts. Must be purchased
online in advance.

For more information on discount pass
options, see www.osaka-info.jp/en/plan/
practical_information/travel_passes.

Hankyū Umeda Station
TUPUNGATO / SHUTTERSTOCK ©

floor of the central north concourse of JR Osaka
Station. There are also branches on the 1st floor
of **Nankai Namba Station** (大阪市ビジターズ
インフォメーションセンター・なんば; Map
p204; ☎06-6631-9100; Nankai Namba Station;
☺9am-8pm; ⑤Midō-suji line to Namba, exit 4,
ℝNankai Namba) and at Kansai International
Airport (KIX). Tourist offices can help book accommodation if you visit in person. The website
is a good resource too.

GETTING THERE & AWAY

Two airports serve Osaka: **Kansai International
Airport** (KIX; 関西空港; Map p195; www.
kansai-airport.or.jp) for all international and
some domestic flights; and the domestic **Itami
Airport** (ITM; 伊丹空港; Map p195; ☎06-
6856-6781; http://osaka-airport.co.jp; 3-555
Hotaru-ga-ike, Nishi-machi, Toyonaka), also
confusingly called Osaka International Airport.
KIX is about 50km southwest of the city, on an
artificial island in the bay. Itami is located 12km
northwest of Osaka.

The Tōkaidō *shinkansen* line connects
Shin-Osaka Station, north of Osaka, and Tokyo
(¥14,140, three hours) to the east. The Sanyō
shinkansen connects Shin-Osaka with Hiroshima
(¥10,230, 1½ hours) to the west; some trains
continue on the Kyūshū *shinkansen* line to
Kagoshima (¥21,900, 4¾ hours).

Osaka is a big hub for long distance coaches,
which service the same destinations as the
shinkansen (and more) for half the price; some
longer trips have night departures. Coaches
depart from the **Willer Bus Terminal** (Willer
バスターミナル; Map p207; ☎reservation
centre 0570-200-770; www.willerexpress.
com; 1st fl, Umeda Sky Bldg Tower West, 1-1-88
Ōyodo-naka, Kita-ku; ☺6am-12.30am; ℝJR
Osaka, north central exit), next to the Umeda
Sky Building.

GETTING AROUND

TO/FROM KIX

Trains depart from Terminal 1; you need to take a
free shuttle bus if you arrive at Terminal 2.

Kuromon Ichiba (p203)

Nankai Express Rapit (¥1430, 40 minutes) All-reserved twice-hourly service (7am to 10pm) between Nankai Kansai-Airport Station (in Terminal 1) and Nankai Namba Station; Nankai Airport Express trains take about 10 minutes longer and cost ¥920.

JR Haruka Kansai-Airport Express Twice-hourly service (6.30am to 10pm) between KIX and Tennōji Station (unreserved seat ¥1710, 30 minutes) and Shin-Osaka Station (¥2330, 50 minutes).

Taxi There are standard taxi fares to Umeda (¥14,500, 50 minutes), Namba (¥14,000, 50 minutes) and Shin-Osaka (¥18,000, one hour). There is a late-night fare surcharge of ¥2500.

TO/FROM ITAMI AIRPORT

Osaka Monorail Connects the airport to Hotarugaike (¥200, three minutes) and Senri-Chūō

(¥330, 12 minutes), from where you can transfer, respectively, to the Hankyū Takarazaka line or Hankyū Senri line for Osaka Station.

TRAIN & SUBWAY

The subway should get you everywhere you need to go (unless you stay out past midnight, when they stop running). There are eight lines, but the one that short-term visitors will find most useful is the Midō-suji (red) line, running north–south and stopping at Shin-Osaka, Umeda (next to Osaka Station), Shinsaibashi, Namba and Tennōji stations. Single rides cost ¥180 to ¥370 (half-price for children). Osaka's local IC-chip transport pass is ICOCA; purchase it (¥2000, including ¥500 refundable deposit) at any ticket machine.

NAOSHIMA

Naoshima

Naoshima (直島) is one of Japan's great success stories: once a rural island on the verge of becoming a ghost town, now a world-class centre for contemporary art. The Benesse Art Site Naoshima project started in the early 1990s, when the Benesse Corporation chose Naoshima as the setting for its growing collection of contemporary art. Many of Japan's most lauded architects have contributed structures, including museums and a boutique hotel – all designed to enhance the island's natural beauty and complement its existing settlements. It has also inspired some Japanese to pursue a slower life outside the big cities, by relocating to Naoshima to open cafes and inns.

Naoshima in Two Days

If you're short on time, it is possible to do Naoshima as a day trip, but considering the time and effort it takes to get here it's worth spending at least one night on the island. In two days you can make your way through the highlights of the Benesse Art Site on Naoshima.

Naoshima in Four Days

With more time, you can explore all the nooks and crannies of Naoshima, getting a feel for the rhythms of island life. You'll also have time to make day trips to some of the less-visited islands that also form part of the Art Site and have their own attractive museums.

Map labels: Inujima, Muneage, Harima Gulf, Tamano, Uno, Teshimaieura, Teshima Island, Hibi, Naoshima Bath – I Love YU, Miyanoura Port, Honmura Port, Miyanoura, Naoshima, Honmura, **Benesse House Area**, Ogi-jima

0 / 0 — 2 km / 1 miles

Arriving in Naoshima

Naoshima is an island in the Seto Inland Sea off the coast of western Honshū. The nearest major city on the mainland is Okayama, a stop on San-yō Shinkansen between Osaka and Hiroshima. Ferries depart from near Uno Station, an hour from Okayama on the JR Uno line. Ferry route maps and the latest timetables can be found on the Benesse Art Site website (www.benesse-artsite.jp/en/access) or at the tourist offices in Okayama.

Sleeping

There's only one hotel on the island, Benesse House, part of Benesse Art Site. Otherwise there are several privately run *minshuku* (guesthouses); not a lot of English is spoken, but locals are becoming increasingly used to foreign guests. There's also the beachfront campsite Tsutsuji-sō (www.tsutsujiso.com) with Mongolian-style *pao* tents. Budget travellers might consider staying in Okayama and visiting Naoshima as a day trip.

Lee Ufan Museum

LEFT & RIGHT: TADASU YAMAMOTO ©

Benesse Art Site Naoshima

This is a captivating blend of avant-garde art and rural Japan, a collection of world-class museums and creative installations in a gorgeous natural setting on the Seto Inland Sea.

Great For...

☑ **Don't Miss**

The yellow *Pumpkin* sculpture by Kusama Yayoi, which has become a symbol of Naoshima.

Art House Project

Naoshima's **Art House Project** (家 プロジェクト; www.benesse-artsite.jp/en/ art/arthouse.html; single/combined ticket ¥410/1030; ⏰10am-4.30pm Tue-Sun), which began in 1998, has turned over half a dozen traditional buildings to contemporary artists. Highlights include Shinrō Ohtake's shack-like **Haisha**, its Statue of Liberty sculpture rising up through the levels of the house; James Turrell's experiment with light in **Minamidera**, where you enter in total darkness...and wait; and Sugimoto Hiroshi's play on the traditional **Go'o Shrine**, with a glass staircase and narrow underground 'Stone Chamber'.

Buy a ticket at Honmura Lounge & Archive or at the Miyanoura ferry terminal.

Kan Yasuda *The Secret of the Sky*

HONMURA
Haisha

Go'o
Shrine

Minami-
dera

*Naoshima
Dam*

*Inland Sea
(Seto-nai-kai)*

*Chichu Art
Museum*

TSUMŪRA

Lee Ufan Museum

Benesse House Museum

❶ Need to Know

The museums (Benesse House Museum, Chichu Art Museum and Lee Ufan Museum) are clustered in the south of the island; Art House Project is on the east side, in Honmura.

✕ Take a Break

There are a few cafes near the port at Miyanoura and in the Art House Project area.

★ Top Tip

March to November is Naoshima's busiest time; some attractions offer the possibility of purchasing a 'timed ticket' for entry; check the website for details.

Benesse House Museum

The **Benesse House Museum** (ベネッセ ハウスミュージアム; www.benesse-artsite. jp/en/art/benessehouse-museum.html; adult/ child/hotel guests ¥1030/free/free; ⊗8am-9pm) was the first art space to open on Naoshima, in 1992. Award-winning architect Andō Tadao designed the stunning structure on the south coast of the island. Among the works here are pieces by Andy Warhol, David Hockney, Jasper Johns, and Japanese artists such as Shinrō Ohtake. Art installations are dotted across the adjacent shoreline and forest, blending architecture into nature.

Chichu Art Museum

A short walk from Benesse House is another Andō Tadao creation, **Chichu Art Museum** (地中美術館; www.benesse-artsite. jp/en/art/chichu.html; adult/child ¥2060/free; ⊗10am-6pm Tue-Sun Mar-Sep, to 5pm Oct-Feb). A work of art itself, the museum consists of a series of cool concrete-walled spaces sitting snugly underground. Lit by natural light, it provides a remarkable setting for several Monet water-lily paintings, a monumental space by Walter De Maria and installations by James Turrell. Outside is the Chichu garden, created in the spirit of Monet's garden in Giverny.

Lee Ufan Museum

The **Lee Ufan Museum** (李禹煥美術館; www.benesse-artsite.jp/en/art/lee-ufan.html; adult/child ¥1030/free; ⊗10am-6pm Tue-Sun Mar-Sep, to 5pm Oct-Feb) houses works by the renowned Korean-born artist (and philosopher) Lee Ufan, who was a leading figure in the Mono-ha movement of the 1960s and '70s.

👍 Beyond Naoshima

With more time, you can explore the other islands in Naoshima's orbit. Teshima (豊島) is the most obvious next port of call. Highlights here include **Teshima Yokoo House** (豊島横尾館; www.benesse-artsite.jp/en/art/teshima-yokoohouse.html; ¥510; ⊘10am-5pm Wed-Mon Mar-Sep, to 4pm Oct-Feb, closed Wed & Thu Dec-Feb), an old house that has been converted into exhibition spaces, and **Teshima Art Museum** (豊島美術館; www.benesse-artsite.jp/en/art/teshima-artmuseum.html; ¥1540; ⊘10am-5pm Wed-Mon Mar-Sep, to 4pm Oct-Feb, closed Wed & Thu Dec-Feb), actually a large concrete shell housing a single artwork where cut-outs frame snapshots of blue sky, clouds, or the green of the surrounding hills.

Or go further off the beaten track to small Inujima (犬島), home to the **Inujima Seirensho Art Museum** (犬島精錬所美術館; Inujima; incl Inujima Art House Project ¥2060; ⊘10am-4.30pm Wed-Mon, closed Wed & Thu Dec-Feb), a copper refinery converted into an eco-building displaying Yanagi Yukinori's art work.

Ferries travel between Naoshima's Miyanoura port and Teshima's Ieura port (¥620, 35 minutes) and between Ieura and Inujima (¥1030, 25 minutes). Check timetables on the Benesse website at www.benesse-artsite.jp/en/access.

Teshima Art Museum
KEN'ICHI SUZUKI ©

🟢 ACTIVITIES

Naoshima Bath "I Love YU"　Sento
(直島銭湯; Map p215; www.benesse-artsite.jp/en/art/naoshimasento.html; adult/child ¥510/210; ⊘2-9pm Tue-Fri, 10am-9pm Sat & Sun) For a unique bathing experience, take a soak at this colourful fusion of Japanese bathing tradition and contemporary art, designed by Shinrō Ohtake, where there really is an elephant in the room. It's a couple of minutes' walk inland from Miyanoura port. Look for the building with the palm trees out front.

🍴 EATING

Cafe Salon Naka-Oku　　　Cafe ¥
(カフェサロン中奥; ☑087-892-3887; www.naka-oku.com; lunch ¥600-790, dinner ¥400-750; ⊘11.30am-9pm Wed-Mon; 🛜) Up on a small hill at the rear of a farming plot, Naka-Oku is a good option in the Honmura area, and one of only a couple of places open in the evenings here. It's all wood-beamed warmth and cosiness, with homey specialities like *omuraisu* (omelette filled with fried rice) at lunchtime and small dishes with drinks in the evening.

Benesse House Museum Restaurant　　　Kaiseki ¥¥¥
(日本料理一扇; ☑087-892-3223; www.benesse-artsite.jp/en/stay/benessehouse/restaurant_cafe.html; breakfast ¥2613, lunch sets ¥2000-2900, dinner sets ¥7722-9504; ⊘7.30-9.30am, 11.30am-2.30pm & 6-9.45pm) The artfully displayed *kaiseki* (Japanese haute cuisine) dinners at this contrastingly austere Benesse House restaurant are almost too pretty to eat. Courses feature seafood, but there is a veg-dominated option (request a couple of days ahead) and the menu changes with the seasons. Breakfast and lunch are also served. Reservations are recommended.

ℹ️ INFORMATION

Honmura Lounge & Archive (☑087-840-8273; ⊘10am-4.30pm Tue-Sun) is next to Honmura port, with a left luggage service.

 Shinro Ohtake Naoshima Bath "I Love YU"

Marine Station Tourist Information Centre (☏087-892-2299; www.naoshima. net; ☉8.30am-6pm) is at the Miyanoura ferry port, with a bilingual map of the island (also downloadable from the website) and a full list of accommodation options (though it can't make reservations).

 GETTING THERE & AWAY

From Okayama, take the JR Uno line to Uno (¥580, about an hour); this usually involves a quick change of trains at Chayamachi, crossing the same platform. Ferries go to Naoshima's main port of **Miyanoura** (Map p215; ¥290; 15-20 minutes; hourly) from the port near Uno Station. There are also ferries from Uno to **Honmura port** (Map p215; ¥290; 20 minutes; five daily). Heading back to Okayama at night, you may find trains from Uno have finished or are two hours away, in which case take a bus to Okayama Station (¥650, one hour, one to two hourly) from bus stop 1 outside Uno Station.

GETTING AROUND

Naoshima is great for cycling. **Cafe Ougiya Rent-a-Cycle** (☏090-3189-0471; rental per day ¥300-500; ☉9am-7pm Mar-Nov, to 6pm Dec-Feb) is inside the Marine Station at the port. A few electric bikes (¥1000 per day) and scooters (¥1500 per day) are also available. Prices are similar at the other rental shops nearby.

Naoshima 'town bus' minibuses (¥100) run between Miyanoura, Honmura, and the Benesse House area (Tsutsuji-sō campground stop) in the south once or twice an hour. From Tsutsuji-sō, there's a free Benesse shuttle, stopping at all the Benesse Art Site museums. In busy seasons buses can fill up quickly, especially towards the end of the day when people are returning to the port to catch ferries. Be sure to check the timetables and allow enough buffer time.

There is one **taxi** (☏087-892-3036) on Naoshima, taking up to nine passengers – this has to be reserved before coming to the island. Walking is also feasible: for example, it's just over 2km from Miyanoura port to the Art House Project area.

HOKKAIDŌ

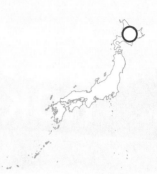

Hokkaidō

Hokkaidō (北海道) is the Japan of wide-open spaces, with 20% of the country's land area but only 5% of its population. There are large swathes of wilderness here, with primeval forests, tropical-blue caldera lakes, fields of alpine wildflowers and bubbling, in-the-rough hot springs. In the summer, all this (plus the cooler, drier weather) draws hikers, cyclists and strollers. Winter is a different beast entirely: copious dumps of dry, powdery snow turn Hokkaidō's mountains into peaks of meringue. In recent decades, Niseko has emerged as Asia's top ski resort and a global destination, backed up by a thriving, cosmopolitan après-ski scene.

Hokkaidō in Two Days

It would be hard to do Hokkaidō justice in two days. In winter, you could base yourself in Sapporo, skiing at Teine during the day and basking in the nightlife of Susukino after dark. Year-round you could pack in a visit to Sapporo, Noboribetsu Onsen and Tōya-ko, the latter two part of Shikotsu-Toya National Park (and easily accessible by train).

Hokkaidō in Four Days

If you're here for the snow, this is a nice amount of time to hole up in one of Hokkaidō top-rate ski resorts, like Niseko or Furano. In the green season, rent a car and head to Shikotsu-Tōya National Park for hiking, hot springs and beautiful vistas. Either way, we recommend budgeting at least an evening for Sapporo.

Arriving in Hokkaidō

New Chitose Airport is located 45km southeast of Sapporo, in Chitose. With flights to more than 25 cities in Japan and many cities in Asia, this is where most travellers will arrive. Sapporo is the largest city and the principal hub for trains and buses. Unless you're spending time in Sapporo, it's most convenient to pick up a rental car at the airport.

Sleeping

Of all of Hokkaidō's ski resorts, Niseko has the best spread of accommodation, as well as the best après scene (centred in Hirafu Village). Furano is quieter, with most guests holed up in one of the two Prince Hotels at the base. The Susukino district in Sapporo makes for a good base, thanks to the high concentration of dining and nightlife options.

Snowboarding at Furano Ski Area

STEVE OGLE / GETTY IMAGES ©

Skiing & Snowsports

Cold fronts from Siberia bring huge dumps of light, powdery snow, which has earned Hokkaidō a reputation as a paradise for skiers and snowboarders; there are international-level resorts here, but also remote backcountry opportunities.

Great For...

☑ Don't Miss

Carving first tracks into Hokkaidō's famous powder.

Niseko

As far as most foreign skiers are concerned, Niseko is how you say 'powder' in Japanese. It gets a whopping 15m of snow every year! **Niseko United** (ニセコユナイテッド; Map p223; www.niseko.ne.jp/en; adult/child ¥7400/4500; ⊙8.30am-8.30pm Nov-Apr) covers the four resorts on Niseko Annupuri (1308m): Annupuri, Niseko Village, Grand Hirafu and Hanazono. While you can buy individual passes for each, part of what makes Niseko so great (in addition to that famous powder) is that you can buy a single all-mountain pass, an electronic tag that gives you access to 18 lifts and gondolas and 60 runs. The all-mountain pass also gets you free rides on the hourly shuttle that runs between the resorts. Eight-hour and multiday passes are available, too.

Deep powder at Niseko United

MIKE SCHIRF / GETTY IMAGES / AURORA OPEN ©

All the resorts have terrain for all levels, though quieter Hanazono is considered best for families. There are plenty of English-speaking instructors and backcountry guides; rental shops (of which there are many) also typically have a few foreign staff on hand. Niseko takes a pretty hard stance against rope ducking. Avalanches do happen; when conditions are deemed safe, gates to select off-piste areas are opened.

Moiwa (モイワ; Map p223; ☎0136-59-2511; http://niseko-moiwa.jp; 448 Niseko, Niseko-chō; lift ticket ¥4300; ⏲8am-4pm) is Niseko's 'fifth Beatle', right next to Annupuri but not part of Niseko United. It's a small resort that's quietly built up a loyal following for its deep powder and backcountry opportunities. Moiwa follows Niseko's policy of no rope-ducking – it just doesn't have any ropes. Experienced skiers can ski from Moiwa over to Annupuri (if the gate is open). As always, check the daily avalanche report (http://niseko.nadare.info).

For information on getting to and around Niseko, see p235.

Need to Know

The ski season runs roughly December to April. February has the best snow but the most crowds.

Take a Break

The village of Hirafu is the centre of Niseko's lively après-ski scene.

★ Top Tip

Book early; accommodation in popular resorts like Niseko fill up months in advance.

Furano

More or less in the centre of Hokkaidō, Furano shot to world fame after hosting FIS World Ski and Snowboarding Cup events. Relatively undiscovered in comparison to Niseko, Furano rewards savvy powder fiends with polished runs through pristine birch forests. **Furano Ski Area** (富良野スキー場; Map p223; www.princehotels.com/en/ski/furano/index.html; lift ticket full day/night ¥5200/1600, children 12yr & under free; ⏲day 8.30am-7.30pm, night 4.30-7.30pm; 👪) has predominantly beginner and intermediate slopes, though there are some steep advanced runs. If you're travelling as a family, a major bonus here is that children aged 12 years and under get a free lift pass. Eleven lifts, including the fastest gondola in Japan, help to keep the crowds in check.

If you're not staying at one of the Prince Resorts, zero in on lodging in the Kitanomine area, which is near the slopes and also has a decent spread of restaurants and bars.

Furano is 125km from New Chitose Airport and 142km to Sapporo. Be extremely careful in the winter months as roads in this area can be icy and treacherous. Ten buses run daily between Sapporo and Furano

(¥2260, 2½ hours), stopping at Kitanomine Iriguchi, for the Kitanomine district, before the terminus at JR Furano Station.

Sapporo Teine

You can't beat **Teine** (サッポロテイネ; Map p223; ☏011-223-5830, bus pack reservations 011-223-5901; www.sapporo-teine.com/snow; day pass adult/child ¥4900/2400; ☺9am-4pm; 🚌) for convenience, as the slopes lie quite literally on the edge of Sapporo – so close that buses run directly from downtown hotels. You can swish down slopes used in the 1972 Sapporo Winter Olympics by day and enjoy the raucous restaurants, bars and clubs of Susukino by night.

Teine has two zones: the lower, more beginner- and family-oriented Olympia Zone; and the higher, more challenging Highland Zone. There are 15 runs and nine lifts. A variety of packages, many including return bus transfer from Sapporo to the slopes, bring the price down. Note that Teine can get very crowded, particularly on weekends and school holidays.

Back Country

Some excellent options for backcountry skiing exist in Hokkaidō, though this is a relatively new sphere of adventure tourism. Daisetsuzan National Park – Daisetsuzan literally means 'Big Snow Mountain' – is a top destination. On the northeastern side of the park, **Kuro-dake** (Map p223; www.rinyu.co.jp/kurodake; pass ¥3800) has one ropeway and lift and is becoming popular with those who like vertical and challenging terrain. Hokkaidō's highest mountain, **Asahi-dake** (Map p223; http://asahidake.hokkaido.jp/en;

Asahi-dake

day pass ¥4200; ⊙1 Dec–6 May), offers an extreme experience on a smoking volcano (not for beginners); there's one ropeway (500 vertical metres), dry powder and scenic views here. Some ski and snowboard operators in Furano run backcountry tours to Asahi-dake and Kuro-dake. If you come on your own, it's advisable to hire a local guide; your accommodation should be able to help with that (ask well in advance).

Extreme skiing is possible on Rishiri-zan, a classic volcanic cone on its own remote island off the coast of northern Hokkaidō. This is true backcountry stuff (think no

> ★ **Top Tips**
> An excellent website for checking out the Japan ski scene is www.snowjapan.com (in English).

KINPOUGEO5 / GETTY IMAGES ©

lifts) with plenty of hiking up, followed by steep descents down the volcano – which sees few skiers or boarders – all the while taking in the breathtaking ocean views. You'll need a guide from **Rishiri Nature Guide Service** (利尻自然ガイドサービス; ☑0163-82-2295; www.maruzen.com/tic/guide). Book early!

For backcountry tours around Niseko, NAC (p234) has experienced English-speaking guides and instructors.

Practicalities

○ **What to Bring** Almost everything you'll need is available in Japan. If you have large feet (longer than 30cm), bring your own boots. If you're on the big side, bring your own clothing and gloves, too.

○ **Costs** Japan is a surprisingly reasonable place to ski or snowboard; Niseko is the priciest of Japan's resorts. Lift tickets and accommodation are competitively priced as the number of domestic skiers has been in decline for years.

○ **Food** The slopes have plenty of pizza, ramen and other snacks. Given its international clientele, Niseko's resort villages have numerous restaurants serving Western food.

☑ **Don't Miss**
Niseko's Hirafu Village has Japan's best après-ski scene.

Shikotsu-Tōya National Park

Shikotsu-Tōya National Park (支笏洞爺国立公園) contains pockets of wilderness – with caldera lakes, mountains and hot spring resorts – carved out of a large area within easy striking distance from Sapporo.

Great For...

☑ **Don't Miss**

Hōheikyō in Jōzankei, often voted Hokkaidō's best onsen.

Jōzankei

Jōzankei (定山渓) sits along the Toyohira-gawa, deep in a gorge. It's the closest major onsen town to Sapporo – only an hour away – and an easy escape for those after some R&R. The resort is especially pretty (and popular) in autumn, when the leaves change colour – a sight that can be viewed from many an outdoor bath.

There are several resort-style hotels here with baths, but none hold a candle to **Hōheikyō** (豊平峡; Map p223; ☎011-598-2410; www.hoheikyo.co.jp; 608 Jōzankei; adult/child ¥1000/500; ☺10am-10.30pm). Set above town on the gorge's forested slope, Hōheikyō can boast of having Hokkaidō's largest outdoor bath. The whole rambling structure is shack-like, which just adds to the appeal of having stumbled upon something great. The door curtains indicating

Tōya-ko (p230)

ℹ Need to Know

Shikotsu-Tōya National Park is spread out 993 sq km southwest of Sapporo; a car is the best way to get around.

✕ Take a Break

All the resort towns have a few restaurants, though many open only for lunch.

★ Top Tip

Hokkaidō is bear country. If you head into the mountains, carry a bear bell and stop in at the nearest visitors centre to check for recent sightings.

which baths are for men and which are for women are swapped daily.

Five buses run between Sapporo Ekimae Bus Terminal and Jōzankei daily (¥770, one hour), continues on to Hōheikyō (¥840, 1¼ hours), the final stop.

Yōtei-zan

The perfect conical volcano **Yōtei-zan** (羊蹄山; Map p223) is also known as Ezo-Fuji because of its striking resemblance to Fuji-san. One of Japan's 100 Famous Mountains, it sits in its own little pocket of Shikotsu-Tōya National Park, just 10km from Niseko. It's a stunning backdrop: the only way to miss it is if it's hidden in cloud.

Be prepared for a big climb if you want to tackle Yōtei-zan. The most popular of four trailheads is Yōtei-zan tozan-guchi (羊蹄山登山口) at 350m, which means a more

than 1500m vertical climb to the summit at 1898m. Most people climb and descend in a day – get an early start and allow six to nine hours return, depending on how fit you are. Be mentally and physically prepared – the weather can change quickly on this exposed volcano, especially above the 1600m tree line. Make sure you have enough food and drink. There is an emergency hut at 1800m.

The upper reaches of Yōtei-zan are covered in alpine flowers during the summer. From the peak, the Sea of Japan, the Pacific Ocean and Tōya-ko are all visible – unless, of course, you are inside a cloud!

Yōtei-zan is best accessed from Niseko. If you want to attempt this by public transport, you have to catch the 6.40am bus (¥300, 11 minutes, Monday to Saturday) from JR Kutchan Station; the last return bus is at 8.07pm. Hiking season is roughly mid-June through mid-October.

Noboribetsu Onsen

Noboribetsu Onsen (登別温泉) is a serious onsen: you can smell the sulphur from miles away. While the town is small, there are countless springs here, sending up mineral-rich waters. The source of the waters is **Jigoku-dani** (地獄谷; Map p223), a hissing, steaming volcanic pit above town. A wooden boardwalk leads out to a boiling geyser. According to legend, this hellish landscape is home to the *oni* (demon) Yukujin. Don't worry: he's kind and bestows luck. You'll find statues of him around town.

Onsen Tengoku (温泉天国; Map p223; www.takimotokan.co.jp/english/onsen; Dai-ichi Takimoto-kan, 55 Noboribetsu Onsen-chō; ¥2000, after 4pm ¥1500; ⊙9am-6pm), the bathhouse attached to the Dai-ichi Takimoto-kan hotel, deserves singling out because it is truly spectacular, an 'onsen heaven' (*tengoku*

means 'heaven'). The sprawling complex, awash in pastel tiles, fountains and mirrors, has more variety than any others here, with seven different springs (all purportedly good for something) and several outdoor baths.

JR Muroran line runs from Sapporo to Noboribetsu (¥4480, 1¼ hours). Frequent buses (¥340, 15 minutes) connect the train station with Noboribetsu Onsen bus terminal, at the southern end of town; a taxi ride between the train station and town should cost ¥2000. Direct highway buses run between Noboribetsu Onsen bus terminal and Sapporo (¥1950, 100 minutes), as well as New Chitose Airport (¥1370, one hour).

Tōya-ko

At the southwestern side of Shikotsu-Tōya National Park, Tōya-ko (洞爺湖) is an

Jigoku-dani

almost classically round caldera lake with a large island (Naka-jima) sitting in the middle. Tōya-ko Onsen (洞爺湖温泉), the small resort on the lake's southern shore, has free hand baths and foot baths throughout town (think of it as an onsen treasure hunt!). There's a fireworks display on the lake every night from April until October at 8.45pm, and paddle steamers running lake cruises. The 50km circumference of the lake can be rounded by car or bicycle.

SMALLDARUMA / SHUTTERSTOCK ©

But what sets Tōya-ko apart is its truly active volcano, **Usu-zan** (有珠山; Map p223; ☎0142-74-2401; www.wakasaresort. com; 184-5 Shōwa Shin-zan, Sōbetsu-chō; ropeway adult/child return ¥1500/750; ⊙8.30am-5pm) at 729m, which has erupted four times since 1910, most recently in 2000. The eruptions at Uzu-zan were among the first to be recorded by modern means (and work here significantly advanced science in early detection). At the **Volcano Science Museum** (火山科学館; Map p223; ☎0142-75-2555; www.toyako-vc.jp; 142-5 Tōya-ko Onsen; ¥600; ⊙9am-5pm; P) you can see video footage of eruptions in action, and before and after photos that clearly show new land masses forming.

Shōwa Shin-zan (昭和新山; 398m), whose name means 'the new mountain of the Shōwa period', arose from a wheat field following the 1943 eruption of Usu-zan. A ropeway runs up to a viewing platform for Shōwa Shin-zan, with Tōya-ko behind it. From the observation deck a trail heads out on a 90-minute circuit (open May to October) around the outer rim of Usu-zan.

The JR Muroran line runs from Sapporo to Tōya (¥5920, two hours). From the train station, it's a 15-minute bus (¥330, twice hourly) or taxi ride (¥1800) to the bus terminal in Tōya-ko Onsen. Buses (one way/round trip ¥340/620, 10.10am, 12.45pm, 1.40pm and 3.50pm) run from the Tōya-ko Onsen bus terminal to the ropeway. A taxi should cost ¥1800; all the way from JR Tōya-ko Station, ¥3000.

Shikotsu-ko

Shikotsu-ko (支笏湖) is the second-deepest lake in Japan and renowned for its clear water. While it is 250m above sea level, its deepest spot is 363m, 113m below sea level. Shikotsu-ko Onsen (支笏湖温泉), on the eastern side of the lake, is the only town. This compact little resort village has some nice short walks, including a nature trail for birdwatchers. Sightseeing boats head out onto the lake and there are rental bicycles, boats and canoes. There is no public transport to Shikotsu-ko.

Sapporo

◉ SIGHTS

Sapporo Beer Museum   Museum

(サッポロビール博物館; ☏011-748-1876; www.
sapporoholdings.jp/english/guide/sapporo; N7E9
Higashi-ku; ⊗11.30am-8pm; 🅿; 🚌88 to Sapporo
Biiru-en, Ⓢ Tōhō line to Higashi-Kuyakusho-mae,
exit 4) **FREE** This legendary Sapporo attraction is in the original Sapporo Beer brewery,
a pretty, ivy-covered brick building. There's
no need to sign up for the tour; there are
plenty of English explanations about Japan's
oldest beer (the brewery was founded in
1876). At the end there's a tasting salon
(beers ¥200 to ¥300) where you can com-
pare Sapporo's signature Black Label with
Sapporo Classic (found only in Hokkaidō)
and Kaitakushi Pilsner, a recreation of the
original recipe (found only here).

Ōkura-yama Ski Jump
Stadium   Museum

(大倉山ジャンプ競技場; Map p223; ☏011-
641-8585; www.sapporowintersportsmuseum.
com; 1274 Miyano-mori, Chūo-ku; combined lift &
museum ticket ¥1000; ⊗8.30am-6pm May-Oct,
9am-5pm Nov-Apr; 🅿) This ski-jump slope
was built on the side of Ōkura-yama for the
1972 Sapporo Winter Games. At 133.6m it's
just slightly shorter than Sapporo TV Tower,
with a 33-degree incline. What would it feel
like to whiz down that? You can hazard a
guess after taking the rickety old lift up to
the top and staring down the slope. Keep
that image in mind when you try the highly
amusing computerised simulator in the
museum below.

Ōdōri-kōen   Park

(大通公園; www.sapporo-park.or.jp/odori/;
Ⓢ Tōzai, Tōhō & Namboku lines to Ōdōri) This
haven in the heart of the city is 13 blocks
(1.5km) long, with the **TV Tower** (さっぽ
ろテレビ塔, Sapporo Terebi-tō; www.tv-tower.
co.jp; Ōdōri-nishi 1-chōme; adult/child ¥720/200;
⊗9am-10pm; Ⓢ Tōzai, Tōhō & Namboku lines to
Ōdōri, exits 2 & 7) at its eastern end. Among
the green lawns and flower gardens are
benches, fountains and sculptures; don't
miss Noguchi Isamu's elegant **Black Slide
Mantra** (ブラックスライドマントラ; Ōdōri
kōen; Ⓢ Tōzai, Tōhō & Namboku lines to Ōdōri).

Sapporo Beer Museum

This is also where many of the city's major events and festivals take place.

EATING & DRINKING

Susukino, south of Ōdōri-kōen, is Sapporo's dining and nightlife centre.

Menya Saimi   Ramen ¥

(麺屋彩未; ☑011-820-6511; Misono 10-jō Toyohira-ku; ramen from ¥750; ⓘ11am-3.15pm & 5-7.30pm Tue-Sun; ℗; Ⓢ Tōhō line to Misono, exit 1) Sapporo takes its ramen seriously and Saimi is oft-voted the best ramen in the city (sometimes the country) – and it's not overrated. You will have to queue, which is annoying, but you will be rewarded with a mind-blowing meal for the same price as a convenience store *bentō*. Get the miso ramen.

A mind-blowing meal for the same price as a convenience store bentō

Daruma   Barbecue ¥¥

(だるま; ☑011-552-6013; http://best.miru-kuru. com/daruma/index.html; S5W4; plates from ¥750; ⓘ5pm-3am; Ⓢ Namboku line to Susukino, exit 5) This is where Sapporoites take friends visiting from out of town for the local speciality, *jingisukan* (all-you-can-eat lamb dish). There's nothing fancy here, just quality meat and a homey vibe. Daruma, in business for more than 60 years, is popular and has a few branches around town, which is good because the main shop draws long lines.

Sapporo Biergarten   Brewery

(サッポロビール園; ☑reservation hotline 0120-150-555; www.sapporo-bier-garten.jp; N7E9 Higashi-ku; ⓘ11.30am-10pm; ☒88 to Sapporo Biiru-en, Ⓢ Tōhō line to Higashi-Kuyakusho-mae, exit 4) This complex next to the Sapporo Beer Museum has no fewer than five beer halls, the best of which is Kessel Hall, where you can tuck into all-you-can-eat *jingisukan* washed down with all-you-can-drink draught beer direct from the factory (per person ¥3900). Reservations highly recommended.

INFORMATION

There is a tourist help desk in the basement of the arrivals hall at New Chitose Airport.

Hokkaidō-Sapporo Food & Tourist Information Centre (北海道さっぽろ「食と観光」情報館; ☑011-213-5088; www.welcome.city.sapporo. jp/english; JR Sapporo Station; ⓘ8.30am-8pm; Ⓡ JR Sapporo, west exit) has maps, timetables, brochures and pamphlets in English for Sapporo and all of Hokkaidō. Staff speak English and are helpful. It's located on the ground floor of Sapporo Stellar Pl, inside the north concourse of JR Sapporo Station.

GETTING THERE & AROUND

Rapid Airport trains (¥1070, 36 minutes) depart every 15 minutes from **New Chitose Airport** (新千歳空港; CTS; Map p223; ☑0123-23-0111; www.new-chitose-airport.jp/en) for JR Sapporo Station. For a taxi to central Sapporo, budget about ¥10,000.

The city's main bus depot is **Sapporo Eki-mae Bus Terminal** (札幌駅前バスターミナル; Map p223; Ⓡ JR Sapporo), beneath the Esta building on the south side of JR Sapporo Station.

Sapporo has three useful subway lines that run from 6am to midnight: fares start at ¥200. Taxis are easy to hail; flagfall is ¥670.

Niseko

ACTIVITIES

Niseko is blessed with more than 25 onsen, including luxurious hotel baths and mountain hideaways.

Goshiki Onsen   Onsen

(五色温泉; Map p223; ☑0136-58-2707; 510 Niseko, Niseko-chō; ¥700; ⓘ8am-8pm May-Oct, 10am-7pm Nov-Apr) At the base (750m) of active volcano Iwaonupuri, Goshiki Onsen has views from the outdoor baths and sulphur-rich, highly acidic (pH 2.6!) waters. It's attached to a deeply rustic ryokan (traditional Japanese inn), but most visitors just come for the baths. You need a car to get here; some lodgings do excursions to the baths.

EATING & DRINKING

After hours, Hirafu has an international spread of restaurants and buzzes during ski season (many places shut in the low season). Kutchan town has lots of *izakaya* (Japanese pub-eatery), especially on Miyako-dōri; there's a supermarket next to JR Kutchan Station.

Niseko Loft Club   Barbecue ¥¥

(ニセコロフト倶楽部; 0136-44-2883; 397-5 Sōga, Niseko-chō; per 300g ¥1900; 5.30-9.30pm; P) Down the road from the Annupuri slopes, Loft Club glitters with fairy lights and the warm, glowing promise of a filling meal washed down with beer and

Niseko Green Season

Niseko is making a big push to become a year-round destination. The buzz isn't quite there yet, but the infrastructure is building, with operators offering rafting, kayaking and mountain-biking tours. The combination of mountains and farmlands means Niseko is excellent for hiking and cycling, too. For a challenging but rewarding ascent, try **Yōtei-zan** (p229), part of Shikotsu-Tōya National Park.

Niseko Adventure Centre (NAC)
(ニセコアドベンチャーセンター; Map p223; 0136-23-2093; www.nacadventures.jp; Yamada, Kutchan-chō; 8am-9pm) is a local pioneer, following examples set in other mountain resorts throughout the world. In summer they offer rafting, cycling, sea kayaking and canyoning tours (and more) with experienced English-speaking guides.

Hiking Yōtei-zan
SHAYNE HILL XTREME VISUALS / GETTY IMAGES ©

lively conversation. The speciality here is *yakiniku* (grill-it-yourself meat), but rather than just the usual beef and pork, there's lamb and venison on the menu, too. Dishes are to share.

Graubunden   Cafe ¥

(グラウビュンデン; 0136-23-3371; www.graubunden.jp; 132-26 Yamada, Kutchan-chō; 8am-7pm Fri-Wed; P 🛜 🍴) This is Niseko's original hang-out spot, in Hirafu East Village, a favourite with season regulars and long-time expats for its yummy sandwiches, omelettes and cakes. You won't find a better breakfast in Niseko than the classic bacon, egg and cheese sandwich here. Friendly service, too.

Sobadokoro Rakuichi   Soba ¥

(そば処 楽一; 0136-58-3170; 431 Niseko, Niseko-chō; lunch from ¥900; dinner course ¥8000; lunch from 11.30am, dinner from 5pm Fri-Wed; P) Niseko's most famous noodle shop is also famously hard to find, though its secluded location (accessed via a wooden boardwalk) is a big part of the appeal. The other part is watching chef Tatsuri Rai behind the counter hand-make the soba (buckwheat noodles) you just ordered. Simple is best: go for the *namako uchi seiro* (生粉打ちせいろ; fresh-made cold noodles) – just ¥900.

Sprout   Cafe

(スプラウト; 0136-55-5161; http://sprout-project.com; N1W3-10, Kutchan-chō; coffee from ¥400; 8am-8pm Wed-Mon; 🛜) This popular hang-out run by a former outdoor guide serves Niseko's best coffee. It's 100m up the road from Kutchan Station, decked out like a very cool campsite. There's a huge library of outdoor books and magazines (in Japanese) here, too.

ℹ️ INFORMATION

Near the Hirafu gondola (and where buses to/from **New Chitose Airport** (p233) originate and terminate), is **Hirafu Welcome Centre** (ひらふ ウエルカムセンター; 0136-22-0109; www.grand-hirafu.jp/winter/en/index.html; 204 Yamada, Kutchan-chō; 8.30am-9pm) with information in English. Open only during the snow season.

Ōdōri-kōen (p232)

Niseko Tourist Information (ニセコ観光案
内所; ☑0136-44-2468; www.nisekotourism.
com; Chūō-dōri, Niseko-chō; ☉8am-5pm; ☎) at
JR Niseko Station, with pamphlets, maps, bus
timetables; can help with bookings.

❶ GETTING THERE & AWAY

Having a car will make it easier to move between
the various ski slopes, though you'll need to
drive with extreme caution. There are outlets of
major car rental companies in Hirafu.

During the ski season, **Chūō Bus** (中央バ
ス; ☑Hakodate terminal 0128-22-3265, Sapporo
terminal 011-231-0600; www.chuo-bus.co.jp)
coaches run from **Sapporo Eki-mae Bus Terminal**
(p233) (one way/return ¥2240/4000, three
hours) and New Chitose Airport (one way/return
¥2600/4500, 3¾ hours) to Niseko; travel times
are dependent on weather conditions. Drop-off
points include the Welcome Centre (p234) in
Hirafu, the Hilton at Niseko Village and Annupuri.
Reservations are necessary, and it's recommended
that you book well ahead of your departure date.

You can also arrive by train: take the JR
Hakodate line from Sapporo to Niseko Station
(¥2680, three hours). You will need to transfer in
Otaru, where you can also get trains directly to
New Chitose Airport.

❶ GETTING AROUND

During snow season, Niseko United Shuttle
(www.niseko.ne.jp) runs a service (roughly
hourly 8am to 11pm) between Hirafu, Niseko
Village and Annupuri (free for all-mountain pass
holders). From 5pm to 11pm, the shuttle route
extends to Kutchan Station, giving you more
dining options. Pick up a schedule from any of
the tourist information centres.

Niseko suffers from a chronic taxi shortage
during the ski season, as most are booked up
in advance. Most likely your lodging will offer to
shuttle you around (for a fee), which is usually
cheaper than taxis and easier to arrange.

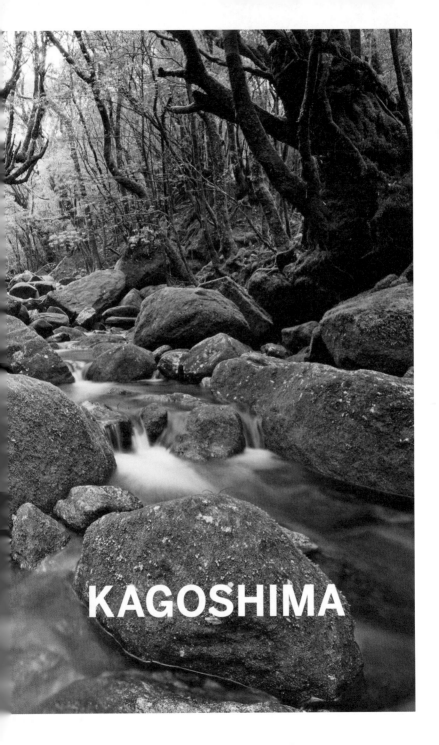

KAGOSHIMA

Kagoshima

Sunny Kagoshima (鹿児島), at the bottom of Kyūshū, has a personality to match its climate, and has been voted Japan's friendliest city nationwide. Its backdrop and deity is Sakurajima, a very active volcano just across the bay. Locals raise their umbrellas against the mountain's recurrent eruptions, when fine ash coats the landscape like snow and obscures the sun like fog – mystical and captivating. The city is also the jumping-off point for trips to Yakushima (屋久島), a Unesco World Heritage Site renowned for its virgin forests, and Ibusuki, where the big attraction is the beachside baths, in which onsen (hot springs) steam rises through sand, heating it.

Kagoshima in Two Days

For a short trip, head straight to Yaku-shima. A night there will give you time to do a short hike and hit a seaside onsen. Take the ferry back to Kagoshima in the afternoon, and spend the evening sampling the food and drink for which the southern city is famous.

Kagoshima in Four Days

More time gives you an opportunity for longer hikes deep into the interior of Yakushima, and also a buffer if bad weather hits. Budget an extra day in Kagoshima, to rent a car and drive out to the volcano Sakurajima and the hot sand baths at Ibusuki.

Arriving in Kagoshima

Kagoshima is at the southern tip of the island of Kyūshū. It is possible to get here by *shinkansen* (bullet train) from Honshū destinations such as Hiroshima, Osaka, Kyoto and even Tokyo, though it's a long ride. If you're short on time, you can fly one-way or both ways to Kagoshima Airport (p243), which has both international connections to Shanghai, Hong Kong, Taipei and Seoul, and convenient domestic flights, including to Tokyo, Osaka and Okinawa (Naha).

Sleeping

Kagoshima has plenty of good-value places to sleep. The station area is a bit quiet; to take advantage of the city's dining and drinking options, stay in or around Tenmonkan. On Yakushima, the most convenient place to be based is Miyanoura. In July and August and the spring Golden Week holiday, it's best to try to reserve ahead as places fill up early.

Yakusugi Land

SARA WINTER / GETTY IMAGES ©

Hiking on Yakushima

Yakushima is covered in primeval forest – some of the last virgin forest left in Japan; hiking into the interior is the best way to experience the island's beauty.

Great For...

☑ **Don't Miss**

The island's famous *yakusugi* (屋久杉; Cryptomeria japonica) – ancient cedar trees.

Jōmon-sugi

This enormous *yakusugi* tree is estimated to be between 3000 and 7000 years old, and though no longer living, it remains a majestic sight. Most hikers reach the tree via the 19.5km, eight-to-10-hour round trip from **Arakawa-tozanguchi** (Arakawa trailhead; 荒川登山口). From March through November, in order to limit traffic congestion and environmental impact, all hikers must transfer to an **Arakawa Mountain Bus** (round trip ¥1740) from the Yakusugi Museum parking lot to get the Arakawa-tozanguchi; you must buy a ticket at least a day in advance.

Shiratani-unsuikyō Hike

Shorter than the Jōmon-sugi hike – about three to four hours return – and arguably more beautiful, this hike passes waterfalls,

Virgin forest, Yakushima

ℹ️ Need to Know

From mid-July through mid-September the trails get very crowded; shoulder season is better (except for Golden Week).

✕ Take a Break

Stock up on provisions from **Yakuden** (ヤクデン; ⏰9am-10pm), a supermarket on the main street in Miyanoura, just north of the entrance to the pier area.

> ### ★ Top Tip
>
> If you're going hiking, you can ask your lodging to prepare a *bentō* (boxed meal) the night before you set out.

moss-lined rocks and towering *yakusugi* to the overlook at Taiko-iwa. The **trailhead** (白谷雲水峡登山口; ¥300), at 622m, is served by up to 10 daily buses to and from Miyanoura (¥550, 40 minutes, March to November).

Yakusugi Land

A great way to see some *yakusugi* without a long trek into the forest, Yakusugi Land (ヤクスギランド; ⏱0997-42-3508; http://y-reku mori.com; ¥300; ⏰9am-5pm)) offers shorter hiking courses over wooden boardwalks, and longer hikes deep into the ancient cedar forest. There are four buses a day to and from Anbō (¥740, 40 minutes).

Know Before You Go

Keep in mind that Yakushima is a place of extremes: the interior of the island is one

of the wettest places in Japan. In the winter the peaks may be covered in snow, while the coast is still relatively balmy. Don't set off on a hike without a good map and the proper gear. **Nakagawa Sports** (ナカガワ スポーツ; ⏱0997-42-0341; http://yakushima-sp.com; 421-6 Miyanoura; rainwear rentals ¥1200-2400; ⏰9am-7pm, closed every other Wed) in Miyanoura rents out everything from rainwear and waterproof hiking boots (also in large sizes) to tents and baby carriers.

The Yakumonkey guide (www.yakumon key.com), available for purchase online, has detailed descriptions of hikes and trails. Also helpful is the detailed Japanese-language trail map Yama-to-Kougen-no-Chizu-Yaku-shima (山と高原の地図屋久島; ¥1080), available at major bookshops in Japan. Even though trails can be very crowded during holidays, be sure to alert someone at your accommodation of your intended route and fill in a *tōzan todoke*de (route plan) at the trailhead.

Kagoshima

◉ SIGHTS

Museum of the
Meiji Restoration   Museum

(維新ふるさと館; Map p239; ☎099-239-7700; 23-1 Kaijiya-chō; ¥300; ☺9am-5pm; ℝ JR Kagoshima-Chūō) This museum offers insights into the unique social system of education, samurai loyalty and sword techniques that made Satsuma one of Japan's leading provinces, with a good smartphone app in English. There are hourly audiovisual presentations about the ground-breaking visits of Satsuma students to the West and the Satsuma Rebellion told by animatronic Meiji-era reformers, including Saigō Takamori and Sakamoto Ryōma.

⊗ EATING & DRINKING

Yamauchi Nōjō   Izakaya ¥

(山内農場; ☎099-223-7488; 2nd fl, 1-26 Higashi-sengoku-chō; dishes ¥410-1250; ☺4pm-2am Mon-Thu, to 3am Fri & Sat, to 1am Sun; ℝTenmonkan-dōri) *Kuro Satsuma-dori*

(black Satsuma chicken) is the name of the bird served here, and also what it looks like after being grilled *sumibi-yaki*-style over open charcoal. Other local dishes: marinated *katsuo* (bonito) sashimi, *kurobuta* (black pork) salad, and *tsukune* (chicken meatballs) with cheese or raw egg. Decor is modern-meets-rustic. Enter around the corner from Remm Kagoshima hotel.

Kagomma Furusato
Yatai-mura   Japanese ¥

(かごつまふるさと屋台村; ☎099-255-1588; 6-4 Chūō-chō; prices vary; ☺lunch & dinner, individual stall hours vary; ℝTakami-bashi) *Yatai-mura* means 'food stall village', and some two dozen stalls near Kagoshima-Chūō Station offer a taste of Kagoshima of old. Follow your nose to your favourite stalls for *sumibi-yaki* (coal-fired chicken), sashimi, teppanyaki beef and fish dishes. Booth No 16 serves delicious Kagoshima *kurobuta* (black pig), *shabu-shabu* style (¥1280).

Street restaurants in Kagoshima

LOKYIN_PHOTOGRAPHY / SHUTTERSTOCK ©

Honkaku Shōchū Bar Ishizue Bar

(本格焼酎Bar 礎; ☑099-227-0125; www.honka
ku-shochu-bar-ishizue.com; 6-1 Sengoku-chō, 4th
fl, Flower Bldg; ¥2000; ◑8pm-3am) This chic,
amber-and-wood *shōchū* (potato vodka)
bar has everything going for it, and is
considered one of the finest places to drink
Kagoshima's prefectural liquor, with over
500 different bottles available, each with
its own story, which the owner can discuss
personally (if time permits). Reservations
are nearly always required.

*One of the finest places to
drink Kagoshima's prefectural
liquor*

 INFORMATION

Tourist Information Centre (鹿児島中央駅総
合観光案内所; ☑099-253-2500; JR Kagoshima-Chūō Station; ◑8am-8pm) provides English
info and the handy *Kagoshima* visitors guide.

Tourism Exchange Centre (観光交流セン
ター; ☑099-298-5111; 1-1 Uenosono-chō; ◑9am-
7pm) is near the Museum of the Meiji Restoration; can make hotel reservations.

 GETTING THERE & AROUND

JR Kagoshima-Chūō Station is the terminus
of the Kyūshū *shinkansen* (bullet train), which
travels from Shin-Osaka (¥21,380, 3¾ hours)
via Hiroshima (¥17,150, 2½ hours). Kagoshima
Airport is north of the city; airport buses (adult/
child ¥1250/630) run to Kagoshima-Chūō
Station (40 minutes), Tenmonkan (for downtown; 45 minutes) and Minamifutō pier (for jet
foils to Yakushima; 50 minutes).

Trams are the easiest way around the city.
Route 1 starts from Kagoshima Station and
goes through the city centre; route 2 diverges at
Takami-baba (高見馬場) to JR Kagoshima-Chūō
Station. Either pay the flat fare (¥170) or buy a
one-day travel pass (¥600) from the tourist information centre or on board. Car-rental agencies can
be found at Kagoshima Airport, Kagoshima-Chūō
Station and Kagoshima Station.

 Shōchū

Shōchū, a distilled spirit strongly
associated with Kagoshima, is made
from a variety of raw materials,
including potato (in which case it's
called *imo-jōchū*), barley (*mugi-jōchū*)
and black sugar (*kokutō-shōchū*). It's
quite strong, with an alcohol content
of about 25% (but can be as much as
45%). Like any spirit, *shōchū* can be
harsh – it's long had a rough image to
match – or deliciously complex and
balanced. The good stuff can be drunk
on the rocks (*rokku de*). Go down a
notch and have it *oyu-wari* (with hot
water) or mixed in a *chūhai* (a highball
with soda and lemon).

TAKASUU / GETTY IMAGES ©

Yakushima

 SIGHTS

Yakusugi Museum Museum

(屋久杉自然館; ☑0997-46-3113; 273 9343
Anbō; ¥600; ◑9am-5pm, closed 1st Tue of the
month) In a forested spot with sea views, the
Yakusugi Museum has informative, beautifully designed exhibits about *yakusugi* and
the history of the islanders' relationship
to these magnificent trees. The museum
offers an excellent audio guide in English.
It's conveniently located on the road leading up to Yakusugi Land (p241). Two daily
buses run to and from Miyanoura (¥960,
80 minutes, March to November).

Nagata Inaka-hama
Beach

(永田いなか浜) On the island's northwest coast, Nagata Inaka-hama is a beautiful beach for sunsets, and it's where sea turtles lay their eggs from May to July. It's beside the Inaka-hama bus stop, served by Nagata-bound buses from Miyanoura.

😊 ACTIVITIES

Yakushima has several onsen, from beautifully desolate seaside pools to upmarket hotel facilities. Seaside onsen here are typically *konyoku* onsen (mixed-sex baths)

Sakurajima

Kagoshima's iconic symbol Sakurajima has been spewing an almost continuous stream of smoke and ash since 1955. In 1914 over three billion tonnes of lava swallowed numerous island villages – more than 1000 homes – and joined Sakurajima to the mainland to the southeast. On the mainland, Kagoshima residents speak proudly of Sakurajima. It is said to have *nanairo* (seven colours) visible from across Kinkō-wan, as the light shifts throughout the day on the surface of the mountain.

Despite its volatility, Sakurajima is currently friendly enough to get fairly close to. Among the volcano's three peaks, only Minami-dake (South Peak; 1040m) is active. Climbing the mountain is prohibited, but there are several lookout points. Frequent passenger and car ferries shuttle around the clock between Kagoshima (departing from Kagoshima Port, a five-minute walk from the Suizokukan-guchi tram stop) and Sakurajima (¥160, 15 minutes).

Sakurajima looming over Kagoshima
SEAN PAVONE / SHUTTERSTOCK ©

where swimsuits are not allowed; women traditionally wrap themselves in a thin towel for modesty.

Hirauchi Kaichū Onsen
Onsen

(平内海中温泉; ¥100; ⊘24hr) Onsen lovers will be in heaven here. The outdoor baths are in the rocks by the sea and can only be entered at or close to low tide. You can walk to the baths from the Kaichū Onsen bus stop, but the next stop, Nishikaikon, is actually closer. From Nishikaikon, walk downhill towards the sea for about 200m and take a right at the bottom of the hill.

Yudomari Onsen
Onsen

(湯泊温泉; ¥100; ⊘24hr) This blissfully serene onsen can be entered at any tide. Get off at the Yudomari bus stop and take the road opposite the post office in the direction of the sea. Once you enter the village, the way is marked. It's a 300m walk and you pass a great banyan tree en route.

😋 EATING

There are a few restaurants in each of the island's villages, with the best selection in Miyanoura. If you're staying anywhere but Miyanoura, ask for the set two-meal plan at your lodgings.

Shiosai
Seafood ¥¥

(潮騒; ☏0997-42-2721; 305-3 Miyanoura; dishes ¥1200; ⊘11.30am-2pm & 5.30-9.30pm Fri-Wed) Find a full range of Japanese standards such as *sashimi teishoku* (sashimi set; ¥1700) or *ebi-furai teishoku* (fried shrimp set; ¥1400). Look for the blue and whitish building with automatic glass doors along the main road through Miyanoura.

ℹ️ INFORMATION

Miyanoura's helpful **Tourist Information Centre** (☏0997-42-1019; 823-1 Miyanoura; ⊘8.30am-5pm) is on the road leading away from the port; you can't miss its dramatic architecture. Staff here can help you find lodgings and answer all questions about the island. For cash, Miyanoura post-office ATMs are your best bet.

Ibusuki Sunamushi Kaikan Saraku

🛈 GETTING THERE & AROUND

Tane Yaku Jetfoil (in Kagoshima 099-226-0128, in Miyanoura 0997-42-2003; ⊗8.30am-5.30pm Mon-Fri, to 7pm Sat & Sun) runs six Toppy and Rocket hydrofoils per day between Kagoshima and Miyanoura (¥8300, one hour 50 minutes for direct sailings). Kagoshima's high-speed ferry terminal is just to the south of the Minamifutō pier, a 15-minute walk from Tenmonkan. There are also two hydrofoils per day between Kagoshima and Anbō Port (2½ hours) – good for visitors headed straight to Yakusugi Land. Booking ahead is wise.

Local buses travel the coastal road part way around Yakushima roughly every hour or two, though only a few head into the interior. You'll save a lot of money by purchasing a Yakushima Kotsu Free Pass (one-/two-day ¥2000/3000), good for unlimited travel on Yakushima Kotsu buses; get it at the Miyanoura TIC. Having your car, though, is handy; there's a **Toyota Rent-a-Car** (☑0997-42-2000; https://rent.toyota.co.jp; up to 12hr from ¥5250; ⊗8am-8pm) north of the port in Miyanoura.

Ibusuki

⊕ ACTIVITIES

Ibusuki Sunamushi Kaikan Saraku
Onsen

(いぶすき砂むし会館 砂楽; ☑0993-23-3900; 5-25-18 Yunohama; sand bath & onsen ¥1080, onsen only ¥610; ⊗8.30am-9pm, closed noon-1pm Mon-Fri) Pay at the entrance, change into the provided *yukata* (light cotton kimono) and wander down to the beach where, under a canopy of bamboo slat blinds, women with shovels bury you in hot volcanic sand. Reactions range from panic to euphoria. It's said that 10 minutes will get rid of impurities, but many stay longer. When you're through, head back up to soak in the onsen bath.

🛈 GETTING THERE & AROUND

Trains depart from Kagoshima-chūō (*tokkyū* ¥2130, 50 minutes) for Ibusuki. It's a 15-minute walk from Ibusuki Station to the sand baths, or a short taxi or bus ride.

OKINAWA

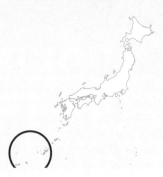

Okinawa

Okinawa (沖縄) reveals a Japan you may not know exists: a chain of semitropical, coral-fringed islands evocative of Hawaii or Southeast Asia. But spectacular nature is only part of it – these islands exude a peculiarly 'un-Japanese' culture. Indeed, they made up a separate country for most of their history, and the Ryūkyū cultural heart still beats strongly here. Okinawa-hontō (沖縄本島) is the largest island, and the historical seat of power of the Ryūkyū dynasty; the modern capital Naha is here. At the southern reaches of the archipelago are the gorgeous Yaeyama Islands (八重山諸島), which include the main islands of Ishigaki-jima and Iriomote-jima as well as a spread of 17 isles.

Okinawa in Two Days

For a short trip, zero in on the cultural (and culinary) attractions of Naha, with its castle, museum, markets and lively *izakaya* (Japanese pub–eateries). From here it's a short ride to the pretty, laid-back Kerama Islands, where you can log some beach time.

Okinawa in Four Days

With more time you can embark on an island-hopping adventure around the truly remote Yaeyama Islands. Each offers a completely different experience: after getting your feet wet on Ishigaki-jima, the main island of the group, take your pick from the old-world charm of Taketomi-jima; the wilds of Iriomote-jima; or the epic diving in Yonaguni-jima.

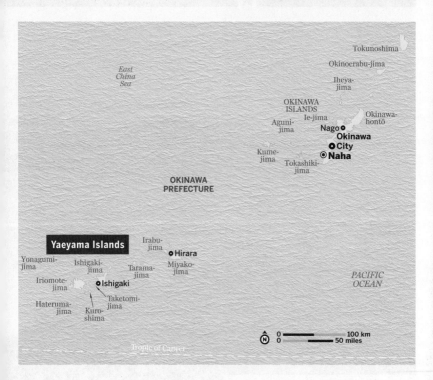

Tokunoshima

Okinoerabu-jima

Iheya-
jima

*East
China
Sea*

OKINAWA
ISLANDS

Aguni-
jima

Ie-jima

Nago○

Okinawa-
hontō

Okinawa

Kume-
jima

○City

Tokashiki-
jima

◎Naha

**OKINAWA
PREFECTURE**

Yaeyama Islands

Irabu-
jima

○Hirara

Yonagumi-
jima

Ishigaki-
jima

Tarama-
jima

Miyako-
jima

Iriomote-
jima

○Ishigaki

Taketomi-
jima

Haterumi-
jima

Kuro-
shima

*PACIFIC
OCEAN*

Tropic of Cancer

⊿
Ⓝ

0 —————— 100 km
0 —————— 50 miles

Arriving in Okinawa

Naha International Airport (OKA) has connections with Seoul, Taipei, Hong Kong and Shanghai and major cities across Japan. From Naha you can fly to other islands further south, or connect to closer ones by jetfoil.

Sleeping

Most visitors in Naha tend to stay on or around Kokusai-dōri, the main tourist strip; you can have your pick from budget guesthouses to reputable chain hotels. On the remote islands, only Ishigaki-jima and Iriomote-jima have resorts; Taketomi-jima has some nice boutique hotels and guesthouses in traditional structures. The most common form of accommodation out here, however, is the family-run *minshuku*.

Kabira-wan

SHIKEMA / SHUTTERSTOCK ©

Yaeyama Islands

*At the far southwestern tip of
Okinawa, near the Tropic of
Cancer, the Yaeyama Islands are
renowned for their sugar-white
beaches, snorkelling and diving
and some of Japan's last intact
subtropical jungles and mangrove
swamps.*

Great For...

☑ Don't Miss

Taketomi-jima and Iriomote-jima's 'star
sand' *(hoshizuna)*, actually the dried
skeletons of marine protozoa.

Perhaps the best feature of the Yaeyamas is
the ease with which you can travel between
them; you can easily explore three or four
islands in one trip.

Ishigaki-jima

Blessed with excellent beaches and brilliant
dive sites, Ishigaki-jima (石垣島) also pos-
sesses an attractive, low-lying geography
that invites long drives and day hikes. A
series of roads branch out from Ishigaki City
and head along the coastline and into the
interior. At the north end of the island, on the
west coast, is **Sunset Beach** (サンセット
ビーチ), a long strip of sand with a bit of
offshore reef. As the name implies, this is
one of the island's best spots to watch the
sun set into the East China Sea. Shower
and toilet facilities are also located here.
Kabira-wan (川平湾) is a sheltered bay

Shiisā (lion-dog roof guardian), Taketomi-jima

SAM DCRUZ / SHUTTERSTOCK ©

Yonaguni-jima (80 km) · **Manta Scramble** · **Sunset Beach** · **Kabira-wan** · **Hoshisuna-no-hama** · Shirahama Port · Iriomote-jima · **Ida-no-hama** · Taketomi-jima · Ishigaki-jima · Shiraho · **Kaiji-hama** · Ishigaki-jima Rittō Ferry Terminal · Ōhara

ℹ Need to Know

Ishigaki-jima is the transit hub for the Yaeyama group. Flights arrive here from Tokyo, Osaka and Naha.

✕ Take a Break

Cafe Taniwha (p259), on Ishigaki-jima, is a great hangout spot.

★ Top Tip

Having a car is best for getting around Ishigaki-jima and Iriomote-jima. If you prefer to avoid the hassle of driving, head to car-free Taketomi-jima.

with white-sand shores and a couple of interesting clump-like islets offshore. Swimming is not allowed in the bay, as pearls are cultivated here, but there's no shortage of glass-bottomed boats offering up a look at the reef life below.

The most popular dive spot on Ishigaki-jima is **Manta Scramble**, off the coast of Kabira Ishizaki. Although you'll likely be sharing with a fair number of dive boats, you're almost guaranteed to see a manta in season. At Kabira-based **Umicoza** (海講座; ☏0980-88-2434; www.umicoza.com; 1287-97 Kabira; 1/2 dives with equipment rental ¥9450/12,600; ⊗8am-6pm), all dive guides speak English, and the shop itself has a long-running reputation for professionalism and reliability.

Taketomi-jima

A mere 15-minute boat ride from Ishigaki-jima, the tiny island of Taketomi-jima (竹富島) is a living museum of Ryūkyū culture, a village of traditional houses complete with red *kawara* (tiled) roofs, coral walls and *shiisā* (lion-dog roof guardians) statues. In order to preserve the island's historical ambience, residents have joined together to ban some signs of modernism. There are a number of modest sights in Taketomi village, though it's best for simply wandering around and soaking up the surrounds. Hiring a bicycle is the ideal way to do this, as you pedal along crushed-coral roads, ceding right of way to placidly plodding ox-carts and admiring the variety of *shiisā* adorning local homes and walls. On the southwest coast is **Kaiji-hama** (カイジ浜; 皆治浜), a lovely stretch of beach. While Taketomi is besieged by Japanese day trippers in the busy summer months, the island remains blissfully quiet at night.

Iriomote-jima

Iriomote-jima (西表島), just 20km west of Ishigaki-jima, feels like Japan's last frontier: Dense jungles and mangrove swamp blanket more than 90% of the island, and it's fringed by some of the most beautiful coral reefs in all Japan. If you're super lucky, you may even spot one of the island's rare *yamaneko,* a nocturnal and rarely seen wildcat (they are most often seen crossing the road at night, so drive carefully after dark).

The majority of the island's beaches are shallow due to the extensive coral reef that surrounds the island. **Hoshisuna-no-hama** (星砂の浜; Star Sand Beach), on the northwestern tip of the island, is a good snorkelling spot. If you are a competent swimmer and the sea is calm, make your way with mask and snorkel to the outside of the reef – the coral and tropical fish here are spectacular. From **Shirahama** (白浜港), at the western end of the north coast road, there are four daily boats (¥500) to the isolated settlement of Funauki. Once there, it's a mere 10-minute walk further to the absolutely gorgeous **Ida-no-hama** (イダの浜).

Several rivers penetrate far into the lush interior of the island and these can be explored by riverboat or kayak. Iriomote has some great hikes, but do not head off into the jungle interior without registering with the police: the trails in the interior are hard to follow – many people have become lost and required rescue. We strongly suggest that you stick to well-marked tracks like the ones along the Urauchi-gawa, or arrange for a guide. **Iriomote Osanpo Kibun** (西表おさんぽ気分; ☎0980-84-8178; www. iriomote-osanpo.com; full-/half-day kayaking &

Hiking on Iriomote-jima

trekking tours from ¥10,000/6000) is a good choice, with an English-speaking guide.

Urauchi-gawa Kankō (浦内川観光; ☑0980-85-6154; www.urauchigawa.com; adult/ child river tours ¥1800/900, full-day trekking & kayak tours ¥8400) runs boat tours 8km up the river (multiple departures daily between 9.30am and 3.30pm). At the 8km point, the boat docks and you can walk a further 2km to the scenic waterfalls of **Mariyudō-no-taki** (マリユドゥの滝), from where a further 200m brings you to another waterfall, **Kanpire-no-taki** (カンピレーの滝).

Yonaguni-jima

About 125km west of Ishigaki and 110km east of Taiwan, Yonaguni-jima (与那国島) is Japan's westernmost inhabited island. It's known for its strong sake, small horses, marlin fishing and the jumbo-sized Yonaguni atlas moth, the largest moth in the world; however, most visitors come to see what lies beneath the waves. In 1985 a local diver discovered what appeared to be human-made 'ruins' off the south coast of the island.

The **Kaitei Iseki** (海底遺跡, Underwater Ruins) look like giant blocks or the steps of a sunken pyramid. Some believe them to be the remains of a Pacific Atlantis; others claim they are just the random result of geological processes. Adding to the underwater allure are the large schools of hammerhead sharks that frequent the waters in winter off the west coast, making Yonaguni perhaps the most famous single diving destination in Japan.

Yonaguni Diving Service (与那国ダイビングサービス; ☑0980-87-2658; 3984-3 Yonaguni; 2-dive boat trips ¥12,500, equipment rental ¥4600) is the most reliable diving outfit on the island. **Mosura no Tamago** (もすらのたまご; ☑0980-87-2112; 4022-380 Yonaguni; per person ¥3700) offers glass-bottomed boat tours of Kaitei Iseki for nondivers.

Island-Hopping

Ferries depart from Ishigaki City's **Ishigaki-jima Rittō Ferry Terminal** (石垣港離島ターミナル) for Taketomi-jima (¥600, 10 minutes, up to 45 daily) and Iriomote-jima (Uehara/Ōhara ¥2060/1570, one hour, up to 20 daily). Uehara port is the more convenient of Iriomote's two ports.

Yonaguni is harder to get to: Ryūkyū Air Commuter flies once daily between Yonaguni and Naha, and operates three flights a day between Yonaguni and Ishigaki-jima. **Fukuyama Kaiun** (福山海運; ☑in Ishigaki 0980-82-4962, in Yonaguni 0980-87-2555) operates two ferries a week between Ishigaki-jima and Kubura Port on Yonaguni (¥3550, four hours). Be warned: these are not for those with a weak stomach.

Okinawan Cuisine

Reflecting the islands' geography and history, Okinawa's food culture is recognisably distinct from that of mainland Japan. Eating your way through the islands – and sampling the signature local ingredients, from both land and sea – is quite literally a treat.

Okinawan cuisine originated in the splendour of the Ryūkyū court and from the humble lives of the impoverished islanders. Healthy eating is considered to be extremely important; indeed, islanders have long held that medicine and food are essentially the same. And it must be noted that Okinawans are among the longest-living people in the world.

Local Specialities

Today one of the island's staple foods is pork, which is acidic and rich in protein. Every part of the pig is eaten. *Mimigā* (ミミガー) is thinly sliced pig's ears marinated in vinegar, perfect with a cold glass of local Orion beer (オリオンビール). *Rafutē* (ラフテー) is pork stewed with ginger, brown sugar, rice wine and soy sauce until it falls apart. If you need some stamina, try some

Great For...

☑ **Don't Miss**

Gōyā (bitter melon), the local ingredient most often associated with Okinawa.

ikasumi-jiru (イカスミ汁), which is stewed pork in black squid ink.

While stewing is common, Okinawans prefer stir-frying, and refer to the technique as *champurū* (チャンプルー). Perhaps the best-known stir-fry is *gōyā champurū* (ゴーヤーチャンプルー), a mix of pork, bitter melon and the island's uniquely sturdy tofu, *shima-dōfu* (島豆腐).

Okinawa-soba (沖縄そば) is udon (thick white noodles) served in a pork broth. The most common variants are *sōki-soba* (ソーキそば), topped with pork spare ribs; and *Yaeyama-soba* (八重山そば), which contains soba topped with tiny pieces of tender pork, bean sprouts and scallions.

Other local specialities bear the imprint of the post-war American Occupation, including *tako raisu* (タコライス), a dish of taco fillings served on sticky rice, and

Blue Seal (ブルーシール) brand ice cream, founded on one of the bases.

Awamori

Okinawa has its own signature distilled spirit called *awamori* (泡盛), actually made of long-grain rice. It has an alcohol content between 30% and 60% and although it's usually served *mizu-wari* (水割; diluted with water), it has a good kick.

Local Ingredients

Gōyā (ごーやー; bitter melon) Gnarly gourd that appears in all kinds of dishes (and cold-pressed in juice), delivering a dose of antioxidants often credited for Okinawan's famous longevity.

Kokutō (黒糖) Dark brown, mineral rich unrefined sugar; used in many dishes sweet and savoury (and also good for snacking).

Shīkuwāsā (シークワーサー) Very sour citrus native to Okinawa and Taiwan, used as a garnish or diluted in cocktails and soft drinks.

Tōfuyō (豆腐餻) Type of *shima-dōfu* whose strong flavour is due to fermentation in *awamori*.

Umi-budō (海ぶどう) Literally 'sea grapes' these are teeny-tiny bunches of spherical algae, usually eaten raw.

Naha

◉ SIGHTS

Naha is fairly easy to navigate, since the main sights and attractions are located in the city centre. The city's main artery is **Kokusai-dōri** (国際通り), a riot of neon, noise, souvenir shops, bustling restaurants and Japanese young things out strutting their stuff. It's a festival of tat and tackiness, but it's a good time if you're in the mood.

Many people prefer the atmosphere of the three covered shopping arcades that run south off Kokusai-dōri: **Ichibahon-dōri** (市場本道り), **Mutsumibashi-dōri** (むつみ橋通り) and **Heiwa-dōri** (平和通り).

The Shuri district is about 3km to the east of the city centre.

Shuri-jō   Castle

(首里城; ☎098-886-2020; http://oki-park.
jp/shurijo; 1-2 Kinjō-chō, Shuri; ¥820, with
1- or 2-day monorail pass discounted to ¥660;
⏰8.30am-7pm Apr-Jun, Oct & Nov, to 8pm Jul-
Sep, to 6pm Dec-Mar, closed 1st Wed & Thu Jul)
This reconstructed castle was originally
built in the 14th century and served as the administrative centre and royal residence of the Ryūkyū kingdom until the 19th century. Enter through the **Kankai-mon** (歓会門) and go up to the **Hōshin-mon** (奉神門), which forms the entryway to the inner sanctum of the castle. Visitors can enter the **Seiden** (正殿), which has exhibits on the castle and the Okinawan royals.

Okinawa Prefectural
Museum & Art Museum   Museum

(沖縄県立博物館・美術館; ☎098-941-8200;
www.museums.pref.okinawa.jp; Omoromachi
3-1-1; prefectural/art museum ¥410/310;
⏰9am-6pm Tue-Thu & Sun, to 8pm Fri & Sat)
Opened in 2007, this museum of Okinawa's history, culture and natural history is easily one of the best museums in Japan. Displays are well laid-out, attractively presented and easy to understand, with excellent bilingual interpretive signage. The art museum section holds interesting special exhibits (admission prices vary) with an emphasis on local artists. It's about 15 minutes' walk northwest of the Omoromachi monorail station.

Kokusai-dōri, Naha

Daichi Makishi
Kōsetsu Ichiba Market
(第一牧志公設市場; 2-10-1 Matsuo; ⊙8am-8pm, restaurants 10am-7pm) Our favourite stop in the arcade area is the covered food market just off Ichibahon-dōri, about 200m south of Kokusai-dōri. The colourful variety of fish and produce on offer here is amazing, and don't miss the wonderful local restaurants upstairs.

Tsuboya Pottery Street Area
(壷屋やちむん道り; Tsuboya Yachimun-dōri) One of the best parts of Naha is this neighbourhood, a centre of ceramic production from 1682, when Ryūkyū kilns were consolidated here by royal decree. Most shops along this old-timey street sell all the popular Okinawan ceramics, including *shiisā* and containers for serving *awamori,* the local firewater. The lanes off the main street here contain some classic crumbling old Okinawan houses. To get here from Kokusai-dōri, walk south through the entirety of Heiwa-dōri arcade (about 350m).

EATING

Yūnangi Okinawan ¥¥
(ゆうなんぎい; ☑098-867-3765; 3-3-3 Kumoji; dishes ¥1200; ⊙noon-3pm & 5.30-10.30pm Mon-Sat) You'll be lucky to get a seat here, but if you do, you'll be treated to some of the best Okinawan food around, served in traditional but bustling surroundings. Try the *okinawa-soba* set (¥1400), or choose from among the appealing options on the picture menu. It's on a side street off Kokusai-dōri – look for the wooden sign with white lettering above the doorway.

Nuchigafu Okinawan ¥¥
(ぬちがふ; ☑098-861-2952; 1-28-3 Tsuboya; set dinner from ¥3000; ⊙11.30am-5pm & 5.30-10pm Wed-Mon) For a memorable, elegant meal in Naha, don't pass up dinner at the hilltop Nuchigafu, off the southern end of Tsuboya Pottery Street (p257). Formerly a lovely Okinawan teahouse, and long before that a historic Ryūkyūan residence, Nuchigafu serves lunch and frothy *buku-buku* tea

during the day and beautifully plated, multi-course Okinawan dinners by night. Children aged 11 years and older are welcome.

Ashibiunā Okinawan ¥
(あしびうなぁ; ☑098-884-0035; 2-13 Shuri Tonokura-chō; lunch sets ¥800-1250; ⊙11.30am-3pm & 5.30pm-midnight) Perfect for lunch after touring Shuri-jō (p256), Ashibiunā has a traditional ambience and picturesque garden. Set meals feature local specialities such as *gōyā champurū*, *okinawa-soba* and *ikasumi yakisoba* (stir-fried squid-ink noodles). On the road leading away from Shuri-jō, Ashibiunā is on the right, just before the intersection to the main road.

> *A traditional ambience and picturesque garden*

ℹ INFORMATION

At Naha airport's helpful **Tourist Information Counter** (☑098-857-6884; 1F Arrivals Terminal, Naha International Airport; ⊙9am-9pm), pick up a copy of the *Naha Guide Map* before heading into town. The city **Tourist Information Office** (那覇市観光案内所; ☑098-868-4887; 3-2-10 Makishi; ⊙9am-8pm), located in the Tenbus Building, gives out free maps and information.

On Kokusai-dōri, **Okinawa Tourist** (沖縄ツーリスト; OTS; ☑098-862-1111; 1-2-3 Matsuo; ⊙9.30am-6pm Mon-Fri, to 3.30pm Sat) is a solid travel agency with English speakers who can help with all manner of ferry and flight bookings.

ℹ GETTING THERE & AROUND

Naha International Airport (OKA) has connections with Seoul, Taipei, Hong Kong and Shanghai and all major cities on mainland Japan. Significant discounts (*tabiwari* on All Nippon Airways and *sakitoku* on JAL) can sometimes be had if you purchase tickets a month in advance. Low-cost carrier Peach Airlines flies to Naha Tokyo's Haneda and Narita and Osaka's Kansai airports.

The Yui-rail monorail conveniently runs from Naha International Airport in the south to Shuri

in the north. Prices range from ¥200 to ¥290; one- and two-day passes cost ¥700 and ¥1200, respectively. Kenchō-mae Station sits at the western end of Kokusai-dōri, while Makishi Station is at its eastern end.

Ishigaki

🔒 SHOPPING

Minsā Kōgeikan Art

(みんさー工芸館; ☑0980-82-3473; 909 Tonoshiro; ⊙9am-6pm) Minsā Kōgeikan is a weaving workshop and showroom with exhibits on Yaeyama Islands textiles. You can also try your hand at weaving a coaster (¥1500); you'll need to reserve ahead by phone. The building is located between the city centre and the airport, and can be reached via the airport bus (there's a Minsā Kōgeikan stop).

❌ EATING & DRINKING

Paikaji Izakaya ¥¥

(南風; ☑0980-82-6027; 219 Ōkawa; dishes ¥700; ⊙5pm-midnight) This Ishigaki City favourite serves all the Okinawan and Yaeyama standards. The boisterous atmosphere and kitchen get top marks, although smokers detract from the experience. Try the *ikasumi chahan* (squid ink fried rice; ¥700), *gōyā champurū* (¥750) or *sashimi moriawase* (sashimi assortment; ¥750–1800 depending on size). Look for the traditional front, with coral around the entryway and a red-and-white sign.

The boisterous atmosphere and kitchen get top marks

Oishiisā-gu Noodles ¥

(おいシーサー遇; ☑0980-88-2233; 906-1 Kabira; meals ¥600-1000; ⊙11am-5pm, to 7pm in summer; ℗) This sunlit soba place in Kabira serves local dishes like chilled *yomogi-soba* (mugwort soba) served in a conch shell, or *tebichi soba* (Okinawan soba topped with stewed pork trotters). Even better, you can

🌴 Kerama Islands

If you don't have time for a trip to the Yaeyama Islands, zip over instead to the Kerama archipelago (慶良間諸島). The islands are surrounded by reefs of diverse corals; their clear, blue waters also provide sanctuary for breeding humpback whales and grazing sea turtles. Several of the islands can be visited as a day trip from Nara (or you can overnight in an island *minshuku* – family-run guesthouse).

Tiny Aka-jima (阿嘉島), 2km in diameter, has some of the best beaches in the Keramas, including postcard-perfect **Nishibama Beach** (北浜ビーチ).

A stone's throw from Aka-jima, Zamami-jima (座間味島) is *slightly* more developed, with its own lovely beaches. **Furuzamami Beach** (古座間味ビーチ), approximately 1km southeast from the port (over the hill), is a stunning 700m stretch of white sand, fronted by clear, shallow water and a bit of coral. The beach is well developed for day trippers, with toilets, showers and food stalls; you can rent snorkelling gear here (¥1000).

Zamami Sonei (☑098-868-4567) has two or three fast ferries a day (¥3140, 70 minutes) and one regular ferry (¥2120, two hours) between Naha's Tomari Port and Zamami-jima. The ferries usually stop at Aka-jima (¥3140, 50 minutes) en route. The Mitsu Shima motorboat also makes four trips a day between Aka-jima and Zamami-jima (¥300, 15 minutes).

Nishibama Beach, Aka-jima
IAN TROWER / ROBERTHARDING / GETTY IMAGES ©

Tsuboya pottery (p257)

follow your lunch with some homemade gelato in novel flavours like Ishigaki beer, *gōyā* or black sesame and soybean.

Cafe Taniwha Bar

(カフェたにふぁ; ☑0980-88-6352; 188 Ōkawa; ☺11am-11pm Tue-Sat) You can't do better than Cafe Taniwha as a first stop in Ishigaki. Owners and citizens of the world Kuri and Fusa have created a snug, welcoming space for local eccentrics and international travellers. They sometimes host live music, and it's a great place to start your evening or park yourself for the duration.

 INFORMATION

There's a small but helpful **information counter** (☑0980-87-0468; airport; ☺7.30am-9pm) in the arrivals hall of the airport.

Ishigaki City's **Tourist Information Office** (石垣市観光協会; ☑0980-82-2809; 1st fl, Ishigaki-shi Shōkō Kaikan; ☺8.30am-5.30pm Mon-Fri) sometimes has English-speaking staff available and always has an English-language *Yaeyama Islands* brochure (which you can also get at the ferry terminal).

 GETTING THERE & AROUND

Ishigaki-jima has direct flights to/from Tokyo's Narita Airport (Vanilla Air) and Haneda Airport (JTA/ANA), Osaka's Kansai International Airport (JTA/ANA/Peach Airlines) and Naha (JTA/ANA).

The bus terminal is across the road from the ferry terminal in Ishigaki City. Several buses an hour go to the airport (¥540, 45 minutes). A few daily buses go to Kabira-wan (¥680, 50 minutes) and Yonehara Beach (¥820, one hour). One-/five-day (¥1000/2000) bus passes are available for purchase directly from the driver.

Rental cars, scooters and bicycles are readily available at shops throughout the city centre. **Ishigaki Rentacar** (石垣島レンタカー; ☑0980-82-8840; 25 Ōkawa; ☺8am-7pm) has reasonable rates.

KII PENINSULA

Kii Peninsula

The remote and mountainous Kii Peninsula (紀伊半島, Kii-hantō), which juts into the Pacific, south of major Kansai cites Osaka, Kyoto and Nara, is a world away from the aforementioned urban sprawl. It's an excellent place to immerse yourself in Japan's ancient traditions and natural beauty – without having to work that hard. (Savvy local tourist boards have made it easy to book traditional accommodation online in English.) Highlights of the region include the historic pilgrimage trails and onsen of the Kumano Kodō, UNESCO World Heritage Sites, and the otherworldly mountaintop temple complex of Kōya-san, one of Japan's most important Buddhist centres.

The Kii Peninsula in Two Days

With just two days you have to make hard choices: either a night in **Kōya-san** (p266), where you can sleep in a temple and spend the days exploring the mossy temple complexes, or head straight to **Hongū** (p268), where you can walk a loop of the **Kumano Kodō** (p264) and visit **Tsubo-yu Onsen** (p269). Having a car helps to make the most of your time.

The Kii Peninsula in Four Days

With four days, you can start in **Kōya-san** and then head to **Hongū**, picking up the **Kumano Kodō** pilgrimage trail there and ending with the river boat ride down to Shingū. Alternatively, you could spend the whole time walking the classic route from **Tanabe** (p265). You'd need a whole week to fully immerse yourself in the charms of Kii.

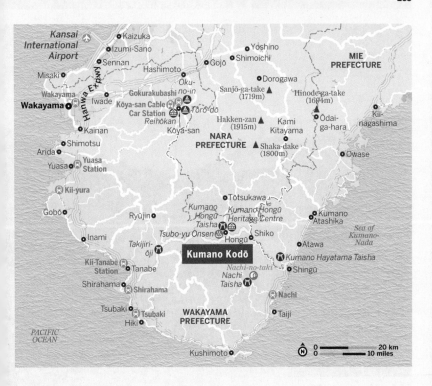

Kansai
International
Airport

Kaizuka
Izumi-Sano
Sennan
Misaki
Hashimoto
Wakayama
Wakayama
Iwade
Kainan
Shimotsu
Arida
Yuasa
Yuasa
Station
Kii-yura
Gobō
Inami
Takijiri-
ōji
Kii-Tanabe
Station
Tanabe
Shirahama
Shirahama
Tsubaki
Tsubaki
Hiki
Kushimoto

Yoshino
Gojō
Shimoichi
Dorogawa
Sanjō-ga-take
(1719m)

**MIE
PREFECTURE**

Hinode-ga-take
(1684m)

Kii-
nagashima

Oku-
no-in
Gokurakubashi
Kōya-san Cable
Car Station
Reihōkan
Tōro-dō
Kōya-san

Hakken-zan
(1915m)

Kami
Kitayama

Ōdai-
ga-hara

Owase

**NARA
PREFECTURE**

Shaka-dake
(1800m)

Tōtsukawa

*Kumano
Hongū
Taisha*
Tsubo-yu Onsen

Ryūjin

Kumano Hongū
Heritage Centre

Hongū
Shiko

Kumano
Atashika

Sea of
Kumano-
Nada

Atawa

Kumano Hayatama Taisha

Kumano Kodō

Nachi-no-taki
Nachi
Taisha

Shingū

Nachi

Taiji

*PACIFIC
OCEAN*

$\overset{\text{N}}{\circledcirc}$

0 ————— 20 km
0 ————— 10 miles

Arriving in the Kii Peninsula

Kansai International Airport (KIX), south of Osaka, is convenient; you can pick up a rental car here. Alternatively, the JR Kinokuni line runs around the peninsula's coast, linking Shin-Osaka and Nagoya Stations (some to Kyoto Station). Special Kuroshio and Nankii *tokkyū* (limited express) trains can get you around the peninsula fairly quickly. Once you step off the express train, however, you're at the mercy of slow local trains and buses.

Sleeping

The Kii Peninsula has fantastic lodging. A highlight of the region is getting to spend a night in a *shukubō* (temple lodging) in Kōya-san. The Kumano Kodō is lined with attractive *minshuku* (traditional guesthouses). Most guests spend a night in Hongū, the main hub of the pilgrimage route. Near Hongū, you have the option to stay in a ryokan (traditional inn) in Yunomine Onsen.

Pagoda at Seiganto-ji, next to Nachi Taisha (p265)

Walking the Kumano Kodō

For over a thousand years, pilgrims have been following the paths of the Kumano Kodō, which link sacred sights throughout the forested Kii mountains. Trails have been expertly restored, leaving an authentic feel.

Great For...

☑ Don't Miss

Climb up the steep steps at Nachi Taisha for views that cross the gorges to the waterfall and down to the Pacific.

History

From earliest times, the Japanese believed the wilds of the Kii Peninsula were inhabited by *kami*, Shintō deities. When Buddhism arrived in the 6th century, these *kami* became *gongen* – manifestations of the Buddha or a bodhisattva – in a syncretic faith known as *ryōbu*, or 'dual Shintō'. Japan's early emperors made pilgrimages to the area. Over time, the popularity of this pilgrimage spread from nobles to *yamabushi* priests (wandering mountain ascetics) and common folk.

The focal points of worship are the Hongū Taisha, Hayatama Taisha and Nachi Taisha 'grand shrines', which are connected via trails, known today as the Kumano Kodō: the Kumano Old Road. The Kumano faith is not defined or standardised, and is open to reinterpretation by those who visit; it's a universal sacred site.

Shrine-keepers at Hongū Taisha

❶ Need to Know

The classic route connects Tanabe, on the west coast of the lower Kii Peninsula with Shingū or Nachi on the east coast. Walking is possible year-round.

✕ Take a Break

There is good accommodation en route; booking ahead is recommended.

★ Top Tip

See the Tanabe City Kumano Tourism Bureau (p268) website for detailed information and maps of the routes and to book accommodation online.

The Classic Route

Most visitors start in Tanabe, with an early morning bus ride to **Takijiri-ōji** (滝尻王子; 859 Kurisugawa, Tanabe-shi). One of five important Ōji shrines, Takijiri-ōji marks the beginning of the passage into the mountains. From here it is a two-day walk to Hongū, home to **Hongū Taisha** (熊野本宮大社) `FREE`, dramatically perched on a tree-covered ridge, and the informative Kumano Hongū Heritage Centre (p268).

From Hongū you can board a bus for Hikari and then a traditional flat-bottomed boat that will carry you down the Kumano-gawa to Shingū. This is the traditional way to end the pilgrimage (well, minus the bus), ending here at **Kumano Hayatama Taisha** (熊野速玉大社; 0735-22-2533; 1 Shingū) `FREE`. The shrine dates from prehistory and celebrates Hayatama-no-Okami, the god said to rule

the workings of nature and, by extension, all life. Meticulously maintained orange pavilions, some tied with impressively thick *shimenawa* (twisted straw ropes), stand in sharp contrast to the greenery all around, including what's said to be Japan's oldest conifer. In town there's a stone staircase, after which a 15-minute climb takes you to a large stone where it is said that the gods originally descended, at Kamikura Shrine.

Alternatively, you can keep walking from Hongū for two days more to **Nachi Taisha** (那智大社) `FREE`. The shrine was built near the waterfall **Nachi-no-taki** (那智の滝), in homage to the its *kami* (Shintō god).

Buses serve key points along the route, so it is possible to do any of these routes as a combination of walking and riding.

Kōya-san

◉ SIGHTS

The precincts of Kōya-san are divided into two main areas: **Garan (Sacred Precinct)** in the west, where you will find interesting temples and pagodas, and **Oku-no-in**, with its vast cemetery, in the east.

A joint ticket (*shodōkyōtsu-naihaiken;* ¥2000) that covers entry to Kongōbu-ji, the Kondō, Dai-tō, Reihōkan, the Tokugawa Mausoleum and more can be purchased at the Kōya-san Shukubō Association (p267) office and the venues themselves.

Oku-no-in   Buddhist Temple

(奥の院; ◷24hr) **FREE** One of Japan's most intensely spiritual places, Oku-no-in is a memorial hall to Kōbō Daishi surrounded by a vast, forested Buddhist cemetery. The tall cedars and thousands of peaked stone stupas along the stone path can be utterly gripping, especially in swirling mist. Important Japanese Buddhists have had their remains, or at least a lock of hair, interred here to ensure pole position when

the Buddha of the Future (Miroku Buddha) comes to earth.

Tōrō-dō   Buddhist Temple

(燈籠堂, Lantern Hall; ◷6am-5.30pm) **FREE** At the northern end of the Oku-no-in cemetery is the complex's main building, Tōrō-dō. It houses hundreds of lanterns donated by dignitaries, including emperors; two lanterns are believed to have been burning for more than 900 years. Here guests are invited to write letters to Kōbō Daishi.

> *Two lanterns are believed to have been burning for more than 900 years*

Kongōbu-ji   Buddhist Temple

(金剛峯寺; ☏0736-56-2011; www.koyasan.or.jp; 132 Kōya-san; ¥500; ◷8.30am-5pm) This sprawling temple is the headquarters of the Shingon sect and the residence of Kōya-san's abbot. The main gate is the temple's oldest structure (1593); the

Konpon Daitō, Garan (p267)

present main hall dates from the 19th century; and the newest annex was constructed as late as 1984, the 1150th anniversary of Kōbō Daishi's passing. The Great Main Hall has ornate *fusuma* (sliding screen door) masterpieces of landscapes and seasonal scenes by famed 17th-century painters, including those of the Kanō school.

Garan   Buddhist Temple
(伽藍; per bldg ¥200; ☺8.30am-5pm) At the western end of central Kōya-san, this complex of eight principal buildings (temples, pagodas) and several other structures is one of Kōya-san's most important sites, along with Oku-no-in (p266) and Kongōbu-ji (p266). Sometimes also called Danjo Garan or Dai Garan, the name comes from Sanskrit for monastery. Among the most important buildings are the **Kondō** (金堂, Main Hall, Golden Hall; ¥200; ☺8.30am-5pm), **Konpon Daitō** (根本大塔, Great Pagoda; ¥200) and **Chūmon** (中門). Even if many of the buildings are 20th- and 21st-century reconstructions, the Garan is well worth a visit.

Reihōkan   Museum
(霊宝館, Treasure Museum; admission ¥600; ☺8.30am-5.30pm May-Oct, to 5pm Nov-Apr) The Treasure Museum has a compact display of Buddhist works of art, all collected in Kōya-san. There are some very fine statues, painted scrolls and mandalas.

EATING
Bononsha   Cafe ¥¥
(梵恩舎; ☎0736-56-5535; 730 Kōyasan; lunch set menu ¥1200; ☺9am-5pm Wed-Sun; ☀) Japanese, English and French are spoken by the delightful couple who own this charming cafe with great old wooden beams. It's a relaxing spot for coffees, organic mains and cakes like chocolate cake and tofu cheesecake. Daily lunch set menus are served until they run out (arrive early). It's also a gallery of local pottery.

Kōya-san Temple Stay

Although it is technically possible to visit Kōya-san as a day trip from Nara, Kyoto or Osaka, we don't recommend it. Instead, take it slow and stay overnight in one of the town's excellent *shukubō* (temple lodgings).

More than 50 temples in Kōya-san offer *shukubō*, which serve *shōjin-ryōri* (Buddhist vegetarian cuisine; no meat, fish, onions or garlic) and typically hold morning prayer sessions that guests are welcome to join or observe.

Lodgings start at about ¥9720 per person including two meals, with a surcharge for solo guests. Prices can vary widely, both between temples and within them, depending upon the room (most without an en suite), meals and season; generally, the more you pay, the better the room and the meals. Most *shukubō* ask that you check in by 5pm.

Reserve at least a week in advance through the **Kōya-san Shukubō Association**; you can fill out a request form online, in English. Many lodgings do not have air-con but do provide fans during warmer months and space heaters during colder months.

Accommodation at Eko-in, Kōya-san (p266)

INFORMATION

In the centre of town in front of the Senjūin-bashi bus stop (千手院橋バス停), Kōya-san's well-equipped tourist information centre **Kōya-san Shukubō Association** (高野山宿

坊協会; 0736-56-2616; http://shukubo.net; ☺8.30am-4.30pm Dec-Feb, to 5pm Mar-Jun & Sep-Nov, to 5.45pm Jul & Aug; 🛜) stocks maps and brochures, and English speakers are usually on hand. The association also makes *shukubō* and dining reservations (in advance) and rents bikes (¥400/1200 per hour/day) and English-language audio guides (¥500) to important sights around town.

GETTING THERE & AWAY

Without a rental car, access to Kōya-san is via the Nankai Railway from Osaka. Trains from Namba Station (*kyūkō* ¥1260, one hour and 40 minutes; *tokkyū* ¥2040, 43 minutes) terminate at Gokurakubashi, at the base of the mountain, where you can board a cable car (gondola; five minutes; price included in train tickets) up to Kōya-san itself. From the cable car station, take a bus into central Kōya-san; walking is prohibited on the connecting road.

Nankai's **Kōya-san World Heritage Ticket** (¥3400, www.nankaikoya.jp/en/stations/ticket.html) covers return train fare (including one-way *tokkyū* fare from Osaka), buses on Kōya-san and discounted admission to some sites.

If you have a Japan Rail Pass, take the JR line from Kyoto to Hashimoto, changing at Nara, Sakurai and Takada en route. At Hashimoto, connect to the Nankai line to Kōya-san (¥830, 50 minutes). Without a Japan Rail Pass, it's easier and quicker to connect to the Nankai line at Namba.

To continue on from Kōya-san to Hongū on the Kumano Kodō, return to Hashimoto on the Nankai line and transfer to the JR line to Gōjō (¥210, 15 minutes), then continue by bus to Hongū (¥3200, four hours).

GETTING AROUND

Buses run on three routes from the top cable-car station via the town centre to Ichi-no-hashi and Oku-no-in (¥410) via the tourist office at Senjūin-bashi (¥290). The bus office by the top cable-car station sells an all-day bus pass (*ichi-nichi furee kippu*; ¥830), but once up the hill, the sights are easily walkable in about 30 minutes. Take note of bus schedules before setting out, as buses run infrequently.

Tanabe

EATING

Shinbe Izakaya ¥¥
(しんべ; 0739-24-8845; www.jpcenter.co.jp/shinbe; Ajikoji; dishes ¥300-1300; ☺5-10.30pm Mon-Sat) In the warren of tiny restaurants called Ajikoji near Kii-Tanabe Station, this boisterous, family-run *izakaya* (Japanese pub-eatery) is famous for *ebi-dango* (shrimp paste balls) with house-made mayo, croquettes and ridiculously fresh fish that the chef himself might have just pulled in from local waters. Sit at the counter for lots of local colour and tons of fun.

INFORMATION

By the train station, the excellent **Tanabe City Kumano Tourism Bureau** (田辺市熊野ツーリズムビューロー; 0739-34-5599; www.tb-kumano.jp; ☺9am-6pm) offers detailed info on the region and lodging options, as well as useful maps, including a 'gourmet map' of local restaurants with English menus.

GETTING THERE & AWAY

The JR Kinokuni line connects Kii-Tanabe with JR Shin-Osaka Station (*tokkyū*, ¥4750, 2¼ hours). Buses running between Tanabe and Hongū (¥2060, two hours, from stop 2) stop at several places that serve as trail heads for the Kumano Kodō.

Hongū

SIGHTS

Kumano Hongū Heritage Centre Museum
(世界遺産熊野本宮館; 0735-42-0751; 100-1 Hongū; ☺9am-5pm) FREE This spiffy, modern multimedia museum has detailed

Tsubo-yu Onsen

information in English about the Unesco World Heritage Sites around the sacred Kumano region. Amid rice paddies behind the heritage centre is Japan's largest *torii* (Shintō shrine gate; 39.9m tall), made out of steel and painted dramatic black.

ACTIVITIES

The picture-perfect village of Yunomine Onsen (湯峰温泉), said to be one of Japan's first onsen towns, is nestled around a rapidly flowing, narrow river in a wooded valley. You can walk here, over a short but steep 3.5km trail from Hongū, in about 1½ hours (or a 20-minute bus ride).

Tsubo-yu Onsen Onsen

(つぼ湯温泉; Yunomine; ¥770; 6am-10pm, enter by 9.30pm) Right in the middle of Yunomine, this hot spring is inside a tiny wooden shack built on an island in the river. Buy a ticket at the *sentō* (public bath) next to Tōkō-ji, the temple in the middle of town, and it's yours for up to 30 minutes. Tsubo-yu Onsen admission includes the *sentō*.

EATING

Cafe Bonheur Vegan ¥¥

(カフェボヌール; 0735-42-1833; 436-1 Hongū; lunch mains ¥850-1000, dinner set meal ¥3000; 11am-3pm, dinner by reservation;) An unexpected treasure at Hongū's southern end is this vegan cafe in a former post office (with the wood floors and clapboard walls to prove it). It does lovely lunches like green curries and delectable sandwiches on house-made bagels. For dinner, ask your innkeeper to make a reservation. The charming owner used to be a designer in Tokyo and Osaka.

GETTING THERE & AROUND

Hongū is served by infrequent buses from JR Gojō Station (¥3200, four hours) and Kintetsu Yamato-Yagi Station (¥3950, five hours and 10 minutes), both to the north; Kii-Tanabe (¥2000, two hours) in the west; and more frequent departures from Shingū (¥1500, 60 to 80 minutes) in the southeast. Most Hongū buses also stop at Yunomine Onsen, but be sure to ask before boarding.

In Focus

Shibuya Crossing (p65), Tokyo

SEAN PAVONE / SHUTTERSTOCK ©

Japan Today

A stubbornly stagnant economy and shrinking population have been a near constant backdrop for political discussion in Japan for decades. Was the post-WWII miracle growth a fluke, or could Japan pull it off again – ideally in time for the 2020 Olympics? There have been glimmers of hope on the economic front, but no one is popping champagne. Meanwhile, the 2011 earthquake has left a legacy of civic engagement.

The Olympics & the Ever-Growing Olympic Budget

When the International Olympic Committee announced in 2013 that Tokyo would host the 2020 Summer Olympics, it felt like the first good news Japan had heard in ages. Now the media could talk about fun things again – like new stadium designs! The enthusiasm didn't last long though: with construction costs for the Zaha Hadid–designed stadium spiralling out of control, the government scrapped it in favour of a cheaper-to-make design by Kuma Kengo. While many locals disliked the Hadid stadium, saying it looked like a giant bicycle helmet, nobody is terribly excited about Kuma's either (it has been compared to a hamburger). With costs still snowballing, firm-fisted Tokyo governor Koike Yuriko has sent more plans back to the discussion table – and possibly the chopping block.

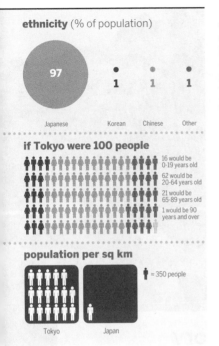

ethnicity (% of population)

97 Japanese | 1 Korean | 1 Chinese | 1 Other

if Tokyo were 100 people

16 would be 0-19 years old
62 would be 20-64 years old
21 would be 65-89 years old
1 would be 90 years and over

population per sq km

Tokyo | Japan | ≈ 350 people

On a darker note, victims of the 2011 earthquake, who lost homes (and even whole communities) in the tsunami or to radiation, have grown increasingly resentful, still living in temporary housing while public funds are spent on showpiece projects. Statistics from the Reconstruction Bureau report that as of 2016, there were more than 100,000 (the majority of whom are from Fukushima) who are still living in temporary housing.

The Nuclear Power Dilemma

More than five years after the meltdown at the Fukushima nuclear power plant, nuclear power is still a hot topic. Before 2011, 30% of Japan's power was nuclear; by 2013, due to a combination of scheduled maintenance and revamped safety inspections, all reactors were offline. Carbon emissions rose 14% as Japan resorted to burning more oil. The government wants Japan back on the nuclear grid; in 2015, two reactors in Kyūshū went live, with more scheduled to follow.

Citizens and local governments, however, have been unusually proactive, some taking legal action to prevent nearby reactors from restarting in a David vs Goliath scenario that pits them against the central government and the national nuclear regulating body. Local residents in Fukui Prefecture petitioned (and succeeded in court) to keep their reactors offline, while Niigata Prefecture elected a governor running as an independent purely on a no-nukes platform in 2016.

The Tourists Are Here!

Japan has long hoped to boost its underdeveloped inbound tourism industry. Then, it got real, by relaxing visa regulations for visitors from its Asian neighbours, which, along with the periodically weak yen, has resulted in a dramatic rise in numbers of foreign visitors. Inbound numbers have more than doubled since 2010; in 2015 the country logged 19.7 million visitors, just shy of the 20 million target set for 2020.

There is hand-wringing, of course: How do we please them? Where are we going to park all these tour buses? And will we ever be able to visit Kyoto in peace again?

But there is also intense fascination: What, exactly, do they find interesting about Japan? There has been an explosion of TV shows trying to figure that out, interviewing tourists (even sending TV personalities to check out places listed in the Lonely Planet guide). The popular show, 'You! ha nani shini nihon e?' ('Why did you come to Japan?') sends cameras to Narita Airport to look for interesting subjects and then follows them around – you've been warned!

After decades of stagnation-bred doldrums, Japan is looking to the outside world for a pick-me-up: if people are willing to spend money to come here, it can't be so bad, right?

Tenryū-ji (124)

History

Japan has been greatly shaped by both its isolation, as an island nation, and its proximity to the massive Asian continent (and particularly by its neighbours, Korea and China). During times of openness it has been a fascinating percolator of the diverse ideas and cultures that have appeared on its shores; in times of retreat it has incubated its own way of doing things. Like most histories, Japan's is also one of conflict, growth and bloodshed.

mid-5th century	710	794
Writing is introduced to Japan by scholars from the Korean kingdom of Baekje (based on the Chinese system of characters).	Japan's first capital is established at Nara. By now, Japan has many characteristics of a nation-state.	The imperial capital moves to Heian-kyō, renamed Kyoto in the 11th century.

Early Japan

The earliest traces of human life in Japan date to around 30,000 years ago, but it is possible that people were here much earlier. Until the end of the last ice age about 15,000 years ago, a number of land bridges linked Japan to the Asian continent. The first recognisable culture to emerge was the neolithic Jōmon, from about 13,000 BC. They lived a quasi-nomadic life in settlements along coastal areas, particularly in northeastern Japan, where they could fish, gather seaweed and wild mushrooms, and also hunt deer and bear.

Sometime between 800 and 300 BC a new culture, which is referred to as Yayoi, began to take shape. There remains much debate regarding the origin of this shift, whether it was brought about by settlers from China or Korea (or both); the earliest known Yayoi settlements were discovered in northern Kyūshū, close to the Korean Peninsula. The Yayoi introduced wet rice farming techniques – a huge game-changer, not just because it demanded more stable settlement but also because the labour-intensive practice was better suited to lowland areas, encouraging population growth in fertile basins.

early 1000s	1192	1223
Lady of the court, Murasaki Shikibu, writes *The Tale of Genji,* considered to be the world's first novel.	Yoritomo takes the title shogun (generalissimo) from a largely powerless emperor, heralding the start of feudalism in Japan.	The monk Dōgen studies Chang Buddhism in China and later returns to found the Sōtō school of Zen Buddhism.

Mythic Origins

According to legend, once upon a time, the male and female deities Izanagi and Izanami came down to a watery world from Takamagahara (the Plains of High Heaven), to create land. Droplets from Izanagi's 'spear' solidified into the land now known as Japan, and Izanami and Izanagi then populated it with gods. One of these was Japan's supreme deity, the Sun Goddess Amaterasu (Light of Heaven), whose great-great-grandson Jimmu became the first emperor of Japan.

Scholars are sceptical of the existence of the earliest emperors. Some believe the 10th emperor, Sujin, was the first to really exist, and was perhaps the founder of the Yamato dynasty. Emperor Kinmei (509–71 AD), who reigned 539–71 AD, is the first emperor of verifiable historical record.

Agriculture-based settlement led to territories and boundaries being established, and the rise of kingdoms, the most powerful of which was ruled by the Yamato clan in the Kansai region. The Yamato clan would go on to found the court in Nara and later Heian-kyō (Kyoto), from where the imperial dynasty would rule for over a millennia.

The Rise & Fall of the Heian Court

Over the next few centuries in Kyoto, courtly life reached a pinnacle of refined artistic pursuits and etiquette, captured famously in a novel *The Tale of Genji,* written by the court-lady Murasaki Shikibu in about 1004. It showed courtiers indulging in diversions such as guessing flowers by their scent, building extravagant follies and sparing no expense for the latest luxury. On the positive side, it was a world that encouraged aesthetic sensibilities, such as of *mono no aware* (the bittersweetness of things) and *okashisa* (pleasantly surprising incongruity), which have endured to the present day. But it was also a world increasingly estranged from the real one. Manipulated over centuries by the politically powerful Fujiwara family, the imperial throne was losing its authority.

Out in the provinces, powerful military forces were developing. Some were led by distant imperial family members, barred from succession claims – they were given new names and farmed out to provincial clans – and hostile to the court. Their retainers included skilled warriors known as samurai (literally 'retainer'). The two main clans of disenfranchised lesser nobles, the Minamoto (also known as Genji) and Taira (Heike), were enemies. In 1156 they were employed to help rival claimants to the Fujiwara family leadership, but these figures soon faded into the background when an all-out feud developed between the Minamoto and the Taira.

The Taira initially prevailed, under their leader Kiyomori (1118–81), who based himself in the capital and, over the next 20 years, fell prey to many of the vices that lurked there. In 1180 he enthroned his two-year-old grandson, Antoku. When a rival claimant requested the help of the Minamoto family, who had regrouped, their leader, Yoritomo (1147–99), was more than ready to agree. Both Kiyomori and the claimant died shortly afterwards,

1543	1603	1638
Portuguese, the first Westerners, arrive in Japan by chance, bringing firearms and Christianity.	Ieyasu becomes shogun, establishing a new shogunate in the small castle town Edo (now Tokyo).	The *sakoku* policy of national isolation is enacted.

but Yoritomo and his younger half-brother Yoshitsune (1159–89) continued the campaign against the Taira. By 1185 Kyoto had fallen and the Taira had been pursued to the western tip of Honshū. A naval battle ensued, won by the Minamoto. In a well-known tragic tale, Kiyomori's widow leapt into the sea with her grandson Antoku (now aged seven), rather than have him surrender.

The Kamakura Shogunate

Yoritomo did not seek to become emperor, but wanted the new emperor to give him legitimacy by conferring the title of shogun, which was granted in 1192. He left many existing offices and institutions in place and set up a base in his home territory of Kamakura (not far from present-day Tokyo) rather than Kyoto. While in theory Yoritomo represented the military arm of the emperor's government, in practice he was in charge. He established a feudal system – which would last almost 700 years as an institution – centred on a loyalty-based lord-vassal system.

When Yoritomo died in 1199 (after falling from his horse in suspicious circumstances) his son succeeded him to the title of shogun. In truth though, the government was now ruled by the clan of Yoritomo's widow, the Hōjō, who acted first as regent before claiming the shogunate outright. It was during the Hōjō shogunate that the Mongols, under Kublai Khan (r 1260–94), twice tried to invade, in 1274 and 1281. On both occasions they were ultimately defeated by storms that destroyed much of their fleet. The typhoon of 1281 prompted the idea of divine intervention, with the coining of the term kamikaze (literally 'divine wind'). Later this term was used to describe Pacific War suicide pilots who, said to be infused with divine spirit, gave their lives to protect Japan from invasion.

Despite victory, the Hōjō suffered: their already depleted finances could not cover the payment promised to the warriors enlisted to fight the Mongols. Dissatisfaction towards the shogunate came to a head under the unusually assertive emperor Go-Daigo (1288–1339), who banded together with the promising young general Ashikaga Takauji (1305–58) to overthrow the Hōjō. Takauji claimed the mantle of shogun, setting up a base in Kyoto.

The Warring States

With a few exceptions, the Ashikaga shoguns were relatively ineffective. Without strong, centralised government and control, the country slipped into civil war as regional warlords – who came to be known as *daimyō* (domain lords) – engaged in seemingly interminable feuds and power struggles. The period from 1467 to 1603 is known as the Sengoku (Warring States) era. In 1543 the first Europeans arrived – another game changer – bringing with them Christianity and firearms. The warlord Oda Nobunaga (1534–82) was quick to apprehend the advantage of the latter. Starting from a relatively minor power base, his skilled and ruthless generalship produced a series of victories. In 1568 he seized Kyoto and held de facto power until, betrayed by one of his generals, he was killed in 1582. Another of

1853–54	**1859**	**1867–68**
US commodore Matthew Perry's 'black ships' arrive off the coast of Shimoda, forcing Japan to open up for trade.	Five international ports are established in Yokohama, Hakodate, Kōbe, Niigata and Nagasaki.	The Meiji Restoration reinstates imperial authority; Japan's capital is moved to Edo, renamed Tokyo.

Traditional samurai war helmet

VLADIMIR ZHOGA / SHUTTERSTOCK ©

his generals, Toyotomi Hideyoshi (1536–98), took up the torch, disposing of potential rivals among Nobunaga's sons and taking the title of regent.

Hideyoshi's power had been briefly contested by Tokugawa Ieyasu (1542–1616), son of a minor lord allied to Nobunaga. After a brief struggle for power, Ieyasu agreed to a truce with Hideyoshi; in return, Hideyoshi granted him eight provinces in eastern Japan. While Hideyoshi intended this to weaken Ieyasu by separating him from his ancestral homeland Chūbu (now Aichi Prefecture), the upstart looked upon the gift as an opportunity to strengthen his power. He set up his base in a small castle town called Edo (which would one day become Tokyo). On his deathbed, Hideyoshi entrusted Ieyasu, who had proven to be one of his ablest generals, with safeguarding the country and the succession of his young son Hideyori (1593–1615). Ieyasu, however, had greater ambitions and soon went to war against those loyal to Hideyori, finally defeating them at the legendary Battle of Sekigahara in 1600. He chose Edo as his permanent base and ushered in two and a half centuries of Tokugawa rule.

Tokugawa Rule

Ieyasu and his successors kept tight control over the provincial *daimyō,* who ruled as vassals for the regime, requiring them and their retainers to spend every second year in Edo, where their families were kept permanently as hostages – an edict known as *sankin kōtai*. This dislocating policy made it hard for ambitious *daimyō* to usurp the Tokugawas.

Early on, the Tokugawa shogunate adopted a policy of *sakoku* (closure to the outside world). Following the Christian-led Shimabara Rebellion, Christianity was banned and several hundred thousand Japanese Christians were forced into hiding. All Westerners except the Protestant Dutch were expelled by 1638. Overseas travel for Japanese was banned (as well as the return of those already overseas). And yet, the country did not remain completely cut off: trade with Asia and the West continued through the Dutch and Ryūkyū empire (now Okinawa) – it was just tightly controlled and, along with the exchange of ideas, funnelled exclusively to the shogunate.

1879	**1923**	**1931**
Japan annexes the Ryūkyū Kingdom (then a tributary of China) and renames it Okinawa.	The Great Kantō Earthquake strikes Japan near Tokyo, killing an estimated 100,000 to 140,000 people.	Japan invades Manchuria and then dramatically withdraws from the League of Nations in response to criticism.

Society was made rigidly hierarchical, comprising (in descending order of importance): *shi* (samurai), *nō* (farmers), *kō* (artisans) and *shō* (merchants). Class dress, living quarters and even manner of speech were all strictly codified, and interclass movement was prohibited. Village and neighbourhood heads were enlisted to enforce rules at the local level, creating an atmosphere of surveillance. Punishments could be harsh, cruel and even deadly for minor offences. Yet for all its constraints, the Tokugawa period had a considerable dynamism. Japan's cities grew enormously during this period: Edo's population topped one million in the early 1700s, dwarfing much older London and Paris. Despite the best efforts of rulers to limit the growing merchant class, it prospered greatly from the services and goods required for *daimyō* processions to and from Edo. A new culture, which thumbed its nose at social hardships and the strictures of the shogunate, began to flourish. Increasingly wealthy merchants patronised the kabuki theatre, sumo tournaments and the pleasure quarters – generally enjoying a *joie de vivre* that the dour lords of Edo castle frowned upon.

The Way of the Warrior

Samurai followed a code of conduct that came to be known as *bushidō* (the way of the warrior), drawn from Confucianism, Shintō and Buddhism. Confucianism required a samurai to show absolute loyalty to his lord, possess total self-control, speak only the truth and display no emotion. Since his honour was his life, disgrace and shame were to be avoided above all else, and all insults were to be avenged. Seppuku (ritual suicide by disembowelment), also known as hara-kiri, was an accepted means of avoiding the dishonour of defeat. From Buddhism, the samurai learnt the lesson that life is impermanent – a handy reason to face death with serenity. Shintō provided the samurai with patriotic beliefs in the divine status of both the emperor and Japan.

The Meiji Restoration

In 1853 and again the following year, US commodore Matthew Perry steamed into Edo-wan (now Tokyo Bay) with a show of gunships – which the Japanese called *kurofune* (black ships), because they were cloaked in pitch – and demanded Japan open up to trade and provisioning. The shogunate was no match for Perry's firepower and agreed to his demands. Soon other Western powers followed suit. Japan was obliged to sign what came to be called the 'unequal treaties', opening ports and giving Western nations control over tariffs. Despite last ditch efforts by the Tokugawa regime to reassert power, anti-shogunal sentiment was high, particularly in the outer domains of Satsuma (southern Kyūshū) and Chōshū (western Honshū). Following a series of military clashes between the shogun's armies and the rebels – which showed the rebels to have the upper hand – the last shogun, Yoshinobu (1837–1913), agreed to retire in 1867.

1941	1945	1972
Japan enters WWII by striking Pearl Harbor without warning on 7 December.	Hiroshima and Nagasaki become victims of an atomic bombing on 6 and 9 August.	The USA returns administrative control of Okinawa to Japan, but keeps many bases in place.

In 1868, the new teenage emperor Mutsuhito (1852–1912; later known as Meiji) was named the supreme leader of the land, commencing the Meiji period (1868–1912; Enlightened Rule). The institution of the shogun was abolished and the shogunal base at Edo was refashioned into the imperial capital and given the new name, Tokyo (Eastern Capital). In truth, the emperor still wielded little actual power. A new government was formed, primarily of leading former samurai from Satsuma and Chōshū. Above all, the new leaders of Japan – keen observers of what was happening throughout Asia – feared colonisation by the West. They moved quickly to modernise, as defined by the Western powers, to prove they could stand on an equal footing with the colonisers. The government embarked on a grand project of industrialisation and militarisation. A great exchange began between Japan and the West: Japanese scholars were dispatched to Europe to study everything from literature and engineering to nation building and modern warfare. Western scholars were invited to teach in Japan's nascent universities. The Meiji Restoration also heralded far-reaching social changes. The four-tier class system was scrapped; after centuries of having everything prescribed for them, citizens were now free to choose their occupation and place of residence.

Rise of a Global Power

A key element of Japan's aim to become a world power was military might. Using the same 'gunboat diplomacy' on Korea that Perry had used on the Japanese, in 1876 Japan was able to force on Korea an unequal treaty of its own. In 1894, using Chinese 'interference' in Korea as a justification, Japan manufactured a war with China; victorious, Japan gained Taiwan and the Liaotung Peninsula. Russia pressured Japan into renouncing the peninsula and then promptly occupied it, leading to the Russo-Japanese War of 1904–05, won by Japan. When Japan officially annexed Korea in 1910, there was little international protest. Japan entered WWI on the side of the Allies, and was rewarded with a council seat in the newly formed League of Nations. It also acquired German possessions in East Asia and the Pacific.

Yet as the 1920s rolled around, a sense of unfair treatment by Western powers once again took hold in Japan. The Washington Conference of 1921–22 set naval ratios of three capital ships for Japan to five American and five British; around the same time, a racial-equality clause that Japan had proposed to the League of Nations was rejected. This dissatisfaction intensified in the Shōwa period (1926–89; Illustrious Peace). In the fall of 1931, members of the Japanese army stationed in Manchuria, who were there to guard rail lines leased by China to Japan, detonated explosives along the track and blamed the act on Chinese dissidents. This ruse, which gave the Japanese army an excuse for armed retaliation, became known as the Manchurian Incident. Within months the Japanese had taken control of Manchuria (present-day Heilongjiang, Jilin and Liaoning provinces) and installed a puppet government. The League of Nations refused to acknowledge the new Manchurian government; in 1933 Japan left the league.

1990	1995	2005
The so-called 'Bubble Economy', based on overinflated land and stock prices, finally bursts in Japan.	The Great Hanshin Earthquake (magnitude 6.9) strikes Kōbe, killing more than 6000.	Japan's population declines for the first year since WWII, a trend that will continue.

Skirmishes continued between the Chinese and Japanese armies, leading to full-blown war in 1937. Following a hard-fought victory in Shanghai, Japanese troops advanced south to capture Nanjing. Over several months somewhere between 40,000 and 300,000 Chinese were killed in what has become known as the Nanjing Massacre or Rape of Nanjing. To this day, the number of deaths and the prevalence of rape, torture and looting by Japanese soldiers is hotly debated among historians (and government nationalists) on both sides.

The Economic Miracle

In the 1950s Japan took off on a trajectory of phenomenal growth that has been described as miraculous. (Though many historians, both Japanese and American, say Japan's role as a forward base for the USA in the Korean War reignited the Japanese economy.) Based on the price paid for the most expensive real estate in the late 1980s, the land value of Tokyo exceeded that of the entire USA. It wasn't until 1990, with the bursting of the 'Bubble Economy', that the country finally came down to earth.

WWII & Occupation

Encouraged by Germany's early WWII victories, Japan signed a pact with Germany and Italy in 1940. With France and the Netherlands distracted and weakened by the war in Europe, Japan quickly moved on their colonial territories – French Indo-China and the Dutch West Indies – in Southeast Asia. Tensions between Japan and the USA intensified, as the Americans, alarmed by Japan's aggression, demanded Japan back down in China. When diplomacy failed, the USA barred oil exports to Japan – a crucial blow. Japanese forces struck at Pearl Harbor on 7 December 1941, damaging much of the USA's Pacific fleet.

Japan advanced swiftly across the Pacific; however, the tide started to turn in the Battle of Midway in June 1942, when much of its carrier fleet was destroyed. Japan had overextended itself, and over the next three years was subjected to an island-hopping counter-attack. By mid-1945, Japan, ignoring the Potsdam Declaration calling for unconditional surrender, was preparing for a final Allied assault on its homeland. On 6 August the world's first atomic bomb was dropped on Hiroshima, killing 90,000 civilians. Russia, which Japan had hoped might mediate, declared war on 8 August. On 9 August another atomic bomb was dropped, this time on Nagasaki, with another 50,000 deaths. Emperor Hirohito formally surrendered on 15 August. When NHK, Japan's national broadcaster, played the message, it was the first time the people of Japan had heard their emperor speak.

The terms of Japan's surrender to the Allies allowed the country to hold on to the emperor as the ceremonial head of state, but he no longer had authority – nor was he thought of as divine – and Japan was forced to give up its territorial claims in Korea and China. In addition, America occupied the country under General Douglas MacArthur, a situation that would last until 1952 (Okinawa would remain occupied until 1972).

2010	**2011**	**2013**
China surpasses Japan as the world's second-largest economy after the USA.	The Great East Japan Earthquake strikes off the coast Tōhoku, generating a tsunami that kills many thousands.	The International Olympic Committee awards Tokyo the right to host the 2020 Summer Olympics.

Traditional Ainu dance performance

The People of Japan

Japan is typically thought of as a homogeneous nation, and it largely is, ethnically (though there are minority cultures), but there are also deep divides between the urban and rural, stubbornly persistent gendered spheres and growing social stratification. Increasingly, the people of Japan are grappling with the same problems as those in developed nations the world over.

Population

The population of Japan is approximately 127 million. That alone makes Japan a densely populated nation; to make things worse, 91% of people live in areas classified as urban. Roughly a quarter of the population (about 36 million) lives within the Greater Tokyo Metropolitan Area, which encompasses the cities of Tokyo, Kawasaki and Yokohama plus the commuter towns stretching deep into the suburbs; it's the most heavily populated metropolitan area in the world. Another nearly 20 million live in the Kyoto–Osaka–Kōbe conurbation (often called Keihanshin).

Besides density, the most notable feature of Japan's population is the fact that it is shrinking. Japan's astonishingly low birth rate of 1.4 births per woman is among the lowest in the developed world, and over a quarter of the population is already aged over 65.

The population peaked at 128 million in 2007 and has been in decline since; it's predicted to reach 100 million in 2050 and 67 million in 2100. Needless to say, such demographic change will have a major influence on the economy in coming decades.

Despite declining population numbers, Japan has shown a reluctance to let immigrants make up the difference. The 2015 census revealed 2.23 million foreigners living in Japan – an uptick of 5% from the year before; the count includes those holding permanent residence status as well as students and temporary workers. The largest non-Japanese group in the country is the Chinese, who number roughly 666,000, or almost 30% of Japan's foreign population, followed by the Koreans (458,000; 20%) and the Filipinos (229,600; 10%).

Minority Cultures

Particularly striking for visitors from multicultural nations is Japan's relative ethnic and cultural homogeneity. The Japanese census does not ask questions pertaining to race, only nationality. As a result, discussions of diversity in Japan tend to fall on divisions of national identity – who is Japanese and who is not. However, buried within the population stats are Japan's invisible minorities – those who are native-born Japanese and appear no different from other native-born Japanese, but who can trace their ancestry to historically disenfranchised peoples. Chief among these are the descendants of the Ainu, the native people of Hokkaidō; Okinawans; and Zainichi Koreans.

Prior to being annexed by Japan in the 19th century, Hokkaidō and Okinawa (formerly the Ryūkyū Empire) were independent territories. Following annexation, the Japanese government imposed assimilation policies that forbade many traditional customs and

Garden at Tōfuku-ji (p105), Kyoto

★ **Books About Japan**

Contemporary Japan: History, Politics and Social Change Since the 1980s (Jeff Kingston; 2010)

Zen and Japanese Culture (Daisetz T Suzuki; 2010)

Handbook of Japanese Mythology (Michael Ashkenazi; 2008)

even the teaching of native languages. The number of Japanese who identify as Ainu is estimated to be around 20,000, though it is likely that there are many more descendants of Hokkaido's indigenous people out there – some who may not know it, perhaps because their ancestors buried their identity so deep (for fear of discrimination) that it became hidden forever. There are maybe 10 native speakers of Ainu left; however, in recent decades, movements have emerged among the younger generation to learn the language and other aspects of their culture. Today's Okinawans, too, have a strong regional identity, though it is less about their ties to the former Ryūkyū Empire and more about their shared recent history since WWII. The Okinawans shouldered an unequal burden, both of casualties during the war and of occupation after it.

The Zainichi Koreans are a legacy of Japan's imperial past. When Japan annexed Korea in 1910 many migrants came to Japan for work; during WWII hundreds of thousands were brought over by the Japanese government to work in wartime factories or stand on the front lines. When the war ended and Korea regained its independence most Koreans returned home, but quite a few stayed. Under the colonial empire Koreans were subjects of the Japanese emperor; however, after the war, the Japanese government did not automatically grant citizenship to those Koreans who stayed. Instead they became Zainichi (temporary residents) and were effectively stateless.

When Japan resumed diplomatic relations with South Korea in 1965, the latter allowed Zainichi Koreans to claim South Korean nationality, which would now be recognised in Japan. Those who chose not to, perhaps because their allegiance or family ties lay with North Korea, and had not become naturalised Japanese citizens, remain stateless. According to the 2015 census, there are 34,000 of them. Up until the 1980s, Zainichi Koreans who wished to become naturalised citizens were required to adopt Japanese-sounding names. While some Zainichi Koreans are now fourth or fifth generation residents of Japan many do still report episodes of discrimination or hate speech.

Religion

Shintō and Buddhism are the main religions in Japan. Shintō, 'the way of the gods', is the indigenous religion of Japan. It locates divinity in the natural world. Its *kami* (gods) inhabit trees, rocks, waterfalls and mountains; they can be summoned through rituals of dance and music into shrines the Japanese have built for them, where they are beseeched with prayers for a good harvest, fertility and the like. The pantheon of deities includes thousands, from the celebrated sun goddess Amaterasu to the humble hearth *kami*.

When Buddhism entered Japan via Korea in the 6th century it didn't so much displace Shintō as envelop it; now there were *kami* and bodhitsattvas (people who put off entry into nirvana in order to save the rest of us stuck in the corrupt world of time). Several waves of Buddhist teachings arrived on Japanese shores; notably meditative Zen, Shingon (an esoteric sect related to Tantric Buddhism), and Pure Land, which preached of the salvation of heaven (the Pure Land). It was the latter that most struck a chord with common Japanese and Pure Land (called Jōdo-shū) remains the most popular form of Buddhism today. Kannon (the bodhitsattva of mercy and an important Pure Land figure) is the most worshipped deity in Japan.

Today, only about one-third of Japanese identify as Buddhist and the figure for Shintō is just 3%; however most Japanese participate in annual rituals rooted in both, which they see as integral parts of their culture and community ties. New Year's visits to shrines and temples are just one example. Generally in Japan, Shintō is concerned with this life: births and marriages for example are celebrated at shrines. Meanwhile, Buddhism deals with the afterlife: funerals and memorials take place at temples.

Rural Japan

Until the beginning of last century, the majority of Japanese lived in close-knit rural farming communities. Today, only one in 10 Japanese lives in the countryside and they are disproportionately elderly. Children who would have followed in the footsteps of their parents now head to the cities for university, often never looking back.

Some do feel a pull to return to their *jika* (hometown), often to take care of ageing parents, but sometimes, too, there is a weariness of city life or a desire to give back to their communities. Meanwhile, there is now a generation of urban Japanese who are so removed from rural life as to think it all sounds very romantic. They dream of fixing up an old *minka* (country house), and starting an organic farm or guesthouse.

Women in Japan

Women have historically been viewed as keepers of the home, responsible for overseeing the household budget, monitoring the children's education and taking care of the day-to-day tasks of cooking and cleaning. Of course this ideal was rarely matched by reality: labour shortfalls often resulted in women taking on factory work and, even before that, women often worked side by side with men in the fields.

As might be expected, the contemporary situation is complex. There are women who prefer the traditionally neat division of labour. This is often seen as the path of least resistance. While gender discrimination in the workforce is illegal, it remains pernicious. And while there is less societal resistance to women working, they still face enormous pressure to be doting mothers. Most women see the long hours that Japanese companies demand as incompatible with child-rearing, especially in the early years; few fathers are willing or, given their own work commitments, able to pick up the slack. Attempts at work-life balance, such as working from home, can result in guilt trips from colleagues or bosses.

Women do in fact make up over 40% of the workforce; however, over half of them are working part-time and often in menial, low-paying jobs. Japan has the third largest pay-gap among developed countries: in 2015 Bloomberg reported that women who are in full-time employment make roughly 30% less than their male counterparts. In the face of Japan's declining birth rate, the central government has acknowledged the untapped labour potential of its female population (while still encouraging women to have more babies, of course). In 2003 the government set a target of having women make up 30% of managerial positions by 2020; it has since scaled back its expectations to 15%. The current rate is 12% in the private sector. Taking all of this into account, the World Economic Forum has given Japan the damning rating of 111 out of 144 countries in its Global Gender Gap Report for 2016.

On the upside: Japanese women have the longest life expectancy on Earth, at 86.83 years of age.

Kaiseki dishes (p287)

Food & Drink

One of the joys of travelling in Japan is experiencing the true breadth of the country's cuisine. Sushi (raw fish on vinegar-seasoned rice) may be synonymous with Japan, but head to the mountains, for example, and you'll discover a hearty cuisine that draws from the land. It's hard not to eat well in Japan: such is the care and thought put into ingredients and presentation. What's more, you can have a superlative meal on any budget.

The Japanese Restaurant Experience

When you enter a restaurant in Japan, you'll be greeted with a hearty *irasshaimase* (Welcome!). In all but the most casual places, the waiter will next ask you *nan-mei sama* (How many people?). Indicate the answer with your fingers, which is what the Japanese do. You may also be asked if you would like to sit at a *zashiki* (low table on the tatami), at a *tēburu* (table) or the *kauntā* (counter). Once seated you will be given an *o-shibori* (hot towel), a cup of tea or water (this is free) and a menu. More and more restaurants these days (especially in touristy areas) have English menus.

Often the bill will be placed discreetly on your table. If not, you can ask for it by catching the server's eye and making a cross in the air (to form a kind of 'x') with your index fingers.

You can also say *o-kanjō kudasai*. At some restaurants, you can summon the server by pushing a call bell on the table.

There's no tipping, though higher-end restaurants usually tack on a 10% service fee. During dinner service, some restaurants, especially *izakaya* (a pub-eateries), may instead levy a kind of cover charge (usually a few hundred yen); this will be the case if you are served an *o-tsumami* (a small appetiser or 'charm') when you sit down. Payment is usually settled at the register near the entrance.

On your way out, if you were pleased with your meal, give your regards to the staff or chef with the phrase, *gochisō-sama deshita*, which means 'It was a real feast'.

Izakaya

Izakaya (居酒屋) translates as 'drinking house' – the Japanese equivalent of a pub – and you'll find them all over Japan. Visiting one is a great way to dig into Japanese culture. An evening at an *izakaya* is dinner and drinks all in one: food is ordered for the table a few dishes at a time along with rounds of beer, sake or *shōchū* (a strong distilled alcohol often made from potatoes). While the vibe is lively and social, it's perfectly acceptable to go by yourself and sit at the counter. If you don't want alcohol, it's fine to order a soft drink instead (but it would be strange to not order at least one drink).

There are orthodox, family-run *izakaya,* often with rustic interiors, that serve sashimi (raw fish) and grilled fish to go with sake; large, cheap chains that are popular with students and often have a healthy (er, unhealthy) dose of Western pub-style dishes (like chips); and there are also stylish chef-driven ones with creative menus. A night out at an average *izakaya* should cost from ¥2500 to ¥5000 per person, depending on how much you eat and drink. Chains often have deals where you can pay a set price for a certain amount of dishes and free drinks.

Kaiseki

Kaiseki is the pinnacle of Japanese cuisine, in which ingredients, preparation, setting and presentation come together to create a highly ritualised, aesthetically sophisticated dining experience. It was born in Kyoto as an adjunct to the tea ceremony; though fish is often served, meat never appears in traditional *kaiseki*. The meal is served in several small courses, giving the diner an opportunity to admire the plates and bowls, which are carefully chosen to complement the food and season. It usually includes sashimi, something steamed, something grilled, soup and finishes with rice and then a simple dessert (though there may be many more courses).

At its best, it's eaten in the private room of a *ryōtei* (an especially elegant style of traditional restaurant), often overlooking a private, tranquil garden. At upwards of ¥20,000 per person, this is about as pricey as dining can get in Japan; reservations are usually required. There are cheaper places though, and lunch can be a good deal as some restaurants do boxed lunches containing a small sampling of their dinner fare for around ¥2500 per person.

Sushi & Sashimi

Sushi (寿司 or 鮨) is raw fish and rice seasoned with vinegar and is a meal unto itself. Sashimi (刺身) is just raw fish and is usually a complement to a larger meal; *sashimi mori-awase* (刺身盛り合わせ; assorted sashimi) is a common dish to order at *izakaya*.

Sushi comes in many varieties: the most recognised kind is *nigiri-zushi*, the bite-sized slivers of seafood hand-pressed onto pedestals of rice. It can be very high-end, served

Miso ramen

★ Local Specialities

Gōyā champarū (stir fry with bitter melon), Okinawa

Tako-yaki (octopus dumplings), Osaka

Hiroshima-yaki (savoury pancake with noodles), Hiroshima

Miso ramen, Sapporo

piece by piece at exclusive *sushi-ya* (sushi restaurants) where a meal of seasonal delicacies could run over ¥20,000 per person. It can also be very cheap, at *kaiten-zushi* (回転寿司), for example, where ready-made plates of sushi (about ¥200 each) are sent around the restaurant on a conveyor belt. Here there's no need to order: just grab whatever looks good.

At an average *sushi-ya*, a meal should run between ¥2000 and ¥5000 per person. You can order à la carte – often by just pointing to the fish in the refrigerated glass case on the counter – or a sampler set; the latter is a better deal (unless you are set on eating only your favourites). These usually come in three grades: *futsū* or *nami* (regular), *jō* (special) and *toku-jō* (extra-special). The price difference is determined more by the value of the ingredients than by volume.

Unless otherwise instructed by the chef (who may have preseasoned some pieces), you can dip each piece lightly in *shōyu* (soy sauce), which you pour from a small decanter into a low dish specially provided for the purpose. *Nigiri-sushi* is usually made with wasabi, so if you'd prefer it without, order *wasabi-nuki*. Sushi is one of the few foods in Japan that is perfectly acceptable to eat with your hands – even at high-end places! Slices of *gari* (pickled ginger) are served to refresh the palate.

Though much is made of the freshness of the ingredients in modern sushi, the dish originated as a way to make fish last longer: the vinegar in the rice was a preserving agent. An older form of sushi, called *hako-zushi* or *oshi-zushi* ('box' or 'pressed' sushi) and more common in western Japan, is made of fish pressed onto a bed of heavily vinegared rice in a wooden mould with a weighted top. Left to rest, it acquires a slight tang of fermentation.

Ramen

Ramen originated in China, but its popularity in Japan is epic. If a town has only one restaurant, odds are it's a ramen shop. Your basic ramen is a big bowl of crinkly egg noodles in broth, served with toppings such as *chāshū* (sliced roast pork), *moyashi* (bean sprouts) and *negi* (leeks). The broth can be made from pork or chicken bones or dried seafood; usually it's a top-secret combination of some or all of the above, falling somewhere on the spectrum between *kotteri* (thick and fatty – a signature of pork-bone ramen) or *assari* (thin and light).

It's typically seasoned with *shio* (salt), *shōyu* (soy sauce) or hearty *miso* – though at less orthodox places, anything goes. Most shops will specialise in one or two broths and offer a variety of seasonings and toppings. Another popular style is *tsukemen*, noodles that come with a dipping sauce (like a really condensed broth) on the side. Given the option, most diners get their noodles *katame* (which literally means 'hard' but is more like al dente). If you're really hungry, ask for *kaedama* (another serving of noodles), usually only a couple of hundred yen more.

Well-executed ramen is a complex, layered dish – though it rarely costs more than ¥1000 a bowl. Costs are minimised by fast-food-style service: often you order from a vending machine (you'll get a paper ticket, which you hand to the chef); water is self-serve.

Japanese Beef

Wagyū (Japanese beef) has cult status both in Japan and abroad. The meat is incredibly tender, largely so because it is heavily marbled in soft, melty fat – a result of careful breeding techniques. Most *wagyū* comes from a breed of cattle known as Japanese Black. Some cows are hand-fed or drink mountain spring water. Within the world of *wagyū* are a few premium brands – such as Kōbe, Matsusaka and Ōmi – that hew to strict quality control and are prized as top-grade meat.

Often the meat is seared at high temperature on a *teppan* (steel hotplate), diced and served with rice and miso soup. You can also grill strips of *wagyū* over coals at Korean-style barbecue restaurants (called *yakiniku*); eat it sukiyaki or *shabu-shabu*

style; or order it at steakhouses paired with wine. Of course none of this comes cheap (prices start at around ¥5000 for a small lunch portion and rise steadily from there). Two things to keep in mind: as the meat is very rich, often a small portion will do. Also, any non-brand *wagyū* with a rating of A4 or, even better, A5 is going to be top-notch (and probably cheaper).

Magic Words for Dining in Japan

If you're generally an adventurous (or curious) eater, don't let the absence of an English menu put you off. Instead, tell the staff (or ideally the chef), *omakase de onegaishimasu* (I'll leave it up to you).

This works especially well when you're sitting at the counter of a smaller restaurant or *izakaya* (pub-eatery), where a rapport naturally develops between the diners and the cooks. It's best said with enthusiasm and a disarming smile, to reassure everyone that you really are game.

This isn't just a tourist hack: Japanese diners do this all the time. Menus might not reflect seasonal dishes and odds are the chef is working on something new that he or she is keen to test out on the willing.

It's probably a good idea to set a price cap, like: *hitori de san-zen-en* (one person for ¥3000).

Japanese Classics

Fugu (ふぐ) Poisonous globefish prepared by licensed chefs; a tasting menu usually consists of different parts of the fish prepared different ways.

Okonomiyaki (お好み焼き) Savoury pancake stuffed with cabbage plus meat or seafood (or cheese or kimchi...), which you grill at the table and top with *katsuo bashi* (bonito flakes), *nori* (seaweed), mayonnaise and Worcestershire sauce.

Shabu-shabu (しゃぶしゃぶ) Thin slices of beef or pork swished briefly in a light, boiling broth then seasoned with *goma* (sesame-seed) or *ponzu* (citrus-based sauce).

Soba (そば) Thin buckwheat noodles, either *to-wari* (100% buckwheat) or cut with wheat; served in hot broth (flavoured with bonito and soy sauce) or with concentrated, room temperature broth on the side for dipping (the latter style is preferred by connoisseurs).

Sukiyaki (すき焼き) Thin slices of beef cooked piece by piece in a broth of soy sauce, sugar and sake at your table, then dipped in a raw egg.

Tempura (天ぷら) Seafood and vegetables deep-fried in a fluffy light batter, flavoured with salt or a light sauce mixed with grated *daikon* (radish).

Sushi restaurant in Tokyo

BLUEHAND / SHUTTERSTOCK ©

Tonkatsu (とんかつ; 豚カツ) Tender pork cutlets breaded and deep-fried, served with a side of grated cabbage.
Udon (うどん) Thick white wheat noodles, served similarly to soba.
Unagi (うなぎ) Freshwater eel grilled over coals and lacquered with a rich, slightly sweet sauce. Note that *unagi* is listed as 'endangered' on the Red List.

Sake

What much of the world calls 'sake' the Japanese call *nihonshu* ('the drink of Japan'). It's made from rice, water and *kōji*, a mould that helps to convert the starch in the rice into fermentable sugars. Sake has existed for as long as history has been recorded in Japan (and odds are a lot longer). It plays an important part in a variety of Shintō rituals, including wedding ceremonies, and many Shintō shrines display huge barrels of sake in front of their halls (most of them are empty). Sake is always brewed during the winter, in the cold months that follow the rice harvest in September. Fresh, young sake is ready by late autumn.

Sake is classed by its *seimai buai* (精米歩合) – the amount of rice that is polished away before fermentation. As a general rule, the more polishing, the better the sake will be, as it is believed that sake made from the inner portion of the rice kernel is the smoothest and most delicious of all. Sake made from rice kernels with 40% to 50% of their original volume polished away is called *ginjō*. Sake made from rice kernels with 50% or more of their original volume polished away is classified as *dai-ginjō*. Sometimes the alcohol content is artificially regulated (either increased or reduced); unadulterated sake is known as *junmai-shu* (pure rice sake). On average the alcohol content of sake is around 15% (by law it can be no more than 22%).

If wine is defined by terroir, then sake is defined by its water, usually mountain snowmelt that flows downstream through rice paddies picking up various minerals on the way. The variety of rice matters too, though many brewers buy rice from elsewhere in Japan (like Yamada Nishiki rice farmed in Hyōgo Prefecture and prized by brewers); there are also countless strains of *kōji* used in secret, proprietary blends. There are over 1500 *kura* (breweries) in Japan; almost everywhere has a *ji-zake* (local sake).

The taste of sake is often categorised as sweet *(ama-kuchi)* or dry *(kara-kuchi)*, though these are just starting points. Sake can also be *tanrei* (crisp), *hanayaka* (fragrant), *odayaka* (mellow) and much more. Naturally, it's the best pairing for traditional Japanese cuisine.

Green Tea

Japan is a treat for tea lovers. Here *o-cha* (tea) means green tea and broadly speaking there are two kinds: *ryokucha* (steeped with leaves) and *matcha*, which is made by whisking dried and milled leaves with water until a cappuccino level of frothiness is achieved. It's *matcha* that is served in the tea ceremony; it is quite bitter, so it is accompanied by a traditional sweet.

When you order *o-cha* in a Japanese restaurant (it's usually free, like water), you'll most likely be served *bancha*, ordinary tea. In summer, you might get cold *mugicha*, roasted barley tea, instead. After a course meal, restaurants often serve *hōjicha* (roasted green tea), which is weaker and less caffeinated. If you want to try out the more rarefied stuff, you'll have to seek out a teahouse or speciality shop. *Sencha* (煎茶) is medium-grade green loose-leaf tea; *gyokuro* (玉露), shaded from the sun and picked early in the season, is the highest grade.

Eat Like a Local

All but the most extreme type-A chefs will say they'd rather have foreign visitors enjoy their meal than agonise over getting the etiquette right. Still, a few points to note if you want to make a good impression: There's nothing that makes a Japanese chef grimace more than out-of-towners who over-season their food – a little soy sauce and wasabi goes a long way (and heaven forbid, don't pour soy sauce all over your rice; it makes it much harder to eat with chopsticks). In Japan, it's perfectly OK, even expected, to slurp your noodles. They should be eaten at whip speed, before they go soggy (letting them do so would be an affront to the chef); that's why you'll hear slurping diners sucking in air to cool their mouths.

Don't stick your chopsticks upright in a bowl of rice or pass food from one pair of chopsticks to another – both are reminiscent of Japanese funereal rites. When serving yourself from a shared dish, it's polite to use the back end of your chopsticks (ie not the end that goes into your mouth) to place the food on your own small dish.

Before digging in, it is customary in Japan to say *itadakimasu* (literally 'I will receive' but closer to 'bon appétit' in meaning). It's considered bad form to fill your own glass. Instead, fill the drained glasses around you and someone will quickly reciprocate; when they do, raise your glass slightly with two hands – a graceful way to receive anything. Once everyone's glass has been filled, the usual starting signal is a chorus of *kampai*, which means 'Cheers!'

Lastly, lunch is one of Japan's great bargains; however, restaurants can only offer cheap lunch deals because they anticipate high turnover. Spending too long sipping coffee after finishing your meal might earn you dagger eyes from the kitchen.

The Year in Food

Spring (March–May) The new growth of spring finds its way onto tables in the form of *takenoko* (bamboo shoots) and *sansai* (mountain vegetables). Especially good if you're in the mountains.

Summer (June–August) The season for cooling dishes like *reimen* (cold ramen) and *zaru soba* (cold buckwheat noodles served on a bamboo tray). And nothing says summer like *kaki-gōri* (shaved ice topped with sweet syrup).

Autumn (September–November) The first sign of autumn is silvery *sanma* (Pacific saury) on menus. Other delicacies: matsutake mushrooms, ginkgo nuts, candied chestnuts and *shinmai,* the first rice of the harvest season.

Winter (December–February) Friends come together for steaming *nabe* (hotpot) dishes; this is also the season for *fugu* (pufferfish) and oysters.

Tokyo Metropolitan Government Building (p68)

SEAN PAVONE / SHUTTERSTOCK ©

Arts & Architecture

Japan has a sublime artistic tradition that has been influenced by the cultures of continental Asia and later the West, and shaped by a tendency to refine techniques and materials to an almost extreme degree. Its traditional design aesthetic of clean lines, natural materials, heightened spatial awareness and subtle enhancement has long been an inspiration to creators around the world.

Traditional Painting

Traditionally, paintings consisted of black ink or mineral pigments on *washi* (Japanese handmade paper) and were sometimes decorated with gold leaf. Paintings of the Heian era (794–1185) depicted episodes of court life, like those narrated in the novel *Genji Monogatari (The Tale of Genji)*, or seasonal motifs, often on scrolls. Works such as these were later called *yamato-e*; one of the most striking conventions of the form is the use of a not-quite-bird's-eye perspective peering into palace rooms without their roofs (the better to see the intrigue!). With the rise of Zen Buddhism in the 14th century, minimalist monochrome ink paintings came into vogue; the painters themselves were priests and the quick, spontaneous brush strokes of this painting style were in harmony with their guiding philosophies.

It was during the Muromachi period (1333–1573) that the ruling class became great patrons of Japanese painters, giving them the space and the means to develop their own styles. Two styles emerged at this time; the Tosa school and the Kano school. The Tosa clan of artists worked for the imperial house, and were torch-bearers for the now classic *yamato-e* style, using fine brushwork to create highly stylised figures and elegant scenes from history and of the four seasons; sometimes the scenes were half-cloaked in washes of wispy gold clouds. The Kano painters were under the patronage of the Ashikaga shogunate and employed to decorate their castles and villas. It was they who created the kind of works most associated with Japanese painting: decorative polychromatic depictions of mythical Chinese creatures and scenes from nature, boldly outlined on large folding screens and sliding doors.

With the Meiji Restoration (1868), when artists and ideas were sent back and forth between Europe and Japan, painting necessarily became either a rejection or an embracing of Western influence. Two terms were coined: *yōga* for Western-style works and *nihonga* for works in the traditional Japanese style. In reality though, many *nihonga* artists incorporated shading and perspective into their works, while using techniques from all the major traditional Japanese painting schools. There are many artists today who continue to create and redefine *nihonga*.

Wabi-Sabi

Wabi-sabi is an aesthetic that embraces the notion of ephemerality and imperfection and is Japan's most distinct – though hard to pin down – and profound contribution to the arts. *Wabi* roughly means 'rustic' and connotes the loneliness of the wilderness, while *sabi* can be interpreted as 'weathered', 'waning' or 'altered with age'. Together the two words signify an object's natural imperfections, arising in its inception, and the acquired beauty that comes with the patina of time. It is most often evoked in descriptions of the tea ceremony, a kind of participatory performance art surrounding the ritual of drinking tea that came into vogue in the 16th century. Ceramics made for the tea ceremony – and this is where Japanese ceramics finally came into their own – often appeared dented or misshapen or had a rough texture, with drips of glaze running down the side. The teahouses too, small, exceedingly humble and somewhat forlorn (compared to the manors they were attached to) also reflected *wabi-sabi* motifs, as did the *ikebana* (flower arrangements) and calligraphy scrolls that would be placed in the teahouse's alcove.

Ukiyo-e

Far from the nature scenes of classical paintings, *ukiyo-e* (woodblock prints, but literally 'pictures of the floating world') were for the common people, used in advertising or in much the same way posters are used today. The subjects of these woodblock prints were images of everyday life, characters in kabuki plays and scenes from the 'floating world', a term derived from a Buddhist metaphor for life's fleeting joys. Edo's particular 'floating world' revolved around pleasure districts such as the Yoshiwara. In this topsy-turvy kingdom, an inversion of the usual social hierarchies imposed by the Tokugawa shogunate, money meant more than rank, actors were the arbiters of style, and courtesans elevated their art to such a level that their accomplishments matched those of the women of noble families. The vivid colours, novel composition and flowing lines of *ukiyo-e* caused great excitement in the West, sparking a vogue that one French art critic dubbed *japonisme*. *Ukiyo-e* became a key influence on Impressionists (for example, Toulouse-Lautrec, Manet and Degas) and post-Impressionists.

★ **Cinema Classics**

Late Spring (Ozu Yasujirō; 1948)

Rashōmon (Kurosawa Akira; 1950)

Ugetsu Monogatari (Mizoguchi Kenji; 1953)

Tampopo (Itami Jūzō; 1986)

Hana-bi (Kitano Takeshi ; 1997).

Superflat & Beyond

The 1990s was a big decade for Japanese contemporary art: love him or hate him, Murakami Takashi brought Japan back into an international spotlight it hadn't enjoyed since 19th-century collectors went wild for *ukiyo-e*. His work makes fantastic use of the flat planes, clear lines and decorative techniques associated with *nihonga*, while lifting motifs from the lowbrow subculture of manga (Japanese comics); his spirited, prankish images and installations have become emblematic of the Japanese aesthetic known as *poku* – a concept that combines pop art with an *otaku* (manga and anime super-fan) sensibility. As much an artist as a clever theorist, Murakami proclaimed in his 'Superflat' manifesto that his work picked up where Japanese artists left off after the Meiji Restoration – and this might just be the future of painting, given that most of us now view the world through the portals of two-dimensional screens.

Naturally, younger artists have had trouble defining themselves in the wake of 'Tokyo Pop', as the highly exportable art of the '90s came to be known. Some artists making a mark include Tenmyouya Hisashi, who coined the term 'neo-nihonga' to describe his works, which echo the flat surfaces and deep impressions of woodblock prints, while singing a song of the street; conceptual artist Tanaka Koki (named Deutsche Bank's Artist of the Year in 2015); and the collection of irreverent pranksters known as ChimPom.

Kabuki

Around the year 1600, a charismatic shrine priestess in Kyoto led a troupe of female performers in a new type of dance people dubbed kabuki – a slang expression that meant 'cool' or 'in vogue' at the time. The dancing – rather ribald and performed on a dry riverbed for gathering crowds – was also a gateway to prostitution. A series of crackdowns by the Tokugawa establishment (first on female performers, then on adolescent male performers) gave rise to one of the most fascinating elements of kabuki, the *onnagata* (adult male actors who specialise in portraying women).

As kabuki spread to Edo (Tokyo), it developed hand in hand with the increasingly affluent merchant class, whose decadent tastes translated into the breathtaking costumes, dramatic music and elaborate stagecraft that have come to characterise the art form. It is this intensely visual nature that makes kabuki accessible to foreign audiences – you don't really have to know the story to enjoy the spectacle. (Tip: if you opt for the cheap seats, bring binoculars.) Over the course of several centuries, kabuki has developed a repertoire that draws on popular themes, such as famous historical accounts and stories of love-suicide, while also borrowing copiously from *nō, kyōgen* (comic drama) and bunraku (classical puppet theatre). Formalised beauty and stylisation are the central aesthetic principles of kabuki;

highlights for many fans are the dramatic poses (called *mie*) that actors strike at pivotal moments.

Golden Age of Japanese Cinema

The Japanese cinema of the 1950s – the era of international acclaimed auteurs Ozu Yasujirō, Mizoguchi Kenji and Kurosawa Akira – is responsible for a whole generation of Japanophiles. Ozu (1903–63) was the first great Japanese director, known for his piercing, at times heartbreaking, family dramas. Mizoguchi (1898–1956) began by shooting social realist works in the 1930s, but found critical acclaim with his reimagining of stories from Japanese history and folklore.

Kurosawa (1910–98) is an oft-cited influence for film-makers around the world. His films are intense and psychological; the director favoured strong leading men and worked often with the actor Mifune Toshirō. Kurosawa won the Golden Lion at the Venice International Film Festival and an honorary Oscar for the haunting Rashōmon (1950), based on the short story of the same name by Ryūnosuke Akutagawa and staring Mifune as a bandit. Japanese cinema continues to produce directors of merit, but has not emerged as the influential cultural force that its heyday seemed to foreshadow.

Temple or Shrine?

Buddhist temples and Shintō shrines were historically intertwined, and centuries of coexistence means the two resemble each other architecturally; you'll also often find small temples within shrines and vice versa. The easiest way to tell the two apart, though, is to check the gate. The main entrance of a shrine is a *torii* (gate), usually composed of two upright pillars, joined at the top by two horizontal crossbars, the upper of which is normally slightly curved. *Torii* are often painted a bright vermilion. In contrast, the *mon* (main entrance gate) of a temple is often a much more substantial affair, constructed of several pillars or casements, joined at the top by a multitiered roof. Temple gates often contain guardian figures, usually Niō (*deva* kings).

Anime

Anime picked up where film left off, piquing the interest of subsequent generations and pointing them in the direction of Japan. Miyazaki Hayao (b. 1941), who together with Takahata Isao founded Studio Ghibli, is largely responsible for anime gaining widespread, mainstream appeal abroad. His *Spirited Away* (2001) earned the Academy Award for best animated film and he was given an Academy Honorary Award in 2014. Thematically, his works are noteworthy for their strong female characters and environmentalism; *Nausicaa of the Valley of the Winds* (1984) is an excellent example.

Among the best-known anime is *Akira* (1988), Ōtomo Katsuhiro's psychedelic fantasy set in a future Tokyo inhabited by speed-popping biker gangs and psychic children. *Ghost in the Shell* (1995) is an Ōishii Mamoru film with a sci-fi plot worthy of Philip K Dick involving cyborgs, hackers and the mother of all computer networks. The works of Kon Satoshi (1963–2010), including the Hitchcockian *Perfect Blue* (1997), the charming *Tokyo Godfathers* (2003) and the sci-fi thriller *Paprika* (2006), are also classics.

One new director to watch is Shinkai Makoto: his 2016 film *Kimi no Na wa* (Your Name) was both a critical and box-office smash – the second highest-grossing domestic film after *Spirited Away*.

★ **Literary Classics**

The Pillow Book (Sei Shōnagon; 1002)

The Narrow Road to the Deep North (Matsuo Bashō, 1702)

The Life of an Amorous Man (Ihara Saikaku; 1682)

Kokoro (Sōseki Natsume; 1914)

Snow Country (Kawabata Yasunari; 1935–37)

Modern & Contemporary Architecture

Modern Japanese architecture really came into its own in the 1960s. The best known of Japan's 20th-century builders was Tange Kenzō (1913–2005), who was influenced by traditional Japanese forms as well as the aggressively sculptural works of French architect Le Corbusier. One of his early commissions was the Hiroshima Peace Memorial Park (1955). He also designed the National Gymnasium built for the 1964 Tokyo Olympics – a structure that looks vaguely like a samurai helmet and uses suspension-bridge technology – and later the Tokyo Metropolitan Government Offices (1991), a looming complex with the silhouette of a Gothic cathedral.

Since the 1980s a new generation of Japanese architects have emerged; they continue to explore both modernism and postmodernism, while incorporating a renewed interest in Japan's architectural heritage. Among the most esteemed is Andō Tadao, whose works are heavy, grounded and monumental; his favourite medium is concrete. Many of his structures can be found in Tokyo and on Naoshima. Other Pritzker Prize winners include SANAA (Sejima Kazuyo and Nishizawa Ryūe), known for their luminous form-follows-function spaces; Itō Toyō, whose designs are light and conceptual; and Shigeru Ban, who makes fantastic use of low-cost and recycled materials.

Traditional Japanese Gardens

Gardening is one of Japan's finest art forms. You'll encounter four major types of gardens during your horticultural explorations.

Funa asobi Meaning 'pleasure boat' and popular in the Heian period, such gardens feature a large pond for boating and were often built around nobles' mansions. The garden that surrounds Byōdō-in in Uji is a vestige of this style.

Shūyū These 'stroll' gardens are intended to be viewed from a winding path, allowing the design to unfold and reveal itself in stages and from different vantages. Popular during the Heian, Kamakura and Muromachi periods, a celebrated example is the garden at Ginkaku-ji in Kyoto.

Kanshō Zen rock gardens (also known as *kare-sansui* gardens) are an example of this type of 'contemplative' garden intended to be viewed from one vantage point and designed to aid meditation. Kyoto's Ryōan-ji is perhaps the most famous example.

Kaiyū The 'varied pleasures' garden features many small gardens with one or more teahouses surrounding a central pond. Like the stroll garden, it is meant to be explored on foot and provides the visitor with a variety of changing scenes, many with literary allusions. The imperial villa of Katsura Rikyū in Kyoto is the classic example.

FAR IEW BOO / SHUTTERSTOCK ©

Onsen

Some locals will tell you that the only distinctively Japanese aspect of their culture – that is, the only thing that didn't ultimately originate in mainland Asia – is the bath. There are accounts of onsen bathing in Japan's earliest historical records, and over the millennia the Japanese have turned the simple act of bathing in an onsen into something like a religion.

Taking the Plunge

Onsen water comes naturally heated from a hot spring, of which there are literally thousands scattered around the archipelago. Some springs have developed into resorts, with strips of hotels and ryokan (traditional inns) housing elaborate bathhouses. Other onsen are hidden in the mountains or along undeveloped coasts; these humble baths may be no more than a pool in a riverbed blocked off with stones or a tidal basin beside crashing waves, in which case bathing is open-air, co-ed and usually free. (Unless stated otherwise, it's okay for a woman to enter rural, unattended baths in a swimsuit or with a 'modesty' towel).

Shy bathers take heart: many resort inns offer what they call 'family baths' (家族風呂; *kazoku-buro*) or 'private baths' (貸切風呂; *kashikiri-buro*), small baths that can be used

★ **Best Onsen**

Hōheikyō (p228), Hokkaidō

Hirauchi Kaichū Onsen (p244), Yakushima

Ibusuki Sunamushi Kaikan Saraku, Kagoshima (p245)

Ōedo Onsen Monogatari (p69), Tokyo

privately (solo, as a couple or as a family) for an hour. This may be free of charge or cost a few thousand yen. High-end inns might offer rooms with private hot-spring baths – the ultimate in luxury.

Sentō, meanwhile, are old-school public bathhouses that date to the era when few Japanese homes had private baths. Most often the water in these baths comes from the tap but some use onsen water. As *sentō* are largely frequented by neighbourhood regulars, they can be a little intimidating – but they can also make for a great local experience. You'll need to bring your own towel and toiletries here, or rent or purchase them from the front desk.

Note that some onsen refuse entry to people with tattoos because of the association of tattoos with the *yakuza* (Japanese mafia). Public *sentō*, however, are usually open to all. If an establishment has a policy against tattoos, it will be cleared stated at the entrance. If your tattoo is small enough to cover with a plaster, you may be able to get away with it.

Onsen Etiquette

Bathing isn't just a pastime, it's a ritual – one so embedded in Japanese culture that everyone knows exactly what to do. This can be intimidating to the novice, but really all you need to know to avoid causing alarm is to wash yourself before getting into the bath. It's also a good idea to memorise the characters for men (男) and women (女), which will be marked on the *noren* (curtains) hanging in front of the respective baths.

Upon entering an onsen or *sentō*, the first thing you'll encounter is a row of lockers for your shoes. After you pay your admission and head to the correct changing room, you'll find either more lockers or baskets for your clothes. Take everything off here and enter the bathing room with only the small towel. That little towel performs a variety of functions: you can use it to wash (but make sure you give it a good rinse afterwards) or to cover yourself as you walk around. It is not supposed to touch the water though, so leave it on the side of the bath or – as the locals do – folded on top of your head.

Park yourself on a stool in front of one of the taps and give yourself a thorough wash. Make sure you rinse off all the suds. When you're done, it's polite to rinse off the stool for the next person. At more humble bathhouses you might have little more than a ladle to work with; in that case, crouch low and use it to scoop out water from the bath and pour over your body – taking care not to splash water into the tub – and scrub a bit with the towel.

In the baths, keep your head above the water and your splashing to a minimum. Whether or not you want to rinse off depends on you and the nature of the waters: some people want to keep the minerals on their skin; others prefer to wash. Before heading back to the changing room, wipe yourself down with the towel to avoid dripping on the floor.

Ryokan

A hotel is a hotel wherever you go. And while some of Japan's hotels are very nice indeed, staying in a ryokan (traditional inn) offers an added cultural experience. Sleeping on futons (quilt-like mattresses), soaking in an o-furo (Japanese-style bath, often communal) or starting your day with grilled fish and rice are all opportunities to connect a little more deeply with Japan.

Choosing a Ryokan

There is a great variety of ryokan: Some are famous for their onsen baths, which may be indoors or outdoors – located along riverbeds or overlooking mountains; others are famous for their food, serving *kaiseki ryōri* (Japanese haute cuisine) that rivals the meals served in the best restaurants. (The priciest will excel in both.) Ryokan can be rambling old wooden buildings that look like they're straight out of a *ukiyo-e* (woodblock) print or they can be modern concrete structures. The latter are more likely to have an elevator, en suites and a few rooms with beds (including a wheelchair accessible room). Older inns may be draughty, with thin walls and shared toilets, but the atmosphere more than makes up for it.

Ryokan exist at all price ranges; note that rates are charged by person rather than by room. For a very nice experience, expect to pay between ¥12,000 and ¥20,000 per

Tawaraya ryokan, Kyoto

LONELY PLANET / GETTY IMAGES ©

★ Best Ryokan

Tawaraya, Kyoto

Arai Ryokan, Shuzen-ji Onsen

Hōshi Onsen Chōjūkan, Minakami

Lamp no Yado, Aoni Onsen

Iwasō Ryokan, Miyajima

person, including meals. If you have food allergies or strong aversions, it's best to inform staff when making a reservation; many inns, especially those used to overseas guests, are accommodating.

The Ryokan Experience

For Japanese guests, a ryokan is a destination in and of itself, and, as a result, most will check in as early as possible (usually 3pm). Most places expect you to check in by 6pm, unless you have arranged otherwise.

Leave your shoes at the entrance and put on the slippers set out for you. After signing in (yes, by hand), you'll be escorted to your room and perhaps given a basic tour of the inn on the way – to show you where the baths and dining rooms are located. Staff will most likely enter the room with you, to show you where the robes and towels are stashed. If you've reserved meals, the staff may then ask what time you would like them. Dinner is typically early, at 6pm or 7pm; breakfast is usually sometime between 7am and 8.30am. You can then make yourself a pot of tea – the supplies should be on the low table, along with some traditional sweets or snacks – and relax.

More on slippers: they shouldn't be worn on tatami mats (so slip them off before walking onto the tatami in your room). Separate slippers will be set out for use just in the toilet. There will also be outdoor slippers (either wooden-soled *geta*, traditional sandals, or clunky plastic ones) at the entrance of the inn, if you need to pop outside. (Given all this sharing of slippers, most guests prefer to wear socks.) Rest assured, slipper etiquette is probably the most stressful thing you'll encounter.

All lodgings in Japan (save hostels) supply sleepwear and at a traditional accommodation this will be a *yukata*, a light, cotton kimono-like robe. Don't be insulted if you're given one marked extra large – they're sized by length not by girth! Put it on over your underwear, left over right; women might want to wear a camisole, as the robes tend to creep open at the top. Men typically tie the *obi* (sash) low on their hips while women tend to secure it snugly at the waist. You can wear the *yukata* anywhere around the inn: to and from the baths and during meals (though of course this is optional). At some onsen resort towns, guests wear them around town as well, while going from bathhouse to bathhouse.

Ryokan staff (often clad in kimonos) tend to be very doting. During meals they'll serve you course by course – and at some fancier inns meals can be taken in your room; during or after dinner, they'll come to lay out the bedding for you. After check-out, you'll be seen off with deep bows.

Tokyo Sky Tree (p53)

ALEKSANDAR TODOROVIC / SHUTTERSTOCK ©

Survival Guide

Directory A–Z

Accommodation

Japan offers a wide range of accommodation. Western-style hotels can be found in most cities and resort areas. Even budget hotels are generally clean and well serviced (though older ones might have smoky rooms). In the top-end bracket, you can expect to find the amenities of deluxe hotels anywhere in the world. For more information on staying in a ryokan (traditional inn), see p299.

Advance booking is highly recommended, especially in major tourist destinations.

Business Hotels

Functional and economical, 'business hotels' (ビジネ

Book Your Stay Online

For more accommodation reviews by Lonely Planet authors, check out http://hotels.lonelyplanet.com/japan. You'll find independent reviews, as well as recommendations on the best places to stay. Best of all, you can book online.

スホテル; *bijinesu hoteru*) are geared to the lone traveller on business, but they're great for any kind of traveller – so long as you don't need a lot of space. The compact rooms usually have semidouble beds (140cm across; roomy for one, a bit of a squeeze for two) and tiny en suites. Business hotels are famous for being deeply unfashionable, though many chains have updated their rooms in recent years. Expect to pay from ¥8000/12,000 for single/double occupancy (more in big cities like Tokyo).

Business hotels are usually clustered around train stations. Some reliable chains with huge networks include **Toyoko Inn** (www.toyoko-inn.com/eng) and **Dormy Inn** (www.hotespa.net/dormyinn/en).

Capsule Hotels

Capsule hotels (カプセルホテル; *kapuseru hoteru*) offer rooms the size of a single bed, with just enough headroom for you to sit up. Think of it like a bunk bed with more privacy (and a reading light, TV and alarm clock). Prices range from ¥3500 to ¥5000, which usually includes access to a large shared bath and sauna. Personal belongings are kept in a locker room. Most only accept cash and do not permit guests with visible tattoos.

Capsule hotels are common in major cities and often cater to workers who have partied too hard

to make it home or have missed the last train. Most are men-only, though some have floors for women, too.

Hostels

Japan has an extensive network of hostels. These include official Japan Youth Hostel (JYH; www.jyh.or.jp/e/index.php) properties as well as a growing number of independent, sometimes quite stylish, hostels. Among the more popular are the K's House (https://kshouse.jp/index_e.html) and J-Hoppers (http://j-hoppers.com) groups. Many hostels are staffed by young travellers who often speak good English. Some, but not all, have kitchen facilities for guests.

Prices average around ¥3000 for a dorm bed. There will usually be some private and family rooms, too (costing about ¥1000 extra per person). Bedding is provided; towels can be hired for about ¥100. Basic toiletries (soap and shampoo) may or may not be supplied.

Customs Regulations

◦ Japan has typical customs allowances for duty-free items; see Visit Japan Customs (www.customs.go.jp) for more information.

◦ Stimulant drugs, which include the ADHD medication Adderall, are strictly prohibited in Japan. To bring in certain narcotics (such as codeine), you need to prepare a *yakkan shōmei* – an import certificate for pharmaceuticals. See the Ministry of Health, Labour & Welfare's website (www.mhlw.go.jp/english/policy/health-medical/pharmaceuticals/01.html) for more details about which medications are classified and how to prepare the form.

Electricity

Tokyo and eastern Japan are on 50Hz, and western Japan, including Nagoya, Kyoto and Osaka, is on 60Hz.

Type A
100V/50Hz/60Hz

Health

Japan enjoys a high standard of medical services, though

unfortunately most hospitals do not have doctors and nurses who speak English. University hospitals should be your first choice; doctors are more likely to speak English and the level of care is usually highest. Larger cities, especially Tokyo, have clinics that specialise in caring for the foreign community; these will have doctors who speak English but they will be pricey. Most hospitals and clinics will accept walk-in patients in the mornings (usually 8.30am to 11am); be prepared to wait. Expect to pay about ¥3000 for a

simple visit to an outpatient clinic and from around ¥20,000 and upwards for emergency care.

No vaccines are required for travel to Japan.

Medical Checklist

○ Pharmacies in Japan do not carry foreign medications, so it's a good idea to bring your own. In a pinch, reasonable substitutes can be found, but the dosage may be lower than what you're used to.

○ Though no prescription is necessary, thrush pessaries

Climate

Hiroshima

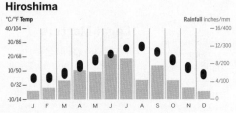

Kyoto

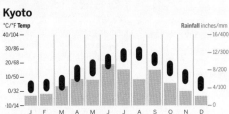

Tokyo

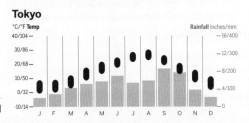

Meal Costs

The following price ranges refer to a standard main meal.

¥ less than ¥1000 (less than ¥2000 in Tokyo and Kyoto)

¥¥ ¥1000 to ¥4000 (¥2000 to ¥5000 in Tokyo and Kyoto)

¥¥¥ more than ¥4000 (more than ¥5000 in Tokyo and Kyoto)

are only stocked behind the counter (you'll have to ask) and many pharmacies don't carry them.

Insurance

A travel-insurance policy to cover theft, loss and medical problems is essential. Worldwide travel insurance is available at www.lonelyplanet. com/travel-insurance. You can buy, extend and claim online anytime – even if you're already on the road.

Note that the only insurance accepted at Japanese hospitals is Japanese insurance. For any medical treatment you'll have to pay up front and apply for a reimbursement when you get home.

Internet Access

Many cities in Japan (including Tokyo, Osaka and Kyoto) have free wi-fi networks for travellers, though the system is still clunky in areas. To avoid frustration, heavy

users might consider hiring a pocket internet device.

Most accommodation now has wi-fi. Hostels and business chain hotels are the most reliable for this; other places might only have a solid connection in the lobby.

Legal Matters

Japanese police have extraordinary powers. They can detain a suspect for up to three days without charging them; after this time a prosecutor can decide to extend this period for another 20 days. Police can also choose whether to allow a suspect to phone their embassy or lawyer, though if you find yourself in police custody you should insist that you will not cooperate in any way until allowed to make such a call. Your embassy is the first place you should call if given the chance.

Police will speak almost no English; insist that a *tsūyakusha* (interpreter) be summoned (police are legally bound to provide one

before proceeding with any questioning). Even if you do speak Japanese, it's best to deny it and stay with your native language.

Note that it is a legal requirement to have your passport on you at all times. Though checks are not common, if you are stopped by police and caught without it, you could be hauled off to a police station to wait until someone fetches it for you.

Japan takes a hard-line approach to narcotics possession, with long sentences and fines even for first-time offenders.

LGBTI Travellers

Gay and lesbian travellers are unlikely to encounter problems in Japan. There are no legal restraints on same-sex sexual activities in Japan apart from the usual age restrictions.

Some travellers have reported being turned away or grossly overcharged when checking into love hotels with a partner of the same sex. Otherwise discrimination is unusual (though you'll likely be given a hotel room with twin beds). One note: Japanese people, regardless of their sexual orientation, do not typically engage in public displays of affection.

Tokyo has the largest and most welcoming gay scene, followed by Osaka. Utopia Asia (www.utopia-asia.com) has good recommendations for Japan.

Maps

Kodansha's *Japan Atlas: A Bilingual Guide* has maps labelled in English and kanji, though the road maps are not terribly detailed.

Money

ATMs

Most Japanese bank ATMs do not accept foreign-issued cards. Seven Bank ATMs at 7-Eleven convenience stores and Japan Post Bank ATMs at post offices accept most overseas cards and have instructions in English. Most towns have one. Seven Bank ATMs are accessible 24 hours a day. Note that many banks place a limit on the amount of cash you can withdraw in one day (often around US$300).

Cash

Many places in Japan – particularly outside the cities – don't accept credit cards. Ryokan and smaller restaurants and shops are common cash-only places. It's wise to keep cash on hand.

Credit Cards

Businesses that do take credit cards will often display the logo for the cards they accept. Visa is the most widely accepted, followed

Media

Newspapers are sold at convenience stores, train-station kiosks and some hotels in major cities. Look for free mags at airports and hotels; and bars and restaurants popular with expats; many cities have expat-run online magazines, too.

- **Japan Times** (www.japantimes.co.jp) Long-running English-language daily.

- **Time Out Tokyo** (www.timeout.com/tokyo) Quarterly magazine on pop culture and events; look for its excellent mini city guides at tourist information centres around Japan.

- **Kansai Scene** (www.kansaiscene.com) Free paper for Kansai's expat community.

- **Kyoto Journal** (www.kyotojournal.org) In-depth articles on arts and culture from Japan and Asia.

by MasterCard, American Express and Diners Club. Foreign-issued cards should work fine.

Exchanging Money

With a passport, you can change cash or travellers cheques at any Authorised Foreign Exchange Bank (signs are displayed in English), major post offices, some large hotels and most big department stores.

For currency other than US dollars, larger banks, such as Sumitomo Mitsui (SMBC), are a better bet. They can usually change at least US, Canadian and Australian dollars, pounds sterling, euros and Swiss francs.

Tokyo-Mitsubishi UFJ (MUFG) operates World Currency Shop (www.tokyo-card.co.jp/wcs/wcs-shop-e.php) foreign-exchange counters near major shopping centres

in Tokyo, Kyoto and Osaka that exchange a broader range of currencies.

Note that you receive a better exchange rate when withdrawing cash from ATMs than when exchanging cash or travellers cheques in Japan.

Opening Hours

Some outdoor attractions (such as gardens) may close earlier in the winter. Standard opening hours:

Banks 9am to 3pm (some to 5pm) Monday to Friday.

Bars From around 6pm to late.

Department stores 10am to 8pm.

Museums 9am to 5pm, last entry by 4.30pm; often closed Monday (if Monday is a national holiday then the museum will close on Tuesday instead).

Post offices 9am to 5pm Monday to Friday; larger ones have longer hours and open Saturday.

Restaurants Lunch 11.30am to 2pm; dinner 6pm to 10pm; last orders taken about half an hour before closing.

Public Holidays

When a public holiday falls on a Sunday, the following Monday is taken as a holiday. If that Monday is already a holiday, the following day becomes a holiday as well.

Ganjitsu (New Year's Day) 1 January

Seijin-no-hi (Coming-of-Age Day) Second Monday in January

Kenkoku Kinem-bi (National Foundation Day) 11 February

Shumbun-no-hi (spring equinox) 20 or 21 March

Shōwa-no-hi (Shōwa Emperor's Day) 29 April

Kempō Kinem-bi (Constitution Day) 3 May

Midori-no-hi (Green Day) 4 May

Kodomo-no-hi (Children's Day) 5 May

Umi-no-hi (Marine Day) Third Monday in July

Yama-no-hi (Mountain Day) 11 August

Keirō-no-hi (Respect-for-the-Aged Day) Third Monday in September

Shūbun-no-hi (autumn equinox) 22 or 23 September

Taiiku-no-hi (Health-Sports Day) Second Monday in October

Bunka-no-hi (Culture Day) 3 November

Kinrō Kansha-no-hi (Labour Thanksgiving Day) 23 November

Tennō Tanjōbi (Emperor's Birthday) 23 December

You will find intercity transport crowded and accommodation bookings hard to come by during the following high-season travel periods. Note that many shops and restaurants close for Shōgatsu and O-Bon.

Shōgatsu (New Year) 1 to 3 January

Golden Week 29 April to 5 May

O-Bon mid-August

Safe Travel

Japan is prone to natural disasters: earthquakes, tsunamis, volcanic eruptions, typhoons and landslides. Sophisticated early warning systems and strict building codes do much to mitigate impact (but they are not foolproof, of course). Smartphone app Safety Tips sends notifications regarding weather alerts, tsunami warnings and impending seismic activity and also lists key phrases to help you get information in the event of an emergency.

Otherwise, the biggest threat to travellers is Japan's general aura of safety. It's wise to keep up the same level of caution and common sense that you would back home.

Taxes & Refunds

Japan's consumption tax is 8% (with an increase to 10% planned for October 2019). A growing number of shops offer tax-free shopping (noted by a sticker in English on the window) if you spend more than ¥5000. Passport required.

Since the tax is not charged at point of sale, there is no need to collect a refund when leaving the country; however, you should hand in a form affixed to your passport to customs officials when you depart. For details see http://enjoy.taxfree.jp.

Telephone

When dialling Japan from abroad, dial the country code (🖉81), followed by the area code (drop the '0') and the number.

Mobile Phones

Japan operates on the 3G network, so overseas phones with 3G technology should work.

Pre-paid SIM cards that allow you to make voice calls are not available in Japan. Data-only SIM cards for unlocked smartphones are available at kiosks at Narita, Haneda and Kansai airports and at large electronics stores (such as Bic Camera, Yodobashi Camera etc) in major cities. You'll need to download and install an APN profile; ask staff to help you if you are unsure how to do this (they usually speak some English).

There is a wide range of options, depending on your data and speed needs (many cards will continue to work after data usage has been exceeded but the speed will be very slow). B-Mobile's Visitor SIM (www.bmobile.ne.jp/english/index.html), which offers 14 days of unlimited data (the speed will be reduced for heavy users) for ¥2380, is a good choice.

Phone Cards

Prepaid international phonecards can be used with any push-button phones, including regular pay phones. Look for the KDDI Superworld Card or the SoftBank Telecom Comica Card at convenience stores.

Time

All of Japan is in the same time zone: nine hours ahead of Greenwich Mean Time (GMT). Sydney and Wellington are ahead of Japan (by one and three hours, respectively), and most of the world's other big cities are behind: New York by 14 hours, Los Angeles by 17 and London by nine. Japan does not have daylight saving time.

Practicalities

○ **Smoking** Japan has a curious policy: in many cities (including Tokyo, Osaka and Kyoto) smoking is banned in public spaces but allowed inside bars and restaurants. Designated smoking areas are set up around train stations. The number of smokers is declining every year; in Tokyo especially, an increasing number of restaurants and bars are banning smoking.

○ **Weights & Measures** Japan uses the metric system.

Toilets

○ You will come across both Western-style toilets and traditional squat toilets in Japan. When you are compelled to squat, the correct position is facing the hood, away from the door.

○ Public toilets are free. The *katakana* for 'toilet' is トイレ, and the kanji is お手洗い. Also good to know: the kanji for female (女) and male (男).

○ Toilet paper is usually provided, but it is still a good idea to carry tissues with you.

Tourist Information

Tourist information offices (*kankō annai-sho*; 観光案内所) can be found inside or in front of major train stations. Staff may not speak much English; however, there are usually English-language materials and staff are accustomed to the usual concerns of travellers (food, lodging and transport schedules). Many have free wi-fi.

Japan National Tourism Organization (JNTO; www.jnto.go.jp) is Japan's government tourist bureau. It produces a great deal of useful literature in English, which is available from its overseas offices as well as its **TIC** (☏03-3201-3331; www.jnto.go.jp; 1st fl, Shin-Tokyo Bldg, 3-3-1 Marunouchi, Chiyoda-ku; ⊙9am-5pm; 🛜; ⑤Chiyoda line to Nijūbashimae, exit 1) in Tokyo.

JNTO has overseas offices in Australia, Canada, France, Germany, the UK and the USA. See the website, which is also a useful planning tool, for more information.

Travellers with Disabilities

Japan gets mixed marks in terms of ease of travel

Japan Helpline

English-speaking operators at Japan Helpline (☎0570-000-911) are available 24 hours a day to help you negotiate tricky situations. If you don't have access to mobile service, use the contact form on the website (http://jhelp.com/english/index.html).

for those with disabilities. On the plus side, many buildings have access ramps, major train stations have lifts, traffic lights have speakers playing melodies when it is safe to cross, and train platforms have raised dots and lines to provide guidance for the visually impaired. You'll find most service staff will go out of their way to be helpful, even if they don't speak much English.

On the negative side, many of Japan's cities are still rather difficult to negotiate, with many narrow streets lacking pavements.

Major sights take great pains to be wheelchair friendly and many have wheelchairs you can borrow for free. Note, however, that 'accessible' at traditional sights (such as castles and temples) might still mean steep slopes or long gravel paths. Often the accessible routes aren't obvious; telling staff (such as those at the ticket counter) that someone in your party is travelling

in a wheelchair (車椅子; *kuruma-isu*) may, literally, open doors.

Train cars on most lines have areas set aside for people in wheelchairs. Those with other physical disabilities can use the priority seats near the train doors.

A fair number of hotels, from the higher end of midrange and above, offer a 'barrier-free' (バリアフリー; *bariafurii*) room or two (book well in advance). Larger attractions and train stations, department stores and shopping malls should have wheelchair-accessible bathrooms (which will have Western-style toilets).

Japan Accessible Tourism Center (www.japan-accessible.com) is a good resource. Download Lonely Planet's free Accessible Travel guide from http://lptravel.to/AccessibleTravel.

Visas

Citizens of 67 countries, including Australia, Canada, Hong Kong, Korea, New Zealand, Singapore, USA, UK and almost all European nations will be automatically issued a *tanki-taizai* (temporary-visitor visa) on arrival. Typically this visa is good for 90 days. For a complete list of visa-exempt countries, consult www.mofa.go.jp/j_info/visit/visa/short/novisa.html#list.

Japanese law requires that visitors entering on a

temporary-visitor visa possess an ongoing air or sea ticket or evidence thereof. In practice, few travellers are asked to produce such documents, but it pays to be on the safe side.

For additional information on visas and regulations, contact your nearest Japanese embassy or consulate, or visit the website of the Ministry of Foreign Affairs of Japan (www.mofa.go.jp).

On entering Japan, all short-term foreign visitors are photographed and fingerprinted.

Women Travellers

Japan is a relatively safe country for women travellers, though perhaps not quite as safe as some might think. Crimes against women are generally believed to be widely under-reported, especially by Japanese women. Foreign women are occasionally subjected to some forms of verbal harassment or prying questions. Physical attacks are very rare, but have occurred.

The best advice is to avoid being lulled into a false sense of security by Japan's image as one of the world's safest countries and to take the normal precautions you would in your home country.

Transport

Getting There & Away

Air

Japan's major international airports include the following:

Narita International Airport (www.narita-airport.jp) About 75 minutes east of Tokyo by express train, Narita gets the bulk of international flights to Japan; most budget carriers flying to Tokyo arrive here.

Haneda Airport (www. tokyo-airport-bldg.co.jp) Tokyo's more convenient airport – about 30 minutes by train or monorail to the city centre – Haneda, also known as Tokyo International Airport, is getting an increasing number of international arrivals; domestic flights to/from Tokyo usually arrive/depart here.

Kansai International Airport (www.kansai-airport.or.jp) Serves the key Kansai cities of Kyoto, Osaka, Nara and Kōbe. Not as many direct international services as the Tokyo airports, but useful if you want to zero in on the Kansai area (or fly in from one and out of the other).

There are also many regional airports with shorter-haul international flights to countries in Asia, such as China, Korea, Hong Kong and Taiwan.

Getting Around

Air

Air services in Japan are extensive, reliable and safe. Flying is often faster and cheaper than *shinkansen* (bullet trains) and good for covering long distances or hopping islands. **All Nippon Airways** (ANA; ☑0570-029-709, in Osaka 06-7637-6679, in Tokyo 03-6741-1120; www.ana.co.jp) and **Japan Airlines** (JAL; ☑0570-025-121, 03-6733-3062; www.jal.co.jp/en) have the largest networks. All local carriers have websites in English on which you can check prices and book tickets.

Tickets & Discounts

○ Both ANA and JAL offer discounts of up to 50% if you purchase your ticket a month or more in advance, with smaller discounts for purchases made one to three weeks in advance.

○ Foreign travellers can purchase **ANA Experience Japan Fare** one-way domestic tickets for the flat rate of ¥10,800. For details, see www.ana.co.jp/wws/th/e/wws_common/promotions/share/experience_jp.

○ JAL's **Visit Japan Fare** offers a similar ¥10,800 flat-rate ticket for domestic routes to foreign travellers flying inbound on any Oneworld carriers. For details, see www.jal.co.jp/yokosojapan.

○ JAL's **Okinawa Island Pass** (www.churashima.net/jta/company/island pass_en.html) is good for affordable island hopping; it's only available for foreign visitors and must be purchased abroad.

Budget Airlines

The recent proliferation of affordable airlines has brought previously expensive and distant destinations like Hokkaidō and Okinawa within the reach of budget travellers.

○ **Air Do** (www.airdo.jp) Connects Hokkaidō's New Chitose Airport with major destinations around Japan.

○ **Jetstar** (www.jetstar.com) Cheap flights from Tokyo's Narita Airport and Osaka's Kansai International Airport to Okinawa (Naha) and Sapporo (New Chitose).

○ **Peach** (www.flypeach.com) Good for flights out of Kansai.

○ **Vanilla Air** (www.vanilla-air.com) Cheap flights from Tokyo (Narita) to Okinawa (Naha) and Sapporo (New Chitose).

Bicycle

Japan is a good country for bicycle touring, and several thousand cyclists, both Japanese and foreign, traverse the country every year. Hokkaidō is a favourite cycling destination.

Baggage Forwarding

Baggage courier services (called *takkyūbin*) are popular in Japan and many domestic tourists use them to forward their bags, golf clubs, surfboards etc ahead to their destination, to avoid having to bring them on public transport. The tourism bureau has been working to open this service up to foreign travellers; see its guide, Hands-Free Travel Japan (www.jnto.go.jp/hands-free-travel), for a list of luggage forwarding counters, mostly at airports, train stations and shopping centres, set up for travellers.

This is a great service except for one caveat: in most cases, your bags won't get there until the following day. (So, for example, if you want to ship your luggage to or from the airport, you'll need a day pack with one night's worth of supplies.) On the other hand, this can free you from large luggage for a one-night detour to an onsen – just send your bags to the following night's destination.

Hotels can also often arrange this service for you (and the couriers will pick up the luggage from the lobby). Costs vary depending on the size and weight of the bag and where it's going, but is typically around ¥2000.

Both KANcycling (www.kancycling.com) and Japan Cycling Navigator (www.japancycling.org) have tutorials on cycling Japan and trip reports.

Bus

Japan has a comprehensive network of long-distance buses. They're nowhere near as fast as the *shinkansen*, but a lot cheaper. Buses also travel routes that trains don't.

Japan Railways (JR) operates the largest network of highway buses in Japan; it tends to be a little pricier than other operators, but is reliable and buses tend to depart and arrive at train stations rather than bus stops elsewhere in the city.

You can purchase these tickets from JR train stations.

Cheaper operators with large networks include **Willer Express** (☏ from outside Japan 050-5805-0383; http://willerexpress.com), which offers three-/four-/five-day bus passes. You can book seats on Willer and other buses through the company's Japan Bus Lines service (http://japanbuslines.com).

Night buses are a good option for those on a tight budget and without a Japan Rail Pass. They are relatively cheap and spacious – depending on how much you are willing to pay – and they also save on a night's accommodation. They typically leave at around 10pm or 11pm and arrive the following day at around 6am or 7am.

There are some truly bargain bus deals out there, but note that, while the government has been cracking down, cheaper operators have been known to skirt safety regulations (by overworking their drivers).

Car & Motorcycle

Driving in Japan is quite feasible, even for just the mildly adventurous. Most roads are signposted in English and major rental agencies offer cars with English-language navigation systems; roads are in excellent condition; road rules are generally adhered to; and although petrol is expensive, it is not prohibitively so.

In some parts of Japan (most notably Hokkaidō and Okinawa), driving is really the only efficient way to get around. On the other hand, it makes little sense to have a car in the big cities, like Tokyo and Osaka, where traffic is thick, a preponderance of one-way streets makes navigation a challenge and parking is expensive.

○ If you're a member of an automobile association in your home country, you're eligible for reciprocal rights with the **Japan Automobile Federation** (JAF; ☏03-6833-9100, emergency roadside help 0570-00-8139; www.jaf.or.jp; 2-2-17 Shiba, Minato-ku; ◷9am-5.30pm Mon-Fri; ⑤Mita line to Shiba-kōen, exit A1), which has an office in Tokyo.

○ Driving is on the left. There are no unusual rules or interpretations of them and most signposts follow international conventions. JAF publishes a Rules of the Road guide (digital/print ¥864/1404) in English, which is handy.

Driving Licences

Travellers from most nations are able to drive (both cars and motorcycles) in Japan with an International Driving Permit backed up by their own regular licence. The International Driving Permit is issued by your national automobile association.

Travellers from Switzerland, France and Germany (and others whose countries are not signatories to the Geneva Convention of 1949 concerning international driving licences) are not allowed to drive in Japan on a regular International Driving Permit. Rather, travellers from these countries must have their own licence backed by an authorised translation of the same licence. These translations can be made by their embassy or consulate in Japan or by the JAF.

Car Hire

○ Typical rates for a small car are ¥5000 to ¥7000 per day, with reductions for rentals of more than one day. On top of the rental charge, there's about a ¥1000-per-day insurance cost. Prices among major agencies are comparable.

○ Car rental agencies are clustered around transit hubs: airports, major train stations and ferry piers. Those at the major international airports are most likely to have English-speaking staff.

○ Toyota Rent-a-Car (https://rent.toyota.co.jp) and Nippon Rent-a-Car (www.nrgroup-global.com) have large rental networks and booking in English is possible online.

○ Japanese law requires children under the age of six to ride in a car seat; rental car agencies provide them for a small extra fee.

ETC Cards

With an ETC card (www.go-etc.jp/english/guidebook/index.html) you can pass through the automated toll booths at 20km/h without stopping. The cards also save money: tolls for ETC users can be up to 30% less than standard tolls (depending on the time of day and distance travelled).

Rental cars have ETC card readers and major agencies will rent the cards for a small fee; you'll be presented with a bill for your tolls when you return the car. If you choose not to use an ETC card, or need assistance, staffed toll booths will be marked in green with the characters 一般 (*ippan*; ordinary).

Navigations Systems

Rental cars come equipped with satellite navigation systems that are generally very reliable; major agencies offer ones that have an English function. As Japanese addresses can be confusing, the best way to set your destination is by inputting the phone number. Many tourist organisations now also provide pamphlets with 'map codes' for major destinations, which you can input into car navigation systems.

Local Transport

Japan's larger cities are serviced by subways or trams, buses and taxis; indeed, many locals rely entirely on public transport. Note that all public transportation except for taxis shuts down between midnight and 5am.

Bus

The city where you'll find yourself relying on public buses is Kyoto. Though the city has a subway system, it is not convenient for all major tourist sites.

Subway & Tram

Kyoto, Osaka, Tokyo and Sapporo have subway systems, which are usually the fastest and most convenient way to get around the city. Stops and line names are posted in English. Kagoshima and Hiroshima have trams.

Fares are typically ¥150 to ¥250, depending on how far your ride (half-price for children). If you plan to zip around a city in a day, an unlimited-travel day ticket (called *ichi-nichi-jōsha-ken*)

IC Cards

IC cards are prepaid travel cards with chips that work on subways, trams and buses in the Tokyo, Kansai, Sapporo and Hiroshima metro areas. They save you the trouble of having to purchase paper tickets and work out the correct fare for your journey. Each region has its own card, but they can be used interchangeably in any region where IC cards are used; however, they cannot be used for intercity travel.

The two most frequently used IC cards are **Suica** (www.jreast.co.jp/e/pass/suica.html) from JR East and **Icoca** (www.westjr.co.jp/global/en/ticket/icoca-haruka) from JR West; purchase them at JR travel counters at Narita and Haneda or Kansai airports, respectively. Cards can also be purchased and topped up from ticket vending machines in any of the cities that support them. Both require a ¥500 deposit, which you can get back when you return your card to any JR ticket window.

To use the card, simply swipe it over the reader at the ticket gates or near the doors on trams and buses.

is a good deal; most cities offer them and they can be purchased at station windows.

Taxi

◦ Taxis are ubiquitous in big cities; they can be found in smaller cities and even on tiny islands, too, though usually just at transport hubs (train and bus stations and ferry ports) – otherwise you'll need to get someone to call one for you.

◦ Transit stations and hotels have taxi stands where you are expected to queue. In the absence of a stand, you can hail a cab from the street, by standing on the curb and sticking your arm out.

◦ Fares are fairly uniform throughout the country and all cabs run by the meter.

◦ Flagfall (posted on the taxi windows) is around ¥600 to ¥710 for the first 2km, after which it's around ¥100 for each 350m (approximately). There's also a time charge if the speed drops below 10km/h and a 20% surcharge between 10pm and 5am.

◦ A red light means the taxi is free and a green light means it's taken.

◦ The driver opens and closes the doors remotely – full service indeed!

◦ Drivers rarely speak English, though fortunately most taxis now have navigation systems. It's a good idea to have your destination written down in Japanese, or better yet, a business card with an address.

Train

Japanese rail services are fast, frequent, clean and comfortable. The predominant operator is Japan Railways, commonly known as 'JR', which runs the *shinkansen* (bullet train) routes. There is also a huge network of private railways.

◦ Most long-haul routes run local (called *futsū* or *kaku-eki-teisha*), express (called *kyūkō* or *kaisoku*) and limited express trains (called *tokkyū*). Limited express trains have reserved seats, with comfortable reclining chairs, and toilets. All trains, save for a few *shinkansen* cars, are nonsmoking. Many different trains run on the same platforms, so be mindful of the signboards that note the schedule of departures.

◦ Many long-haul trains have 'green car' carriages, which are akin to business class. Seats are a little more spacious and the carriages tend to be quieter and less crowded; they're also usually the last to sell out.

◦ Tickets can be purchased from touch-screen vending machines in major train stations; most have an English function and those for *shinkansen* journeys accept credit cards.

◦ If you are booking a series of journeys, have questions or just want the reassurance of buying a ticket from a person, major JR stations have what are called *midori-no-madoguchi*, which function as JR's inhouse travel agency; these days most staff speak enough English to answer basic questions. Private line trains will have their own ticket windows.

○ Reservations can only be made for limited express (*tokkyū*) liners and *shinkansen* services. There are also unreserved *shinkansen* seats; the policy on limited express trains varies by route and operator (some are all-reserved; others are not). Reserved-seat tickets can be bought any time from a month in advance to the day of departure.

○ It is generally not necessary to make reservations in advance except on weekends and national holidays and during peak travel seasons – such as Golden Week (late April to early May), Obon (mid-August) and the New Year period.

○ The website HyperDia (www.hyperdia.com) is useful for searching routes and travel times/costs in English.

Travel Passes

Rail passes, which include the classic, country-wide Japan Rail Pass to a growing number of passes that zero in on specific regions,

are excellent value. These passes are only available to foreign passport holders entering Japan on a tourist visa (station staff will check). Children between the ages of six and 11 qualify for child fares, while those under six ride for free.

Note that JR passes are valid only on JR services; you will still have to pay for private-train services. However, as the JR network is the country's largest, the coverage is good. The value is in getting to ride *shinkansen* and limited express (*tokkyū*) trains, though of course you can use the passes on ordinary express and local trains, too.

New passes are being created all the time (and unpopular ones retired), so check websites for the latest information.

Japan Rail Pass

The Japan Rail Pass (www.japanrailpass.net) is perfect for first-time visitors who want to zip around to see the highlights. It covers travel on all *shinkansen* lines, though on some routes you may not be allowed to ride the very fastest trains (such as Nozomi and Mizuho). A 'green' pass is good for rides in 1st-class 'green' train cars.

A one-way reserved-seat Tokyo–Kyoto *shinkansen* ticket costs ¥13,910, so you only need make one round trip between Tokyo and Kyoto on the *shinkansen* to make a seven-day pass come close to paying off (add a round trip between Narita Airport and Tokyo and you're already saving money).

The Japan Rail Pass must be purchased outside Japan. In order to get a pass, you must first purchase an 'exchange order' outside Japan at a JAL or ANA office or a major travel agency. Once you arrive in Japan, you must bring this order to a JR Travel Service Centre (in most major JR stations and at Narita, Haneda and Kansai international airports). When you validate your pass, you'll have to show your passport in addition to the exchange order.

When validating, you select the date on which you want the pass to become valid. You can choose to make it valid immediately or on a later date. So, if you just plan to spend a few days in Kyoto or Tokyo before setting out to explore the country by rail, set the validity date to the day you start your journey outside the city.

Japan Rail Pass Costs

Duration	Regular (adult/child)	Green (adult/child)
7 days	¥29,110/14,550	¥38,880/19,440
14 days	¥46,390/23,190	¥62,950/31,470
21 days	¥59,350/29,670	¥81,870/40,930

Once you've validated your pass, you can make seat reservations from any *midori-no madoguchi* ('green window' ticket counters) at JR train stations. You can also just show your pass at the ticket gates and hop on any unreserved train car (though you'd be wise to book ahead during peak travel times).

JR West Passes

JR West (www.westjr.co.jp) offers several regional rail passes useful for travellers who are giving Tokyo a miss. In addition to the routes outlined following, all Kansai area passes cover transport on JR lines to/from Kansai International Airport to Kyoto and Osaka.

o **Kansai Area Pass** (one-/two-/three-/four-day pass ¥2200/4300/5300/6300, children half-price) Unlimited travel on all JR lines – except *shinkansen* lines – between major Kansai cities, including Himeji, Osaka, Kyoto and Nara. Perfect for exploring the Kansai region in depth.

o **Kansai Wide Area Pass** (adult/child ¥8500/4250) Valid for five consecutive days; covers the same destinations as the Kansai Area Pass plus travel on the San-yō Shinkansen between Osaka and Okayama. Good for visiting Kansai with detours to Himeji and Naoshima (accessed from Okayama).

o **Kansai–Hiroshima Area Pass** (adult/child ¥13,000/6500) Valid for five consecutive days. Good for everything covered in the Kansai Wide Area Pass, plus Hiroshima.

Kansai Thru Pass

The Kansai Thru Pass (two-/three-day pass ¥4000/5200; www.surutto. com) is a real bonus to travellers who plan to explore the Kansai area. It's good for travel on city subways, private railways and city buses in Kyoto, Nara, Osaka, Kōbe and Kōya-san, plus discounts at many attractions. It is available at the Kansai International Airport travel counter on the 1st floor of the arrivals hall and at the main bus information centre in front of Kyoto Station, among others.

Language

Japanese pronunciation is not difficult as most of its sounds are also found in English. You can read our pronunciation guides as if they were English and you'll be understood just fine. Just remember to pronounce every vowel individually, make those with a macron (ie a line above them) longer than those without, and pause slightly between double consonants.

To enhance your trip with a phrasebook, visit **lonelyplanet.com**. Lonely Planet iPhone phrasebooks are available through the Apple App store.

Basics

Hello.
こんにちは。 konnichiwa

How are you?
お元気ですか? o-genki des ka

I'm fine, thanks.
はい、元気です。 hai, genki des

Excuse me.
すみません。 sumimasen

Yes./No.
はい。/いいえ。 hai/ iie

Please. (when asking/offering)
ください。/どうぞ。 kudasai/dōzo

Thank you.
どうもありがとう。 dōmo arigatō

You're welcome.
どういたしまして。 dō itashimashite

Do you speak English?
英語が話せますか? eigo ga hanasemas ka

I don't understand.
わかりません。 wakarimasen

How much is this?
いくらですか? ikura des ka

Goodbye.
さようなら。 sayōnara

Accommodation

I'd like to make a booking.
部屋の予約を heya no yoyaku o
お願いします。 onegai shimas

How much is it per night?
1泊いくらですか? ippaku ikura des ka

Eating & Drinking

I'd like ..., please.
…をください。 ... o kudasai

What do you recommend?
おすすめは何 o-susume wa nan
ですか? des ka

That was delicious.
おいしかった。 oyshikatta

Bring the bill/check, please.
お勘定をお願い o-kanjō o onegai
します。 shimas

I don't eat ...
…は食べません。 ... wa tabemasen

chicken	鶏肉	tori-niku
fish	魚	sakana
meat	肉	niku
pork	豚肉	buta-niku

Emergencies

I'm ill.
気分が悪いです。 kibun ga warui des

Help!
たすけて! taskete

Call a doctor!
医者を呼んで! isha o yonde

Call the police!
警察を呼んで! keisatsu o yonde

Directions

I'm looking for (a/the) ...
…を探しています。 ... o sagashite imas

bank
銀行 ginkō

... embassy
大使館 taishikan

market
市場 ichiba

museum
美術館 bijutsukan

restaurant
レストラン restoran

toilet
お手洗い/トイレ o-tearai/toire

tourist office
観光案内所 kankō annaijo

Behind the Scenes

Acknowledgements

Climate map data adapted from Peel
MC, Finlayson BL & McMahon TA
(2007) 'Updated World Map of the
Köppen-Geiger Climate Classification',
Hydrology and Earth System Sciences,
11, 163344.

Illustrations pp44-5, pp146-7 by
Michael Weldon.

This Book

This edition of Lonely Planet's *Best of Japan* guidebook
was curated by Rebecca Milner, who also researched and
wrote for it along with Ray Bartlett, Andrew Bender, Craig
McLachlan, Kate Morgan, Simon Richmond, Tom Spurling,
Phillip Tang, Benedict Walker and Wendy Yanagihara. This
guidebook was produced by the following:

Destination Editor Laura Crawford
Product Editor Joel Cotterell
Senior Cartographer Diana Von Holdt
Book Designer Wibowo Rusli
Assisting Editors Katie Connolly, Victoria Harrison
Assisting Cartographers Mark Griffiths, Corey Hutchison
Cover Researcher Naomi Parker
Thanks to Naoko Akamatsu, Janice Bird, Kate Chapman,
Bruce Evans, Liz Heynes, Kate Mathews, Lauren O'Connell,
Martine Power, Lyahna Spencer

Send Us Your Feedback

We love to hear from travellers – your comments keep us on our
toes and help make our books better. Our well-travelled team reads
every word on what you loved or loathed about this book. Although
we cannot reply individually to postal submissions, we always guar-
antee that your feedback goes straight to the appropriate authors,
in time for the next edition. Each person who sends us information
is thanked in the next edition, the most useful submissions are
rewarded with a selection of digital PDF chapters.

Visit lonelyplanet.com/contact to submit your updates and sug-
gestions or to ask for help. Our award-winning website also features
inspirational travel stories, news and discussions.

Note: We may edit, reproduce and incorporate your comments in
Lonely Planet products such as guidebooks, websites and digital
products, so let us know if you don't want your comments repro-
duced or your name acknowledged. For a copy of our privacy policy
visit lonelyplanet.com/privacy.

Index

A

Symbols & Map Key

Look for these symbols to quickly identify listings:

- ◉ Sights
- ✪ Activities
- ✦ Courses
- ✪ Tours
- ✪ Festivals & Events

- ✪ Eating
- ✪ Drinking
- ✪ Entertainment
- ✪ Shopping
- ✪ Information & Transport

These symbols and abbreviations give vital information for each listing:

- ✿ Sustainable or green recommendation
- **FREE** No payment required

- ☎ Telephone number
- ⊙ Opening hours
- ℗ Parking
- ⊖ Nonsmoking
- ❄ Air-conditioning
- @ Internet access
- ☎ Wi-fi access
- ☈ Swimming pool

- ▣ Bus
- ⊕ Ferry
- ⊟ Tram
- ▣ Train
- ▣ English-language menu
- ✈ Vegetarian selection
- ⊞ Family-friendly

Find your best experiences with these Great For... icons.

 Art & Culture

 Beaches

 History

 Local Life

 Budget

 Nature & Wildlife

 Cafe/Coffee

 Photo Op

🚲 Cycling

 Scenery

 Detour

 Shopping

🍷 Drinking

 Short Trip

🎟 Entertainment

 Sport

✨ Events

👪 Family Travel

🚶 Walking

🍽 Food & Drink

❄ Winter Travel

Sights

- ⊛ Beach
- ⊛ Bird Sanctuary
- ⊛ Buddhist
- ⊛ Castle/Palace
- ⊕ Christian
- ⊛ Confucian
- ⊛ Hindu
- ⊛ Islamic
- ⊛ Jain
- ⊛ Jewish
- ⊕ Monument
- ⊛ Museum/Gallery/ Historic Building
- ⊛ Ruin
- ⊛ Shinto
- ⊛ Sikh
- ⊛ Taoist
- ⊛ Winery/Vineyard
- ⊛ Zoo/Wildlife Sanctuary
- ◉ Other Sight

Points of Interest

- ⊙ Bodysurfing
- ⊖ Camping
- ⊖ Cafe
- ⊖ Canoeing/Kayaking
- ⊙ Course/Tour
- ⊘ Diving
- ⊙ Drinking & Nightlife
- ⊗ Eating
- ⊙ Entertainment
- ⊛ Sento Hot Baths/ Onsen
- ⊙ Shopping
- ⊙ Skiing
- ⊜ Sleeping
- ⊜ Snorkelling
- ⊜ Surfing
- ⊜ Swimming/Pool
- ⊙ Walking
- ⊙ Windsurfing
- ⊙ Other Activity

Information

- ⊛ Bank
- ⊕ Embassy/Consulate
- ⊕ Hospital/Medical
- @ Internet
- ⊘ Police
- ⊘ Post Office
- ⊘ Telephone
- ⊕ Toilet
- ⊕ Tourist Information
- ● Other Information

Geographic

- ⊛ Beach
- ⊶ Gate
- ⊛ Hut/Shelter
- ⊛ Lighthouse
- ⊛ Lookout
- ▲ Mountain/Volcano
- ⊛ Oasis
-)(Park
-)(Pass
- ⊛ Picnic Area
- ⊛ Waterfall

Transport

- ⊛ Airport
- Ⓑ BART station
- ⊗ Border crossing
- ⊙ Boston T station
- ⊛ Bus
- ⊕ Cable car/Funicular
- ⊛ Cycling
- ⊖ Ferry
- Ⓜ Metro/MRT station
- ⊕ Monorail
- ℗ Parking
- ⊛ Petrol station
- Ⓢ Subway/S-Bahn/ Skytrain station
- ⊛ Taxi
- ⊕ Train station/Railway
- ⊟ Tram
- ⊖ Tube Station
- Ⓤ Underground/ U-Bahn station
- ● Other Transport

Craig McLachlan

Craig has covered destinations all over the globe for Lonely Planet for two decades. Based in Queenstown, New Zealand, for half the year, he runs an outdoor activities company and a sake brewery, then moonlights overseas for the other half, leading tours and writing for Lonely Planet. Describing himself as a 'freelance anything', Craig has an MBA from the University of Hawai'i and is also a Japanese interpreter, pilot, photographer, hiking guide, tour leader, karate instructor and budding novelist. Check out www.craigmclachlan.com.

Kate Morgan

Having worked for Lonely Planet for over a decade now, Kate has been fortunate enough to work as a travel writer covering destinations such as Shanghai, Japan, India, Zimbabwe, the Philippines and Phuket. She has done stints living in London, Paris and Osaka but these days is based in one of her favourite regions in the world – Victoria, Australia. In between travelling the world and writing about it, Kate enjoys spending time at home working as a freelance editor.

Simon Richmond

Journalist and photographer Simon Richmond has specialised as a travel writer since the early 1990s and first worked for Lonely Planet in 1999 on their *Central Asia* guide. He's long since stopped counting the number of guidebooks he's researched and written for the company, but countries covered include Australia, China, India, Iran, Japan, Korea, Malaysia, Mongolia, Myanmar (Burma), Russia, Singapore, South Africa and Turkey.

Tom Spurling

Tom Spurling is an Australian travel writer and high school teacher who has worked on 13 travel guides for Lonely Planet. His titles include *Australia, Turkey, Central America, China, India* and *South Africa*. On his second *Japan* guide he covered the mythical northeast where the wild things roam but the *shinkansen* Green Car still runs.

Phillip Tang

Phillip Tang grew up on typically Australian pho and fish'n'chips. A degree in Chinese and Latin American cultures launched him into travel and writing about it for Lonely Planet's *Canada, China, Japan, Korea, Mexico, Peru* and *Vietnam* guides. Phillip has made his home in Sydney, Melbourne, London and Mexico City. His travels include most countries in Europe, much of Asia and Latin America, as well as the greatest hits of North America.

Benedict Walker

Born in Newcastle, Australia, notions of the beach are core to Ben's idea of self, having travelled hundreds of thousands of kilometres from the sandy shores of home. Ben was given his first Lonely Planet guide *(Japan)* when he was 12. Two decades later, he'd write chapters for the same publication: a dream come true. A communications graduate and travel agent by trade, Ben whittled away his twenties gallivanting around the globe. He speaks fluent Japanese and has contributed to LP's *Japan* guide twice. Ben has also written and directed a play, toured Australia managing the travel logistics for top-billing music festivals and is experimenting with a return to his original craft of photography and film-making.

Wendy Yanagihara

Wendy serendipitously landed her dream job of writing for Lonely Planet in 2003, and has since spent the intervening years contributing to titles including *Southeast Asia on a Shoestring, Vietnam, Japan, Mexico, Costa Rica, Indonesia,* and *Grand Canyon National Park*. In the name of research, she has hiked remote valleys of West Papua, explored the tiny nooks and alleys of Tokyo sprawl, trekked on a Patagonian glacier, and rafted Colorado River whitewater.

Our Story

A beat-up old car, a few dollars in the pocket and a sense of adventure. In 1972 that's all Tony and Maureen Wheeler needed for the trip of a lifetime – across Europe and Asia overland to Australia. It took several months, and at the end – broke but inspired – they sat at their kitchen table writing and stapling together their first travel guide, Across Asia on the Cheap. Within a week they'd sold 1500 copies. Lonely Planet was born.

Today, Lonely Planet has offices in Franklin, London, Melbourne, Oakland, Dublin, Beijing, and Delhi, with more than 600 staff and writers. We share Tony's belief that 'a great guidebook should do three things: inform, educate and amuse'.

Our Writers

Rebecca Milner

California-born. Longtime Tokyo resident (14 years and counting!). Co-author of Lonely Planet guides to Tokyo, Japan, Korea and China. Freelance writer covering travel, food and culture. Published in the *Guardian, the Independent, the Sunday Times Travel Magazine, the Japan Times* and more. After spending the better part of her twenties working to travel, she was fortunate enough to turn the tables in 2010, joining the Lonely Planet team of freelance authors.

Ray Bartlett

Ray Bartlett has been travel writing for nearly two decades, bringing Japan, Korea, Mexico and many parts of the United States to life in rich detail for top industry publishers, newspapers and magazines. His acclaimed debut novel, *Sunsets of Tulum,* was a *Midwest Book Review* 2016 Fiction pick. Among other pursuits, he surfs regularly and is an accomplished Argentine tango dancer. Contact him for questions or motivational speaking opportunities via www.kaisora.com, his website. Ray Bartlett currently divides his time between homes in the USA, Japan and Mexico.

Andrew Bender

Andrew is a native New Englander who worked in the financial industry in Tokyo and the film industry in Los Angeles before setting out to pursue his dream of travelling and writing about it. He has since authored more than three dozen Lonely Planet titles to regions as varied as Japan, Korea, Taiwan, Norway, Amsterdam, Germany and his current home of Southern California. He also writes the Seat 1A travel site for Forbes.com, and contributes to the *Los Angeles Times* and airline magazines. Catch his work at www.wheres-andy-now.com.

More Writers

STAY IN TOUCH LONELYPLANET.COM/CONTACT

AUSTRALIA The Malt Store, Level 3, 551 Swanston St, Carlton, Victoria 3053
☏ 03 8379 8000,
fax 03 8379 8111

IRELAND Unit E, Digital Court. The Digital Hub, Rainsford St, Dublin 8, Ireland

USA 124 Linden Street, Oakland, CA 94607
☏ 510 250 6400,
toll free 800 275 8555,
fax 510 893 8572

UK 240 Blackfriars Road, London SE1 8NW
☏ 020 3771 5100,
fax 020 3771 5101

 twitter.com/lonelyplanet

 facebook.com/lonelyplanet

 instagram.com/lonelyplanet

 youtube.com/lonelyplanet

 lonelyplanet.com/newsletter